Education, Justice, and Democracy

Education, Justice, and Democracy

EDITED BY DANIELLE ALLEN
AND ROB REICH

THE UNIVERSITY OF CHICAGO PRESS   CHICAGO AND LONDON

DANIELLE ALLEN is the UPS Foundation Professor of the School of Social Science at the Institute for Advanced Study in Princeton, New Jersey. She is the author of *Why Plato Wrote*, *The World of Prometheus*, and *Talking to Strangers*, the last published by the University of Chicago Press. ROB REICH is associate professor of political science with courtesy appointments in the Department of Philosophy and the School of Education at Stanford University. He is the coeditor of *Toward a Humanist Justice* and the author of *Bridging Liberalism and Multiculturalism in Education*, the latter published by the University of Chicago Press.

The publication of this book was supported by a grant from the Spencer Foundation.

The University of Chicago Press, Chicago 60637
The University of Chicago Press, Ltd., London
© 2013 by The University of Chicago
All rights reserved. Published 2013.
Printed in the United States of America

22 21 20 19 18 17 16 15 14 13   1 2 3 4 5

ISBN-13: 978-0-226-01262-9 (cloth)
ISBN-13: 978-0-226-01276-6 (paper)
ISBN-13: 978-0-226-01293-3 (e-book)

Library of Congress Cataloging-in-Publication Data

Education, justice, and democracy / edited by Danielle Allen and Rob Reich.
     pages ; cm
   Includes bibliographical references and index.
   ISBN 978-0-226-01262-9 (cloth : alkaline paper)—ISBN 978-0-226-01276-6 (paperback : alkaline paper)—ISBN 978-0-226-01293-3 (e-book)   1. Educational equalization—United States. 2. Democracy and education—United States. 3. Educational equalization. 4. Democracy and education. 5. Education—Philosophy.   I. Allen, Danielle S., 1971– II. Reich, Rob.
   LC213.2.E39   2013
   379.2'6—dc23
                                                                2012030963

Contents

Acknowledgments

The idea of this book emerged from many conversations between the editors; and the contents, in turn, came from a great many—and many great—conversations among its contributors. Unlike most edited volumes, where the book is an assembly of papers presented at conferences or a collection of essays brought together by the editors, the chapters here were written as part of a long-term seminar aimed at understanding the connections among education, justice, and democracy.

Essays were developed over the course of three separate workshops, held in 2009–10 at the Institute for Advanced Study in Princeton, New Jersey. Authors chose their topics in conversation with one another and wrote and revised in light of our ongoing dialogue. We owe our contributors our largest debt of gratitude, both for these conversations and for the essays they produced.

We also thank our institutional host, the Institute for Advanced Study, where sturdy and steadfast protection is given to open-ended inquiry. We are especially indebted to Laura McCune for her expert arrangements for the workshops, for formatting the essays and creating a bibliography, and for support of virtually every administrative detail concerning this book.

These workshops could not have taken place without generous grants from the Spencer Foundation and the Ford Foundation. We thank Mike McPherson at Spencer and Alison Bernstein and Jeannie Oakes at Ford.

During the course of the workshops and while finishing the volume, we received comments and assistance from a great many other friends and colleagues. We thank Stephanie Sutton, Anne-Claire Defossez, Andrew Jewett, Catherine Ross, Leif Wenar, Debra Satz, and Josh Cohen, as well as all the faculty, members, and visitors in the School of Social Science who contributed so richly to the study of education, state, and society in the 2009–10 academic year.

Elizabeth Branch Dyson at the University of Chicago Press championed the idea of the book and, once a manuscript was in hand, championed the book itself. We are very grateful for her wise editorial advice and ever-present enthusiasm for the project. Russ Damian at the Press provided expert assistance, and Alice Bennett was a magnificent copy editor. And we thank Meira Levinson for a detailed and extremely helpful review of the entire manuscript; we also thank an anonymous reviewer for the Press.

Finally, we should like to express special gratitude to the partners without whose support, intellectual as well as familial and of a hundred other kinds, this project would not have been possible. Rob thanks Heather Kirkpatrick. Danielle thanks James Doyle.

A book about education, justice, and democracy inevitably takes up questions about how education is a crucial means of sustaining justice and democracy across generations. It is a book about the future as much as about the present. All the more appropriate, then, to dedicate this book to our children: Rob to Gus Kirkpatrick and Greta Reich, Danielle to Nora and William Doyle.

Introduction

Danielle Allen and Rob Reich

Education, Justice, and Democracy

Education is an ancient and universal practice whose importance has had, in different times and places, diverse defenders and explicators. We now live in an era when everyone—from parents to business leaders to community groups to politicians of every partisan stripe—speaks of education, especially the education of children, with reverence and urgency. What the US Supreme Court announced in its landmark 1954 decision *Brown v. Board of Education*—"Today, education is perhaps the most important function of state and local governments"—can now be stated without qualification. A telling fact: expenditures for public schooling are the single largest outlay in most local and state budgets.[1]

In short, no one contests the significance of education. Yet almost always contested are its meaning, content, and purpose. In our democratic society, we take for granted the basic principle that every individual should have access to educational opportunities. But what is education for? What ideals should guide our practice of education? What is required—of families, of teachers, of communities, of politicians, of institutions—for education to succeed? How would we know if we were succeeding in educating? What would we be measuring?

Consider perhaps the simplest and most fundamental question of all: What are the aims of education in a democratic society? Do we educate children to prepare them for economic success in the workforce, to succeed as citizens, or to flourish as human beings? Are these goals compatible or tension-ridden? Can we achieve all three simultaneously?

Education: the ubiquity of its invocation is matched only by the superficiality of its contemporary use.

For instance, political leaders often espouse the view that to have a secure job everyone needs a college education, yet this is literally a nonsense goal. Our economy does not consist solely of jobs that require a college degree, nor is it about to. Buried in this aspiration are more complicated views about social competition, equality, and the meaning of democracy. Our national conversation—one that includes teachers, school leaders, parents, students, and policymakers—fails to orient schooling around a thorough understanding of the meaning, content, and purpose of education, and consequently our educational choices are limited or, worse, muddled and confused.

This volume seeks to bring some clarity and content to that muddled, shallow rhetoric, but not by adding our voices to the already cacophonous arena of policy proposal or partisan political sniping. We do not advance blueprints for our education system: the policy conversations, we believe, too often obscure rather than illuminate the meaning, content, and challenges of education. There are no silver bullets or panaceas.

We intend rather to step back and consider the larger social, political, and developmental contexts in which educational aspirations and anxieties play out. In particular, we believe we can gain clarity and content in our discussion about education by deepening our understanding and appreciation of three core ideals—education, justice, and democracy—that structure, implicitly or explicitly, nearly every discussion about schooling in the United States. Then, in addition to clarifying ideals, we must also hone our understanding of the constraints on their realization.

We are not the first to take up such an aspiration. When John Dewey published *Democracy and Education* nearly one hundred years ago, he too argued that "the reconstruction of philosophy, of education, and of social ideals and methods . . . go hand in hand." His social moment was not so different from our own. Now as then, changes in the structure of the global economy and in national labor markets raise questions about the levels of achievement and attainment that prepare individual students and particular nations for competitive success. Now as then, population growth and global patterns of migration raise questions about the capacity of democracies to build civic cultures where citizens can bridge difference and where opportunity is equitably distributed. And now as then, record income inequality, shrinking social mobility, and hardened residential segregation in the United States raise questions about whether educational institutions can function as engines of advancement for those born into difficult and disadvantageous circumstances.

Yet two fundamental contrasts between Dewey's moment and our own force a differentiation of our project from his. A century ago, educational policy was not a federal matter. Now the federal government, more than the variegated national tapestry of local and state administrations, sets the direction for our educational institutions. Not only in the United States but around the world, nations are directing significant policy attention to education, and as governments choose one or another policy framework for their educational institutions, they implicitly make choices that affect whether they are building educational systems that advance the intertwined, though distinct, ideals of justice and democracy. So too, they implicitly make choices about whether and how to balance educating young people for economic success, civic functioning, and human development and flourishing. Because local, state, and national governments bring such vast power, funds, and human resources to bear on the activity of educating, these choices are more consequential than ever—for the lives of individual students, but also for the ongoing evolution of democracies.

The second difference between our moment and Dewey's relates to social diversity—both that arising from internal demographic evolution and that flowing from high rates of immigration. When Dewey wrote *Democracy and Education*, the legal framework of segregation was very much still under construction, but the country's doors were wide open to immigrants, except for Chinese and Japanese migrants (Chinese exclusion had been established in 1890, and restrictions on Japanese immigration were put in place in 1908).[2] Congress legislated the first broad numerical restrictions on immigration, of the kind we know today, only in 1921.[3] Alongside the policies of segregation and openness to European immigration, a discourse of assimilation—illustrated by the proverbial melting pot, a metaphor that dates from this era—grew to shape the terms on which those outsiders who were invited in should enact their membership.[4] In response to this discourse, Dewey advocated hyphenated identity. Clearly, much has changed between Dewey's time and our own. One the one hand, we have dismantled much of the legal structure of segregation—though not all of it and not its de facto instantiations (see Rothstein, this volume). On the other, we have greatly expanded the project of immigration restriction. Alongside these changes, the ideal of melting-pot assimilation has been thoroughly discredited.

We have, then, a different context than Dewey's for thinking about the role of power—national power—in education and for thinking about social difference. On these questions, the essays in this volume generally share a set of answers.

With regard to the question of power, the essays gathered here are egalitarian, not libertarian. They express an acceptance of the role of government power in educational policy but seek to constrain and direct that power by tying it closely to the ends of democratic egalitarianism. Some of the essays connect justice and democracy to distributive equality, others to the equal standing of citizens, where this is a matter not merely of formal legal status but of a richer, relational equality (see Laden, this volume, for the most explicit treatment). Whichever approach they take, these essays limn an egalitarianism in which equality itself is the ground of freedom: where we are not able to protect equal standing in relation to one another, we are not free. A discerning reader will notice that across these essays, our contributors aspire to identify the conditions for achieving equal standing for all members of a diverse and highly socially differentiated polity. Schools are central sites for pursuing and sustaining this democratic egalitarianism.

With regard to the question of social difference, the essays here by and large express sympathy with *Brown*'s integrationist project, but on new, and decidedly not assimilationist, grounds. They steer away from identity-based politics while nonetheless embracing difference as a feature both ineradicable and enriching of democratic life. Across the essays one finds traces of a recognizable ideal: No citizen must be required to become like any other—the goal of assimilation—but all need to understand the linkages among themselves and others who are unlike them, so that the members of a polity can come to recognize how the good of different others is their good too.

Dewey sought to reconstruct the whole of philosophy through his philosophy of education. In *Democracy and Education* he offered new definitions of the human being, of knowledge and thinking, of mind and body, of experience, labor, leisure, and art, of science and culture, of morals, democracy, and philosophy. Our project is far more modest. We identify places where policy conversations and social science research have an impact on one or another of these philosophical questions, and we try to push forward our philosophical understanding. But we by no means aspire to answer, or even to raise, all the philosophical questions implicit in either the practice or the politics of education. Nor do we cover the full range of policy concerns; any number of important educational topics go unaddressed: for example, school choice, special education, educational entrepreneurship such as Teach for America or the creation of charter schools, issues of gender, and the impact of technology on education. Rather than a comprehensive set of philosophical or practical answers, we offer readers an invitation to participate in a particular method of thinking.

Methodology

Every education policy and practice involves implicit or explicit claims about the relations among education, justice, and democracy. Our aspiration as individual scholars was to bring to the surface the definitions of these core ideals that lie behind our educational policy choices, as well as to refine our understanding of how ideals interact with social realities. Consider the following as an illustration of the method of this volume.

Our current situation presents a very large challenge: Can we identify the kind of education—where "education" is understood as the combination of specific curricula and pedagogies with an institutional infrastructure of delivery—that attenuates the well-documented relationship between inherited socioeconomic position and life outcomes, that makes the quality of one's education and likelihood of future success depend less on accidents of birth? And can we do this without leveling down but instead by raising up the educational achievement of any given generational cohort while also ensuring that the highest peaks of achievement are accessible to students from the full range of social backgrounds?

Notice that the goal of attenuating the relationship between inherited socioeconomic position and life outcomes is a democratic one. The hereditary accrual of privilege to particular families or groups of citizens undermines the egalitarian foundation that a democracy needs if citizens are to be in a position to protect their rights and liberties and to stand in a relation of equality to one another. And democracies draw their legitimacy from, among other things, the claim that of all types of political regime, they best enable every individual to achieve his or her fullest human flourishing.

Attenuating the relationship between inherited position and life outcomes without leveling down educational achievement and while opening up the highest levels of achievement to students from all backgrounds is also a goal of justice: it is giving children what they are due. Limiting the growth of any particular student would be an injustice; conversely, activating each student's potential for growth is a requirement of justice.

And finally, what we mean by educational achievement in the first place is a question, simply, of what we see as the possibilities for human development, both individual and collective. That is, what are our ideals for education in itself, as a process by which human potentialities are identified and unleashed?

How are we to meet the challenge of developing, delivering, and governing an education that rests on an intelligent account of what achievement is and promotes the ideals of democracy and justice? The animating impulse of this volume is that we can meet that challenge only by more directly considering the ideals that are in play in educational research, policy, and practice and by being explicit about the relation between our ideals and the constraints on their realization.

Yet educational researchers, policymakers, and practitioners do not have a professional mandate to address how best to think about these guiding ideals. That work is more conventionally assigned to philosophers. But there is a problem in that direction too, for the conventional philosopher these days interacts infrequently with social scientists and policymakers (and almost never with practitioners) and addresses the topic of education even more infrequently. If we as a society are to strengthen our capacity to understand, and then deliver, the kind of education that can best support democracy and advance justice, we need a new conversational framework.

Here we present such a new, paradigm-shifting conversation. These collected essays emerged from an eighteen-month seminar among scholars across the social sciences and from philosophy and the literary humanities. A sociologist, an anthropologist, an economist, public policy researchers, psychologists, and political scientists are joined by literary critics, ethicists, and political philosophers. It was our conviction, as conveners, that a multidisciplinary conversation would break some new ground. Such conversations are especially important, we believe, at the crossroads between normative, or value-oriented, scholarship and positive, or empirically oriented social science. Questions about justice and democracy have been at the center of an amazing output of philosophical scholarship over the past forty years. During the same period, social scientists have increased their methodological rigor and amassed vast data sets to study important social phenomena. Both normative and positive scholars have been working hard on questions concerning education, but they too rarely engage one another.

The intermingling of scholars whose work is primarily philosophical or normative with those whose work is primarily social scientific or empirical was purposeful. Just as philosophers can help social scientists orient their research toward normatively significant questions, so too can social scientists direct philosophers' attention to socially urgent topics. We began with the belief that a tangible benefit of dialogue between philosophers and social scientists is to guide the pursuit of justice in a non-ideal world. Political philosophers engaged in ideal theory are trying to get as clear as possible about what values are important and how valuable they are relative to one another. An ideal theory attempts to sort these values into principles that, taken together, can guide the design of ideally just institutions. But it is only by knowing something about feasibility in the real world that philosophers can guide action for policy design here and now. Identifying the feasible set requires careful description of existing states of affairs: to judge well where we can realistically hope to get to from here, we need to know precisely where we are. It also requires predictions, with probabilities and timescales, about the likely effects of anything we might do to change things, which itself presupposes adequate understanding of social mechanisms and causal processes.

There are other questions too: What sort of real world outcomes would actually count as the manifestation of the ideals examined by philosophers? What phenomena should social scientists investigate to best judge how well our social and political institutional arrangements are realizing ideals of democracy and justice and to ascertain the kinds of interventions that might be more effective? Answering these questions requires collaboration between theorists of the ideal and analysts of the real, between scholars of the normative and experts at the positive. Moreover, each discipline of the social sciences brings to bear a different, but important, type of expertise. These forms of expertise function best, we believe, when brought together; alone, they are like the proverbial blind men, each grasping a part of the elephant but claiming to know the whole. This volume brings all the human sciences together to address a broadly human question. One important result of these conversations was the discovery that the interactions between normative and positive theory are intricate and delicate and come in even more forms and styles than we have outlined above.

Finally, then, our essays seek to show by example how a coordinated multidisciplinary conversation can clarify, more effectively than work from within a single discipline, the stakes of policy choices by bringing analytical rigor to bear on relating ideals and the horizons of possibility to each other. The illuminating light so created emerges now from one part of the intellectual terrain, now from another. Sometimes ethical commitments underlying policy choices become visible; sometimes we catch a glimpse of what our ideals, clothed in the garb of social realities, would look like; sometimes we are brought face to face with the moral consequences of empirical discoveries. Which of these things happened at which time over the course of our conversation was unpredictable. For each of us, the points of contact between theory and empirical scholarship were different—we will identify some examples below. Nonetheless, such moments of illumination strengthen our capacity both to understand the type of education that can support democracy and meet the requirements of justice and also to see how to deliver it. The quality of the essays in this volume reflects this mode of thinking.

Structure

Following from this strategy, we have organized this volume into three main parts, titled "Ideals," "Constraints," and "Strategies." The section on ideals sets out the normative terrain where debates about education, justice, and democracy take place. The section on constraints examines a variety of limits or obstacles to the advancement or realization of these ideals. The section on strategies takes up some policy-guiding frameworks that combine the ideals of education, justice, and democracy with an appreciation of the real world obstacles with which every policymaker and practitioner must grapple. Taken all together, the essays of this third section offer a panoramic view of some concrete forms that democratic agency can take.

Ideals

The essays in this section anatomize a set of orienting ideals currently guiding conversations about education policy. Some of these ideals—the contrast between the ideals of equal educational opportunity and the adequacy movement in education—are at present more to the fore in policy-making contexts. Others—education for justice, education for democratic citizenship—are part of an American tradition for thinking about education that flows in and out of policy conversations at different times. One central lesson of this section is the recognition that providing educational opportunities to children and adults raises deep questions not only about distributional justice—who receives an education and how—but also about relational justice—how people stand in relation to one another as citizens and as fellow human beings. Another lesson is that thinking about justice and education in the context of a democratic society leads, as John Dewey understood well a century ago, to questions about citizenship and civic education, where an education simultaneously prepares students for life in a democracy and where the school context itself might embody a democratic ethos.

The contributors take up our core ideals of education, justice, and democracy in different ways. The first essay, "The Challenges of Measuring School Quality: Implications for Educational Equity," shows the benefit of placing philosophical and empirical scholars in dialogue. Helen Ladd and Susanna Loeb examine the complex challenges of identifying and then measuring what a quality education might be. They consider three proxies for quality education—school resources, internal processes and practices of schooling, and student outcomes—then evaluate these proxies against various normative conceptualizations of equal quality schooling. In the next chapter, "Equality, Adequacy, and K–12 Education," Rob Reich considers what a theory of distributive justice has to say about the provision of education, identifying two possible principles of distribution, equality and adequacy, and argues ultimately for the superiority of equality to adequacy. The analysis is not a simple matter of abstraction, however. He embeds the argument in a historical account of the shift in US education policy from equality to adequacy as the orienting ideal of reform. Anthony Laden's chapter, "Learning to Be Equal: Just Schools as Schools of Justice," sits in illuminative contrast to Reich's, arguing that the relevant picture of justice, especially when one is thinking about the place of education in democracy, is relational, not distributive; the pressing question for education in democracy is to develop a system of education that fosters equal standing as citizens, and he draws lessons about both the content of such an education and the ethos of a school that delivers it. Laden's arguments about democracy in the classroom evolved as he synthesized his approach with an enriched sociological understanding of the necessary status of educators as leaders in the classroom. Finally, Sigal Ben-Porath's contribution, "Education for Shared Fate Citizenship," begins from the assumption that a primary task of education in a democracy is to develop students into equal and able citizens, but she transitions from a view of citizenship as a stable individual identity to a view of citizenship as shared fate, a dynamic and relational affiliation. She then translates the normative ideal into the concrete by drawing out various curricular implications.

Constraints

The section on constraints contains essays that identify various problems in seeking to forward or realize certain of the ideals discussed in the first section. These essays are therefore the most straightforwardly empirical in orientation. They identify concrete phenomena that count as evidence of our failure to achieve some measure of the ideals explored in the first section and identify the reasons for those failures. Their anatomies thus provide a rich analysis of the sorts of constraints we should take into account as we pursue ideals of justice and democracy in the arena of educational policy.

Take as an example the achievement gap. The achievement gap—identifying the gaps in test scores between students from different racial and ethnic groups—is now also a shorthand for our failure to reach ideals of equality, equity, or adequacy in distributing the good of education. Because educational attainment and achievement are so strongly correlated with socioeconomic success and active political engagement, among other life outcomes, the achievement gap also names an obstacle to the achievement of relational justice or an ideal of "shared fate." To understand the constraints or limits on our realization of our ideals, we need to understand phenomena like this.

Angel Harris's essay, "Can Members of Marginalized Groups Remain Invested in Schooling? An Assessment from the United States and the United Kingdom," begins this section by refuting the often-heard claim that an "oppositional culture" among black students explains the achievement gap. Harris's data show that black families actually exhibit a greater commitment to learning and the value of education than white families do and have more positive views about what they can gain from education. The existence of the achievement gap should be understood as flowing not from a putative oppositional attitude but from cumulative skill deprivation. In "Conferring Disadvantage: Immigration, Schools, and the Family," Carola and Marcelo Suárez-Orozco make a similar argument about immigrant students. Such students, in fact, show high aspiration to learn English, but the aspiration is not matched by success in language learning. What are the obstacles to their successful academic performance? The Suárez-Orozcos focus, first, on psychosocial factors that affect students' learning and, second, on the fact that, for immigrant families, the demands of the school context are often poorly aligned with the realities of immigrant family life. Immigrants are often not in a position to provide the sort of support that schools implicitly demand of parents.

Both these essays—empirically grounded as they are—remind us of an important moral truth embedded in the etymology of the word student. Its original meaning in Latin is simply "the eager one." If we begin our analyses of education, then, from a presumption of eagerness on the part of the students and their families, what new research questions should we ask? Where should we focus our efforts at reform? A focus on the normative significance of empirical discoveries can lead to a reorientation of worthy and interesting research questions. We find ourselves asking, for instance, How do we rectify earlier stages of skill deprivation that set the stage for achievement gaps down the line? Both Harris and the Suárez-Orozcos turn our attention to how the larger social context in which particular students find themselves, as well as the school context, establishes or fails to establish a foundation for learning.

Gregory Walton's essay "The Myth of Intelligence: Smartness Isn't Like Height," third in this section, offers a subtle argument, drawing on recent work in psychology, to demonstrate the socially situated nature of human intelligence. Not only do our social contexts provide or fail to provide solid foundations for learning, they can elicit better or worse performance from us as learners. Individual performance on intelligence tests can change dramatically as the social context surrounding the testing situation changes. This, of course, means there are fundamental problems with our many attempts to define and measure intelligence as a fixed and internal trait, like height, and then to base all manner of educational decisions and distributions of resources on such measurements. But more important, it means we cannot pursue our ideals in education without reflecting on whether broader social patterns support or work against the intellectual development of any particular student or group of students. It seems that Plato, the first philosopher of education, was right in arguing that the educational achievement of any given generation of students broadly depends on the preexisting capacity of adults to build a society that provides a solid foundation for learning.

With regard to our contemporary context, both Harris and the Suárez-Orozcos pinpoint ethnic and socioeconomic segregation as part of the explanation for the skill deprivation that lowers achievement for the groups of students being discussed. Richard Rothstein's essay, "Racial Segregation and Black Student Achievement," directly tackles this topic, which has largely fallen away as a subject of conversation in the arena of education policy. He too connects the achievement gap to racial segregation and analyzes the capacity of the US policymakers, including our justice system, to tackle the problem. He takes as a starting point the observation that US courts seem to have concluded that residential segregation is no longer de jure but entirely de facto, the product not of government policy but of individual choice about where to live. By examining a wide array of social policies, Rothstein shows how astonishingly alive de jure segregation and its effects still are today, and he gives the lie to assumptions about de facto segregation embedded in major court decisions on school desegregation. He takes us, in other words, from social to political constraints on our ability to realize ideals of justice and democracy in the domain of education. Rothstein's exploration of assumptions about de facto segregation and of the continued reality of de jure segregation raises, of course, the question of what strategies might be used to pursue educational ideals in the face of such social and political constraints. And so we turn, in the third section, to strategies.

Strategies

The final section—on strategies—examines novel frameworks or actual initiatives that seek to make progress toward greater justice and democracy in schooling. The chapters in this section provide four pathways for combining the ideals laid out in the first section with a recognition of the constraints identified in the second. That our contributors examine different pathways reflects that we, as a group of authors, are not proposing a single strategy for approaching questions of educational policymaking. Rather, taken together the essays are panoramic, showing the multiple venues and leverage points where reform is possible or needed. They begin with action in and through the family, move to action through legislatures and courts, and conclude with action through social organizations and associations.

The four pathways do, however, share something: each contributor presents the strategy under consideration as democratic. We use this adjective with two meanings. How should a democratic society organize and govern institutions of education? The question raises issues both of pedagogy and curricular content, on the one hand, and of method and the infrastructure for the delivery of education on the other. Education for democracy, and democracy in education. The strategies outlined seek both to build a curriculum and set of pedagogic methods that are appropriate to a democratic citizenry and also to develop, deliver, and, where necessary, defend that education by means that are themselves democratic. These essays, then, offer four pictures of how democratic agency can be enacted in the context of advancing the intertwined causes of education, justice, and democracy.

The essay by Harry Brighouse and Adam Swift, "Family Values and School Policy: Shaping Values and Conferring Advantage," begins the section by exploring the tension between the family and the state in the pursuit of educational goals. The authors provide a strategy by which philosophical reflection can be brought into the policy arena and propose protections for but also limits to the rights of parents to transmit values and confer advantages on their children through formal education.

Patrick McGuinn's essay, "The Federal Role in Educational Equity: The Two Narratives of School Reform and the Debate over Accountability," analyzes how justice, equality, and education intersect in the contemporary US debate about the federal No Child Left Behind legislation and its coming reauthorization. His close examination of the politics of policy evolution allows us to understand how the debate about expansive federalism in education unfolded historically and, in particular, to track a shift in the debate from a focus on broad social reform as necessary to improve educational outcomes to a focus on the pedagogic capacity of schools. His account also allows us to see how political and educational ideals take the form of policy. His own argument is ultimately optimistic. He sees great potential in the connection between an expanded federal role and a focus on the local matter of school governance and management.

In "Reading Thurgood Marshall as a Liberal Democratic Theorist: Race, School Finance, and the Courts," Anna Marie Smith moves us from the executive to the judicial branch of government. She analyzes and endorses Justice Thurgood Marshall's jurisprudence in a set of Supreme Court education cases as a strategy for pursuing ideals of justice in the realm of education in a democratic context. She reads Marshall as making a case for an expansion of federal powers in the realm of education and sees the preservation of public interest litigation and judicial review as indispensable elements in the tool kit of democratic advocates for education rights, especially in the face of asymmetrical socioeconomic structures and deeply entrenched majoritarian interests.

Finally, Seth Moglen's "Sharing Knowledge, Practicing Democracy: A Vision for the Twenty-First-Century University" takes us away from the political arena and to the university as a site for strategic pursuit of the ideals of education, justice, and democracy discussed in the first section. Moglen sees the university as a critical starting point because it is, after all, the institution responsible for tending to the culture of knowledge of any given society—for knowledge production and dissemination. A university rightly configured, he argues, would help build a social context that supports effective learning across many socioeconomic divides, for its students as well as for the community where it is located.

Collectively, the essays in this section make an important point about the relationship between democracy and educational policy. When we consider the kinds of decisions that are made about education at different points within the US political system and by different methods (voting, judicial decision, constituent deliberation), it becomes clear that a multiplicity of institutional arrangements meet the criteria of democracy. No particular institutional arrangement is the sine qua non of democratic practice; the question is rather whether a citizenry is equipped, and equipped intergenerationally, to wield institutional forms democratically: that is, to avoid concentrations of power in elites, to maintain transparency, to maintain accountability, to limit majoritarianism with the protection of minorities, and to train the next generation of democratic citizens. In short, the question how a democracy should govern institutions of education turns out to collapse, as Dewey also realized, into the question whether it can develop adult citizens who are prepared to sustain and protect responsible democratic governance across generations.

Conclusion

Citizens of a democracy are decision makers the whole of their lives, and their job of equipping themselves for that work ceases never. A central feature of life in a democracy is the need for citizens to engage in their own ongoing education. "Adult education," understood not as remedial but as simply a continuing experience for all adults, is a building block of democratic life.

It is no exaggeration to claim, therefore, that much of the current failure of schools to improve themselves is best understood as a failure not of teachers, not of schools, not of school systems, not of families, not of politicians, but rather of adult education.

This volume as a whole represents a commitment to the view that, if adults are to succeed in educating their children to steer democracy effectively when it is their turn, those adults must constantly work to educate themselves so they might become better educators. The work of this volume—to clarify both the goals we pursue with educational policy and the constraints on their realization—itself exemplifies the process of adult education that is necessary to protect democratic governance and a successful education delivered by democratic means.

Thomas Jefferson, who designed a system of democratically controlled local school districts that would contribute to the political education and engagement of adult citizens as well as the schooling of children, seems to us correct: "If a nation expects to be ignorant and free, it expects what never was and never will be." Can we improve our ability to think about our goals as well as our ability to think about our methods? This is the hope that bore this project aloft.

PART I
Ideals

CHAPTER I

The Challenges of Measuring School Quality

Implications for Educational Equity

Helen Ladd and Susanna Loeb

Introduction

N early all countries, including the United States, view elementary and secondary education as so important for the well-being of both individuals and society that they make schooling compulsory through some age, whether that age is fourteen as in many developing countries or sixteen or eighteen as in various states of the United States. In addition, there is a worldwide consensus that all students, but especially those in primary school, should have access to publicly financed schools with no fees. In practice many countries, especially developing countries with limited resources, do not meet this latter requirement, and they often permit schools to charge fees that in some cases are substantial (see Ladd and Fiske 2008, chap. 16). The policy throughout the United States has been clear: public schools, including both traditional schools and publicly funded charter schools, cannot require parents to pay to enroll their children. Compulsory schooling, supported by full public funding, reflects the observation that elementary and secondary education not only provides private benefits to those who attend school and their families but also brings public benefits to the broader society.

Among the private benefits are consumption benefits to the enrolled students of being in a safe, engaging, and potentially enjoyable school environment; consumption benefits to their parents in the form of child care and satisfaction in their children's development; and future investment benefits to students in the form of higher-paying jobs, better health, and a more fulfilling life (Card 2001; Haveman and Wolfe 1984). These private benefits—both the consumption and the investment benefits—can also be categorized as intrinsic or extrinsic. Intrinsic benefits arise when education is valued for its own sake, such as the pleasure of being able to solve a complex problem or to appreciate artistic expression. Extrinsic benefits arise when education serves as an instrument for attaining other valued outcomes such as the higher income working parents can earn by having children in school, or the potential for the recipients of education to seek higher-paying jobs and more fulfilling careers. Regardless of the classification, it is clear that education provides a variety of private benefits, many of which accrue long after the students have left school.

If the only benefits were private, one might expect families to pay for a significant part of their children's education, as they typically do at the higher education levels. Even in the case of exclusive private benefits, however, there would be a compelling argument for making education compulsory and providing public support. The argument rests on the government's responsibility for protecting vulnerable groups, in this case children, who are not in a position to protect their own interests. Thus it can be viewed as both unfair and undesirable for children whose families invest little in their education—regardless of whether that reflects limited resources or weak preferences for education (see essays by the Suárez-Orozcos and Harris in this volume for the debate)—to be denied access to the skills and orientations needed to lead a productive life and to unlock their potential.

Clearly, however, the benefits of schooling accrue to more than just children and their parents. Among the public benefits of schooling are short-run benefits for others from keeping idle children off the streets and away from crime or other antisocial behaviors, and the longer-run benefits of having an educated citizenry capable of participating in the democratic system and a workforce that is productive and innovative. These longer-run benefits accrue not only to the residents of the children's local community, but also to the broader society. Low educational investment in students in one jurisdiction spills over to other jurisdictions because people move across jurisdictions, citizens participate in the political life of the nation as well as that of their local community, and the productivity of one geographic area of the country can affect overall productivity.

Even without government financing of education, families would have an incentive to invest in their children's education to generate future benefits for themselves. Parents gain directly from the future earnings of children who care for them when they are elderly. Parents also gain from investing in education when having flourishing, happy children increases their own happiness. Many families, however, might invest less than would be most beneficial for the larger community because they do not take into account the benefits that would accrue to others. Such underinvestments are likely to be largest for low-income families, for whom the public benefits of educating their children, including the creation of conditions for democratic participation, could be large relative to their perceptions of the private benefits. In addition, they may have less information as well as fewer resources to invest currently for future returns.

Governments have the potential to overcome some of these underinvestments. They can raise taxes and make schooling less expensive so that people invest more to account for the externalities of education, the benefits others get from an individual's schooling. Governments can also give loans to make it easier for families to invest, and they can require attendance.

Given the benefits of education, almost all societies invest in an education system, and the vast majority provide free education to young children. In so doing, each government needs to make many choices about how to fund and govern schools. These decisions have implications for the quality of schools and the educational opportunities available. Well-informed choices require a clear definition of education quality and an understanding of how to measure it.

In this chapter we explore the complexity of defining and measuring education quality in a way that can help public decision making. We discuss common approaches to measuring education quality and explore the advantages and disadvantages of each in terms of accuracy and reliability. We then turn to a discussion of the distribution of education quality in relation to the normative standards of equal quality schooling, equal educational opportunity, and adequacy, and we highlight the merits of the different approaches to measuring school quality with respect to each equity standard.

What Is Education Quality?

In its simplest form, education quality can be conceptualized as the investment and consumption value of the education. The investment portion

captures benefits in the form of higher earnings, better health, contributions to the arts, effective participation in the democratic process, and
other outcomes that education enhances. The consumption portion of education quality captures the benefits to children and their families of having safe, supportive, and happy environments. From the perspective of the
community, the quality of an education system refers not only to the sum
of the investment and consumption benefits, but also to how they are distributed across individuals. The value of any particular pattern is likely to
differ across societies. For example, highly unequal patterns of education
consumption across individuals may be unacceptable in some societies,
while in others they may be more acceptable provided all children receive
a minimum floor of consumption. As another example, some communities
may look for equality in the investment benefits of education, while others
may want to provide greater investment benefits to students whose families are less able to provide them, compensating for low family resources.
The distribution of both consumption and investment benefits may also
affect the robustness of the democratic process and the degree of societal
cohesion, both of which are valued in a democratic society.

Of course, it is unlikely that all members of a community will agree on
the value of different components of education quality or on how they
should be distributed. Children and their parents often differ on what
constitutes a high-quality day at school. Families also disagree on what
is high-quality education—with some valuing investment returns of one
type and other families another type. For example, some parents value
the development of art and music skills and appreciation for its own sake,
while others value the arts primarily for motivating students to learn more
math or develop better reading skills. In addition, families disagree on the
values children should be learning in school. Educators also often differ
with children, with parents, and among themselves about worthwhile outcomes as well as worthwhile types of education consumption.

Communities and their government representatives have to decide how
to balance these differing perspectives, much the way they need to balance
perspectives in other areas of public decision making. Education may be
particularly sensitive because it touches on parenting, rights, and values.
It is further complicated in federalist systems where many different communities have a say in public education. Certainly in the United States,
local, state, and federal governments all play important roles in the public
education system and often disagree on the best approach to schooling.
While much could be and has been written about how best to govern and
finance education in a federalist system, those issues are not the subject

of this essay. We have a more limited, but nonetheless challenging, goal of better understanding what education quality is and how to measure it.

In keeping with this discussion, ideally we would measure the quality of an education system by the investment and consumption benefits it provides. Measuring education this way is not an easy task, however, in part because some of the benefits of education are difficult to quantify and in part because investment benefits do not emerge immediately. We do not know, for example, how much income a first-grade child will earn two or three decades in the future. Moreover, even if we could look at data thirty years after the child attended school, we would be learning about the quality of the education system thirty years earlier, which is not much use for current decision making. As such, we need proxies for education quality. Not surprisingly, none of the available proxies is perfect.

In what follows we discuss the relative merits of commonly used proxies for education quality.

One set of proxies aims to capture the inputs to schools that are the building blocks or ingredients for a high-quality education system. Measures of resources—in the form of either spending per pupil or specific school inputs such as the number of teachers per pupil—are the most concrete proxies for school quality and are the most commonly used. Although resources may be necessary for a high-quality school or district, they may not be sufficient given that some schools are likely to use their resources more effectively than others. Thus, direct measures of school processes, as observed by external evaluators, can serve as alternative measures of school quality. For a number of reasons, including the complexity of schooling and the difficulty of standardizing evaluators' ratings, even measures of school processes are flawed as a measure of education quality. A third type of quality measure uses proximal student outcomes such as test scores and educational attainment. Although these measures do not fully capture the investment outcomes of interest, they are often justified on the grounds that they predict such outcomes. One of the challenges in using outcome-based proxies for quality is determining what student outcomes would have been in the absence of the schooling system so as to uncover the contribution of schools to the outcomes in question.

Proxies for School Quality

The three most common proxies for school quality are measures of resources, of internal processes and practices, and of student outcomes. In this section we discuss each of these measures and evaluate their strengths and weaknesses in light of the framework just presented.

Resources

Spending per pupil is an intuitively appealing rubric for measuring education quality. Setting aside for the moment that price levels may differ across places, we all have a sense of the scale of a dollar, what it can and cannot buy. Such a measure can be interpreted as a weighted average of the various inputs a school uses, with the weights being the prices of each input. According to such a measure, a school or district with more teachers who are experienced (and hence have higher salaries) would be spending more than a school or district with fewer experienced teachers, all other factors held constant. Thus, to the extent that the differential salaries paid to teachers reflect their true quality, a measure of spending per pupil appears to be a reasonable way to capture both the quantity and quality of the resources available to a school.

An advantage of using spending per pupil as a measure of school quality is that it is not based on any specific assumptions about the best, or preferred, way for schools to allocate their total resources among specific inputs. For example, the same amount of (per pupil) spending in two schools could be used for smaller classes with less experienced teachers in one school and larger classes with more experienced teachers in the other. In the absence of evidence that certain configurations of resources are preferred to others in all schools regardless of their context, it would be inappropriate to attribute higher quality to one school than another. Finally, this single-dimensional measure allows for straightforward comparisons across schools or districts with statements of the form: district A spends 40 percent more than district B, with an implied comparable statement about the relative quality of the two districts.

In the United States in 2007, the average current expenditure per pupil for public elementary and secondary education equaled $9,683 (US Department of Education 2007). This average masks great variation in spending both across states and across districts within states. On average, for example, schools in Utah spent $5,706 per pupil, while those in New York State spent an average of $15,546. By one estimate, about 70 percent of the variation in spending per pupil across US school districts is attributable to variation across states and about 30 percent is attributable to variation across districts within states (Corcoran and Evans 2008, table 19.2). Largely as a result of the school finance and property tax reform efforts in many states that reduced variation both within state and across states, spending inequality across school districts throughout the country declined substantially between 1972 and 2000 but then rose slightly in subsequent years.[1]

There is far less information on the distribution of dollars across schools within districts. Because of the single salary schedule and the associated well-documented propensity for the more experienced—and hence, more costly—teachers to leave schools with high proportions of low-achieving, low-income, and black students, one might expect spending per pupil to be lower in these schools than in more advantaged schools. Working in the other direction, these schools may receive more funds from state and federal governments targeted toward needy students. As one example, New York City public schools spent an average of almost $12,800 per pupil during the 2003–2004 school year, with school-level spending ranging from approximately $3,500 to $24,500 per pupil. In this district, schools with higher proportions of poor students, low-achieving students, and especially special education students spent more per pupil on average than other schools, though much of the variation across schools is not easily explained by student characteristics (Schwartz, Rubenstein, and Stiefel 2009).

Despite the intuitive appeal of spending per pupil as a measure of school quality, it suffers from serious drawbacks even as a measure of a school's resources. First and most important, the costs of any given quality-adjusted input often differ significantly across districts and may also differ across schools within a district. As a consequence, at a minimum spending would need to be adjusted for the costs of inputs to be used as a measure of a school's resources.

Costs of inputs differ for a number of reasons. The costs of facilities, or the annual debt service needed to finance them, are likely to be higher in large cities, where land prices are higher than in smaller cities or rural areas. Probably most important, that college-educated workers earn different wages in different parts of the country means that districts in high-wage areas typically have to pay higher salaries to attract teachers than districts in low-wage areas. As an example, Taylor and Fowler (2006) found that in 1999–2000 starting teacher salaries were 27 percent higher in California than in Kansas ($32,190 versus $25,252). Because most of this difference was attributable to the higher wages for college-educated workers in California, the cost-adjusted teacher salaries in the two states were almost the same ($29,481 and $29,528, respectively).

Cost differences for teachers also arise across districts or across schools within a district because teachers prefer some neighborhoods and some types of students to others (Boyd et al. 2011; Jackson 2009; Clotfelter, Ladd, and Vigdor 2011). In particular, schools serving educationally advantaged or high-achieving students may be able to recruit higher-quality teachers at any given salary level than schools serving less advantaged or lower-achieving students. Disadvantaged schools are likely to end up with lower-quality teachers unless they can override the single salary schedule and raise the salaries of teachers in their schools. One recent study shows that the additional salary required to retain high-quality teachers in disadvantaged schools at the same rate as in more advantaged schools could exceed 50 percent, with the required salary differential depending on the extent of school segregation (Clotfelter, Ladd, and Vigdor 2011).

Given the imperfections of spending per pupil as a measure of school resources, it may be tempting to measure resources directly. For example, one could look at the number of teachers per pupil in a school, access to computers, the length of the school day or year, the availability of after-school programs, or all of these. In US public elementary and secondary schools in 2007 there were 15.7 students per teacher on average, down from 17.9 students per teacher twenty years earlier (US Department of Education 2009). As with other resources, the number of teachers per student varies substantially across and within schools and districts. The main benefit of using specific school resources as a measure of school quality is that quantifying resources instead the dollars avoids the difficulty of adjusting for cost differences.

As we have already suggested, when using resources as a measure of school quality, one must measure the quality of resources as well as the quantity. Clearly, not all classroom books or computers are the same. Similarly, not all teachers are the same. Two schools might employ the same number of teachers per pupil, but these teachers may come with very different skills and knowledge that affect their teaching ability. Unfortunately, just as it is difficult to measure the quality of the overall education system, it is difficult to measure the quality of teachers for generating educational benefits. Instead, until recently, most studies of the distribution of teachers across schools used proxies such as teachers' experience, certification, and academic ability (as typically measured by licensing test scores) when assessing differences in the quality of teachers serving different students. While these proxies are not ideal measures, they are likely to capture differences in the appeal of teaching in different places and thus, at least in part, adjust for differences in quality. Studies using such proxies in North Carolina and New York found that, regardless of the proxy used, schools serving the high-poverty student populations had far higher proportions of teachers with weak credentials than did schools serving more affluent students (Clotfelter, Ladd, and Vigdor 2007; Lankford, Loeb, and Wyckoff 2002).

Although using school inputs to measure education quality has some advantages relative to spending per pupil, it too has drawbacks. First, as discussed above, there is no consensus on the correct measure of quality for many education resources, particularly for the key human resources in schools—teachers and other staff. Second, the best configuration of resources probably differs across schools, and again there is no consensus on optimal configurations. Third, either measures of school resources focus on only one of the relevant inputs or, if they are intended to represent a bundle of inputs, the question arises of how to weight the inputs within the bundle. That brings us back to some form of spending measure, with the elements of the bundle weighted by their prices.

As a measure of education quality, however, cost-adjusted spending still suffers from two additional problems. First, it takes no account of differences in how effectively or efficiently dollars are spent. At the extreme, some school leaders simply may be corrupt and not use the dollars to benefit students. Even without corruption, more knowledgeable and effective leaders can achieve greater education quality for the same cost-adjusted spending level by implementing school processes and practices directed toward the valued outcomes.

Second, cost-adjusted spending levels take no account of the fact that some schools need more resources than others to offer equivalent schooling. For example, consider two schools, one with a far higher proportion of special needs students whose legally mandated individual education plans require that they be taught in small classes. The first school would need more teachers per student on average to provide an equivalent quality of schooling to the students without special needs. For a more general example, consider two students, A and B, who are similar except that they attend different schools. If the other students in the school student A attends are more likely to be disruptive or the variation in the achievement levels of students is much greater than in the school student B attends, the school serving student A may need more resources, either more teachers or more teachers with special qualifications, to provide an education equivalent to what student B receives in the other school.

The Dutch have used arguments like these to justify their system of weighted student funding. Ever since 1917, with the extension of public funding to religious schools, the Dutch objective has been to provide equal quality schools, regardless of whether such schools were operated by Roman Catholics, Protestants, or the government. Historically, that meant providing equal funding for each school. With the influx of low-skilled immigrants in the 1960s and 1970s and the resulting concentrations of immigrant children in some schools, however, the Dutch realized that equal resources did not translate into equal quality. Thus, starting in 1985 they implemented a system in which immigrant children whose parents had low education would bring almost twice as much funding to the school they attended as would native Dutch with well-educated parents (Ladd and Fiske 2009).

This argument for the need for more resources in one school than in another is based on the goal of providing *equivalent* quality education to all students, regardless of the schools they attend. It is not grounded in the view that educationally disadvantaged students may require higher-quality education in order to have equal—or, possibly, adequate—educational opportunity. Questions of how best to distribute education quality across students raise a different set of issues than those of interest in this discussion of how to define and measure school quality. We address the arguments for providing different quality of education to different students in the final section of the chapter. For now, we are still working on how to measure quality.

Observational Measures of Internal Processes and Practices

As suggested by some of the previous examples, even schools—or broader education systems—with similar cost-adjusted levels of resources may differ in quality because of the way they use those resources. An alternative approach to measuring education quality is to observe what goes on within classrooms, schools, districts, or broader education systems. Such measures typically focus on internal processes and practices. The best quality measures of this type would be generated by trained observers and would be based on formal rubrics or protocols designed to produce consistent measures across units.

Examples of process measures of education quality include evaluations of teacher quality based on observing their practices in the classroom (Grossman et al. 2010; Kane et al. 2010) and inspection reports on individual schools. Such reports typically are based on periodic visits to individual schools by external review teams. Although multiple countries around the world use such an approach, it is less common in the United States. Only recently have some states and cities begun experimenting with school or district inspection systems of this type. The New York City Department of Education, for example, currently sends review teams to individual schools as part of its larger effort to promote school quality, and for several years Massachusetts has had various permutations of a state-wide system for evaluating both districts and individual schools. Interest in charter schools has induced some states, including Massachusetts, to send review teams to all their charter schools to evaluate their quality, both early in the life of the school and just before the reauthorization decision.

This observational approach is advantageous in that it can provide a more nuanced and comprehensive measure of quality than can measures based on resources or spending. Moreover, by highlighting areas of quality shortfalls, such information can be useful to the units observed in that it provides guidance on areas that need improvement. For observational measures to provide valid measures of school quality, however, the observed measures must be closely linked to valued educational outcomes.

One area in which observational measures of quality are relatively well developed and well justified by research is early childhood education. In this context, research documents that the way teachers interact with children in the classroom affects children's learning and development (Pianta, LaParo, and Stuhlman 2004; Pianta et al. 2007). Classroom observations can therefore provide more valid information on the quality of a preschool program than simple measures of resources such as the number of teachers or their educational achievement. This example not only illustrates the potential for observational measures to be useful measures of quality but also suggests that the case for using direct observation is most compelling when it is difficult to get crucial information on quality in other ways.

Even with their potential benefits, observational measures are rarely used on a large scale in the United States at either the early education or K–12 levels. Both the early stage of development of most of the measures and the cost of effectively implementing a system of assessment based on observation limit their current use. The experience of New Zealand illustrates the challenges involved in measuring school quality by direct observation. An innovative part of the country's reform package of the early

1990s, which turned operating responsibility over to individual schools, was the establishment of an Education Review Office (ERO) designed to monitor school quality through periodic school visits. The initial intent was to evaluate each school in terms of its own mission statement, but the vagueness of the mission statements made that approach unworkable. The ERO instead turned its attention to how well the school was complying with national guidelines for school policies and also how well the school itself was using information on student performance to make internal policy. Despite ERO efforts to focus on learning outcomes, the reviews often became mechanistic, were heavily focused on management procedures, and did not necessarily foster better educational outcomes. Starting in 2003, the country introduced a new planning and reporting framework for schools. Under this new system, the ERO now focuses on process questions of the following type: How well is information on student achievement used, both formally and informally, to develop programs to meet the needs of individuals and groups of students? How well is available time used for learning purposes? How effective are the systems for identifying and meeting staff professional development needs? And how well does the school establish partnerships around learning with its community (Ladd 2010)? The focus is not on learning outcomes themselves but rather on the robustness and coherence of the internal processes and practices that policymakers believe are associated with good outcomes.

The focus on how well schools use data on student achievement to allocate resources and on the coherence of policies for supporting student learning emerge as central components of all the inspection systems of which we are aware. The logic underlying such evaluation systems is at one level quite compelling. Because schools differ so dramatically in their students and, in many cases, in the resources available to them, it makes intuitive sense to judge quality by how well the school uses those resources to meet the needs of its students.

At the same time, there are some potential drawbacks to this approach. One is the danger of emphasizing processes that are in fact not ultimately related to valued educational outcomes, either because the processes have not been validated in the literature as being linked to those outcomes or because the validation is based on measures of quality that are themselves imperfect or narrow. For example, if the reviewers place a lot of emphasis on the use of data, and those data are all based on tests of basic skills in math and reading, then the observational measure may provide a narrow measure of school quality. Working in the other direction, the review protocol could be so broad that the reports are not useful for distinguishing between processes that contribute significantly to quality and those that are less directly predictive. Furthermore, because it relies on human judgment, the observational approach may be subject to variation in ratings that reflect differences across reviewers rather than differences in education quality. Unless the reviewers are well trained and the reports tested for reliability across reviewers, the system could provide misleading information.

While the validity of many current observational measures can be questioned, the most common concern about the observational approach is its high cost. As the school-based approach has been implemented in practice, costs include the reviewers' time and the costs of their training as well as the time school officials use preparing for reviews and responding to them. These costs depend on the nature of the program, including the size of the review team for each visit, the salaries of the reviewers, the frequency of visits, and the costs of training high-quality reviewers and of ensuring reliability. Offsetting some of these costs, however, are any school improvements the process generates.

The well-developed English inspection system as it operated in the 1990s was very expensive, with visits to primary schools costing about $20,000 and visits to secondary schools about $37,500 (Kogan and Maden 1999; converted from pounds to dollars). The smaller-scale system in Charlotte/Mecklenburg, North Carolina, that built on the English model but made greater use of internal personnel was far less expensive, with an estimated cost of each school evaluation below $9,000. The program of charter school evaluations in Massachusetts has an average cost of about $3,500 per charter school visit. The potentially high costs of the observational approach tend to make US policymakers wary of this approach and skeptical of the potential for taking it to scale. At the same time, many other countries have historically made much greater use of the observational approach and have used it for all their schools. In some countries, most notably England, the school visits have become less extensive and comprehensive in recent years as emphasis has shifted to a greater reliance on outcome measures, most prominently test scores.

The processes approach to measuring school quality, while potentially better at measuring the quality of schooling than purely resource-based measures, requires an understanding of how the benefits of education are produced. For example, to measure teacher quality or the quality of school leadership, observers need to know what good teaching and good school leadership look like. Although school systems have made substantial recent progress in measuring processes, most education processes have no protocols for observation, much less well-validated protocols. To the extent that schools continue to diversify—for example, through multiple pathways to high school completion, homeschooling, or distance learning—the job of directly measuring education practice becomes more challenging. Given the complexities of measuring quality through the inputs (either resources or processes), it is appealing to consider whether it is feasible to measure the outcomes of education directly.

Student Outcomes

As described above, education quality encompasses the consumption and investment benefits of schooling. These benefits could include general satisfaction, earnings, nonpecuniary job benefits, health, low crime, and a range of other outcomes. Most of the returns to education accrue long after students have completed school, and certainly too far in the future to provide meaningful measures of the current state of education quality or to be useful to education decision makers.

More immediate measures of student outcomes such as achievement and educational attainment may serve as proxies for these later outcomes. Ample evidence confirms that student test performance is associated with higher educational attainment and with earnings (Johnson and Neal 1998). The contribution of cognitive skills to future earnings, as measured by test scores, also appears to have risen over time (Murnane, Willett, and Levy 1995). Given this link between test performance and subsequent earnings, one might use measures of the student achievement gains attributable to schooling as a proxy for school quality. This approach is currently popular in the United States, arising from state-level test-based accountability programs introduced in the 1990s and currently represented at the national level by the No Child Left Behind Act.

The benefits of using outcome-based measures of school quality are clear. Directly measuring outcomes negates the need to know how education is or should be produced. If we measure quality by how much a student learns, we do not need careful analyses of how to adjust spending for costs across regions or across schools serving different populations of students, or careful observational measures of good teaching. If it were easy to measure education quality directly through observation, this advantage of outcome-based measures would not be important, but measuring education quality directly is difficult and costly.

Not surprisingly, using student outcomes to measure education quality has meaningful drawbacks. First, measures of student outcomes used in current education systems do not capture the breadth of student outcomes that individuals and society value and that therefore are central to the concept of school quality. By requiring that all states annually test all students in grades three through eight in math and English language arts, No Child Left Behind (NCLB) has dramatically increased the availability of student test performance data in those two subjects and has required that those test scores serve as the basis of measures of school quality. Those two subjects, however, represent only a portion of the content that may generate future education benefits. They completely ignore other skills and dispositions that could, at least in principle, be measured at the time of schooling and that are likely to be important for future outcomes—such as the ability to work effectively in groups and to empathize, as well as achievement in science, history, and the arts (see Rothstein, Jacobson, and Wilder 2008 for a fuller discussion). Moreover, current tests do not even attempt to measure the consumption benefits of education, such as student happiness and health. Even within the domains of math and English language arts, tests focus on skills that are more easily tested and thus emphasize the importance of some content over other content, creating outcome weights that do not necessarily align with society's values. While the tests may be highly reliable measures of student achievement in the content tested, they are unlikely to be valid measures of the full set of education goals.

The focus of current testing programs on math and English language arts stems from a variety of sources. It is impractical to measure all outcomes of interest for all students each year, even if the outcomes are limited to current (in contrast to future) knowledge and skills. The time necessary to measure each domain reliably is simply too great. To get a sense of the success of an overall education system, one could measure outcomes for different students or in different years, but this approach is more complex and sacrifices some comparability across students and over time. In addition, while reliable measures of student outcomes span areas broader than math and English language arts, many important outcomes are not as easy to measure with instruments currently available. Whether a broader approach to testing would better capture education outcomes (both consumption and investment benefits) of interest is an empirical question that has yet to be answered. Logically, tests covering broader content should capture a broader set of valued outcomes and should also reduce the tendency of narrow tests to lead to a narrow curriculum. At the same time, though seemingly broader, the tests may simply pick up skills similar to those measured by the current tests (using different questions), whether those are test-taking skills or skills important for future success. Broader tests may sacrifice both time and reliability for little gain if they do not improve our ability to measure the consumption and investment benefits that characterize high-quality education. Although we cannot directly measure the long-run outcomes of education, we can judge a testing regime that aims to measure education quality on the extent to which it appears to measure the outcomes of ultimate value.

A second difficulty of using student outcomes as a proxy for school quality is that, even if current outcomes such as test scores well represent the long-run outcomes of interest, it is often difficult to correctly determine the portion of a student's outcome that is due to schools. We have defined school quality as the benefits students and society get from their schooling. The benefits of interest arise, however, not only from the schooling itself but also from other parts of their lives, particularly from their families but also from their communities and other experiences. If we simply use student test performance to measure school quality, we would falsely attribute to schools differences in performance that are due to ability and to family background. A first step is to look at gains in student performance instead of levels, so as to separate initial differences from changes during schooling. In fact, however, the evidence shows that ability and family background affect gains as well as levels. Despite the development of sophisticated approaches to estimating the effects of schools on student outcomes, even the most well considered does not cleanly isolate school effects from other effects. For example, most empirical models of student outcomes adjust statistically for differences in achievement gains by family background, but these adjustments inappropriately eliminate any components of school quality that are systematically associated with family background. That is, some of the difference in the achievement gains of students in schools with a higher proportion of students in poverty is due to fewer educational opportunities outside school, but some is probably due to lower-quality schools. Statistical adjustments eliminate both these sources of lower achievement from the measure of school quality when ideally the differences in achievement due to lower-quality schools would remain in the measure of school quality. The models could be run without adjustments, but then we would inappropriately attribute to the schools differences in educational opportunities outside schools. The bottom line is that it is very difficult to separate the contributions of differences in average quality of schools across groups from those of differences in other inputs to the variation in student outcomes across groups. As we discuss further below, if the goal is to understand the quality of educational opportunities available to students overall (both inside and outside school), then this difficulty of attribution is not important. If the goal is to assess the quality of schools themselves, however, then attribution is both important and difficult.

Education Quality in the Context of Education Equity

Thus far we have introduced the concept of education quality and different approaches to measurement: resources, observational measures of internal processes and practice, and proximal outcomes. Each of these measures has advantages and disadvantages. In the context of equity discussions, the relative salience of these advantages and disadvantages depends on how one conceptualizes educational equity. Setting aside the voluminous literature by philosophers, lawyers, public finance economists, and education researchers, we focus here on three concepts: equity as access to equal quality schools, equity as equal educational opportunity, and equity as adequacy.

Equity as Access to Equal Quality Schools

One plausible equity goal is that all schools should be of equal, or equivalent, quality. By this we mean that student A would do equally well, or badly, by going to school X, Y, or Z. Average student outcomes would probably still differ across schools, but those differences would be attributable to differences in the abilities, motivations, and outside-school supports of the students in each school and not to differences in school quality. This definition of equal guarantees that students would receive equal quality schooling regardless of which school they attend; it does not guarantee that all students would receive the same quality education, since education quality can vary between students within a school. One consequence of this equity standard is that the systematic sorting of students across schools (for example, as a result of residential segregation by income or race) would not increase achievement gaps between groups beyond those associated with the background characteristics of the students themselves. Nor, however, would schools narrow those gaps.

Our goal here is to consider the relative merits of the different approaches to measuring school quality in the context of this equity standard. As discussed above, resource measures can take the form of cost-adjusted spending or direct measures of resources. There is very little merit to spending measures that do not include cost adjustments. On one hand, although appropriate cost adjustments can be difficult to estimate, cost-adjusted spending measures may be preferred to direct resource measures because they allow for differences in the allocation of funds to meet the needs of students, needs that may vary widely across contexts. On the other hand, cost-adjusted spending measures will not capture differences in school quality that are due to inefficiency (including corruption) in the use of dollars. Schools may appear to be of equal quality on cost-adjusted spending but not on direct measures of resources if they differ in how effectively they use their money to buy resources. Direct measures of resources (such as the number of equal quality computers or equal quality teachers) would uncover some of the differences in quality due to ineffective use of funds, as long as the measures of resources appropriately identify the quality, as well as the quantity, of resources.

The quality of the school is a function not only of the quality of the specific resources but also of how those resources are utilized together; thus, direct measures of resources will not identify all quality differences across schools even if they are a better measure than cost-adjusted spending for assessing the quality of the individual resources. Observational measures of processes in schools aim to carefully measure quality differences not only in each specific resource but in how the resources are used. In theory, these observational measures would be a productive way to determine whether the quality of education provided is equal across schools. The technology for measuring the quality of processes is just emerging, however, and it is currently impractical to measure the quality of all the key schooling processes. Although instruments are in development, it is likely to be many years before comprehensive measurement of schooling is feasible. Finally, the third measure, proximal student outcomes, may at first appear to have some advantages. As discussed further below, however, the difficulty in attributing outcomes to schools limits its usefulness for assessing whether the quality of education is the same across schools.

In summary, if the goal is to assess the extent to which schools are of equal quality, then some combination of the resource measures and process measures would constitute the best approach in most situations.

Equity as Equal Opportunity

A second standard, equity as equal opportunity, goes beyond the principle of "do no harm" and calls for schools to compensate for, or redress, background disadvantages that students bring with them to school so that all children have the opportunity to participate equally in the political and economic life of the community. According to this more demanding equity standard, social disadvantage would not be an excuse for differential outcomes. Because students come to school with different family backgrounds and capacities to learn, providing equal quality schools would not meet this equal opportunity standard. Instead, some schools would have to offer higher-quality schooling than others to compensate for the differences society deemed unacceptable contributors to unequal outcomes.

Because this standard focuses on educational outcomes, the relative merits of the three approaches to measuring educational quality change. In particular, the difficulties of attributing educational outcomes to schools become less problematic. Consider first an extreme—and admittedly unrealistic—example in which the community defines educational equity as equal outcomes for all students. In this case the cause or attribution of the outcomes is irrelevant. All that matters is whether the outcomes differ, not why they differ. Of course, any limitations associated with the use of a set of outcome measures that do not reflect the full range of investment outcomes of actual interest remain a problem. Defining educational equity in this extreme way of equal outcomes for all students may in fact be an undesirable conception of equity, for the reasons emphasized by Amy Gutmann (1987). Children differ in their aptitudes and interests, and requiring them all to reach the same level on each outcome of interest is unrealistic. Moreover, equalizing outcomes at the level of the individual would undoubtedly require a level of government intervention into family life, and perhaps into the gene pool, that most people would deem inappropriate.

A somewhat more realistic conception of this equity goal would require equality of average outcomes across groups of students defined by their demographic characteristics (Roemer 1998). For instance, equity could require similar outcomes on average for males and females, blacks and whites, southerners and northerners, or children from low-income and more affluent households. This interpretation of the equity goal may require too much of schools alone to be fully achievable in practice, but it at least provides guidance about background differences for which schools would need to provide higher-quality education and thus probably would require greater inputs. Once again, though, because this equity concept is based on outcomes, the problem of attributing outcomes to schools is less salient than when the equity standard is equal quality schools.

An equity concept that is based on educational outcomes, rather than on school inputs, is appealing because it aligns well with an ultimate goal of an equitable distribution of outcomes such as income and health. Such an equity concept, however, is not by itself very useful to makers of educational policy. Because many factors besides schooling contribute to educational outcomes, policymakers need information on the schooling component if they are to make wise decisions that balance schooling, income redistribution, housing programs, individual incentives, and other potential approaches to equalizing individual or group outcomes. As such, some direct measures of education quality—in the form of cost-adjusted spending measures and observational protocols—are warranted in combination with outcomes-based measures.

Equity as Adequacy

Yet a third standard of educational equity shifts the focus away from equality to the sufficiency or adequacy of the education system. According to an adequacy standard, every child should receive a level of education quality sufficient to achieve some specified goal or goals. Once that standard was met, it would be acceptable, from a normative perspective, for some children to receive a far higher quality of education than others. Thus, adequacy need not require equality.

The concept of adequacy can be applied either directly to educational inputs or, as is more common in practice, to educational outcomes. As applied to inputs, the standard might require schools to have qualified teachers and manageable class sizes and to provide safe and healthy learning environments. As one part of the first phase of the New York *Campaign for Fiscal Equity* (*CFE*) case, for example, the court specified that children are "entitled to minimally adequate physical facilities and classrooms," "reasonably current textbooks," an adequate number of qualified teachers, and schools in which "reasonably up-to-date curricula such as reading, writing, mathematics, science, and social studies" are being taught according to "minimally adequate" standards (*Campaign for Fiscal Equity v. State of New York*, 295 A.D. 2d 1 [2002], 317). Measuring educational quality for the purposes of assessing compliance with this equity standard would clearly require information on the specific input measures of interest, including information on teacher quality, and might well require some attention to school processes. The main focus would be only on whether schools did or did not meet the threshold. The outcome approach to measuring educational quality would be neither useful nor necessary.

The *CFE* case also defined adequacy in term of outcomes for students, as has been done in many other court cases. Interpreted in terms of outcomes, the adequacy standard raises the central question, "Adequate for what?" One answer might lie in the Rawlsian concept of primary goods and the notion that all students attain a minimum set of educational outcomes connected to their long-term life chances (Rawls 2001, 57–61). Another might draw on philosopher Amy Gutmann's concept of a democratic threshold. In her view, the primary role of education is to promote a democratic society, characterized by deliberative and collective decision making, and hence the threshold is that level at which a person has the ability to participate effectively in the political process (Gutmann 1987; see also the discussion in Ladd and Hansen 1999, 102 6). Combining these two views, an adequate education may be conceived of as one that is sufficient for someone to participate fully in both the economic and the political life of the country (see also Allen, n.d.; Smith, this volume, for such a combined view).

In general the definition of educational adequacy would allow for disparities above the adequate threshold. To the extent that education is viewed as a "positional good," however, adequacy defined in terms of outcomes becomes more complicated and in fact may require that educational outcomes be equalized. A positional good is one in which one's position in the queue matters for one's outcome. In other words, "the absolute value of the good one holds, to the extent it is positional, can only be determined by referring to one's standing in the distribution of that good" (Koski and Hahnel 2008, 45; Reich, this volume). Hence, if education is viewed as a positional good, the only way to ensure that everyone gets an adequate education is to make sure educational outcomes are similar.

Regardless of whether education is or is not viewed as a positional good, judging the adequacy, defined in terms of outcomes, of an education system raises most of the same issues for the measurement of education quality as does the equal opportunity standard. Specifically, because the focus is outcomes, one need not necessarily isolate the contribution schools make to student outcomes to measure the quality of the system. Thus, while equity as equal opportunity and equity as adequacy differ conceptually, the use of proximal outcome measures of quality makes them quite similar in terms of the relative merits of different approaches to measuring quality. Although US policymakers have not pursued equality of educational outcomes, broadly defined, as a serious policy goal, both the courts and the federal government have embraced outcome adequacy with various degrees of ambition. Some state courts, including the Kentucky court in a 1989 adequacy case, conceived of the outcome goals very broadly.[2] In practice, however, adequacy is typically defined more narrowly. In the New York *Campaign for Fiscal Equity* case (see Smith, this volume), for example, the issue was whether an eighth-grade education was adequate (though this position lost and a much higher standard was adopted), and under the federal No Child Left Behind Act adequacy is defined narrowly in terms of proficiency on math and reading tests.

As is the case for the equal opportunity standard, while proximal outcome measures may be necessary and useful for assessing the adequacy of an education system, that approach alone is not sufficient for makers of educational policy because it sheds no light on the contributions of schools relative to other generators of the outcomes of interest. Even with an adequacy standard, therefore, some combination of the three approaches to assessing school quality would be needed.

Conclusion

Education quality has been and continues to be the focus of policy debates, as well as academic discussions within a range of disciplines from political theory to economics and sociology. Yet the definition of education quality in these deliberations is often hazy, relying on examples of spending patterns or patterns of specific resources available across schools, observations in schools, or student test performance. None of these approaches to measuring education quality is perfect; each brings with it advantages and disadvantages. In this chapter we began by defining education quality as the benefits of education to students and other members of the community—benefits that can be described as consumption and investment benefits, intrinsic and extrinsic benefits, private and public benefits, or in a variety of other ways. Higher-quality schools provide more benefits than do low-quality schools.

None of the available measures of education quality perfectly capture these benefits of schooling, at least in part because most education benefits accrue long after students leave school. School spending adjusted for cost differences is an appealing measure of quality because it is easy to understand and, as a ratio scale, allows for quantitative comparisons such as one school spending 25 percent more than another school. Unfortunately, because of meaningful efficiency differences as well as unknown cost differences across schools, school spending poorly approximates school quality. Direct measures of education practices can account for efficiency and cost differences in ways spending measures cannot. Unfortunately, validated observational measures are available for only a very limited number of school processes, which is especially problematic in the quickly changing and diversifying education sector. Using students' test performance as a measure of school quality eliminates the need to understand or agree on the best way to teach or to run schools. It also is not affected by rapidly changing approaches to schooling. Thus, measuring education quality by test performance has benefits. However, while current test performance is predictive of future job market opportunities, it does not capture the full range of benefits of value. In addition, attributing the portion of test performance that is due to schooling in contrast to educational opportunities outside school is not easy.

Given that none of the available measures of school quality fully (or sufficiently) capture actual quality, which measure is most useful? The answer depends on the reason for measuring education quality. If the goal is equal or adequate education outcomes for students, as would be consistent with the normative standards of equal educational opportunity or adequacy, measuring quality in terms of student outcomes may be appealing, since determining whether students achieve specified outcomes is more important than correctly attributing quality to particular schools. Even in the context of this relatively compelling case for using an outcomes-based measure, however, the limited range of measurable contemporaneous outcomes for students makes it useful to supplement the outcome measure of quality with information on school resources and processes. In addition, resource and process measures can help policymakers choose where to target investments and interventions. Thus, while student outcome measures are clearly useful for understanding how fully equal opportunity or adequacy goals are achieved, they are best supplemented with other quality measures.

If the normative goal is equal quality schools, so that a student (and society) receives the same level of benefits regardless of which school that student attends, then attributing outcomes to specific schools is of great importance. Consequently, the advantages of resource and process measures of education quality increase relative to measures based on student outcomes. The point is that all three approaches to measuring quality are imprecise, and each has its own strengths and weaknesses. All three are potentially useful, but how much emphasis to put on one approach differs depending on the normative standard of interest.

CHAPTER 2

Equality, Adequacy, and K–12 Education

Rob Reich

Introduction

Questions about distributive justice occupy a place of central and long-standing importance in political philosophy. The basic task of a theory of distributive justice is to identify what principle or principles should govern or structure the distribution of benefits and burdens in a society and to identify to whom—what people or class of persons—these benefits and burdens are to be distributed. Schooling is a paradigm of a good that is distributed in some manner or another by virtually every society. The introduction early last century of compulsory attendance laws provides a definitive answer to the question of what persons are to receive the benefit of schooling: each and every child. But compulsory attendance laws do not address the question *how* to distribute education to a universal class of recipients, namely, all children.

In this chapter I examine two ideals that could guide a state's provision of primary and secondary schooling: *equality* and *adequacy*. Should all children receive equal educational opportunities? Or is the state's obligation to ensure that all children receive *enough* or an *adequate* education? What is the connection, if any, between equality and adequacy?

The question is of much more than academic interest. The backdrop for posing it is the undeniable significance of educational attainment and achievement in the modern world. As recently as 1950, only one-third of Americans twenty-five and older had attained a high school degree. In 2000, 85 percent had done so. Today education is central to individual

flourishing, economic growth and innovation, and the health of a democratic society. This fact is reflected in the extraordinary expenditures on
primary and secondary schooling.[1] It is reflected in compulsory attendance
laws that represent, with the possible exception of taxation, the most visible intrusion of the state into the average citizen's daily life. Put simply,
education has a profound influence on an individual's opportunities and
life prospects; increasing educational achievement and attainment are correlated with labor market opportunities, income, health, and political participation, among other things. Education is important not only because
of its instrumental value; it has intrinsic value in helping to unlock the
potential and develop the talents and interests of each person. Insofar as
states attempt to improve or equalize life chances and opportunities, or
to provide an opportunity for each person to flourish, education has been
described as the closest we have to a "universal solvent," the best lever at
the state's disposal to promote equal opportunity.[2]

Yet despite the centrality of education to modern life and the amount
taxpayers spend on it, policymakers and citizens have surprisingly little
clarity about the differences between equality and adequacy and how the
two ideals have woven themselves into educational law and policy. As a
result, our debates about educational provision and reform are conceptually muddied.

This essay lays out at a conceptual level the difference between equality and adequacy and shows what these conceptual differences mean for
educational policy and practice.

The chapter proceeds as follows. The next section outlines the historical evolution in education law and policy from an equality orientation
to an adequacy orientation. The following section provides a conceptual
primer on equality and adequacy. The final section relates these conceptual differences to current educational policy debates.

History of Equality and Adequacy in Education Law, Policy, and Practice

In 1954 the United States Supreme Court famously held in the landmark
case *Brown v. Board of Education* that when a state provides children
an education, such an opportunity "is a right which must be made available to all on equal terms." This orientation toward equality continued in
American educational law and policy for several decades, focusing first

and foremost on the desegregation of public schools. But the equality orientation is also visible in federal educational policy, in particular in the
Title I provisions of the 1965 Elementary and Secondary Education Act
(ESEA) that directed significant federal support for low-income children.
And equality is central to the school finance battles—usually known as
school finance *equalization* battles—that began in the late 1960s and continue today. Equality was the guiding norm in the provision of schooling
across each of these policy domains.

During the past two decades, however, the rhetoric and policy of equal
educational opportunity have given way to the rhetoric and policy of providing an "adequate" education for all. As a result, the concept of "educational adequacy" has framed contemporary discussion among scholars,
courts, and policymakers, and this is evident across each of the policy domains just mentioned.

The contested arena of school finance—the hobgoblin of virtually every state in the union, in which over the past thirty years *no fewer than
forty-five states* have had their school funding schemes challenged in state
courts—provides perhaps the most obvious example of this shift from
equality to adequacy.

According to a standard narrative describing the evolution of school
finance, litigation has come in three waves, the first two defined by their
aspiration toward *equality* and the third defined by its move to *adequacy*.

The first and briefest wave lasted from 1971 to 1973. The distinguishing feature of initial efforts during this period was to challenge unequal
school funding between districts based on the United States Constitution's
Fourteenth Amendment, or Equal Protection Clause. The basic argument
was that the equal protection guaranteed to citizens under the Fourteenth
Amendment prohibited substantially unequal funding of schools that was
the product of the wealth of the people or property within any particular
district. It was a version of this argument that prevailed in California's
1971 *Serrano v. Priest*, leading to the centralization of school funding
at the state level. In 1973, however, the federal equal protection theory
reached a dead end when the US Supreme Court rejected the argument in
San Antonio Independent School District v. Rodriguez, finding that there
was no fundamental right to education under the US Constitution.

With no recourse at the federal level, the battleground over school finance shifted to the states and to the language in the fifty state constitutions. This began the second wave of school finance litigation, which
lasted from 1973 through 1989. The essence of the claim in second-wave

cases, according to the wave typology, was the *equality* of school funding schemes. Most courts primarily sought to achieve "horizontal equity" across school districts such that revenues per pupil were roughly equalized by the state. Alternatively, courts sought "fiscal neutrality" such that the revenues available to a school district would not depend solely on the property wealth of the school district. Instead, funding between school districts could be unequal, but the inequality would be a product not of varying degrees of property wealth but of the varying democratically decided preferences of localities to levy taxes at higher or lower levels to support public education. In practice, horizontal equity and fiscal neutrality usually meant greater state involvement in educational funding through the institution of state-guaranteed tax base, or "foundation," plans and, on rarer occasions, state-backed equal yield, or "district power equalization," plans, which captured revenues from wealthy districts and redistributed them to poorer districts.

The third wave marks the shift from an equality to an adequacy orientation, and it can be dated with precision. In 1989 the Kentucky Supreme Court rendered its decision in *Rose v. Council for Better Education*. The court interpreted the education article in Kentucky's constitution to require that the state legislature provide Kentucky children with an adequate education, or a "sound basic education," which the court specified by identifying seven capabilities that all students would be expected to attain. Since 1989, many other states have followed Kentucky's path, with court decisions frequently invoking the terms sufficient education and basic education.

The difference in language is obvious, and so too are the educational policy repercussions of the shift to adequacy. These are captured well in the following assessments of longtime observers of school finance wars. According to Paul Minorini and Stephen Sugarman,

> What is most distinctive about the adequacy approach is that, unlike the traditional school finance cases, it does not rest on a norm of equal treatment. Indeed, the adequacy cases aren't about equality at all, except in the sense that all pupils are entitled to at least a high minimum. In other words, adequacy is not a matter of comparing spending on the complaining group to spending on the others. It is rather about spending what is needed (and its focus is in some respects more on the school or the pupil than on the district).[3]

Similarly, James Ryan and Michael Heise observe, "Even successful adequacy suits . . . presuppose that existing funding inequalities will remain.

More precisely, adequacy suits abandon the idea of tying districts together financially by requiring access to equal resources. Those districts that can fund a more-than-adequate education are free to do so."[4] Another difference is that the equality orientation of the first two waves tended to focus on school inputs, chiefly dollars, and the new adequacy orientation brought along a focus on school outputs. As we shall see later, this was a matter of historical contingency, not conceptual necessity.

The school finance cases focus almost exclusively on efforts to change education law and policy through the courts. But courts are not the only venue of change, of course. A similar story can be told about the evolution from equality to adequacy in other prominent educational policy domains.[5] The equality orientation of Title I in the 1965 ESEA has given way to a new emphasis on standards-based reform in the 2001 congressional reauthorization of Title I, better known as the No Child Left Behind Act (NCLB). Under NCLB, states must establish "challenging content standards" and "student academic achievement standards" in reading, math, and science that reflect an adequate educational outcome for all students in the state.[6] States then must use assessments aligned with those standards to hold schools accountable for ensuring that their students make adequate yearly progress (AYP) toward proficiency on the state's standards with the goal of reaching proficiency by 2014.

The design of current accountability regimes is based on an adequacy principle, the idea that the school system ought to press all students toward some predefined level of proficiency in various subject matters. AYP, for instance, is based on progress toward a specific goal of proficiency. It is not a measure of how poor and minority students perform relative to their wealthier peers.

Most standards-based reform and accountability schemes also possess disequalizing incentives in their design. Specifically, NCLB and the accountability regimes it has supported or spawned create incentives that may exacerbate current racial and socioeconomic segregation and its resulting educational disparity (see Rothstein, this volume); decrease graduation rates for minority students faced with high-stakes testing; discourage high-quality teachers from accepting difficult assignments in relatively low-performing schools; and narrow the curriculum in low-performing schools, increasing the deficit in the opportunities for poor and minority children to enjoy a rich curricular and educational experience.[7]

A more detailed history of the past fifty years of school reform would also identify legislative efforts at both the federal level and at the state level. I omit these to focus exclusively on how equality and adequacy are at the conceptual foundation of any kind of education reform concerning the distribution of educational opportunity, judicial or legislative. In short, if we are to answer the question, "What is the state's obligation to provide K–12 education to children?" we must answer by discussing whether the obligation is satisfied by an equal education, whatever that might mean, or an adequate education, whatever that might mean. It is toward the task of conceptually distinguishing equality and adequacy that I now turn.

Conceptual Distinction between Equality and Adequacy

To appreciate more precisely the contrast between equality and adequacy, it is instructive to consider how philosophers have distinguished equality from sufficiency. "Sufficiency," not "adequacy," is the term philosophers use; the two should be understood here as equivalent in meaning.[8]

The fundamental conceptual difference between equality and sufficiency is that equality is necessarily *comparative or relational,* while sufficiency is not. To ask if somebody or something is equal, we must engage in a comparative evaluation. Does X have as much as Y? Is the outcome in situation A the same as the outcome in situation B? To ask if somebody or something is sufficiently well off, however, we need not make any such comparison; we simply identify what constitutes the level of sufficiency and then make the appropriate allocation or redistribution of resources. Put another way, the sufficiency framework aims to combat *absolute* deprivation; the equality framework aims to combat *relative* deprivation. For the sufficiency advocate, we should not care that people are equal but only that they have enough. But it is bad, the egalitarian claims, for some people to be worse-off than others through no fault of their own.[9] (And for some strict egalitarians, it is bad just to be worse-off.)

The sharpness of this distinction requires a qualification. Sufficiency encompasses relational or comparative assessments in two respects. What constitutes a sufficient level of resources will be relative to the norms of any given society at a particular time. In light of vastly different levels of GDP and different occupational market structures, what counts as a sufficient level of education in Ghana will be different from a sufficient level of education in the United States at present. Sufficiency is also relative to historical developments within societies. What seemed a luxury a generation ago can now seem a necessity. Fifty years ago sufficient education in the United States was less than a high school degree. Today, however, what constitutes a sufficient education is more demanding because social norms and the economy have changed.[10] A sufficient education in the twenty-first century, most policymakers and courts agree, must prepare all children for postsecondary education without remediation.

But this relational aspect of sufficiency is unimportant here. While standards for what is sufficient will vary across societies and over time within societies, sufficiency at any given moment is an absolute, or noncomparative, thing. This is not true for equality, which is always and necessarily comparative. In addition, it is important to be mindful of the practical consideration that when a society wishes to place "sufficiency" into institutional operation—as is the case with the adequacy movement in American school reform—policymakers will be strongly attracted to absolute outcome standards, static definitions of subject matter proficiency.

A few observations about the conceptual differences between equality and sufficiency. First, with respect to any particular policy issue, it is entirely possible to employ an equality analysis and a sufficiency analysis simultaneously, for the simple reason that one can simultaneously be both absolutely deprived and relatively deprived. A person living on two dollars a day, for example, is absolutely deprived, below a threshold of sufficient income, and also relatively deprived, possessing a lower income than richer members of society. Desperate poverty is objectionable for both equality and adequacy reasons. But only an egalitarian framework can capture what is wrong with relative deprivation, once levels of sufficiency have been established and absolute deprivation has been eliminated.

Second, the sufficiency framework, to be sure, can justify equality-enhancing transfers from the well-off to the needy. If many people have more than enough and a few have less than enough, then taking from the many to boost the few above the threshold that marks the level of adequacy looks like a good thing. But if all are above the threshold, then transfers from the well-off to those who already have enough no longer seems justifiable.

Third, adequacy might seem less demanding than equality—fiscally and politically. All that appears to be required is that those below a specified threshold (of inputs or outcomes) be brought up to that level. Equality, by contrast, demands that all people be brought into an equal relationship (of whatever metric equality is being applied to). In practice, pursuing equality often *is more* demanding. But clarifying the conceptual relationship between the two ideals reveals that adequacy can also demand far more than equality. Consider a scenario in which the level of adequacy of some good is one hundred units per person. A has ten units, B has fifteen units, and C has twenty units of the good. Equality can be attained by giving A five units from C. Adequacy, obviously, would be much more difficult to attain. Indeed, as I shall argue below, some versions of educational adequacy are far more fiscally demanding than educational equality, and objectionable for this very reason.

Finally, to draw the conceptual contrast between equality and adequacy most clearly, consider two powerful criticisms to which the equality advocate is vulnerable but not the adequacy advocate. The first criticism is often called the leveling down objection. Simply stated, the egalitarian should be satisfied if the well-off were brought down to the same level as the worst-off, for this would eliminate the inequality between them. If A has five units of some good and B has two, equality is served by making A and B equal at five units each, but also at two units each. In leveling down, of course, there is a loss in overall utility; some are made worse-off while no one is made better-off. In an example from philosopher Derek Parfit, the egalitarian appears forced to claim, perversely, that it must in some way be an improvement if equality of vision between the sighted and the blind is brought about by blinding those who can see.[11] Though philosophers prefer to illustrate the leveling down objection in formal algebraic terms or with ludicrous examples such as the equally blind, its bearing in the real world is perhaps nowhere greater than in school finance. It is a genuine concern that in equalizing school resources among districts with varying degrees of wealth, the actual effect will be to level down the resources of the wealthy districts rather than leveling up the resources of the poor districts. Leveling down might increase equality of educational resources, but in the process it will significantly affect the *absolute* quality of education provided, worsening the better-off and failing to improve the worse-off.[12] Who could possibly prefer this outcome?

The second criticism suggests that equality conflicts with other worthy values and that, at least sometimes, equality should give way. That this may happen within education is quite clear. Consider, for instance, the following comment by Nathan Glazer:

> To be sure, the case for both [racial] integration and equality of expenditure is powerful. But the chief obstacle to achieving these goals does not seem to be the indifference of whites and the non-poor to the education of nonwhites and the poor. . . . Rather, other values, which are not simply shields for racism, stand in the way: the value of the neighborhood school; the value of local control of

education and, above all, the value of freedom from state imposition when it affects matters so personal as the future of one's children.[13]

In short, pursuing equality in education can, and often does, conflict with other values, most prominently the value of parental liberty. And when it does, sometimes it is equality that should yield or bend to accommodate the other value. Some parents, for instance, seek to provide better or more education for their children, perhaps because they assign a very high value to being educated or perhaps because they want to share certain interests with their children that can be developed only through formal schooling. If providing one's child with better or more education requires additional resources that would make a public school unequal to other schools (in inputs, opportunities, or outputs), it might be within the proper scope of parental liberty to pursue such education. Pursuing only equality might unduly constrain parental liberty. (Harry Brighouse and Adam Swift discuss exactly this tension in their chapter in this volume, arguing that parents do *not* possess a right to choose or use schools to confer advantage or shape their children's values.)

In light of these two criticisms, many philosophers argue that the strict egalitarian position must be flawed. What is important here is to recognize that the person committed to sufficiency or adequacy is not vulnerable to these criticisms. Leveling down is no threat to the sufficiency advocate, who is concerned only that people have enough. This might require redistribution from the wealthy to the poor to bring everyone up to the tolerable or decent minimum. But the sufficiency advocate is not oriented around leveling or equalizing and has a clear way to choose between a situation in which A and B have two units of some good and one in which A and B have five units. So long as the level of sufficiency is greater than two units, sufficiency points to the latter distribution as preferable; the egalitarian is indifferent. As for the parental liberty objection, this might be pressed against adequacy as strenuously as against equality. But adequacy seems to weigh more lightly against parental liberty, for adequacy can be construed to give wide latitude to parental liberty so long as all children receive an adequate education. Equal education *appears to require more* than an adequate education, especially if it is directed in practice to level up all students, schools, or districts to the spending or opportunities at the top end of the distribution and therefore seems to conflict more sharply with the liberty of parents who want to give their children the very best education they can provide.

Equality, Adequacy, and Educational Reform and Resource Distribution

With the conceptual distinction between equality and adequacy now clear, this section discusses how the two concepts relate to educational reform and resource distribution. Let us begin with three general points about equality and adequacy as applied to educational policy.

First, it is conceptually coherent to connect both equality and adequacy to *inputs*, *opportunities*, or *outcomes*. As discussed in the section above on education law, policy, and practice, as a historical matter equality has most often been applied to educational inputs, particularly to the financing of school districts. The equality framework has frequently been deployed to ask, Why should funding levels between districts be unequal, with some districts spending far more than others? And in this case, equalizing inputs is thought to be a vehicle for equalizing educational opportunities, though defining opportunities in a precise manner has been notoriously difficult (see Ladd and Loeb, this volume). Adequacy, by contrast, has usually incorporated educational outcomes—academic attainment or achievement—into its framework. Adequacy asks, "What level of educational resources is sufficient to generate a specific set of educational outcomes?" Adequacy represents an attempt to move beyond considering the fairness of fiscal inputs toward the broad-based improvement of educational outcomes. For many, this difference is taken to be one of the virtues of adequacy over equality. And indeed, it seems a truism that any school reform initiative that is indifferent to academic achievement must be counted as flawed. Long experience has shown that additional dollars do not automatically translate into educational achievement. The so-called production function of schooling is not a linear connection between dollar inputs and achievement outputs.[14]

But as the preceding conceptual analysis reveals, the ideal of equality, just as much as the ideal of adequacy, can be hooked to educational opportunities and outcomes. An equality orientation need not revolve only around inputs to education. An egalitarian might seek equal educational outcomes or equality of educational opportunity or equal access to schooling.[15] Take the familiar and important discussions about the achievement gap, where education reforms aspire to equality of educational outcomes between races and socioeconomic classes. We might assess, for instance, whether equality of opportunity exists by looking to see if students from different racial and class backgrounds were equally represented in the distribution of educational achievement. Indeed, this is what motivates the prevailing concern over the black-white test gap in the United States.[16]

Second, as alluded to earlier, one fundamental distinction between equality and adequacy as applied to educational resource distribution is that adequacy seeks to ensure that all students have *enough* education and, if this condition is reached, will tolerate inequalities above this threshold. Imagine that the state's provision of schooling was judged adequate in the event that students were prepared for postsecondary education, the labor market, and able citizenship. Suppose at some point this standard is actually reached. But then some well-off school districts begin spending more money, generating greater opportunities for students, spurring greater academic achievement, and thereby securing for their students significant advantages in selective college admissions and entry to the labor market. Are there any grounds for complaint, since adequacy has been achieved? The adequacy framework sees no grounds; the equality framework, concerned with relative, not absolute deprivation, will indeed find grounds for complaint.

Third, it is commonplace to assume that equality-oriented reforms are more fiscally demanding than adequacy-oriented reforms. To avoid leveling down, equality appears to require that the state give every district the same level of resources as the highest-spending district in the state. But clarifying the conceptual relationship between equality and adequacy reveals that adequacy can sometimes be the more fiscally demanding. And some adequacy critics believe this is exactly the case in adequacy-oriented school reform. If states specify certain academic outcomes and insist that all children have the resources necessary to achieve them, then the marginal cost of the last batch of the most difficult to educate children will be enormous. Indeed, literally to have "no child left behind" would cost nothing less than the entirety of each state's budget, and even then it is doubtful that the last child would achieve to the adequate standard. (Imagine the marginal cost of that final child!) So while the equality ideal in its most fiscally demanding form required that the state level up expenditures to the rate of the highest-spending district, this was at least an expense imaginable within the constraints of the state's overall budget, even if reaching this spending goal was not politically viable. But one interpretation of the adequacy ideal, matching high outcome standards for all children to the resources necessary to attain these standards, appears to represent a tapline into the state treasury that could drain it of every last dollar.

In short, the fiscal and political advantages of adequacy over equality, or equality over adequacy, are unclear. Whether achieving equality costs more than attaining adequacy depends on contingent features of how the two are applied to educational resource distribution and on assumptions about the connection of resource inputs to educational outputs. It depends, in other words, on design features of educational policy, not on conceptual differences between equality and adequacy.

With a clearer understanding of the conceptual differences between equality and sufficiency and of how these differences manifest themselves in the institutional context of school reform, we are now better positioned to confront our initial question: Adequacy or equality in education—which is the state's obligation? The answer, I submit, concerns how one views the very purposes of education. I argue that equality is the more defensible ideal, not because equality is conceptually to be preferred to adequacy, but because equality is superior given an understanding about the state's interests in providing education to its citizens.

The State's Obligations That Adequacy Serves

To the extent that the purposes of education are seen as strictly civic—about the creation of able citizenship—adequacy is the appropriate ideal to govern the public provision of K–12 education. What is important is to establish a threshold of educational provision *sufficient* to whatever is considered to define able citizenship. For instance, public education should ensure that children acquire certain civic capacities (e.g., they can read and write), that they learn certain facts (e.g., about the structure of government and some history), and that they will have nondiscriminatory access to higher education and the labor market. Inequalities in educational provision above the threshold necessary to produce these outcomes are unobjectionable on the civic view.

To capture this in more precise philosophical terms, consider the position of Elizabeth Anderson. In a series of articles Anderson has developed an adequacy principle of distribution that is rooted in an egalitarian view of citizenship she calls "democratic equality."[17] What equality demands is that citizens stand in equal relation to one another, that no citizen is subjugated or oppressed, that there exist no castelike groups in society, that all can appear in public without shame or humiliation. (For an elaboration of a related view, see the chapter in this volume by Anthony Laden.) Democratic equality is therefore a theory of social justice rooted in a view about people in their capacities as citizens. It has implications for the distribution of goods and resources, but it is fundamentally a relational view about citizenship. The upshot for education is clear: adequate, not equal, provision is all that is required.

Democratic equality is egalitarian in its conception of just relationships among citizens, but sufficientarian in its conception of justice in the distribution of resources and opportunities. What is important is not that everyone has equal opportunities to acquire resources and fulfilling jobs, but that everyone has "enough." The ideal of democratic equality specifies how much this is: enough to secure the conditions of citizens' freedom and civic status as an equal to other citizens. On this view, as long as everyone has enough to function as an equal, inequalities beyond this threshold are not of particular concern.[18]

Of course, what is enough to establish the conditions of citizens' freedom and civic status as an equal may be a matter of considerable debate. Anderson has her own view, an expansive one that includes not merely the capacity to function as a political agent (voting, petitioning government, etc.), but also the capacity to function in civil society (to be free to form private groups, have access to public space, etc.) and certain minimum levels of human functioning (adequate nutrition, shelter, clothing, etc.).[19] Defining the equal standing of citizens in a robust manner, such that opportunities to participate in civic life are roughly equal, will bring the adequacy orientation much closer to the equality orientation in practice. But the essential point is that equality need not guide the distribution of educational resources; the distribution must give every student enough, must be *sufficient* to establish equal standing as a citizen. Inequalities above the threshold of adequate provision, potentially even vast inequalities, are a matter of indifference to the state. Note also that vast inequalities in educational achievement are also unobjectionable, so long as all children attain an education sufficient to establish equal standing as citizens. In short, adequacy sets a floor of educational provision and attainment below which no child or no group of children should fall. The connection to educational inputs, such as actual school finance litigation, should be obvious.

Debra Satz has taken the ideal of democratic equality one step further, showing that a concern for equal civic status not merely establishes a floor but also has implications for a ceiling of provision.[20] Thus a proper understanding of how the adequacy ideal guides educational provision gives us on Satz's account both a minimum and a maximum threshold. The reason is that equal standing as a citizen can be undermined when persons or groups of persons are so far above the adequate standard that they form an ingrained and perhaps self-perpetuating elite. "Great inequalities," writes Satz, "regarding who has a real opportunity for important goods above the threshold might relegate some members of society to second-class citizenship, where they can be effectively denied effective access to positions of power and privilege in the society."[21] Adequate provision of education has to be understood not as a fixed level of inputs, opportunities, or outcomes. The level of adequate inputs, opportunities, or outcomes will sit in dynamic relation to whatever the highest spenders or highest achievers are doing. Only such a dynamic relationship can ensure equal standing as a citizen and ward off the creation of entrenched and segregated elites.

Anderson and Satz derive a principle of educational distribution—adequacy—from an understanding of what equal citizenship entails. Which is to say, they understand the purpose of the state's involvement in educational distribution to be strictly public or civic, related to preparing able citizens and to sustaining the flourishing of democratic life. When the purpose of the state's involvement in education is confined to a civic rationale, the adequacy ideal has undeniable attractions. One might quibble that neither offers much in the way of operational specifics—exactly how equal standing as a citizen is to be measured in terms of dollar inputs or achievement outcomes in education[22]—and it is notable that no recent adequacy litigation or legislation I am aware of has attempted to define the adequate threshold of educational resources as a dynamic function of whatever the wealthiest districts in a state spend on education. In the real world, educational adequacy has been pursued as legislatively defined static outcome standards—typically minimal—and countless attempts are now under way to determine the cost of an "adequate" education that will get all students to these outcome standards.[23]

Adequacy defenders such as Anderson and Satz show us how an ideal of democratic equality—equal standing as a citizen—can bring an adequacy principle of educational distribution into close alignment with an egalitarian principle of educational distribution. And they also show—as does Laden's chapter in this volume—the interconnection between democracy and justice in education: a conception of democratic equality in the space of civic standing is at the heart of the relational view of justice he articulates.

It is perhaps tempting to suggest that Anderson and Satz show that equality and adequacy are inextricably linked, that they are not separate and distinct ideals. When Satz defends a dynamic view of adequacy, where what counts as adequate is sensitive to those students or schools at the top end of inputs, opportunities, or outcomes, it might seem to undercut the analysis offered in the preceding section, where I defined adequacy as conceptually unconcerned with vast inequalities above the specified adequate threshold. But equality and adequacy are not inextricably linked. Anderson and Satz simply identify different spaces in which the ideals of equality and adequacy might be deployed. They are egalitarians in the space of civic relations and "sufficientarians" in the space of distribution of educational resources. For Anderson and Satz, insofar as we concern ourselves with *relational justice*, equal standing between citizens is the correct view. And insofar as we concern ourselves with *distributional justice*, adequacy is the correct principle of distribution. Equality and adequacy are linked here only in the sense that adequacy in distribution flows from a view about equality in civic standing. Neither Anderson nor Satz defends equality in the space of distribution, as a distributional ideal.

But more important, I believe Anderson's and Satz's defenses of adequacy as a principle of educational distribution miss something important. There is something objectionable about the use of formal public institutions, such as public schools, to deliver resources over and above the level of sufficiency. Private individuals can thereby deploy public institutions to deliver private advantages to their own children. In doing so, the state confers its imprimatur on the advantage, and this can constitute a dignitary harm to individuals.

What Anderson and Satz fail to recognize is that, while sufficient provision of education may satisfy the conditions necessary to establish equal standing as a citizen, the state has special obligations to administer public institutions—or at least the public institution of K–12 schools—in a way that does not permit individuals to enlist them as vehicles for delivering private advantages.[24] This is because the state's concern with education is not only civic, where the purpose is to develop people into citizens who stand in equal relation to one another with certain capacities for civic participation. The state's concern with education, as I now shall discuss, also extends to the private advantages schooling can confer on individuals.

The State's Obligations That Equality Serves

The adequacy ideal is inadequate if we move beyond the view that the purpose of education is only civic. Education has private returns in addition to public purposes that are quite properly within the purview of the state.

It is a commonplace today to observe that the economic or vocational purposes of education have eclipsed its civic or public purposes. Parents do not see schooling as a vehicle to acquire the skills and dispositions necessary for good citizenship and for sustaining democracy. They see it as necessary for entry into the labor market and financial security. Similar things might be said about policymakers, who, when they argue about how to reform schools, see the main issue as how best to educate children so they will become productive, high-skilled workers. Finally, economists tend to examine educational provision as a question of how to fulfill local or private preferences about educational consumption most efficiently, how best to match the public supply of schooling with the private demand for it. In short, public education is seen less and less as an institution necessary to preserve healthy citizenship, or equal standing as a citizen, and more and more as necessary to ensure the ability to obtain a well-paid or simply middle-class job and to maintain the competitive advantage of the state's economy in a globalized world.

When the purposes of education are seen as economic and deliver significant private returns, equality has a strong claim as the appropriate ideal to govern its public provision. The reason is that private returns to education are very much a state concern. The state's interest in the private returns to education rests in the fact that education is a "positional good." Equality is normatively important in the provision of education because education is in part, and has historically become in larger part, a positional good. Education has positional aspects because, while acquiring some absolute level of educational attainment matters, the possession of education relative to one's peers also matters a great deal to one's life chances.

The term positional good comes from economist Fred Hirsch's *Social Limits to Growth*,[25] where he discusses the way the value of a certain good to a person depends on other people's not possessing that good, or not possessing as much of it. Positional goods fuse the notions of absolute and relative value. The absolute value of the good one holds, to the extent it is positional, can be determined only by referring to one's standing in the distribution of that good. Positional goods are competitive goods and valued as a means to achieving some other end or goal. As an illustration, Hirsch quips, "If everyone stands on tiptoe, no one sees better."[26]

The contrast, of course, is with goods whose absolute value to their possessor is independent of how much of that good others possess. Most goods, when examined closely enough, have some positional aspects. But consider the following example of a noncompetitive, nonpositional good.

Suppose I find a working television left out with the trash. The value of the television as something to use in my house is unaffected by how many televisions other people have. (Its marginal value to me may of course be different from its marginal value to others who occupy different places in the income distribution, but that is not the point here.) If televisions had positional value, in terms of their operation, then another person's finding a television on the street would affect the value of the television in my house.

Notice that in the case of positional goods, the typical understanding of the value of goods to a possessor can come apart. If a distribution of positional goods to A and B increases the holdings of each but in unequal amounts, a greater gain for B may ultimately harm A. Though A's absolute holdings have increased, and aggregate holdings of A and B have increased, A experiences a decline in welfare.

Education is said to be a "paradigm" positional good.[27] As Brian Barry observes, "In the job market, what matters is not how much education you have but how much you have in relation to others. If half the population have a degree, then a degree will become the minimum qualification for entry-level positions in many jobs that previously would have been filled by those who had completed secondary education but gone no further."[28] Because education is instrumentally valuable for obtaining other scarce goods, such as well-paid jobs, securing more educational resources for myself affects the absolute value of education to others; relative standing in the distribution of education modifies the absolute value of education to me.[29]

If education does indeed possess these positional aspects, the case in favor of equality over adequacy as the distributional principle of education becomes clearer. In its most sympathetic interpretation, educational adequacy connects different levels of resources (different levels of spending for different categories of students) with high outcome standards so that all students reach a level of proficiency or have adequate educational opportunities to learn. The state then turns a blind eye toward districts or schools that choose to spend far above the level required for adequacy and those where achievement flies high beyond the specified level of proficiency. In effect, the state confers its imprimatur on educational inequalities in both inputs and outcomes above the threshold of adequacy. Yet if education is positional, then even in a miracle world in which no child is left behind and all achieve the high outcome standards, those who rise beyond the adequacy threshold will gain positional advantages and will do so with the official sanction of the state.

Thus, to the extent that education has positional value, adequacy threatens to entrench or exacerbate the positional advantages of the well-off. If education is a strong positional good, then inequalities in educational opportunity above even an adequate threshold are objectionable, since possessing educational goods above an adequate or even high minimum creates a positional advantage for their possessors, affecting the value of the education of those at the minimum. Moreover, the adequacy paradigm not only tolerates this but provides new incentives for the well-off to maintain and increase their positional advantage. If the lowest-performing schools and students begin to perform better, or gain proficiency, the advantage of the well-off is threatened. Parents and communities who seek to protect their children's positional advantages will now have reason to increase their educational goods and opportunities even more.

Adequacy, with its failure to focus attention conceptually on the worse-off (instead of insisting uniformly that every child receive and achieve at adequate levels), is insensitive to positional advantages. Only equality, which is necessarily comparative, directs attention to those who are worse-off than others, and therefore only equality can fully account for and if necessary redress any unfair positional advantages in education.

Simply put, the more strongly education is a positional good, the more necessary it becomes to be an egalitarian. Any alternative framework that tolerates inequalities will condone worsening the position of the comparably worse-off, even if their absolute quantity of educational resources or achievements increases. For positional goods, the relative amount of the good determines its absolute value. With respect to education, this is why adequacy is not good enough.

Let me be clear, however, about the implications of this discussion. The concern is not that education is positional and that egalitarianism therefore requires that the state attempt to eliminate the availability of positional advantages children can gain through educational opportunities in K–12 schooling. It is probably inevitable that education has strong positional aspects.[30] The egalitarian implication is not to break the causal link between the acquisition of educational resources and opportunities and success in later competitions, to overcome the positional advantages education can afford.

The concern is that with the adequacy paradigm, the public institution of the schoolhouse is being used, or can be used, with state sanction, to compound or extend the positional advantages of the already privileged and advantaged for reasons having nothing to do with whether they merit this additional benefit. That is to say, when a child, however talented, has at his or her disposal the educational opportunities of a wealthy school that spends and achieves far above the adequacy threshold, the child in a poorer school is denied the opportunity to benefit from such an educational environment for reasons that cannot have anything to do with what the child deserves. Moreover, given the strong positional aspects of education, the additional advantages gained by the child in the wealthy school will harm the child in the poorer school, even if the poor child's school meets the adequacy standards. The child is made worse-off through no fault of his or her own. And all of this will happen with the sanction, indeed the endorsement, of the state. This is why acknowledging the positionality of education requires the state to pursue egalitarian, not sufficientarian, policies in education.

The ideals of adequacy and equality both have a place in any discussion of the just distribution of education. In the end, the relevant question is whether the state's obligation to provide education is based on a view about the civic purpose of education, where its distribution is intended to cultivate the skills necessary for able citizenship. If this is the case, then adequacy is a strongly appealing framework. Alternatively, the state's obligation to provide education might go beyond producing good schools for all that cultivate good citizens and require that opportunities to attend college and compete for jobs in the labor market be not merely adequate but equal. If so, then inequalities in resources and outcomes above the level of adequacy will undermine equal opportunity, and the equality paradigm is needed to address these relative deprivations.

CHAPTER 3

Learning to Be Equal

Just Schools as Schools of Justice

Anthony Simon Laden

Introduction: Redrawing Our Conceptual Maps

As citizens of a democratic society, we are collectively responsible for governing ourselves. Self-government requires certain skills and knowledge. As citizens of a diverse society, we must bridge all sorts of differences. Living with others who disagree with us or who have ways of living that are unfamiliar to us or that we disapprove of also requires knowledge and skills. Discussions of civic education tend to focus on these kinds of knowledge and skills: active political participation, knowledge of government, and the skills of deliberation and tolerance.[1] But as citizens we are also equals. Being equal is not merely a matter of what we are or what we have, but of what we do, and so it too requires knowledge and skills. The practices and habits of relating to one another as equals do not come naturally. Schools can prepare children to be citizens only if they also help them learn to be equal. Or so I want to argue.

The thought that schools should teach children how to be equal, in addition to teaching them that they *are* equal or what follows from their being equal, is not common in discussions of civic education. This chapter

Work on this chapter was funded in part by the Spencer Foundation's initiative for Philosophy and Education. I am grateful to Rob Reich and Danielle Allen for including me in the Dewey Workshop on Justice, Education, and Democracy at the Institute for Advanced Study and to all the participants, from whom I have learned much more than is contained in this essay. This chapter is dedicated to Jun Shihan, Nancy Lanoue, Sarah Ludden, and everyone who makes the Thousand Waves Martial Arts and Self-Defense Center a school for justice.

has the relatively modest aim of urging this topic on our attention. It takes up the philosophical task of shifting our conceptual focus. Understanding equality as something we do requires changing how we think about such concepts as justice, democracy, and education. Shifting our conceptual focus is not a matter of arguing for new theories or policies. Its practical effects lie in how we argue for particular policies rather than directly in which policies we argue for. Changing our conceptual focus involves the mental analogue of optometry, and its value is similar. Just as new glasses can bring into focus some things that were previously obscure, so new conceptual lenses can direct our attention and understanding in new ways and toward issues that were obscure. Shifting our focus thus requires realigning a whole set of conceptual lenses, like twisting the various dials on an optometrist's phoropter. To see why our thinking about civic education may benefit from a new prescription, consider a familiar map of the conceptual terrain this volume focuses on. Three big concepts—justice, democracy, and education—occupy the points of a triangle. Between any two of these points there is a set of familiar questions and controversies. Among those that lie between "democracy" and "education" are questions of civic education and the civic mission of schools, as well as about school governance. Between "education" and "justice" some of the central questions involve equality in the allocation of various goods as well as the adjudication of competing rights claims (e.g., between parents, children, teachers, and the wider public). Finally, between "democracy" and "justice" reside questions about whether democracy is a means to justice or a constituent of justice, understood once again as the equitable distribution of a certain set of goods and the proper allocation of rights.

The two sides of this triangle with the common point at "education" cover rather separate debates and questions, and to the extent that either brings in the third term, it is not as a fundamental aspect of the basic question, but as it constrains our answers or provides us with a means of realizing them. Even if justice demands a certain pattern of inputs to education, it might turn out that they are unlikely to meet with democratic approval. Even if diverse and well-integrated schools teach their students to work deliberatively together across differences and thus provide democratic civic benefits, this consequence is thought to say nothing about the justice of a system that works to create and maintain such schools. At the risk of oversimplifying, questions concerning education and justice turn out to be questions about equality and rights, whereas questions concerning education and democracy turn out to be questions about either difference or politics.

Of course this map is too crude: not every important debate in education that touches on democracy or justice is easily contained in it. But its basic contours should strike you as familiar. One feature of this map is that the very middle, where all three terms converge, is strangely empty: uncharted territory, if you will. Focus your attention on that empty spot as I turn several conceptual dials, starting with "justice."

Two Pictures of Justice

The concept of justice that generates the debates alluded to above has a certain shape.[2] At the heart of justice lies a distributive ideal: distributive justice involves the nonarbitrary distribution of goods, so that each subject of justice has what is rightly hers.[3] What, precisely, distributive justice demands depends on how we specify the set of relevant goods to be distributed, the criteria for determining rightful versus arbitrary claims, and the proper recipients of the goods as well as what, if any, concerns of justice extend beyond questions of distribution. But some philosophers have raised questions about the ways that approaching justice as centrally a matter of distribution shapes our thinking.[4]

Let me note three effects of adopting a distributive picture. First, this approach makes the subjects of justice basically passive recipients. Justice here involves handing out a more or less fixed quantity of goods to a fixed set of recipients, with no attention paid to the role of the recipients in the production of the goods to be distributed. Distributive justice, so conceived, is not a matter of regulating cooperative schemes, but of handing out products, including perhaps such goods as political voice, meaningful work, prerogatives of office, and leisure time. Moreover, since according to this picture distributive justice treats its subjects as passive recipients, it makes no difference to the justice of a distribution that some people neither accept nor understand it. While "buy-in" to a given distributional scheme may help with its implementation, and complaints from the unfortunate may alert us to a miscalculation in our determination of the space of or the formula for justice, its acceptance by those it covers is not conceptually necessary for the distribution to be just. One consequence of this feature is that justice is easily thought of as realized by policies worked out and implemented by experts.

Second, distributive justice so conceived has no tight connection to democracy. Unless we add political participation or certain political rights to the list of goods to be distributed and specify that the proper distribution of these goods is universal and equal, democracy is not conceptually necessary for distributive justice. Equipped with the right formula for a just distribution and the knowledge of the appropriate social levers to pull to bring it about, justice could be achieved by a machine or a dictator. Justice here is not a matter of standing in certain interpersonal relations to others, but rather of relative or absolute standing.

Third, the objects of distributive justice must be conceived as distributable goods. If political power or a set of rights or social positions is an object of distributive justice, it must be imagined as a good. We thus speak about bundles of rights, equal access to or voice in political decisions, or the various ingredients necessary to shape a good life. If education is an object of distributive justice, it too must be characterized as a distributable good. This leads to a focus on measurable and distributable quantities associated with education: inputs to education or achievements that education yields rather than the values and processes of education itself. So we focus on funding levels or test scores or lifetime earnings potential rather than the relationships brought about by teaching, the horizons of thought and appreciation opened, or, to use Plato's phrase, the turning of souls toward the light.[5]

This picture of justice, then, occludes certain issues of particular importance to education in general and civic education in particular as matters of justice. Turning the justice dial, we can replace a picture of justice as distributive with a picture of relational justice. Relational justice requires that no one is in a position to rule arbitrarily over another. Rule is arbitrary when it cannot be justified to the person being ruled. The justification involved here is essentially intersubjective: it is justification *to* those ruled, rather than a justification that grounds the rule in some theoretical apparatus that others may not accept or understand. Rainer Forst describes this feature of just rule in terms of reciprocal accountability.[6]

If I am to successfully justify our relationship to you (including perhaps my decisions or my right to make decisions for you), then from your standpoint you must be able to accept what I say as an adequate justification, and it must be the case that your rejection would have mattered. Moreover, this requirement holds from your end as well: accountability regimes create justice only when they hold in all directions.[7]

Note that conditions of reciprocity are, by and large, egalitarian, insofar as they require a rough balance of power. But it is the sort of relational equality achieved when no one is standing on someone else's neck rather than the distributional equality achieved when we both have the same size slices of pie. Relational equality is both more robust and more flexible than purely distributional conceptions of equality. One aspect of its flexibility that is relevant for discussing education is its compatibility with certain forms of hierarchy.[8]

Since relational justice is fundamentally a matter of offering reasons to others and evaluating the reasons others offer us, the subjects of justice cannot be pictured as passive recipients. They must be regarded as equal participants in realizing justice. Justice, in this model, is no longer a matter for experts and theorists to figure out and implement. It comes about only through our shared implementing of our shared ideas about how to live together. Relational justice thus cannot be thought of primarily as a possible goal of government policy; rather, it is a constraint on it. We are not to figure out what relational justice demands and then work out which policies bring it about. We must ask of various policies, regardless of the ends they seek to promote, Are these consistent with relational justice? Can they be justified to our fellow citizens? This yields a rather different view of how political philosophy, in offering ideal conceptions of justice, impinges on more concrete and practical questions.[9]

Justice and Equality

Shifting our picture of justice then frees up the equality dial for turning. According to the distributional picture of justice, equality is a matter of mirroring. A distribution is nonarbitrary when it mirrors some more or less natural feature of the population among whom it is distributed. So we can justify an equal distribution by pointing to traits we have in common, or criticize an unequal distribution by arguing that it is based on differences that are morally irrelevant. Alternatively, we can justify an unequal distribution that does not mirror a morally relevant difference in terms of some other end it serves, such as efficiency or the protection of liberties or the advantage of such schemes to the less well-off.

What is significant in this approach to equality is that it starts from a premise about the world or about people that is taken as a given at least in the short term. The basis for equal claims is a fact, so teaching students to be equal or unequal makes no more sense than teaching them to be blue-eyed or long-fingered. The question that remains for policy and the design of social institutions as well as a subject for teaching is whether our society adequately responds to this presocial fact.

According to the relational picture of justice, equality involves standing in certain relations (reciprocally accountable ones) and not in others
(those marked by arbitrary rule). Which kinds of relations we stand in is
not a natural or presocial fact about us, but a result of how our society is
organized and how we act within its various rules and possibilities. Although a large part of what determines our possibilities in the short run is
a result of social factors that may well be beyond our individual control,
there are also plenty of aspects of our relationships that are the direct
result of how we and others act within them. I can be servile toward or
contemptuous of some or all of my peers, teachers, and fellow citizens, or
I can respect them as equals. Whether we stand in relations of reciprocity
with one another as citizens depends on how we treat one another, including whether we see others as appropriate subjects of our love or respect
or moral regard.[10] Since being equal is in large part a matter of acting one
way rather than another, it is something we can and must learn.[11]

Equality, Justification, and Reasoning

Next we turn the dial marked "reasoning." Here it helps to distinguish
two practices of justification I contrasted briefly above. Consider a teacher
who justifies a course of study to her students in terms of a state mandate
or her own expertise and takes these justifications to be final and sufficient. Secure in her justification, she can fail to take seriously her students'
criticisms of her decisions. Their failure to follow her orders is just one
more sign of their immaturity, and their resistance demonstrates their lack
of self-control and thus lack of full rationality. Here the teacher justifies
her action by grounding it in a system of thought, rules, or authority that
she takes to hold regardless of whether the person to whom she is justifying her actions also accepts these premises. Justification here is a way of
securing a kind of warrant from the universe or the existing social structure that what she is doing is rational, backed by the appropriate norms
and facts and reasons. Understood this way, justification need not have
anything to do with equality.

The kind of justification that is required by a relational picture of justice and that serves as a practice of equality aims at uptake from the one
to whom it is offered and, with several qualifications that we can ignore
for the moment, succeeds only when it is accepted as adequate. I treat you
as an equal when I treat you as one whose words and concerns matter as

much as my own. I do this when I justify what I do to you in this second intersubjective sense. If I try to dismiss your rejection as a sign of your irrationality, like the teacher described above, then I fail at this activity of justification. Intersubjective justification can advert to inequalities in knowledge or expertise or the need for some to make decisions for others. But these considerations have to be ones that those to whom we offer our justifications accept as grounds for allocating decision-making power un-equally. So, engaging in the practice of justification that secures relational justice requires being responsive and accountable to those to whom you are offering justification.

Our teacher can shift to this second kind of justification by explaining that her greater knowledge of the subject allows her to see why this ap-proach makes it easier to learn, although her students' lack of knowledge at the moment makes it impossible to explain to them what she knows. In offering a justification of this sort, the teacher is asking her students to trust her and perhaps reminding them why she is trustworthy rather than baldly asserting her authority to make these decisions without challenge. Her justification succeeds only to the extent that her students find her trustworthy. Among the many things that might make her trustworthy is her responsiveness to them, considered as the particular individuals they are, and not merely as abstract placeholders or possible test scores or dis-ciplinary problems to be managed.[12]

This egalitarian practice of offering justifications that are accountable to others is part of a larger practice of reasoning understood as an essen-tially social and responsive activity rather than a process of calculation and problem solving. Picturing reasoning this way involves thinking about the activity of reasoning as a way of neither commanding nor blindly deferring to others, but of treating them as equals, as people whose words and ideas and points of view matter and to whom our own actions are accountable.[13] Excellence at reasoning in this sense involves being reasonable. A skilled reasoner according to this picture is someone who is fully responsive to the people she talks and relates with, rather than someone who is particularly skilled at maneuvering within formal and symbolic systems. Reasoning, so understood, is a central practice of equality, and so something democratic citizens need to learn. It requires, in addition to the skills of critical think-ing, calculation, and analysis regularly described as goals of education, skills like listening to others, understanding them and allowing their words to matter, as well as, when appropriate, being able to trust others, which may require openness to being vulnerable to them.

Schools of Justice?

If relational justice is to be brought about in part by initiating democratic citizens into the habits of equality, which centrally include reasonableness, then it might seem obvious that schools have a clear role in this process. They do, but it turns out to be less straightforward than it might appear at first. There are at least two reasons to think that schools, and in particular elementary and secondary schools, are actually bad places for the kind of training in reasonableness that justice requires. First, the recipients of the training that schools provide are children, and children, especially young ones, are for all sorts of complex psychological and developmental reasons not yet completely suited to be reasoners in the sense I am using. Even as they learn to maneuver and manipulate formal and symbolic symbols, they may not be able to be fully responsive to one another. In some cases, when a young child refuses to accept a justification offered to her, it is appropriate to say that the justification is adequate, but the child is not able to appreciate it.[14] This problem does not arise for theories of educational justice that adopt the distributive picture of justice. The psychological facts about children that may interfere with their capacity to be fully reasonable do not make them unsuitable as the claimants to or recipients of proper shares of various goods, including education.

Second, schools' central mission is education, and even the most progressive and child-centered account acknowledges that in large part education (at least lots of primary and secondary education) involves someone who knows more about a topic bringing those who know less about it to learn more. In other words, at some important level, education takes place across certain types of hierarchy. This is a feature of education in the sense that it involves teaching, rather than learning generally.[15]

So schools cannot initiate children into the practices of equality that involve reasonableness by turning their core mission of teaching into a fully egalitarian activity. Fully democratic kindergartens, where each five-year-old has an equal vote in the school's budget or pedagogical methods, are not likely to be paths to democratic citizenship. Some of these worries can be addressed by noting that initiating someone into any practice or activity requires more than dropping her into it. Sometimes we engage with children in a simplified form of the practice (e.g., T-ball rather than baseball) or an activity that, while not even a form of the practice, serves to develop some of the necessary skills (e.g., catch). It may also help if there are clear examples around them, so they can get a clearer sense of what it is to engage in the practice or do it well. So, in the case of young children, adults can help initiate them into the practices of equality such as reasonableness by engaging them in simpler activities, such as careful listening or acknowledging the contribution of others to their own success or safety or well-being. And they can further encourage and aid in the development of reasonableness by displaying it as fully as possible in their own interactions. Finally, teachers and others can accept a duty of accountability to children that does not depend on the children's demanding that account. A teacher who plans lessons so she can justify them to her students may thus contribute to their learning how to be equal. She is, for instance, likely to thereby make herself more trustworthy, and so begin to build the basis of trust necessary for reciprocal relationships. Behaviors like these can initiate young children into reasonableness in the absence of fully equal teacher-student relationships.

But to see the full potential that schools provide in teaching us to be equals, we need to turn a final dial, the one marked "schools." Initiating students into the practices and habits of equality is not merely a matter of adding topics to the curriculum. So we need to think of schools not only as a series of lessons and assignments and tests, but as social institutions in their own right, structured by principles and rules and norms, some explicit, some hidden. We can then ask what roles schools, as institutions, play in fostering or hampering various forms of moral development.

When we focus on the educational impact of the school as an institution, the question to ask is no longer *whether* schools should or can have as one of their missions advancing civic purposes or fostering the development of citizens. Institutions necessarily have developmental and psychological effects on those who interact within them. So the choice here is not between having no effect and deciding to be influential, but rather among the kinds of influence a school has. Schools (like all other social institutions) can be schools of justice, where children learn to be equals, or they can be schools of despotism, where children learn to dominate, or to accept subjection, or any number of other things. But they cannot escape from being, in virtue of their institutional shape, schools of something or other. Since the worries raised in the previous section addressed the "whether" question, we can sidestep them, if not totally avoid their implications, by shifting our focus in this way.[16] A further consequence of this shift is that the practical lesson to be drawn from this chapter takes the form not of a particular set of pedagogical practices or institutional designs, but of a recognition of the need to pay attention to this dimension of both pedagogical practice and institutional design in our assessment of schools. Beyond asking whether a particular teaching method or school program raises test scores or prepares students for college, we ought to ask whether it initiates students into practices of equality.

The Justice of Schools

What sort of institutional structures and norms are likely to teach students to be equal? One consequence of a focus on relational justice turns out to be that schools need not be perfect miniature democracies to foster the practices of equality in children. As I argue below, schools can have hierarchical authority structures and yet foster reciprocal accountability, so the choice we face is not between thoroughly democratic schools and arbitrarily authoritarian ones. Moreover, all sorts of nonpolitical institutions within a just democratic society can helpfully contribute to citizens' reasonableness without being fully democratic or egalitarian. Thus, for instance, families that are characterized by deep and sincere love and care for the well-being of their children and where the parents' partnership is marked by love, respect, and equality may help develop children who are willing to trust, and who do not confuse love and domination, even if the family does not rely on democratic procedures to make its decisions or assign equal rights to its members. Similarly, a school may be able to foster reasonableness and other practices of equality while maintaining many of the hierarchical authority structures it relies on to fulfill its other educational missions.

Here it helps to distinguish hierarchy from arbitrariness of rule. Hierarchy involves some having authority over others, and thus having the status to make decisions or take actions that others cannot. Teachers who determine lesson plans and assessment mechanisms and assign grades and enforce classroom rules without consulting their students or receiving their approval stand above them in a hierarchy. But an institution can have within it hierarchical relations of this sort without granting those in higher positions the further privilege of nonaccountability, of arbitrary rule. A teacher has this further privilege when he can peremptorily refuse his students' demands that he justify his decisions based on his position in the hierarchy, with "because I know better" or "because I'm the teacher" or "because that's what the rules say," where these are offered as final answers. But it is possible to stand in a hierarchical relation to others while still being accountable to them. In such cases deference to one's authority must rest on earned trust and the ability to justify one's decisions, neither of which requires handing authority to one's subordinates. Again, to return to the language of accountability, it requires only that those in authority are accountable to those below them just as those under their jurisdiction are accountable to them. So a school can incorporate and foster habits of reasonableness by making sure relationships are reciprocally accountable, without having to do away with all hierarchies. Such a school would, despite being neither fully democratic nor egalitarian, play a role in teaching students to be equals in virtue of its institutional structure. It would be, in the sense developed here, a just school and thus a school of justice.

What sorts of institutional structures, practices, and rules might make classrooms, schools, and educational systems more adequate as schools of justice? Here is an illustration. Clearly, empirical work would be needed to find out what, if any, effect such structures had on students' moral development, and there are no doubt many other institutional features that could be added to this or put in its place.[17] But I hope this illustration will give a better sense of the kinds of issues these conceptual shifts illuminate as well as make clear just what those shifts involve.

One way for an educational environment at any level both to value and to encourage reasonableness would be to place the practice of intersubjective justification at the heart of its organizational structures and norms and to reward and encourage those who properly demand and offer justifications, who show the proper responsiveness to others. One rather direct way to do this would be for a classroom, school, or district to adopt the right to demand justifications as a kind of fundamental right of all its stakeholders, and to pair this with the concomitant duty to offer acceptable justifications when asked.[18] Such a right could be explicit and formal or implicit and merely widely understood to structure practice.[19]

Institutionalizing something like a right within the practice of an institution does not require legal changes, although legal changes would also produce this shift. The suggestions offered here could be adopted or pursued at any of these levels, from the smallest to the largest, without requiring the wholesale changes in the political landscape that would be necessary for this to be a guiding idea in a nation's education policy more broadly. And while institutionalizing such a right within a classroom can be a means of the kind of civic education I have in mind,[20] it would also have educative effects when applied at higher levels of educational structure. Both Deborah Meier, of Central Park East, and the founding teachers of KIPP schools, Dave Levin and Mike Feinberg, seem to have been motivated in their creation of new schools by their experience with the failures of such accountability (in particular, of principals and administrators to teachers) in the districts and schools where they worked.[21]

The presence of this right would allow for some of the following kinds of conversations to take place within and around a school: A student could ask a teacher why a particular topic was being covered or why it was being taught that way, as well as why certain work was being assigned or certain facts and interpretations were being presented as they were. A parent could ask similar questions of a principal or a teacher. A teacher could ask a principal to justify certain rules and regulations governing how she ran her classroom or what she taught, and a principal could ask a teacher why he was teaching as he did. A janitor could ask a teacher why her classroom was always such a mess and a principal why working conditions for support staff were so poor. A student could ask another student why she was bullying him or ignoring him or failing to be helpful, and a teacher could ask a student similar questions, or ask why he was not paying attention in class or doing better work. The point of having the right to ask such questions is not the right itself or even the questions themselves, but to begin to shift a classroom, school, or district away from certain arbitrary hierarchical institutional features whereby key decisions are in the hands of experts who are not accountable to those below them, and toward one that teaches and encourages reasonableness.

Such conversations might not *produce* better results, whether higher test scores, more manageable classrooms, or more egalitarian distributions of educational outcomes, though they might have all of these effects. Their value lies elsewhere. Participation in and observation of such conversations would initiate students into a practice of reciprocally relating to others. For the presence of such a right to justification to succeed at that wider mission, however, it needs to be paired with a set of practices for offering and evaluating justifications and for understanding what is involved in the very asking of questions.

Reasonable Demands

Demands for justification are often issued and heard as challenges to authority or expertise or competence: "How dare you? Who do you think you are?" Sometimes such challenges may be warranted, but even then they come across as obnoxious, lacking respect rather than extending it. Given this picture of questioning and demanding justification, the thought that any institution should build such a right into its foundations looks like a recipe for disaster, all the more so when many of those in possession of this right would be children and adolescents. But we need not ask such questions in such a voice, and we need not hear them that way even when that is how they are asked. I can ask someone what she is doing or why she thinks it is appropriate not because I secretly think she is misbehaving and want to call her on it, but because I think she is generally trustworthy and competent but I just don't see what is going on. That is, I might ask the question not as a challenge but as a sincere attempt to understand. Even when a question is asked as a challenge, others could learn to hear it as a request for illumination and thus respond without defensiveness. The raising of the question and my attempt to give an answer can lead me to see that the answer I have is lacking or that things are not as clear-cut as I thought, not because a challenge to my authority has succeeded in undermining it.[22]

One of the differences between questioning as challenge and questioning as genuine request is how the two situate the relationship between the questioner and questioned. If I raise a question as a challenge, then I either rely on or try to establish a hierarchical relationship, either by calling into question your claim to superiority or by showing that insofar as you are accountable to me, I am your superior. That is why, when we first imagine a student questioning a teacher or a principal, we think of the questions as challenges. But when we pose a question as a request, we often place ourselves in a relation of equality or rely on our relationship as equals. In such a relationship there is no danger in displaying our vulnerability by confessing that we do not know the answer, yet we would be in a position to understand if the other explained. It is questioning in the second sense that is a genuine practice of equality, and the kind that a school for justice ought to model and foster. In large part, this requires that the adults in schools have the skill to hear children's questions in this way and ask their own questions in this tone.

It helps here to contrast the kinds of reasoning I am describing with uses of reason and argument that serve as unanswerable assertions of the authority of various forms of privilege. In *Unequal Childhoods*,[23] Annette Lareau argues that a set of reasoning practices play a large role in the family structures of middle-class but not working-class and poor families, and that initiation into these practices gives middle-class children an advantage in navigating and using a variety of social institutions that expect and reward them. Lareau argues that middle-class children in the United States tend to be brought up into practices of reason giving and justification as well as questioning and challenging authority figures by demanding that they provide justifications, whereas these practices are not present in poorer families, who tend to be deferential toward social authorities (teachers, principals, doctors, government agents) and to give their children commands and expect obedience. To someone familiar with Lareau's work, it may appear that I am suggesting schools be structured to reinforce these middle-class lessons, possibly to the detriment of poorer children. But reasonableness understood as a practice of equality differs from the reasoning practices Lareau describes.

These practices can be divided into two types, neither involving the kind of reasoning I have been describing. First, children in middle-class families are taught and encouraged to have reasons for their opinions and positions and requests, not as a preparation for reciprocal conversations but to arm them against challenges. When a parent asks a child to justify an opinion or a request, that question is an implicit challenge, or at least it is designed to prepare the child to handle future challenges. Having reasons and being skilled in their deployment prevents one's having to cede ground.

The second practice—asking questions of authority figures—is also not a practice of equality. The point of asking questions in these exercises is to make sure one can navigate various institutions in ways that allow effective pursuit of one's ends. When a parent demands that a teacher or principal justify a decision affecting her child, it serves as a challenge to his judgment and an assertion of the parent's superior status, as a customer, a client, to whom the other is accountable. It is decidedly not an exercise in equality, in finding out something not known, or an entry into a reciprocal discussion about what to do. The accountability demanded here flows in only one direction. Teachers and others are questioned by such parents when the parents are dissatisfied, not when they are confused. The parents in Lareau's study who question teachers and doctors and others whose decisions affect their children's lives do not cede ground, and they do not expect to. The middle-class families Lareau discusses use reason as a tool for maintaining superiority and privilege, not as a practice of equality. Justifications are demanded as an assertion of privilege, and reasons are marshaled to prevent others from similarly asserting privilege. What is missing here is the importance of listening as well as arguing, of trusting and earning the trust of others by being trustworthy, of openness to being changed by and thus vulnerable to one's reasoning partner.

There are at least two lessons to draw from the difference between reasonableness as a practice of reciprocity and the reasoning practices Lareau describes. First, reasonableness in my sense involves humility and trust as much as assertiveness and a lack of blind deference. It is neither a vision of a democratic society as a society of lawyers nor one that shows no recognition that some people know more or better or with greater maturity and depth than others. It merely holds that in a democracy, recognition and trust of our fellow citizens must be earned and freely given. They cannot be imposed from above. What makes an activity an activity within the practice of reasonableness described here is not its connection to cognition or its approximation of logical form, but its display of proper responsiveness to others, of treating them reciprocally and thus as equals.

The second lesson concerns how schools' charge to be schools of justice interacts with various practices of inequality in the wider society. In particular, the training in reasonableness that students need may differ depending on the lessons they are learning from the other institutions they participate in. Children of privilege, who are taught to use and defend their privilege even as they are taught to be ignorant of it, may most need to be taught how to listen and to take other people's views seriously, to see their privilege and to avoid deploying it. All this would help them find their way to the possibility of equal and reciprocal relationships with others, whether their classmates, other children, or teachers.[24] Children lacking in such privilege, who are taught to defer quietly to assertions of authority, may need to be taught how to assert themselves, demand justifications, and ask questions. It may also be incumbent on those teaching such children to go out of their way both to be trustworthy and to manifest that trustworthiness so that disadvantaged children, who are taught to protect their real vulnerabilities as a matter of survival, might be willing to enter into the kind of trusting relationship necessary for true reciprocity.[25]

At the same time, being reasonable is not a matter of always accommodating stubborn, doctrinaire, or obstructionist forces in the name of peace and harmony. Just because reasoning is not a form of bullying does not mean it cannot stand up to bullying. Here it helps to distinguish the search for agreement from the process of reasoning together. Those whose main end is to find agreement and compromise at all costs are very likely to be pushed into accommodating the bullies they deal with in the name of finding common ground. But the practices of reasonableness that are constitutive of standing in reciprocal and thus equal relations with others do not aim at agreement, even if they produce it. Being reasonable involves being properly responsive to the concerns and criticisms and demands of others, but being properly responsive need not mean always giving in to their demands. And so teaching reasonableness involves encouraging respectful responsiveness, not privileging or celebrating or pushing for agreement. It is more about the process than the product. Just as bullying others is not a way of being equal to them, accepting their bullying is not a practice of equality.[26]

Finally, it is important to note that the practices of reasoning and reasonableness I have been discussing do not presume that the only valid reasons are grounded in the advancement of an individual's interests and ends. Being reasonable involves being responsive to others' demands and to their requests for justification of our actions and principles and policies. If the only response I ever give to such demands is to advert to my particular interests and how what I do is in their service, then I am not being responsive. Relating to each other on terms of reciprocity and respect, being accountable to each other, involves more than merely coordinating our own individual pursuits.

Being reasonable thus means being open to justifying not only one's means and tactics, but also one's ends and goals. We should be able to ask why a teacher insists on teaching the way he always has, despite all sorts of evidence that it is ineffective. But he should also be able to ask the principal or district superintendent or the wider polity why it insists on measuring the effectiveness of his teaching in terms of math and reading test scores or according to some narrow conception of education as merely instrumental.

My aim in the foregoing discussion, again, has not been to recommend policies, either of school organization or of adopting particular pedagogical methods or regimes of accountability. Such questions go well beyond the scope of the chapter and my expertise. Nor by focusing on practices of justification and the demand for justification do I mean to imply that these are the only features of school structures that would teach the practices and habits of equality, or are even necessary ones. There are no doubt other ways of training students into these practices and creating norms of reciprocal accountability. My aim here has been to clarify just what the practices of reasonableness involve in order to suggest more clearly where we need to direct our attention once we confront the questions raised in the opening sections.

Can Just Schools Just Be Schools?

Even accepting these modest aims, won't this shift of focus inevitably detract from what must be the core mission of education: instilling knowledge and certain basic skills? Such a worry might take a number of forms. In the weakest form, it might merely amount to a worry that allowing everyone to continually ask for justification would be rather time consuming. Given the definite limits to the school day, time devoted to justification is time taken away from learning history or science or math or reading. A somewhat stronger worry holds that that even if the time devoted to justification did not prove terribly great, the disruptive possibility of such demands would no doubt undermine the effectiveness of other lesson plans. Imagine a teacher's explanation of long division or some of the issues and events that led to the Missouri Compromise routinely being disrupted by demands that she justify her whole approach to math or history or the very teaching of these subjects. It isn't unreasonable to suppose that such interruptions would make such lessons less effective, even if they might provide other forms of education.

Any aspect of school design that led to these kinds of disruptions and distractions from the core educational mission of a school would be a real problem. But rather than seeing these possibilities as reasons not to create just schools, I think we should see them as feasibility constraints on the ways we create such schools, constraints that do not undermine the basic idea of creating institutional structures that foster reasonableness. Any fully developed practice of justification and reasoning includes rules and norms about when and where demands for justification are appropriate. This does not restrict this basic right, but merely regulates it. A teacher could forestall constant interruptions to her class by setting aside a regular period every week for addressing such demands and encouraging students to keep track of their questions. Alternatively, she might allow for interruptions as they occur to her students but postpone lengthy responses until some allotted time. A school might institutionalize a class delegate system that allows classmates to bring up issues regularly with their teacher or school administrators in a context where they know they will be taken seriously. In turn, by modeling respectful and sincere questioning and showing themselves to be trustworthy, school administrators and teachers can initiate students into similar patterns. In doing so, they teach students that having a right carries a responsibility not to invoke it

frivolously or irresponsibly, and that asking questions is a way not of asserting authority but of seeking information.

Whatever accommodations a school makes to these concerns, however,
we should keep in mind that if we look at justice, education, democracy,
and reasoning as I have suggested here, then it turns out that among the
many things children learn as they learn to be equal in a just school is how
to reason. Reasoning is, or should be, toward the top of any list of what
we want children to learn in school. I hope I have made a case here that
properly understood, learning to reason can be part and parcel of learning
to be equal, and thus not only part of the educational mission of schools,
but part of their wider contribution to democratic justice as well.

CHAPTER 4

Education for Shared Fate Citizenship

Sigal Ben-Porath

Introduction

Contemporary democratic societies are diverse in many ways. Schools are charged with responding to the diversity of affiliations, preferences, ideologies, languages, values, and memberships. They are expected to celebrate the diversity of the student body, but also to minimize it by developing civic capacity and a host of shared dimensions, including language, civic knowledge, academic competency, and patriotic sentiments. This chapter suggests a political and educational response to the fact of diversity that focuses on conceptualizing national citizenship as a form of shared fate.

Political and theoretical responses to diversity focus on containing it through a liberal emphasis on core democratic values like respect or liberty;[1] on minimizing it through a civic-republican focus on virtues and participation;[2] or on celebrating it with a multicultural commitment to accommodating a wide range of differences.[3] All these responses tend to be identity-based, or "groupist"—conceptualizing nationality as a stable, tangible, concrete, and enduring category. As an alternative, national membership is conceptualized here as based on "shared fate"—as a relational, process-oriented, dynamic affiliation that arises from cognitive perceptions as well as from members' preferences and actions.[4] Such an approach can allow liberal democracies to accommodate diversity while maintaining a common foundation. A view of education for citizenship[5] based on this idea of citizenship as "shared fate" envisions schools that build on and develop a holistic notion of society while maintaining a commitment to the well-being of individuals whose complex identities arise from their memberships in multiple groups.

Aren't We Postnational?

This focus on a nation's shared fate and on education for citizenship within a national context might seem surprising to many who are committed to cosmopolitan visions of affiliation and education. The notion of shared fate is sometimes invoked in the global context to indicate the interdependence of all humans (or all living things). Shared fate in this context is envisioned not as nation-based, but rather as an interest, shared globally, in preserving the planet, avoiding wars, or developing sustainable practices. Legally and socially, some argue, other forms of membership born of globalization are replacing national citizenship as sources of affiliation and loyalty.[6] In this view, communities based on ethnicity, religion, sexual orientation, and other ascriptions, which can reside within the nation or transcend it, provide their members with the sense of belonging that the nation used to provide. I suggest that, even in a world where global forces and cosmopolitan affiliations are on the rise, the nation-state still plays an important role, both on the world stage and in the moral realities of individuals. Citizenship therefore maintains the qualities that Hannah Arendt identified in it decades ago, when writing on the possibility of world citizenship:

> A citizen is by definition a citizen among citizens in a country among countries. His rights and duties must be defined and limited, not only by those of his fellow citizens, but also by the boundaries of a territory. Philosophy may conceive of the earth as the homeland of mankind and of one unwritten law, eternal and valid for all. Politics deals with men, nationals of many countries and heirs to many pasts; its laws are the positively established fences which hedge in, protect, and limit the space in which freedom is not a concept, but a living, political reality.[7]

As Arendt's words indicate, nations are not a philosophical necessity but a political reality that philosophers who focus on politics must contend with. While nation-states clearly are historically contingent rather than necessary or organic entities, it is still worth asking, What values, interests, and ends do nation-states serve that other institutions may not be able to provide?[8]

Belonging to a group and pursuing shared social and political ends through membership is a human practice that, even if neither natural nor universal, is widespread and significant enough to merit theoretical attention and normative justification. The nation may serve a purpose like the one tribes and other pre- and subnational groups served in earlier historical periods, and in this sense it is not unique as an institution that can satisfy the human aims of political belonging and the shared pursuit of social aims. Subnational affiliations (or membership in groups based on ethnic, ideological, geographic, and other identities) as well as cross-national affiliations (in institutions that bring together individuals from various nations around a shared cause, like Oxfam or the Catholic Church) provide opportunities for membership, some of which parallel those underlying the nation-state. In addition, in the past century or so global institutions have developed additional opportunities for collaboration and belonging. But under the current institutional structure, global institutions and processes still rely on nation-states as the key players in the global arena. For individuals, the nation-state provides a vehicle for developing, expressing, and validating social and political forms of belonging that are not similarly served by the thin institutions of global allegiance. The nation-state provides a unique set of opportunities that neither global nor subnational forms of membership currently provide.

In the context of the nation-state, and in no other, individuals can pursue broad social and political goals, congruent with key demands of justice, along with diverse others who share a broad and sustained set of interests, needs, and goals. Because the nation connects diverse individuals through practices and institutions that call for their cooperation to advance shared interests, needs, and preferences and to develop shared value systems that can sustain this pursuit, it offers forms of political expression and action unparalleled in more homogeneous groups or in groups based on a single shared cause. The context of the democratic nation-state specifically—the context this chapter focuses on—offers a unique structure that allows members to develop and pursue their shared political and social goals in ways that correspond to the expectations and requirements of justice.[9] This focus on the shared fate of members of a nation-state gives rise to a notion of citizenship that is unique to the political context that today is most significantly available through the nation-state and evolves as the citizens' political preferences and interests evolve, as well as with the constant reconstitution of the civic body. This concept of citizenship as an aspect of the fate we share with others can enable nations and their publicly funded school systems to respond effectively to the nation's need for a shared foundation while simultaneously respecting and protecting value pluralism (and other forms of diversity).

I turn now to whether membership in the nation should be portrayed as an attribute or an aspect of the member's identity and consider the difference between the common view of citizenship as identity and the argument for shared fate.

Shared Fate as Common Ground

In deeply diverse societies, education that aims to develop common values is continually challenged by individuals and groups who subscribe to value systems that they assume would be upended by certain aspects of substantive democratic citizenship. The pursuit of commonality seems always to trigger concerns about the loss of identity. An important response to these concerns is offered by diversity liberalism, or the view that liberal democracies must "afford maximum feasible space for the enactment of individual and group differences, constrained only by the requirements of liberal social unity."[10] The challenge, then, is to identify exactly what "liberal social unity" might require from the liberal "diversity state" and to consider how schools can contribute to the development of that unity.

One approach is simply to minimize the shared elements to be taught. The political philosopher William Galston provides an example of this approach. A key advocate of diversity liberalism, Galston suggests that "to the extent that we accept shared citizenship, we have something important in common, a set of political institutions and of principles that underlie them. What we share, beyond all our differences, provides the basis for a civic education valid across the boundaries of our differences."[11] Galston maintains that the diversity state (the liberal democratic state committed to diversity rather than to autonomy) establishes a political common ground that does not rest on membership in a specific religion, race, ethnicity, or other social group. Like certain other liberal visions, Galston's is strongly committed to tolerance. He develops a system of civic education that focuses primarily on teaching tolerance and, contrary to most liberal views, rejects the inculcation of political virtues and other value commitments in schools, restricting the normative reach of schools to developing respect for the law and tolerance for difference. In other words, Galston seeks to solve the problem of the tension between commonality and identity by minimizing the impact of politics and civic education on identity.

Like Galston, I argue that "what we share, beyond all our differences, provides the basis for a civic education valid across the boundaries of our differences." But I argue that by understanding citizenship as a matter of shared fate, we can achieve a rich view of commonality while simultaneously respecting the depth of diversity in a pluralistic democracy. My view differs from Galston's most significantly with regard to what shared citizenship might entail. In my argument, what we share is not minimal, but neither does it impinge on the development or preservation of additional group-based identities.

Shared fate envisions membership in the nation-state as based on ties to the state in its political and historical forms, but most significantly on horizontal ties with fellow members and linkages among citizens along a host of shared dimensions. In a nutshell, a conception of national citizenship as entailing shared fate focuses on linkages among members of a nation that include connections to a shared territory, merged historical narratives, shared language(s), and interconnected visions of past and future, of institutions and values. Understanding nationality in terms of cognitive schemas, cultural practices, discursive frames, collective representations, and political projects[12] means, first, overcoming the vision of the nation as a group linked ultimately by kinship (thus overcoming ascriptive notions of nationality) and, second, acknowledging the workings of "everyday nationalism"—again, in schemas, practices, frames, representations, and projects—that touch everyone and evolve and are continuously reinterpreted as part of the shared project of political membership. Shared fate citizenship does not require active participation in formal aspects of politics or the development of virtues deemed central to the national character (as some civic republican views demand), nor does it require the containment of diversity and the acceptance of overarching liberal values (as many liberal views demand). Understanding the content of citizenship as shared fate requires, instead, focusing on the schemas, practices, frames, representations, and projects that members of a nation share, even if unwittingly or divergently.

A conception of citizenship as shared fate thus views the common ground of citizenship—the shared political sphere that offers the backdrop for the multiplicity of diverse affiliations—as consisting of more substantial practices than tolerance alone (the focus of diversity liberalism's prescription). In this way, it aligns with liberal views like those of Anthony

Laden (this volume), who advocates teaching citizenship through introducing substantial elements of liberalism, such as mutual justification, autonomy, and critical thinking; however, this focus on citizens' shared fate aims to give citizenship political rather than moral substance, thus hoping to minimize some of the conflicts that teaching moral principles and practices generates among those who feel that their worldviews are threatened by these values. The conceptualization of citizenship as involving a shared fate allows for a thick description of the commonality among citizens, but that thickness stems from political rather than moral substance.

Thinking about citizenship as a shared project, born of and evolving through the multiple links shared by members of the political community, while accepting their deep differences in a variety of other affiliations and commitments, allows for a more inclusive, accommodating, and tolerant membership than other concepts, while maintaining a shared political liberal-democratic basis. Sharing a fate is different from just having a fate in common. Building the visions and practices that continue the civic-political project into the future requires relating to other citizens in a variety of ways, some of which are captured by Laden's view of mutual justification (this volume).

What does citizenship as shared fate add to other theoretical and practical accounts of citizenship and particularly to the relation between citizenship and nationality? As depicted in liberal-democratic scholarly debates, citizenship is an aspect of one's identity. That members of a national community should regard themselves as members of that community by virtue of their ascribed identity is often seen as conducive to their political cooperation. Seeing one's membership in a national community as a matter of identity can support the processes of choosing personal ends and pursuing them within the context of that community; when citizens generally think of their membership this way, their outlook promotes construction of a public agenda and deliberation over desirable ways to advance it. Additionally, such an outlook, widely shared, can enhance mutual cultural (and other communal) practices that maintain justice and a sense of belonging.

The focus on citizenship as an aspect of identity arises because citizenship is a type of membership that links an individual with a nation-state. Moreover, membership in the nation-state commonly rests either on birthright or on formal naturalization, where the would-be citizen must manifest certain meritorious characteristics as a matter of identity. A web of virtues, procedures, emotions, and histories (including national, ethnic, and racial pasts), as well as ascribed or naturalized characteristics, is presumed to capture and cultivate aspects of identity that make one a member in good standing of a particular nation. This vision of citizenship requires an assumption that unity is more important than diversity, as well as political insistence on the idea.[13] For instance, individuals are assumed to possess a multiplicity of identities, but their national identity is expected to trump conflicting demands from the others. The affective attachments to fellow citizens as members of the same identity group are expected to guard against demands for secession by subgroups within the nation-state. Liberal theorists thus tend to focus on containing diversity within the polity and define citizenship as a form of identity as a way of responding to challenges from individuals' affiliation with other subnational (or supranational) groups.

The concept of citizenship as solely a form of identity, however, may be questionable as a foundation for a liberal democratic national project. Specifically, if it can generate the kind of affiliation and commitment that are the marks of a healthy democracy, it may do so at the expense of the public sphere's ability to accommodate deep diversity, as well as migration.

Yet because of its now long-lived status as a source of affiliation for many individuals, the role of national identity is too strong simply to will away. A diversity vision of the nation-state requires supplementing the idea of identity as ascription with an idea of identity as emerging from actual and desired social ties. Many countries are rethinking their birthright laws and requiring more than the accident of birth to allow for legal membership (citizenship).[14] In a parallel conceptual move, we should supplement accounts of citizenship that rest on ascriptive identity with accounts that rest on lived social ties and the shared fate they give rise to.

Augmenting the vision of citizenship as identity with the notion of shared fate can help reflect and maintain democratic inclinations, including motivation and a sense of efficacy. In other words, the common basis for understanding citizenship as shared fate rather than solely as identity can frame an argument for citizenship and citizenship education in a diverse society. This view, like some republican and communitarian views, focuses on membership in the nation as a key aspect of democratic citizenship. However, its focus is not so much on participation and civic virtue as on the ties and relationships among members and on the effects their political choices have on one another. Members of a democratic society share a voice in choosing representatives and in holding those representatives accountable to them as a citizenry. They share access to public institutions and a commitment to at least some basic symbols of their national group as expressed in the democratic processes and the basic structure of their society. Their decisions mutually affect their lives through the institutions that govern, regulate, and organize them. They can take action together on issues that affect them through voluntary associations; they are bound together by the cognitive and emotional representations of the national group, the myths and narrations of its history, the cultural and political practices that represent the nation, and the political projects that they pursue with (and sometimes against) each other. While many of these aspects can be contested, and most of them regularly are, the procedural and substantive opportunities to contest and debate these shared dimensions of civic life, and the affiliation of various overlapping groups with different civic aspects of shared fate, create a relational context for citizens to affiliate with and act within.

Some recent writings on multiculturalism and on citizenship rely to some extent on the notion of citizenship as shared fate. The suggestion that institutional linkage creates a unique obligation to our compatriots can be traced to Robert Goodin's argument from affected affect (2007), which prioritizes the interests of our fellow citizens because our political choices will result in laws that they too must obey. Similarly, some republican visions of solidarity[15] parallel the view of citizenship as shared fate by relying on shared institutions and practices to sustain the common good, and by relying on educational (and other) practices to generate among the citizenry a predisposition to act in ways that promote the common good.[16] In other words, citizenship based on conceptions of identity and citizenship based on the idea of shared fate can be understood as complementary approaches.

Thus, citizenship as shared fate can be based on a shared if evolving cultural connection, but its focus on linkages among citizens—institutional linkages (such as a representative government), material linkages, and "seeing our own narratives as entwined with those of others"[17]—engenders a greater sense of agency among citizens. In a related discussion, Rogers Smith[18] advocates for constituting citizenship based on historical rather than naturalistic perceptions. Historical notions of citizenship can be revised, criticized, reinterpreted, and amended by the individuals and groups who make up the national community. The historical understanding of national affiliation transforms citizens' conception of themselves as belonging to a group and helps them own it in a different and more active way, as they see themselves as individuals (or members of groups within the nation) responsible for reinterpreting their national group over time. Addressing the role of constitutive myths in the narration of what it means to be a member of a nation, Smith concludes that, at least to some extent, the narratives we share with others turn us into compatriots in the fuller sense. This conclusion is echoed (with a different view on the truth-value of the stories) by Williams: "Having a sense of ourselves as members of a community of fate entails telling ourselves (true) stories about how we came to be connected."[19] Alongside their historical narratives, members of the nation tell stories about how they come to be connected through current or desirable shared practices, institutions, visions, and values; these stories, together with the historical narratives, construct the nation.

Shared fate citizenship thus aims both to recognize and to construct public and common goods; it also aims to respond to the sense of connection among members of the same nation. A shared structure that is open to interpretation provides a basis for citizens to offer open-minded responses to a wide range of conceptions about the community. Social life, communal perceptions, and understanding oneself as a citizen are all contingent on the constant construction and reinterpretation of the shared aspects. Thus shared fate citizenship does not call for an uncritical endorsement of historical "facts" or myths, or of membership as a pillar of one's identity. Rather, it is an invitation to participate in constructing a community that is not constrained by a static vision of social life and the common good. A national community of shared fate would ideally engage in continual debate over its boundaries and character and would express a social and institutional commitment to giving voice to diverse views. Like any vision of citizenship, therefore, the vision of shared fate requires an account of citizenship education, for it is through such education that the young are engaged in the continuing debate over the boundaries and character of the community of shared fate they are part of.

Shared Fate Citizenship Education

The common school—inasmuch as it is democratically attainable—has long been deemed the best context for learning to live a shared life with others who espouse different subnational affiliations. As Reich argues, "The fact of pluralism . . . makes the common school necessary in that the schoolhouse is perhaps the best vehicle available to the state to unite a diverse citizenry under common ideals and to help forge a common national identity."[20] Schools often express in their practices, beyond the mandated curricular focus on social studies or civics, views of "everyday nationalism."[21] It is these expressions that are frequently targeted at developing national identity and that the shared fate argument rethinks.

Early twentieth-century accounts of democratic education considered the diversity of the civic body—along ethnic, class, and other lines—to be a challenge that common or universal schooling would be able to overcome, not necessarily by erasing differences but by creating a sufficient common basis for shared civic action. The early forms of universal schooling envisioned the development of a common identity—an American identity in the case of the United States, though parallels exist in many other democracies—an identity that would override other affiliations, moral commitments, and group memberships. In this sense identity is a property, an attribute, and to a significant extent it is restricted to a limited group of people who often relate it to other aspects of their identities such as their ethnic origins or religious commitments.[22] Becoming a member of the nation under this description of identity citizenship requires taking on, or at minimum accepting, these attributes that are assumed to constitute the essence of national identity.

In his important contribution to the scholarly debate on education for citizenship, Eamonn Callan portrays the emotional attachment of citizens to each other as a basis for liberal patriotism, which he sees as a condition of liberal justice in a democratic state, but he suggests that we see these relationships as ones that "connect our very identity to the good of others."[23] As we have seen, thinking of citizenship as a form of shared fate requires considering social ties, ways for citizens to relate to one another, horizontal connections among citizens, and their connections to the shared project of constructing the nation and developing and advancing its aims. Shared fate aims not to replace but rather to augment, and in this way to reframe, the view of membership in the nation as a matter of a common identity. Rather than thinking of the citizen as a member of the political community by virtue of her identity (for example, as an American), shared fate portrays her as developing a view of herself as member of the community by virtue of her relationship with other members, by her way of relating to the nation-state as a project she takes part in, and by her multiple linkages to the national community and its institutions and practices. A central dimension of shared fate citizenship education is thus to introduce the evolving social and institutional context in which citizens live and to develop an understanding of the cultural, cognitive, and discursive dimensions of national membership.

Citizenship education based on the idea of shared fate calls for starting with the fact of enduring pluralism in American society (as in other democratic nations) and developing democratic citizenship and its skills as the common basis that informs education for membership in the nation-state. A focus on shared fate gives a central role in citizenship education to the nation as a shared political community, with the diversity of affiliations it encompasses. A firm grounding in social and moral realities contextualizes citizenship education as a project based on the connectedness of individuals who share the same fate by virtue of their membership. Shared fate requires citizenship education that acknowledges and promotes visions of shared histories, struggles, institutions, languages, and value commitments. It takes into account and builds on the tension and struggles over how we define and recognize many of these shared dimensions. Teaching citizenship as a form of shared fate incorporates the understanding of an individual's relation to the state with discussions of her relationships with other members of the nation. Notably, thinking of citizenship as shared fate entails understanding how webs of relationships form in the context of the nation, some chosen, some given. This understanding is a key aspect of citizenship education, and it can constitute the foundation for viewing our fate as intertwined with that of others. It then gives rise to obligations we have toward one another, and to actions we are expected to take and see ourselves as capable of taking based on these obligations. The first step to developing civic skills is for individuals to see themselves as participants in a shared, cooperative project that includes diverse others. Shared fate citizenship education can thus help bridge the gap between political knowledge and motivation while recognizing that each school's capacity to introduce visions of good citizenship is continually challenged by the particular population it serves.[24]

Group membership envisioned as shared fate can reasonably include a commitment to one's nation-state and to the democratic principles and institutions that signify its values, including the opportunity to revise them within democratic guidelines. Shared fate citizenship education thus introduces an acknowledgment of the various ways one's fate is shared with one's compatriots. This form of citizenship education focuses on the nation (rather than subgroups or the global community) as key to the pursuit of shared political goals.

Like other kinds of citizenship education, shared fate citizenship education has both responsive and aspirational components. It responds to

the ties among nation members that arise from shared territoriality, institutional affiliation, affected interests that arise from institutional and
geographic linkages, shared histories, linguistic ties, and shared views of
national myths. At the same time, it aspires to build on such linkages to
promote the skills and attitudes required for good citizenship, thus enhancing the sense of belonging among the young members of the nation.

Significantly, shared fate sees the nation-state as the institutional and
territorial location for a continuous project of nation building. It thus
pulls apart the nation-state and the nation and maintains that while the
nation-state is relatively stable (barring civil and other wars), the nation
is always a work in progress. The continuing process of nation building
is bound to raise some anxiety, both among those who are trying to join
the nation and among those who feel they have accomplished a satisfac-
tory—maybe laudable—version of the nation and are loath to allow for
its reinterpretation. Learning to see one's connection to the nation-state
as horizontal as well as vertical can alleviate some of these concerns, inasmuch as members consider their citizenship not solely or centrally as an
attribute or acquired status but rather as a form of relational affiliation.
The identity such citizenship provides is based on achieved ties and connections rather than on ascription; as a continuing project, it provides an
opportunity to participate in constructing and striving for shared goals.
This can be empowering for those identified as "the next generation of
citizens"—children—because their education is based on their role not
in taking on an existing vision of the nation but rather in reimagining and
recreating the nation for the society they envision. In this way citizenship
education, like education in general, is rooted both in the present, with its
social realities, and in the future vision of what society might be like for
the next generation.

The focus on the future must not outweigh the importance of the present. Citizenship education requires not only the future-oriented development of civic virtues, commitment to justice, and creating the conditions
for legitimacy—all areas addressed in contemporary political theory. Citizenship education must also look at the lived experiences of children as
they go through the educational process. It must be rooted in the social and
psychological conditions for the development of virtues, skills, and habits
of mind that enable the current political structure to continue and to improve. Education for citizenship is expressed in the structures and practices
of the education system as much as in explicit curricular and pedagogic
mandates, and through this "everyday nationalism" educational structures must not only promote shared fate but also exhibit a commitment

to it. Citizenship education starts with the moral realities of the nation in all their complexity and seeks forms of attachment, belonging, and commitment that would enable children to become positive members of diverse communities of fate, including the shared national fate.

Shared Fate Education across Divides

Because the concept of shared fate is based on actual links among members of the nation-state, it has to acknowledge contexts in which fate is and is not shared.[25] Asymmetries and differences regularly interrupt the project of shared fate. Focusing on shared fate offers an alternative to the common scholarly responses to families, communities, and ideologies that oppose certain civic values. These responses tend to either demand adherence to the civic ethos above other values or accommodate competing value sets by minimizing the content and reach of the shared civic foundation. How does educating for shared fate citizenship respond more effectively to particular forms of difference, asymmetry, and pluralism within a diverse nation? Citizenship education based on shared fate cannot address all children similarly, without regard to the particularities of their lives.

Competing group affiliations create one challenge to this and other forms of citizenship education. Some have suggested that citizenship should be thought of not as a universal but as a differentiated status, carrying multiple meanings for diverse populations.[26] Ethnic and racial minorities' road to citizenship differs from that of the majority; immigrant children, both documented and undocumented, face unique challenges when learning citizenship; and though some religious beliefs coincide with certain citizenship virtues and strengthen them, others may be (or may be perceived as) incongruous to some of citizenship's demands. A related challenge to conceptualizing citizenship as shared fate, and to teaching it as such, arises from the different living conditions that children and families face as a result of their socioeconomic status. There are significant differences between a child who enjoys the benefits of a family with a stable income and available leisure time and a child who lives with the stresses of hunger and homelessness.

Linguistic differences, diverse value commitments (including religious values), and social class differences present key contexts for the shared fate approach to citizenship education. Before I consider them in turn, it is important to make three preliminary notes. First, in all cases the shared fate approach treats differences not as challenges but rather as resources that inform and enrich shared national membership. There is no assumption of existing, given, "natural," or ascriptive forms of membership that "other" groups need to be assimilated into, but rather an assumption of complex social structures and personal affiliations that need to coexist within a shared sphere of institutions and practices. Second, shared fate does not require active participation in the national project as a way to affirm or "overcome" difference. Rather, it provides all members of society, as well as aspiring members, an opportunity to contribute in diverse ways to the common, public sphere. Third, because diversity is an infinite social reality and individuals can affiliate with multiple groups and maintain a host of diverse commitments, the differences discussed in the following pages by no means exhaust the list of key resources in contemporary democratic societies.

Because the project of citizenship education is political, it is by nature contextual and relates to a particular community with its specific forms of diversity and shared spaces. As Galston puts it, civic education "is by definition education within, and on behalf of, a particular political order."[27] I now consider divides and forms of diversity in contemporary American classrooms and the ways they can contribute to and inform the project of shared fate citizenship.

Language

Linguistic communities often provide individuals with a cultural horizon, a context to which they can relate and through which they learn to navigate their social environment. Linguistic diversity generates particular challenges to a common national foundation, since the boundaries that language divides create can sometimes undermine attempts to maintain a shared public sphere. French-speaking Canadians, Spanish-speaking Americans, speakers of dialects of the official language in Thailand, Arabic-speaking Israelis, and Turkish-speaking Germans are all examples of the web of relations and differences that a linguistic minority expresses and reproduces. Despite the understanding developed in political, linguistic, and educational scholarship regarding the role of language as a cultural indicator and an aspect of identity,[28] education practice often treats language as a skill. This educational view sometimes justifies imposing the majority's language on students with other home languages, as a way to open educational and other opportunities that are more abundantly

available to those who can speak the majority language. In addition, practitioners, like other citizens, sometimes view the acquisition of majority
language as an indicator of the individual's acceptance of mainstream political identity.

Shared-fate citizenship encourages alternative responses to linguistic diversity, responses that do not require students to leave their native
tongues at home and that do not insist on instruction exclusively in the majority language. Because shared fate allows for competing memberships
to exist alongside the national one, linguistic diversity does not threaten
its realization. Pathways to expanding linguistic capacities, including the
opportunity to acquire the majority language, would be desirable in many
political contexts as a way to promote and sustain communication in the
public sphere and the sharing of institutional affiliations and linkages. But
in different national and local contexts, this goal can be pursued without
the pressure to prioritize the majority language over minority ones, based
on an understanding that linguistic respect and the generation of shared
public spaces are not the responsibility of the minority group(s) alone. In
addition, even if language is a pathway to educational and employment
opportunities, bilingualism provides greater opportunities to children of
both majority and minority home languages (as well as smaller-minority
languages). The Canadian context has been extensively discussed in the
literature, and a growing body of work indicates related perspectives in the
context of English and Spanish in the United States.[29] A shared fate vision
should thus be constructed without excluding the diversity of languages
represented in the public domain from being used and promoted in communal, educational, and other public settings.

Cultural and Religious Diversity

Acknowledging diversity as a foundation of citizenship education stands
at the heart of shared fate visions, though diversity informs other visions
of citizenship education as well. Callan suggests that to develop a vision of
patriotism that is an ally of cosmopolitan morality rather than an alternative, children can learn to think about their nation as "an open venture
of collective self-rule."[30] However, like other liberal scholars, Callan sub-
scribes to the notion of the school as a "great sphere"[31] whose civic charge
is to teach students about the choices open to them for membership in different cultural and other groups. Politically speaking, this emphasis on the
opportunity to switch cultures risks alienating members of cultures who

believe their set of values reflects the truth. Religious groups and sects are likely to be suspicious of institutions that aim to support their children in a journey that can end outside their belief system. Other groups that are committed to a definitive set of values, as well as minority groups that define themselves through their affiliation to other nations,[32] may share this concern. The concerns of religious and other comprehensive communities and families raise an important point for democratic citizens to consider. While schools are indeed charged with widening students' horizons, directing much of these efforts toward culture or religion seems to miss the point. A devotion to one set of values may be disconcerting to those who believe in the democratic power of choice, but that is mostly because they neglect some of the major features of this important value. In this context, choice should not be construed as encouragement to abandon your way of life for another. Rejecting the set of values one was raised with is a possibility that should not be denied, but neither should it be an aim of democratic schooling. If they do not wish to argue for abolishing religion and nonreflective cultures, liberal democrats must acknowledge that public schools—like society itself—can accommodate a variety of affiliations without serious harm to democracy. The aspiration should not be to introduce, or instill, the possibility of self-authorship or even a more minimal version of autonomy.[33] As long as children are able to participate as civic equals—a requirement that should be understood procedurally rather than as a matter of soulcraft—their particular affiliations are beyond the realm of justifiable public (including educational) intervention.

Class

Contrary to other divides, significant class differences pose a challenge rather than an opportunity to democracies and to the process of educating for citizenship. One of the greatest challenges to equal civic standing, and by implication to shared fate, is class-based civic exclusion.[34] Recent research has identified a gap in civic achievement between students of different races and socioeconomic and immigration status.[35] Poor and minority students seem to demonstrate lower levels of civic and political knowledge, skills, positive attitudes toward the state, and participation than their wealthier and white counterparts, insofar as these measures are focused on formal aspects of knowledge and practices such as voting.[36] Access to school-based opportunities to develop civic commitments and capacities are unevenly distributed among high school students: college-bound students have significantly more access to these opportunities than students not tracked to attend college. The range between the best- and worst-prepared students is exceptionally large in the United States compared with other countries.

Much of the difference has to do with underperforming and resource-poor schools, resulting in an achievement gap and in exclusion from appropriate schooling.[37] The effects of lack of knowledge, including formal civic knowledge, and educational opportunities include the lack of political self-efficacy, diminished trust in institutions including the government, and disengagement from formal and shared aspects of the public sphere.

A growing body of educational research indicates that children from underserved communities, including minority and poor children, exhibit the best educational results when they attend institutions that are focused on a shared mission.[38] Although I do not explore educational achievement, this fact is relevant here for two reasons. First, as I suggested above, there is some indication of a correlation between educational attainment and political participation/efficacy. Inasmuch as this research provides us with a link between education—not specifically citizenship education—and a sense of membership, as well as active membership in the political community, this is another reason to support efforts to minimize the achievement gap to promote civic equality. Therefore, finding promising directions for improving the educational results of those least well served by the current education system is important.

Moreover, there is a political message in the success of schools that are committed to a mission, in which adults trust each other and work together to advance a common goal, whether this goal is Afrocentric education, better test results, leadership for girls, or other missions. The willingness and capacity to work together to change current political and social conditions not only improves the test results of underserved children but also indicates, to them and to others, that a shared action can be meaningful and successful. Developing partnerships and forms of listening and acting across difference can support the civic capacities of those who have both greater and fewer opportunities, as Seth Moglen illustrates in his contribution to this volume. The sense of efficacy that can arise from the experience of partnering for a shared mission, and the development of positive attitudes toward civic participation, could be another important outcome.[39]

Children who are members of excluded, disenfranchised, and marginalized groups have an additional lesson to learn in their education for citizenship. Their teachers should present them not only with knowledge of current shared institutions, practices, and histories (although these are important components of any valuable education for citizenship), but also with the context of their own exclusion. On the other hand, shared fate citizenship education would require that middle-class and wealthy children learn about their reciprocal relationships and interdependency with poorer citizens. Unlike identity-oriented civic education, which could teach wealthy students principles of equality, liberty, and patriotism while ignoring class-based inequities entirely, civic education oriented toward shared fate demands that advantaged students learn about and with conationals with whom they are interlocked in webs of political, economic, social, and cultural relationships.[40] Shared fate does not gloss over the realities of economic and cultural marginalization; it gives individuals who are harmed by these realities, as well as those advantaged by them, a context and an incentive to work across these gaps. Although the burden of overcoming current exclusionary practices should by no means rest on the shoulders of children (and adults) who are currently excluded, shared fate in the context of exclusion is more an aspiration than a reality. In this sense, the institutions (including schools) that serve marginalized groups—schools that are becoming increasingly homogeneous (or effectively segregated)—should not only account for current exclusion but also equip their students with a sense of self-efficacy. Similarly, institutions that serve children and families who benefit from the current social order should expose these children to the ways their position in society is a result of institutions and practices shared with others, and the ways these institutions and practices disadvantage some of their fellow nation members. This could help motivate them to view themselves as equal citizens who can work to advance their own interests as individuals and as members of the shared community. Schools that endorse a mission of preparing citizens can support students from marginalized communities in enacting their full membership.

Conclusion

Publicly supported educational institutions are charged with responding to the fact of diversity and with advancing a shared vision of civic political membership. Considering citizenship as membership in diverse democratic nation-states, I argued here that the fate citizens share with each other—the institutional, historical, linguistic, cultural, territorial, and other dimensions that bind them together—should constitute the shared foundations of political membership, and that the project of defining and realizing shared national projects should serve as a key dimension of citizenship and citizenship education. Shared fate citizenship requires that a publicly supported education system be positioned to facilitate shared civic knowledge, skills, and dispositions, and that it views competing value systems as part of the civic sphere it teaches and endorses. The goal of continuously interpreting the shared dimensions of nationality, the sense of commitment and affiliation it generates, and the ways its institutions serve and promote it can provide a sound and evolving shared foundation for membership in a diverse democratic society.

PART 2
Constraints

CHAPTER 5

Can Members of Marginalized Groups Remain Invested in Schooling?

An Assessment from the United States and the United Kingdom

Angel L. Harris

Introduction

The research reported in this chapter was meant to determine whether belonging to a marginalized group is associated with academic disinvestment. Can members of marginalized groups remain invested in schooling despite their persistent encounter with barriers to upward socioeconomic mobility? If the answer is no—if members from marginalized groups perceive barriers to upward mobility in a manner that compromises their academic investment—it will be difficult to achieve racial parity in educational outcomes as long as the factors that lead to perceptions of barriers persist. However, if the answer is yes—that members from marginalized groups can remain invested in schooling—then the narrative of blacks' resistance to schooling needs to be reassessed; explanations (and solutions) for the racial achievement gap should be shifted away from the narrative that blacks resist schooling.

This chapter is divided into two parts. First I examine the intergenerational transmission of beliefs regarding upward socioeconomic mobility among black Americans. Studying perceptions of barriers and beliefs about education as a mechanism for upward mobility among black parents is important for understanding how members from marginalized groups orient themselves toward education, because adolescent youths have limited firsthand experiences in the labor market. Although normative expectations of achievement can be transmitted through a number of social contexts, youths' perceptions about the opportunity structure are likely to stem from the messages they receive from older family members. Therefore it is important to determine whether parents who belong to a marginalized group—black Americans—perceive barriers to upward mobility in a manner that results in their children's academic disinvestment. In the second part of this chapter I examine whether youths from marginalized groups disinvest from schooling. In order to provide a robust assessment, I show evidence from youths in both the United States and the United Kingdom.

Below I discuss the factors that might contribute to racial differences in perceptions about the opportunity structure within the United States, followed by a brief description of how black parents might respond to their perceptions of barriers to upward mobility. I then provide results for the implications of parents' views about barriers for youths' academic investment and assess whether youths from marginalized groups have lower levels of academic investment than youths from nonmarginalized groups in both the United States and the United Kingdom. I conclude by discussing the theoretical and policy implications of the findings.

Basis for Cynicism about Opportunities among Black Americans

The black American experience is deeply rooted in socioeconomic disadvantage and a history of being targets of government-sanctioned discriminatory treatment, dating back to the era of slavery (pre-1865) through the era of Jim Crow laws that mandated de jure racial segregation in public spaces (1876–1965). State-mandated discrimination ended with the Civil Rights Act of 1964 and the Voting Rights Act of 1965. Yet racial inequality on many socioeconomic indicators—education in particular—has persisted. This persistence has fueled a narrative about "black cultural deficits" (Ogbu 1978, 2003). According to this narrative, the vestiges of past discriminatory practices lead blacks to go beyond disinvesting from schooling to outright resistance. Some scholars claim that because of these barriers, the larger black community has an antagonistic attitude toward education that stems from negative perceptions about the opportunity structure (Fordham and Ogbu 1986; Ogbu 1978, 2003; Steinberg, Dornbusch, and Brown 1992).

Previous research suggests that there is a legitimate basis for blacks' perceptions of an unfair opportunity structure (Baldi and McBrier 1997; Elliott and Smith 2004; Smith 2005). For example, using data from the National Organizational Study—interviews conducted with the employers of respondents from the National Opinion Research Center's General Social Survey (GSS)—Baldi and McBrier (1997) find that, relative to whites, black workers with comparable education, experience, and training and in similar types of firms are only half as likely to receive a promotion. In a study on differential access to workplace power, Elliott and Smith (2004) find that racial inequality in promotion increases at higher levels of power. Specifically, using data from the Multi-city Survey of Urban Inequality (MCSUI)—a multistage stratified area-probability sample of respondents in Atlanta, Boston, Detroit, and Los Angeles—they find that both females and black males are less likely to receive promotions at the higher end of the occupational hierarchy than white males. These differences exist even if the comparisons are made among individuals with similar years of education, total work experience, prior job-specific experience, and employer tenure. In the case of black women, this form of inequality appears to be a result of direct discrimination, since family considerations that might lead females to opt out of consideration for higher-level positions were taken into account. Thus, studies on racial differences in promotion suggest that these disparities cannot be attributed to differences in human capital or type of firm. In sum, blacks' human capital credentials receive more intense scrutiny than whites' credentials when vying for managerial (Wilson, Sakura-Lemessy, and West 1999) and supervisory positions (Smith 2001).

In addition to racial differences in upward mobility within the workforce, another factor that might contribute to blacks' perceptions of discrimination is racial differences in wages. Studies based on the National Longitudinal Survey of Youth (NLSY)—which contains panel data spanning four decades on the school-to-work transition and labor market experiences of a nationally representative sample of over twelve thousand men and women—show that while no black-white wage gap exists at labor force entry, a racial wage gap develops as experience accumulates, primarily because blacks reap smaller gains from job mobility (Oettinger 1996; Tomaskovic-Devey, Thomas, and Johnson 2005). The black wage disadvantage persists net of education, experience, hours worked, occupation, authority, region, and city size (Smith 1997). Many of these patterns also exist among women. Anderson and Shapiro (1996) show that black women are less likely to hold high-wage occupations than their white counterparts, even if they have the same levels of education, work experience, tenure, and type of occupation. They also find that black women must have higher levels of education, work experience, and tenure than their white counterparts to access high-wage occupations. Thus there is ample empirical evidence suggesting that blacks have a basis to perceive barriers within the labor market that education might not help them overcome. But do these barriers and the perception of them lead to disinvestment? In contrast to scholarly and journalistic orthodoxy since Ogbu, my answer is a resounding no.

Parents, Race, and Messages about the Opportunity Structure

Given that blacks and whites differ in their experiences within the workforce, it is reasonable to expect that the values and norms parents impart to their children—particularly around race—will differ by race. Let me refresh our understanding of the story that is now, as a consequence of Ogbu's influence, conventionally told. On Ogbu's line of analysis, parents' experiences are major conduits for black children's knowledge about the opportunity structure, and parents' experiences with an opportunity structure that underrewards blacks' educational accomplishments relative to whites' compromise black children's motivation to achieve academically (Ogbu 1978, 2003; Fordham and Ogbu 1986; Mickelson 1990). According to Ogbu (1978) and Fordham and Ogbu (1986), parents' experiences with discrimination limit children's confidence in the system of social mobility and in education. Mickelson (1990, 59) puts the view thus: "Young blacks are not bewitched by the rhetoric of equal opportunity through education; they hear another side of the story at the dinner table."

In fact, the opposite is true. Parents who experience discrimination are more likely to anticipate that their children will also experience discrimination and to provide them with coping mechanisms (Hughes and Chen 1997; Hughes 2003; Coard et al. 2004). Whereas Ogbu (1978) argued that an overemphasis on racial barriers and discrimination undermines children's self-worth and promotes distrust and anger toward mainstream institutions, numerous studies show that black children who are socialized to be aware of racial barriers generally have a more positive racial identity, which studies consistently show is associated with better academic outcomes (Bowman and Howard 1985; Edwards and Polite 1992; Sanders 1997; Sellers, Chavous, and Cooke 1998; Wong, Eccles, and Sameroff 2003). A more positive racial identity also makes youths better prepared to deal with prejudice, stigmatizing, and discrimination (Bowman and Howard 1985; Oyserman et al. 2003; Thomas and Speight 1999).

In the first part of this chapter I focus on parents' beliefs about the discrimination they have experienced and the discrimination they anticipate for their children: Are their beliefs on those two points determinants either of youths' perceptions about schooling as a mechanism for upward mobility or of their academic achievement? I also consider whether parents' beliefs about the importance of schooling are a determinant of youths' perceptions about the importance of school. To seek connections between parents' beliefs and youths' perceptions and achievement, I analyze survey data from the Maryland Adolescence Development in Context Study (MADICS), which contains a unique collection of measures on 1,407 black and white families (66 and 34 percent, respectively) from a county on the eastern seaboard of the United States. The sample was selected from approximately five thousand adolescents in the county who entered middle school during 1991 via a stratified sampling procedure designed to get proportional representations of families from each of the county's twenty-three middle schools. The mean family income in the sample is normally distributed (that is, most family incomes cluster around the mean in a bell curve that tails off at the low and high ends), with white families reporting significantly higher incomes ($50,000 to $54,999) than black families ($40,000 to $44,999).

The MADICS provides a good opportunity to examine the intergenerational transmission of beliefs about upward mobility because it contains data on children and parents throughout adolescence (from middle school through high school). It also contains a wealth of survey items, not usually found in national data sets, regarding perceptions about the opportunity structure, chances for upward socioeconomic mobility, and academic orientation from both parents and youths. Numerous data sets contain basic indicators of academic orientation unrelated to race (e.g., educational aspirations), but the MADICS is particularly rich on indicators that measure racialized perceptions of barriers to upward mobility at various stages of adolescence.

I begin my assessment in figure 1, which displays findings for black-white racial comparisons on survey questions intended to measure parents'

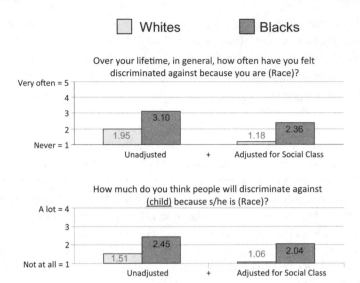

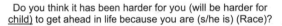

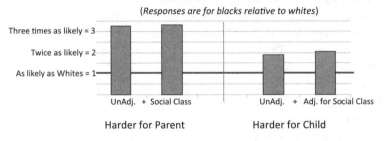

Note: Comparisons on the right-hand side account for family income, parental education, family structure, and youths' sex and can be interpreted as the scores for blacks and whites similarly situated with regards to social class. All racial differences are statistically significant ($p < .01$).

FIGURE 1. Parents' perceptions of discrimination toward self and child (means).

perceptions of racial barriers, including their subjective experiences with discrimination and their beliefs concerning the potential barriers their children may experience owing to race.[1] I display two pairs of estimates for each question. The first pair simply shows the average score for each group. The second pair represents the average scores for both groups if they had similar family income, parental education, and family structure (i.e., single- or two-parent household) and can be interpreted as the scores for blacks and whites similarly situated with regard to social class. The figure shows that black parents experience more racial discrimination over the life course than whites. Parents' expectation that their children will experience discrimination is also greater among blacks than whites. The second pair of estimates shows that these patterns are the same even if the comparison is between blacks and whites with similar socioeconomic backgrounds.

The bottom part of figure 1 shows group comparisons on the odds of responding yes to whether parents think it has been harder for them to get ahead in life because of their race, and whether they expect the same for their children. The bold line along the y-axis highlights 1.0, which is intended to provide a basis for comparing the estimates for black parents with those of white parents. Thus, an estimate of 1.0 would indicate that blacks are just as likely as whites to affirm the question. The first pair of estimates show that black parents are over three times as likely as their white counterparts to view their race as a liability for advancement in life. They are nearly twice as likely to believe race will make it challenging for their children to advance in life. These patterns remain nearly identical when socioeconomic background is taken into account.

The findings in figure 1 confirm what most readers already know; relative to whites, black parents report having more experiences with discrimination and greater belief that their children will experience a similar fate. It seems logical that they would attribute less value to education as a mechanism for upward mobility. However, it also seems logical that black parents would promote a positive academic orientation in order to increase their children's chances of overcoming barriers to upward mobility that they themselves experienced.[2] It is important to note that parents' experiences of discrimination and perceptions of barriers are not synonymous with their beliefs about the importance of education. Even the anticipation that their children will experience barriers within the labor market does not necessarily mean parents will attribute little value to education. I show this in figure 2, which displays black-white comparisons on indicators that gauge how important parents believe education is for their children. Despite reporting a greater belief in barriers, black parents' educational aspirations for their children are not lower than those of their white counterparts. Figure 2 suggests that they actually hold higher educational aspirations and believe more strongly than whites that success in school is essential for their children's success in life.

The greater importance black parents attribute to education despite their greater perceptions of discrimination might reflect overcompensation.

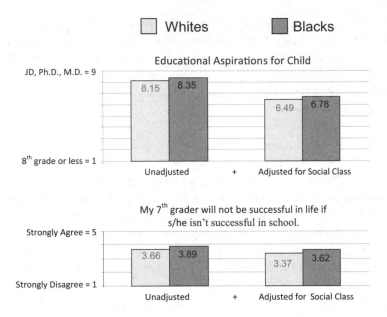

Note: Educational aspirations and expectations are coded as 1 = eighth grade or less, 2 = grades 9-11, 3 = high school graduate, 4 = post-HS vocational training, 5 = some college, 6 = graduate from a 2-year college, 7 = 4-year college graduate, 8 = Masters degree, and 9 = J.D., M.D., Ph.D. The comparisons on the right-hand side account for family income, parental education, family structure, and youths' sex. All racial differences are statistically significant ($p < .05$).

FIGURE 2. Parents' perceptions of the importance of education (means).

In anticipating greater obstacles for their children, black parents may offer more encouragement for school achievement than white parents. In fact, given comparable family backgrounds based on ordinary measures of social class (without even taking wealth into account), blacks display higher levels of educational attainment than whites. Mason (1997) found that black students are 6 to 7 percent more likely than white students to graduate from high school if the comparison is made among students with similar socioeconomic backgrounds. Mason (2007) also shows that both black men and black women obtain more years of education than their white counterparts raised in similar family environments. Mason's work suggests that black students translate a given set of family status characteristics into more years of educational attainment than otherwise similarly situated white students, which is consistent with an overcompensation effect attributable to parents' and family characteristics.

The findings that black parents have higher educational aspirations for their children and attribute more importance to schooling than their white counterparts are consistent with analysis conducted by Cook and Ludwig (1997). Using nationally representative data from the National Education Longitudinal Study, they find that, on average, black parents are at least as involved in their children's educations as white parents. Their results show that black parents are more likely than white parents to telephone their children's teachers (65 to 58 percent) and attend a school meeting (65 to 56 percent), and there are no racial differences in parents' attending school events (63 percent) or helping their children with homework (54 percent). However, when they controlled for family socioeconomic status, the racial differences increased on all outcomes in favor of black parents. Further evidence of this pattern can also be found in a national poll commissioned by the National Center for Public Policy and Higher Education, which showed that black parents place higher value on obtaining an education as a means for advancement than whites do (Public Agenda 2000). Therefore these findings show that the results in figure 2 should not be considered an artifact of the MADICS data.

Do Parents' Beliefs about the Opportunity Structure Have Implications for Youths?

The answer to whether black parents contribute to an antiacademic ethos is not yet clear from the data discussed above. The findings appear paradoxical and contravene expectations. What should be made of the findings displayed in figure 2 suggesting that black parents hold education in as high regard as white parents, or even higher? And what about black parents' negative experiences and negative perceptions about opportunities? Are those experiences and perceptions irrelevant? To determine whether black parents indeed help precipitate an antipathy toward school among black youths, one must consider which set of factors—discriminatory experiences, beliefs about barriers, or views about education—mediate this process.

I address these questions by assessing whether parents' experiences and beliefs have implications for the value youths attribute to school, for their educational aspirations and expectations, for the barriers they anticipate in the future, and for their academic achievement. I present these findings in figure 3, in a series of minigraphs. I show the youth averages on various

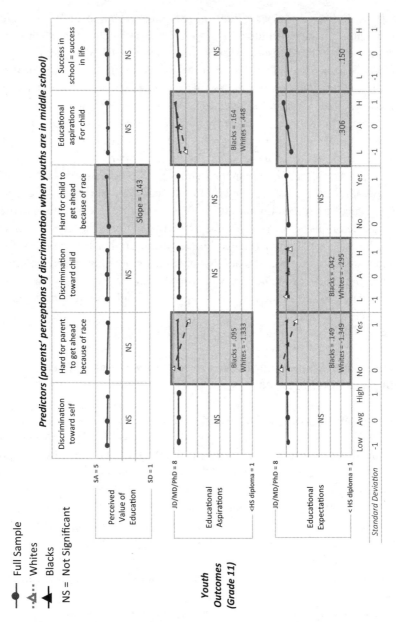

FIGURE 3. The implications of parents' perceptions of discrimination and value of school for selected youth outcomes.

Predictors

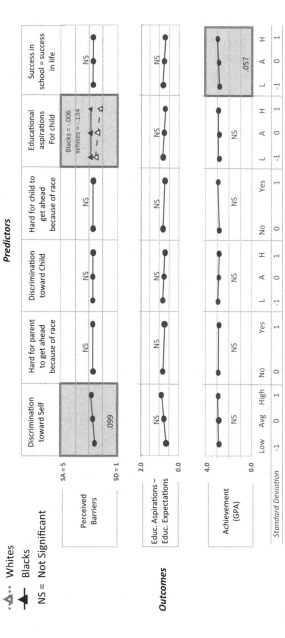

Note: Several points of clarity are warranted apropos of figure 3. First, each mini-graph shows the slope or changes in the youth outcome—listed along the left side of the figure—associated with increases in the parental indicator listed across the top of the graphs. Each panel represents one equation; all slopes for each outcome were obtained from the same statistical regression model that includes race, sex, all parental beliefs listed across the top of the figure, and socioeconomic background (i.e., family income, parents' education, and family structure). Second, in order to convey both youths' averages on the outcomes and how they are associated with the parental factors, I graph the slopes through the mean of the youth outcomes. Third, each mini-graph displays the association as the average score for youths at two levels of the parental indicator: one standard deviation (or the average difference of each parent from the mean of all parents on the parental indicator) below and above the mean of the youth outcomes. Fourth, in cases where the slope differs by race, the slope is graphed separately for blacks and whites. Finally, whereas graphs that show no significant association are labeled NS for *not significant*, those which display a significant association at the .05 level of significance are highlighted (see the methodological appendix A for further details).

outcomes for parents who are low, average, and high on the measures for parents' perceptions of discrimination, beliefs about barriers, and views about education. Graphs that represent a statistically significant relation are highlighted, and those that do not are labeled NS for not significant. The top panel shows that only one parental indicator is associated with the value youths attribute to education (pairings for which a systematic relationship exists are highlighted). Parental concern over the potential barriers to upward mobility their children will encounter because of race has a *positive* association with the value youths attribute to school. Thus, youths with parents who believe race will make it harder for them to succeed (labeled no/yes along the bottom of the figure) attribute more value to school than those whose parents do not view race as an obstacle for their children.

The next two panels show that parents' perceptions of racial barriers are not significantly related to black children's educational aspiration or expectations. Instead, it is white youths for whom parents' beliefs in barriers and a parental expectation of discrimination for their children seem to have adverse consequences. Parents with greater educational aspirations for them have children with higher educational aspirations and expectations than parents with lower educational aspirations. Also, parents' beliefs about the value of schooling are positively associated with youths' educational expectations. Basically, in the three pairings (out of twelve) for which parents' negative experiences and beliefs have adverse consequences for children, the declines are observed only on the outcomes for whites.

Figure 3 also contains findings for the links between parents' beliefs regarding the opportunity structure and, first, the barriers youths anticipate and, second, their academic achievement. The anticipation of barriers is high among youths whose parents experience more discrimination. I also estimate youths' perception of barriers by an indicator I call perceived limited opportunities for upward social mobility—this is the discrepancy between educational aspirations and expected educational attainment. A greater discrepancy between the amount of schooling students *wish* to attain (i.e., educational aspirations) and the amount of schooling they believe they will attain (educational expectations) reflects that the student more keenly perceives a limited opportunity set. The findings show that none of the parental indicators is associated with this outcome.

Finally, the findings for academic performance suggest that only one parental indicator is associated with achievement. Achievement is higher for youths whose parents believe their children cannot be successful in life without being successful in school. Supplemental findings also show that increases in parents' educational aspirations for their children and in their belief that schooling is important for their children's success are associated with an increase in the odds of college enrollment for youths. More important, parents' perceptions of racial discrimination and barriers—for themselves or their children—have no connection to youths' academic outcomes.

Does Membership in a Marginalized Group Lead to Academic Disinvestment among Youths?

The previous analysis shows that, despite belonging to a marginalized group and having a reason to be skeptical about education as a mechanism for upward mobility, black parents maintain a positive outlook about it. Furthermore, their perceptions of barriers are not associated with academic disinvestment for their children. In this next section I examine whether membership in a marginalized group is associated with academic disinvestment for youths. In addition to reporting findings for youths within the United States, I extend the analysis to include British youths.

Most people are aware of the racial achievement gap, and many believe that black students have a ubiquitous "culture" of underachievement, since there is a tendency to invoke culture to explain persistent patterns of inequality in academic outcomes. However, it would be a mistake to attribute a culture of resistance to blacks based on their academic achievement. A racial achievement gap can still exist without a pervasive oppositional culture. Similarly, black youths could display an oppositional culture even if they did not have lower levels of achievement than whites. When scholars invoke oppositional culture in the context of discussing the poor academic achievement of black youths, they do not mean that oppositional culture is synonymous with poor academic achievement; they mean it explains poor achievement.

In my previous work (Harris 2006), I found that black students report greater perceptions of educational returns and higher educational aspirations than whites. I also found that blacks have more positive affect toward school and rate enjoyment of classes as more important for their school attendance than whites. Although these results suggest that blacks do not perceive fewer educational returns or have less favorable affect toward schooling than whites, Ogbu (1991, 446) argues that black Americans' pro-school attitudes merely reflect "wishful thinking . . . [because blacks] simply do not match their aspirations with effort." He argues that using students' attitudes toward school to measure school resistance is inadequate because "direct questions will generally elicit responses similar to those given by white Americans" (1991, 444).

In other words, according to Obgu's hypothesis, black students do not walk the talk; they mouth pieties about education but do not act on them. Ogbu is correct that school resistance is better gauged by assessing students' behavior—what they do or fail to do to improve academically. But my findings on this point go in the opposite direction from Ogbu's argument. Black students do make an effort. In the previous section I argued that the problem for black student achievement is not aspiration. In this section I will argue that neither is it the absence of an effort to make good on that aspiration. Below I report findings for analyses that compare black and white youths on behavioral indicators for students' academic investment and school resistance.

Academic investment is measured by five indicators: the frequency with which youths seek help when they are having trouble in school, time spent on school activities/clubs, time spent on homework, time spent on learning outside school, and the importance youths attribute to academic activities. School resistance is measured as the frequency with which youths skip school or cut classes, the number of times they have been suspended from school, and the importance they attribute to nonacademic activities. Sports serve as the nonacademic activity because Ogbu notes (2003, 28), "One major issue in prioritizing was deciding between sports and academics." Ogbu (1978) argues that the American caste system encourages a dual system of social/status mobility leading ethnic minorities to disinvest from academics and focus on perceived nonwhite domains such as sports, which they perceive will be more rewarding. Therefore, if Ogbu's resistance model were correct, our data would show blacks scoring lower on indicators that measure academic investment and higher on the indicators of school resistance. But the data do not show this.

The relevant racial comparisons are displayed in figure 4. The names of the survey indicators are listed on the side of the expected "effect" as posited by the resistance model; indicators for which we would expect blacks to score lower than whites, if Ogbu's resistance model were correct, are labeled on the negative side of the graph, while those on which blacks would be expected to score higher, according to his argument, are labeled on the positive side. Since each indicator is measured differently, the estimated racial differences should not be interpreted across indicators. Rather, the focus should be on the location of the estimates—whether they are on the negative or positive side of the graph. I display two estimates for each indicator. The first shows the black-white difference on the indicator (triangle), and the second shows this difference once social class is taken into account (circle). That is, the circle represents how black youths would differ from their white counterparts if they had similar family income, parental education, and family structure. The standard errors are represented by the tails on both sides of the estimates.[3]

The top portion of figure 4 shows little support for the claim that blacks exert less effort to improve academically than whites. Findings show blacks seek help more often than whites when they are having trouble in school. They also spend the same amount of time on homework and educational activities as whites. Although blacks spend less time on school activities/clubs, the adjusted estimate suggests that this can be attributed to their lower socioeconomic status. Blacks actually place greater importance on academic activities than whites (a black advantage of .416 for both unadjusted and adjusted estimates). The bottom portion of figure 4 shows that although blacks do not skip school/cut classes more than whites, they are suspended more often than whites. Only a little more than one-third of their higher suspension levels can be attributed to socioeconomic differences (from .375 to .232). Finally, they also place greater importance on sports, though not when compared with whites of similar socioeconomic status.

It is important to note that suspension from school is not necessarily equivalent to school resistance. Several studies on blacks' differential discipline rates suggest school practices are partially to blame (e.g., Delpit 1995; Lewis 2003; Ferguson 2000; Tyson 2003; Morris 2005). Specifically, these studies find that cultural discontinuity between black families and the institutionalized structure of schools, which value cultural norms and standards of "mainstream" white middle-class society, results in school personnel's placing greater emphasis on black children's behavior. For example, Ferguson (2000) finds that school personnel view the dress and behavior of black males as recalcitrant and oppositional and exert strict control over them. She notes that culturally based assumptions about black males result in their facing constant regulation of their dress, behavior, and speech. Similarly, Morris (2005) finds that whereas white and Asian American children are viewed as nonthreatening, black (and

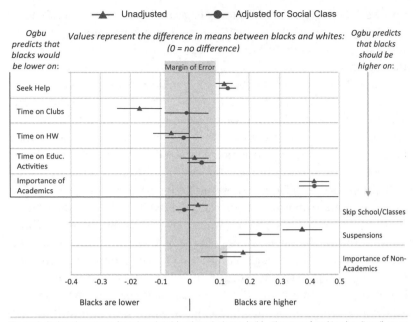

The graph displays the estimate (triangle and circle) and standard error (tails). The means for whites (unadjusted) are as follows: *seek help* (2.87), *time on clubs* (1.81), *time on HW* (4.70), *time on educational activities* (3.03), *importance of academics* (4.95), *skip school or classes* (1.52), *suspension* (0.33), and *importance of non-academics* (4.26). Changes in these means are negligible after adjusting for social class. Adjusted estimates illustrate the group differences after accounting for parents' education, family income, family structure, youths' sex, and grade in school. Values within the margin of error suggest that the racial difference is not significant (*p* is *not* less than .05). Values were obtained from pooled cross-sectional regression models (OLS) using robust standard errors. All indicators are self-reported. See Appendix A for further details on the analytic plan and appendix B for a description of measures.

FIGURE 4. Blacks' scores on measures of academic investiment relative to whites' scores.

Latino/Latina) children are considered dangerous and therefore face constant surveillance and greater discipline for behavioral infractions. In sum, these studies show that "schools react to students based on perceptions of race and gender and use these concepts as a basis for specific patterns of regulation" (Morris 2005, 28). Thus, suspension might reflect differential treatment black children experience in schools. The causal ordering might be reversed; receiving a suspension could be an effect of being a target of school personnel.

The point of this figure, then, is to show that black youths do match aspiration with effort. They seek help and spend time on homework and educational activities equivalent to the time whites spend. But if neither a lack of aspiration nor a lack of effort can explain the achievement gap, what can? Before we return to that question, we need to take one more step to confirm that marginalized students do not disinvest in schooling.

The University of Chicago Press

REVIEW COPY

Education, Justice, and Democracy

Edited by Danielle Allen and Rob Reich

Domestic Publication Date: March 25, 2013
Foreign Publication Date: April 8, 2013

Paper $30.00 £19.50 ISBN 978-0-226-01276-6

For more information, please contact Ryo Yamaguchi by phone at (773)834-8708, by fax at (773)702-9756, or by e-mail at ryamaguchi@press.uchicago.edu

Please send a PDF of your published review to: **publicity@press.uchicago.edu**
Or, by mail to: **Publicity Director, THE UNIVERSITY OF CHICAGO PRESS**

1427 E. 60th Street, Chicago, Illinois 60637, U.S.A. Telephone 773-702-7740

ORDERING INFORMATION

Orders from the U.S.A., Canada, Mexico, Central and South America, East and Southeast Asia, and China:
The University of Chicago Press
Chicago Distribution Center
11030 S. Langley Avenue
Chicago, IL 60628
U.S.A.
Tel: 1-800-621-2736; (773) 702-7000
Fax: 1-800-621-8476; (773) 702-7212
PUBNET @ 202-5280

Orders from the United Kingdom, Europe, Middle East, Africa, and West and South Asia:
The University of Chicago Press
c/o John Wiley & Sons Ltd. Distribution
Centre
1 Oldlands Way
Bognor Regis, West Sussex PO22 9SA
UNITED KINGDOM
Tel: (0) 1243 779777
Fax: (0) 1243 820250
Email: cs-books@wiley.co.uk

Orders from Japan can be placed with the Chicago Distribution Center or:
United Publishers Services Ltd.
1-32-5 Higashi-shinigawa
Shinagawa-ku
Tokyo 140-0002
JAPAN
Tel: 81-3-5479-7251
Fax: 81-3-5479-7307
Email: info@ups.co.jp

Orders from Australia and New Zealand:
Footprint Books Pty Ltd
1/6A Prosperity Parade
Warriewood NSW 2102
AUSTRALIA
Tel: (+61) 02 9997-3973
Fax: (+61) 02 9997-3185
Email: info@footprint.com.au
http://www.footprint.com.au

For Information:
International Sales Manager
The University of Chicago Press
1427 E. 60th Street
Chicago, IL 60637
U.S.A.
Tel: (773) 702-7898
Fax: (773) 702-9756
Email: sales@press.uchicago.edu

Rethinking the Implications of Marginalization for Educational Engagement

Thus far the findings suggest that belonging to a marginalized group does not necessarily result in disengagement from the system of social mobility. This pattern has implications for the study of social stratification because it challenges the general notion that actual or perceived marginalization compromises social (or educational) engagement. The connection between group status—marginalized versus nonmarginalized—and academic investment requires greater inquiry. Specifically, are the patterns observed within the United States a universal indication of how groups marginalized within any given society orient themselves toward education? This is important for stratification research in general, particularly considering that education is increasingly becoming the primary mechanism for upward mobility in industrialized and postindustrialized countries. Therefore I examine whether youths who belong to marginalized groups remain invested in schooling within a non-US context.

Marginalization and Academic Investment beyond the United States

The United Kingdom is an ideal setting for examining whether youths from marginalized groups disinvest from school. Ethnic minorities in the United Kingdom have historically faced difficulties in using education to become upwardly mobile. For example, Bernard Coard's (1971) classic study on the educational experience of West Indian children in England identified a process of programmed retardation of black youths in British schools. A report by the Parliamentary Select Committee (1973, 38) documents that of the more than five thousand youths enrolled in special schools—particularly for "mentally retarded" children—in England and Wales in 1971, 70 percent were West Indian. This is startling considering that West Indians constituted less than 1 percent of the national population. Mortimore et al. (1988) found that a large proportion of black youths in the Inner London Education Authority were placed in schooling tracks lower than those prescribed by their test scores rather than the level that leads to entry into secondary school. Similar to British blacks, Asians in the United Kingdom can be considered as belonging to a marginalized minority group. Over four-fifths of British Asians are descended from residents of India, Pakistan, or Bangladesh (British National Statistics 2001). Since India was under British rule until 1947, along with the territories that now constitute Pakistan and Bangladesh, most British Asians belong to a group that was incorporated into the United Kingdom by colonization.

It is not surprising that Britain was one of the six countries Ogbu (1978) highlighted in his early work to underscore the cross-cultural applicability of his framework. Despite the introduction of state-sponsored comprehensive schools in the late 1960s to allow all students access to postsecondary education (Kerckhoff 2000, 2003), the British education system is more stratified than the US system (Modood 1993). Furthermore, ethnic minorities with qualifications similar to those of whites have experienced higher unemployment (Smith 1981). Therefore it is reasonable to expect that ethnic minorities—both Asian and black—within the United Kingdom are less likely than whites to regard education as a mechanism for upward mobility. I assess whether youths from marginalized groups within the United Kingdom disinvest from schooling using the Longitudinal Study of Young People in England (LSYPE), which contains data on 13,529 whites, 981 Asians, and 381 blacks born in England between September 1989 and August 1990. The LSYPE was developed to understand the factors affecting young people's transition from the later years of compulsory education through any subsequent education or training and into the labor market. Data have been collected annually since the respondents were in year nine or equivalent on February 2004.

Figure 5 displays findings for racial comparisons among youths on four indicators of academic orientation: the frequency with which they read for pleasure, how happy they are at school, the value they attribute to school, and their academic disengagement. Three estimates are shown for each indicator. The first represents how each group differs from whites. The next two estimates show the group differences after accounting for social class (measured according to parents' occupation) and social class and perceived discrimination. The LSYPE measure of discrimination is specific to discrimination based on ethnicity, race, or religion from teachers within the school setting. Why should we control for discrimination? Remember that, according to Obgu's theory, ethnic minorities, as members or marginalized groups, are expected to have lower levels of academic engagement resulting from their perceptions of marginalization. If Ogbu is right, then controlling for their perceptions of discrimination should

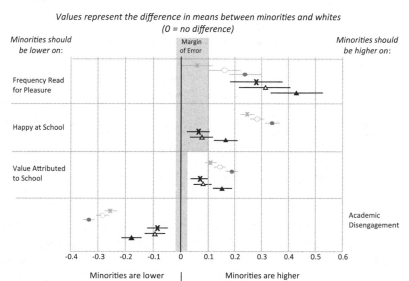

The graph displays the estimate (x, circle, or triangle) and standard error (tails). The means for whites (unadjusted) are 4.32, 3.01, 3.30, and 2.28 for *frequency read for pleasure, happy at school, value attributed to schooling,* and *academic disengagement,* respectively. Changes in these means are negligible after adjusting for social class and discrimination. Estimates adjusted for social class illustrate the group differences after accounting for social class (i.e., parents' occupation). Discrimination is measured as youths' yes/no response to the following question: "Do you think you have ever been treated unfairly by teachers at your school because of your skin, ethnicity, race, or religion?" Values within the margin of error suggest that the racial difference is not significant at the .05 level. Values were obtained from regression models (OLS). See Appendix A for further details on the analytic plan and appendix B for a description of measures.

FIGURE 5. Racial differences in academic orientation among British adolescents.

account for their lower academic engagement. In other words, any lower academic engagement should disappear in their scores. The results are very different from what Ogbu's theory would predict.

The first three indicators suggest that racial minorities do not have lower pro-school orientation than whites. The unadjusted estimates show that relative to whites, black youths read for pleasure more often, Asians are happier at school, and both groups attribute greater value to school. These advantages become greater when comparing youths with similar socioeconomic backgrounds. Making such a comparison shows that Asian youths also read for pleasure more than whites. The third estimate shows that controlling for discrimination further widens ethnic minorities'

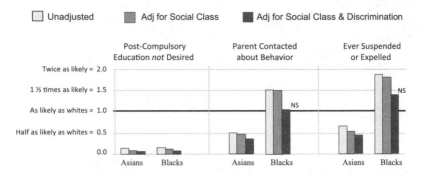

Note: Estimates adjusted for social class illustrate the group differences after accounting for parents' occupation. NS denotes that the racial difference from whites is not significant at the .05 level. Post-compulsory education not desired is youths' yes/no response to whether they want to continue schooling beyond age 16 (reverse coded). See appendix A for further details on the analytic plan and appendix B for a description of measures.

FIGURE 6. Odds ratios for school resistance among British adolescents.

pro-school orientation relative to whites'. Estimates for the three indicators suggest that racial minorities are *more* engaged in academics than whites. In the case of this data set, the perception of greater discrimination does lower engagement, but ethnic minorities start from a high enough level that even in the face of discrimination they remain more engaged than whites.

Figure 6 displays group comparisons on indicators of school resistance. Specifically, I compare the groups on the odds of *not* desiring postcompulsory education and on two indicators that gauge behavioral resistance to schooling: whether the youths' parents were contacted about their behavior and whether the youths have ever been suspended or expelled. The bold line is intended to provide a basis for comparing the estimates for Asians and blacks; an estimate of 1 would indicate that the group is just as likely as whites to exhibit the behavior captured by the indicator.

The bars for the first indicator show that both Asians and blacks have lower odds than whites of *not* desiring postcompulsory education. However, only Asians have lower odds on the behavioral indicators of school resistance. Blacks have higher odds of having their parents' contacted by their schools for behavioral issues and of ever having been suspended or expelled from school, and these findings remain even when the comparisons are made between blacks and whites with similar socioeconomic status. These findings are consistent with those found among black youths within the United States. The third estimate for blacks shows that they do not differ significantly from whites on these indicators after discrimination is taken into account. Thus, the higher odds for blacks of having parents contacted and of ever having been suspended or expelled from school can be attributed to their greater perception of being targets of discrimination. If youths' perception of discrimination is accurate, then this would suggest that blacks' higher odds of experiencing these behavioral sanctions are an artifact of differential treatment by school personnel rather than actual misbehavior. This scenario has been shown to occur within the United States. Specifically, several studies on US youths suggest that blacks' differential disciplinary rates can be partially attributed to school practices that emphasis stricter behavioral control over black youths (e.g., Delpit 1995; Lewis 2003; Ferguson 2000; Tyson 2003; Morris 2005).

Conclusion

This was done to determine whether belonging to a group with a history of being marginalized is associated with academic disinvestment. Youths from marginalized groups often have lower academic achievement than those belonging to nonmarginalized groups. I began by assessing whether being marginalized within a given society results in youths' being socialized by their parents in a manner that compromises their academic investment. I then assessed whether youths from marginalized groups resist school. I provide a more robust assessment than previous studies by extending my analysis beyond the United States to include British youths. In general, two important findings emerged that contradict the claim that the larger black community has an antagonistic relationship with education.

First, although black parents expect their children to experience racial discrimination, they also attribute more value to education than white parents. Specifically, black parents believe education is essential for their children's future success, and they have higher educational aspirations for them than white parents have for their children. Figure 3 shows that parents' beliefs regarding discrimination and the challenges associated with race—for themselves or their children—were related to youths' educational outcomes in a manner consistent with the notion that perception of barriers compromises achievement in only five of the twenty-four minigraphs (twenty-eight if I include the analysis for college enrollment). Furthermore, none of the minigraphs show a negative association between parents' belief in barriers and the youth outcomes for blacks. In contrast, parents' beliefs about the importance of education were associated with improvements in youth outcomes in five of the twelve minigraphs that display these connections in figure 3. Thus, although black parents—youths' primary socializing agents—report experiencing more discrimination than their white counterparts and have a greater belief than whites that their children will experience barriers to upward socioeconomic mobility, these beliefs do not compromise youths' academic investment. Rather, it is parents' beliefs and messages about the value of schooling that are positively related to youths' academic orientation.

The finding that parents' perceptions of discrimination and racial barriers do not compromise the academic measures is consistent with the research literature on racial socialization. This research suggests that in addition to instilling group pride and exposing their children to the culture, history, and heritage of their group, black parents attempt to make children aware of racial bias and prepare them for it (Bowman and Howard 1985; Cross, Parham, and Helms 1991). Parents' transmission of views regarding race and ethnicity has been found to help children cope with racial discrimination and predict positive youth outcomes (Bowman and Howard 1985). This suggests that while minority parents may make their children aware of the potential racial barriers facing them in the future, they also transmit messages of racial pride, which leads to a higher sense of self-efficacy and personal mastery that prevents minority children from disinvesting in school.

My second major finding is that the data analyzed here do not support the cultural deficit model often used to explain the lower achievement of racial minority groups. This narrative fails to account for the high variability within the black student population. This finding even extends to racial minorities within the United Kingdom (Asians and blacks), who also have lower academic achievement than whites yet score either the same or higher on pro-school measures, are less academically disengaged, and are *less* likely than their white counterparts to *not* desire postcompulsory education. These findings are consistent with others showing that blacks in the United Kingdom are more likely than whites to persist in school beyond compulsory level (Tomlinson 1991) and are overrepresented in higher education (Bird, Shebani, and Francombe 1992). It appears that marginalized racial groups do not respond to their marginalization by resisting school. These findings contribute to our understanding of the implications for upward mobility of belonging to a marginalized group; it appears that membership in a marginalized group does not necessarily mean one will resist schooling.

To be clear, I am neither arguing that blacks do not have a counter-productive approach to schooling nor assessing that question; their lower academic achievement suggests that the way they approach school is in-effective given the current standards and modes of evaluation. But if the evidence fails to support that black youths have lower academic orienta-tion than whites, then the counterproductive approach to schooling ob-served among blacks by proponents of the cultural deficit model does not reflect a *deliberate* attempt by black youths to sabotage their own academic achievement. In other words, whatever counterproductive approach may be affecting black students' achievement, the approach does not consist of resistance to schooling. An alternative explanation for blacks' poor aca-demic achievement and counterproductive approach to schooling is nec-essary. Black youths who want to succeed academically may simply not know how.

In a strict sense, the findings of this chapter that members of marginal-ized groups are invested in schooling despite their lower academic achieve-ment yields a paradox only if the value a student places on schooling and that student's academic orientation are the only factors affecting achieve-ment. However, achievement is essentially a summary measure represent-ing a collection of contributing effects from various factors, some based on personal, home, school, and neighborhood characteristics. This point becomes easier to grasp if one considers that a love of golf does not neces-sarily translate into an ability to play like Tiger Woods, regardless of how much importance one places on golf and even regardless of how much one practices. What matters is not merely that one practices, but that one knows how to practice effectively. It is important to distinguish one's in-tended or desired behavior from one's actual behavior. The result of a student's effort is not evidence of the intent or aspiration behind the effort. Blacks' greater academic orientation and lower achievement than whites is not paradoxical when we recognize that basic fact.

In a previous study (Harris and Robinson 2007), I found that the achievement gap between blacks and whites is driven primarily by unequal exposure to instruction and content—that black students disproportion-ately are deprived of the prior skills necessary to be successful at the mid-dle school and especially the high school level. The findings clearly show that the cumulative effect of prior acquisition of academic skills is far more important in determining educational outcomes than student behaviors or attitudes. Ultimately, I do not find much of a difference across racial lines in behaviors and attitudes of students; in fact, black students' attitudes to-ward schooling are mildly better than white students'. The process of skill deprivation connects directly to mechanisms producing racialized tracking and, hence, uneven schooling between black and nonblack students, even in racially mixed schools. This skill deprivation—not reduced aspiration or the absence of effort—is at the heart of the achievement gap.

Appendix A: Methodology

I begin my analysis in figure 1 by determining whether a racial difference exists in how frequently parents perceive that they have experienced discrimination because of their race and believe that their children will experience discrimination because of race (see appendix B for a description of all measures used). The left-hand panel of figure 1 shows simple mean comparisons that can be expressed as an equation as such:

$$Y = \alpha + \beta \text{ (black)} + e, \tag{1}$$

where Y is the outcome or measure for which the racial comparison is being made, α represents the constant, β represents the estimate for blacks, e represents the error term, and whites are the omitted category. This means that α actually represents the mean score for whites (the lighter bar in figure 1) on the outcome and β the mean score for blacks *relative to* whites (the black mean is $\alpha + \beta$, represented by the darker bar in figure 1).

Since blacks have lower socioeconomic standing than whites, the comparison as specified in equation (1) (which shows the raw *unadjusted* group means) is apples to oranges; it is unclear whether any observed black disadvantage relative to whites can be attributed to blacks' lower socioeconomic status (SES). Thus it is important that the racial comparison be apples to apples. I do this by showing the racial comparison after adjusting for SES, such as:

$$Y = \alpha + \beta_1 \text{ (black)} + X\beta_2 + e, \tag{2}$$

where X represents the matrix of SES variables and observations specified in the model (family income, parents' education, single or two-parent household, and youth's sex) and β represents its associated vector of coefficients. Equation (2) shows the estimated racial difference on the outcome after accounting for social class. That is, β represents the black estimate *relative to* whites if both groups had similar SES (e.g., family income, parents' education, and family structure) and $\alpha + \beta$ can be interpreted as the score for blacks if blacks and whites were similarly situated with regard to social class.

The bottom part of figure 1 shows racial comparisons for whether black parents are more likely than whites to believe that their race has made it harder for them to get ahead in life and that their race will make it more difficult for their children to get ahead in life. To show both the unadjusted and SES-adjusted odds for black and white parents, I estimate the log of the odds of responding yes to the aforementioned measures. Since it is difficult to model a dichotomous measure (yes/no), log odds are employed because they expand the range of the probability of yes beyond 0 (no) and 1 (yes) from negative infinity to positive infinity. The estimate from the log of the odds is known as the logit-transformed probability and is calculated as such:

$$\text{Logit } P = \text{Log odds} = P/(1 - P) = \alpha + \beta_1 \text{ (black)} + e, \qquad (3)$$

where α and β represent the estimates for whites and blacks, respectively, and e represents the error term. The SES-adjusted estimates are obtained as such:

$$\text{Log odds} = P/(1 - P) = \alpha + \beta_1 \text{ (black)} + X\beta_2 + e, \qquad (4)$$

where X represents the matrix of SES variables and observations specified in the model and β represents its associated vector of coefficients. Thus, logit-transformed probability allows for the estimation of linear relations with predictor variables (i.e., being black and SES factors).

A final racial comparison is made on parents' views about the importance of schooling. Specifically, I examine whether black parents differ from whites in the belief that their children will not be successful in life if they are not successful in school, and in their educational aspirations for their children. The comparisons on these measures are made using equations (1) and (2) and displayed in figure 2.

The findings in figure 3 show the results for whether parents' perceptions of barriers and the importance of schooling have implications for youths' academic outcomes. I present these findings in a series of mini-graphs. I show the youth averages on various outcomes for parents who are low, average, and high on the measures for parents' perceptions of discrimination, beliefs about barriers, and views about education. Specifically, I employ the following equation:

$$Y_{G11} = \alpha + \beta_1 \text{ (black)} + \delta_1 \text{ (DiscrimPar}_{G7}) + \quad \text{(5)}$$
$$\delta_2 \text{ (RaceBarrierPar}_{G7}) + \lambda_1 \text{ (DiscrimChild}_{G7}) +$$
$$\lambda_2 \text{ (RaceBarrierChild}_{G7}) + \xi_1 \text{ (EducAsp}_{G7}) + \xi_2 \text{ (EducSuccessLife}_{G7}) +$$
$$\gamma_1 \text{ (DiscrimPar}_{G7} * \text{black)} + \gamma_2 \text{ (RaceBarrierPar}_{G7} * \text{black)} +$$
$$\gamma_3 \text{ (DiscrimChild}_{G7} * \text{black)} + \gamma_4 \text{ (RaceBarrierChild}_{G7} * \text{black)} +$$
$$\gamma_5 \text{ (EducAsp}_{G7} * \text{black)} + \gamma_6 \text{ (EducSuccessLife}_{G7} * \text{black)} +$$
$$\beta_2 (Y_{G7}) + X\beta_3 + e,$$

where youth outcomes are measured when youths were in grade eleven (Y_{G11}), δ_1 and $_2$ represent the estimates for parents' belief that they have experienced discrimination (DiscrimPar) and that race has made it harder for them to get ahead in life (RaceBarrierPar), respectively. The next two estimates, λ_1 and λ_2, represent the estimates for parents' belief that their children will experience discrimination because of race (Discrim Child) and that race will make it harder for them to get ahead in life (Race BarrierChild), respectively. The estimates represented by ξ are for parents' educational aspirations (EducAsp) for the youth and their belief that their children will not be successful in life if they are not successful in school (EducSuccessLife). The next six estimates (γ) are intended to examine whether parents' beliefs about discrimination toward themselves and their children and their views about the importance of education have a stronger association with the youth outcomes for blacks than whites. Finally, X represents the matrix of the aforementioned SES variables and observations specified in the model, and β_3 represents its associated vector of coefficients. The findings from this equation are displayed in minigraphs, which show the *slope* or changes in the youth outcome—listed on the *y*-axis—associated with increases in the indicator for parents' beliefs about discrimination—listed along the *x*-axis. These slopes were obtained using the following equation:

$$\mu_{outcome} +/- [(\eta) (\sigma_{\text{predictor}})], \quad \text{(6)}$$

where μ is the mean of the youth outcome, η refers to the estimate obtained from equation (5) for the parental measure listed along the top of the x-axis, and σ represents the standard deviation for the *parental measure*. When the parental measure is dichotomous, such as when parents assess whether "race has made (will make) it difficult for them (for youths) to get ahead in life," the following equation is employed:

$$\mu_{outcome} +/- [\eta / 2]. \tag{7}$$

Thus, *minigraphs* enable me to convey both youths' averages on the outcomes and how the outcomes are associated with the parental factors. The association between the parental and youth measures is displayed as the average score for youths at two levels of the parental indicator: one standard deviation below and one standard deviation above the mean of the parental indicator (labeled low and high, respectively), passing through the mean (labeled average) of the youth outcomes. In cases where the slope differs by race, the slope is graphed separately for blacks and whites.

The findings in figure 4 were obtained using equations (1) and (2), with one exception; the adjusted estimates in these figures (obtained using equation [2]) also include a control for students' grade level (grades eight and grade eleven, grade seven omitted). The racial comparisons in these figures are based on pooled cross sections. Because an individual can enter the sample three times (grades seven, eight, and eleven), robust standard errors are used to account for correlation across individuals.

The next set of analyses is contained in figures 5 and 6. These findings are intended to test the resistance model in the United Kingdom and are based on the LSYPE. The analytic strategy differs in three ways. First, British Asians are included in the analysis. Second, as is conventional within the British context, social class is measured as parents' occupation. Third, perception of barriers (or discrimination) is included to explain potential minority disadvantages in academic orientation. Therefore the findings in figure 5 were obtained using the following equation:

$$Y = \alpha + \beta_1 \text{(black)} + \beta_2 \text{(Asian)} + \beta_3 \text{(SC)} + \beta_4 \text{(Sex)} \tag{8}$$
$$+ \beta_5 \text{(Discrim)} + e,$$

where SC is an indicator of parents' occupation, β_4 is the estimate for youths' sex, and β_5 is the estimate for youths' experiences of discrimination (i.e., whether they have ever been treated unfairly by teachers because of their skin color, ethnicity, race, or religion).

Three estimates are displayed for black and Asian youths in figure 5. The first estimate shows the unadjusted means for black and Asian youths on the outcomes relative to whites. The second estimate for each group was obtained from an equation that includes social class and youths' sex. Finally, the third estimate is based on the full model shown in equation (8). The same analytic approach was applied to the measures displayed in figure 6. However, since the measures in figure 6 are dichotomous (yes/ no), the findings were estimated using logistic regression with the same predictors shown in equation (8). I graph the odds ratios in figure 6 for each group based on the same three model variants described for figure 5 above.

Since an analysis using listwise deletion rapidly reduces sample size, particularly with an increase in covariates, I include missing values as dummy categories within each predictor variable. Thus, missing cases for the predictors were bottom coded, and each predictor was entered into the models along with a flag or "missing information" measure—coded as o if not missing and 1 if missing. This has certain advantages, since it prevents the loss of explanatory power that would come from listwise deletion; allows for the direct modeling of missing data rather than imputing values, for example, by mean substitution, which has its own interpretative problems; ensures a consistent base in terms of the sample size across a range of regression models including increasingly large numbers of explanatory variables; yields estimates identical to those attained via listwise deletion for the variable with the substituted values; and allows all cases with values on the outcome to remain in the analysis. Therefore the number of cases (n) in all analyses totals the N that responded to the outcome being assessed.

Appendix B: Means, Standard Deviations, and Descriptions for Variables Used in This Chapter

Variable Name	Description	Metric	Whites	Blacks	N	Alpha	Data
				Means (SD)			
Figure 1[a]							
Parents' Perceptions of Barriers for Self							
Parent discrim	Over your lifetime, in general, how often have you felt discriminated against because you are (race)?	1 = Never 5 = Very often	1.95 (1.08)	3.10 (1.29)	923	—	MADICS
Parent get ahead	Do you think it has been harder for you to get ahead in life because you are (race)?	0 = No 1 = Yes	.03	.40	923	—	MADICS
Parents' Perceptions of Barriers for Child							
Child dDiscrim	How much do you think people will discriminate against (child) because s/he is (race)?	1 = Not at all 4 = A lot	1.52 (.67)	2.45 (.80)	924	—	MADICS
aAhead	ahead because s/he is (race)?	1 = Yes					
Figure 2[a]							
Parents' Perceptions of Importance of Schooling							
Educational Aspirations	If finances were not a problem and everything else went right, how far would you like to see (child) go in school?	1 = < HS diploma 9 = J.D./Ph.D./M.D.	8.15 (1.14)	8.35 (1.20)	948	—	MADICS
School = life	My seventh grader will not be successful in life if s/he isn't successful in school.	1 = SD[b] 5 = SA	3.66 (1.01)	3.89 (.98)	937	—	MADICS
Figure 3[a]							
Youth Outcomes (Parental predictors are described above under figures 1 and 2)							
Perceived Value of Education	(a) I have to do well in school if I want to be a success in life. (b) Getting a good education is the best way to get ahead in life for the kids in my neighborhood. (c) Achievement and effort in school lead to job success later on. (d) Education really pays off in the future for people like me.	1 = SD 5 = SA	4.06 (.75)	4.16 (.72)	860	.812	MADICS
Educational Aspirations	If you could do exactly what you wanted, how far would you like to go in school?	1 = < HS diploma 8 = J.D., Ph.D., M.D.	7.51 (1.51)	7.75	846	—	MADICS

| | | | Means (SD) | | N | Alpha | Data |
Variable Name	Description	Metric	Whites	Blacks			
Educational Expectations	We can't always do what we most want to do. How far do you think you *actually will* go in school?	1 = < H.S .diploma 8 = J.D., Ph.D., M.D.	6.86 (1.58)	6.93 (1.63)	844	—	MADICS
Perceived Barriers	People like me aren't treated fairly at work no matter how much education they have.	1 = SD 5 = SA	2.39 (.90)	2.91 (.94)	869	—	MADICS
Limited Educ. Opportunities	Discrepancy between educational aspirations and educational expectations.		.66 (.94)	.82 (1.20)	844	—	MADICS
Achievement	Student GPA in grade eleven	0–4.0	3.04 (.79)	2.82 (.72)	789	—	MADICS

Figure 4
Academic Investment

| | | | Means (SD) | | N | Alpha | Data |
			Whites	Blacks			
Seek Help	When you're having trouble on schoolwork, how often do you go to (a) your teachers for help? (b) Other adults in the school, like a tutor, for help? (c) Other students for help? (d) Your parent(s) for help? (e) Your friends for help?	1 = Almost never 5 = Almost Always	2.87 (.76)	2.99 (.74)	3,197	.600	MADICS
Time on School Activities/Clubs	During the past year, how often did you spend time on any other school activities (such as clubs or student government)?	1 = < once a month 6 = Usually every day	1.81 (2.00)	1.64 (2.09)	3,344	—	MADICS
Time on Homework [b]	Think about the past two weeks. About how often did you do homework?	1 = Never 6 = Daily, > an hour	4.70 (1.42)	4.64 (1.42)	2,316	—	MADICS
Time on Educational Activities [b]	Think about the last two weeks, about how often did you: (a) Watch news, educational, or cultural shows on TV? (b) Read books or magazines for pleasure? (c) Read newspapers?	1 = Never 6 = Daily, > 1hr	3.03 (1.05)	3.04 (1.13)	2,326	.581	MADICS

Construct	Description	Coding				N	α	Data
Importance of Academics	Compared with other things you do, how important are each of the following activities to you? (a) Math. (b) Other school subjects.	1 = Much less, 7 = Much more	4.95 (1.34)	5.37 (1.31)		3,241	.810	MADICS
Resistance to Schooling								
Skip School / Cut Classes	How often, if ever, have you skipped school or cut classes?	1 = Never, 4 = Often	1.52 (.87)	1.54 (.92)		3,303	—	MADICS
Suspensions [c]	Number of times youth has been suspended from middle school and high school (asked in grades eight and eleven, respectively).	1 to 10 or more	.33 (1.19)	.70 (1.62)		1,845	—	MADICS
Importance of Nonacademics	Compared with other things you do, how important are sports to you?	1 = Much less, 7 = Much more	4.26 (1.93)	4.43 (1.88)		3,325	—	MADICS
Figure 5 *Academic Orientation among British Youths*								
Read for Pleasure	Frequency with which youth reads for pleasure.	1 = Never, 6 = Most days	4.32 (1.60)	4.38 (1.60)	4.60 (1.50)	13,221	—	LSYPE
Happy at School	I am happy when I am at school.	1 = SD, 4 = SA	3.01 (.71)	3.26 (.60)	3.07 (.69)	12,699	—	LSYPE
Value of School	(a) School is a waste of time for me.* (b) Schoolwork is worth doing. (c) The work I do in lessons is a waste of time.*	1 = SD, 4 = SA	3.30 (.54)	3.41 (.50)	3.36 (.49)S	12,272	.601	LSYPE
Academic Disengagement	(a) Most of the time I do not want to go to school. (b) On the whole, I like being at school.* (c) I work as hard as I can in school.* (d) In an lesson, I often count the minutes until it ends, (e) I am bored in (all or most) of my lessons.	1 = SD, 4 = SA	2.28 (.56)	2.02 (.48)	2.19 (.53)	11,249	.764	LSYPE
Figure 6 *Resistance to Schooling*								
No Postcomp School Desired	Youth does *not* want to continue schooling beyond age sixteen.	0 = Stay on, 1 = Do not stay	.16	.03		12,561	—	LSYPE
Behavior	Whether youth's parents have ever been contacted by school(s) about youth's behavior.	0 = No, 1 = Yes	.24	.14	.33	12,758	—	LSYPE

Variable Name	Description	Metric	Means (SD)		N	Alpha	Data
			Whites	Blacks			
Suspended	Whether youth has ever been temporarily suspended or excluded from school.	0 = No 1 = Yes	.08	.14	12,807	—	LSYPE
Controls for all Analyses Based on LSYPE							
Discrimination	Do you think you have ever been treated unfairly by teachers at your school because of your skin color, ethnicity, race, or religion?	0 = No 1 = Yes	.09	.45	12,401	—	LSYPE
Social Class	Highest level of education by either parent coded as follows: (4) higher managerial and professional occupation; (3) lower managerial and professional and intermediate occupation; (2) small employers, low supervisors, and technical semiroutine and routine labor; (1) never worked or long term unemployment.	1 to 4	2.65 (.73)	2.16 (.81)	2.45 (.86)	12,479	—	LSYPE

Notes:

* Item is reverse coded. Also, SD refers to strongly disagree and SA refers to strongly agree.
[a] The sample is restricted to youth present in grade eleven; these measures (grade seven) were predictors for youth outcomes measured in grade eleven.
[b] These measures were not collected in the eighth grade and consist of 94 percent or greater of the total seventh and eleventh grade sample.
[c] These measures were not collected in the seventh grade and consist of 94 percent or more of the total eighth and eleventh grade sample.

CHAPTER 6

Conferring Disadvantage

Immigration, Schools, and the Family

Carola Suárez-Orozco and Marcelo M. Suárez-Orozco

Introduction

Immigration generates a powerful echo over time and across generations. Where migrant workers arrive, their families follow. Immigration,
in its fullest sense, is about families, communities, and ultimately the next
generation. State and local policies and practices, however, are misaligned
with this reality: in the United States, the integration of families and the
transition of immigrant-origin children to their new societies are not now,
and perhaps have never been, the object of systematic immigration policy
coordination.

Although on paper immigration policies appear quite lofty—placing
family values and reunification at their center—de facto current practices
generate dystopia. Family members originating in the countries that send
the most immigrants to the United States face an intolerable bureaucratic
gridlock with no orderly queues or tenable timelines. Immigrant families
are systematically torn apart for long periods, and many settled immigrants
are forced to miss their children's infancy and childhood. Family intimacy
and autonomy, lauded by Brighouse and Swift (this volume) as basic rights,
are thus an elusive mirage for millions of immigrant families whose claims
to cherished family values—coded and enacted differently in different
immigrant-origin communities—are routinely interrupted, usurped, and
denigrated by the architecture of current immigration policy.

Educational policies are equally misaligned in relation to immigration.
Accountability, high-stakes testing, and charter schools swept the nation

as the largest educational policy initiative in recent history, coinciding with a large influx of immigrant-origin students. Immigrant children enter an implacable high-stakes testing regime, with dire consequences to learning, engagement, and future opportunities. These educational policies as well as a number of widely accepted schooling practices that focus on parents' involvement and homework have been blind to the needs of immigrant-origin students and have unintended consequences. These policies align with other structural arrangements so that too many immigrant families end up joining other stigmatized families (see Harris, this volume) in imposing disadvantage on their children—in a most unhappy binary opposition to the normative portrait sketched by Brighouse and Swift (this volume).

The children of immigrants are the fastest-growing sector of the child and youth population in disparate high-income countries around the world, including Australia, Canada, Germany, Italy, the Netherlands, Spain, and Sweden. In the United States, approximately a quarter of all youths are of immigrant origin (over sixteen million in 2010), and it is projected that by 2020 over a third of all children will be growing up in immigrant households. Because of migration, by the year 2030, fewer than half of all children in the United States will be of white European origin.

In this chapter we treat the family as the center of immigration, reveal just how dislocating immigration becomes to its form and coherence, point out how school policies and practices undermine the immigrant family in unanticipated ways, and clarify how the family elements of the immigration experience intersect negatively with the structure of the educational system.

Policy and Nonpolicy as Policy

While there are multiple pathways in immigration, the principles of "love and work" are the bedrock of United States immigration policy. According to the Congressional Budget Office, US immigration policy

> first, serves to reunite families by admitting immigrants who already have family members living in the United States. Second, it seeks to admit workers with specific skills and to fill positions in occupations deemed to be experiencing labor shortages. Third, it attempts to provide a refuge for people who face the risk of political, racial, or religious persecution in their country of origin. Finally, it seeks to ensure diversity by providing admission to people from countries with historically low rates of immigration to the United States.[1]

Over the past two decades between half and two-thirds of all authorized immigrants arrived through family reunification.

The bulk of unauthorized migration to the United States is also work- or family-related. Unauthorized immigrants are not from the other side of the moon. The majority are like most other migrants—yet they find themselves in an extreme state of liminality that is destabilizing to them and to their new societies. On September 12, 2001, America's traditional "swinging back door" of immigration—feeding capital's predilection for "flexible" and cheap labor—overnight became a trapdoor for millions of legal and illegal workers. A new cycle of family separations began as involuntary deportations skyrocketed: in 2009, 393,000 immigrants were deported— the seventh consecutive record high and approximately 100,000 more than during President George W. Bush's last year in the White House.

Immigration may destabilize the societies where immigrants settle. Ironically, however, what becomes most unsettled by immigration are the very families the process was motivated to safeguard. Immigration is often precipitated by a destabilizing event—a death in the family, the disappearance of adequate work, the outbreak of war, or an environmental disaster. In other cases a beacon of opportunity calls from other lands, and families mobilize to take advantage of better jobs and educational opportunities. As elders consider the decision to migrate, the family may become divided about how to proceed. Many migrations begin tentatively, with the ambition of an eventual return.

Migrations, however, often result in protracted separations that threaten the identity and cohesion of the family, transforming well-established roles, creating new loyalties and bonds, and destabilizing cultural scripts of authority, reciprocity, and responsibility. Even in the best of circumstances, the family is never the same after migration.

There is a wide array of transnational family configurations. Most typically, migrations take place "stepwise," with one family member going ahead, to be followed by others.[2] Historically the pattern was of the male going ahead and establishing a beachhead in a new land while sending remittances home. Over time, when it was financially possible, he began bringing relatives—wife, children, and others. But in recent decades immigration has achieved a nearly perfect gender balance, with approximately half of all global migrants being women.[3] In the high-income countries, demand for service workers draws women—many of them mothers—from a variety of developing countries to care for what Hondagneu-Sotelo aptly terms "other people's children."[4] And in rapidly aging countries these immigrant workers are summoned to care for "other people's parents" as well. When immigrant mothers are forced to leave their children behind, complicated new arrangements must be left in place. Extended family members, such as grandparents or aunts, become the primary caretakers with the help of the father (if he remains locally and is still part of the family). In many other cases both parents may go ahead, leaving the children in the care of extended family.[5]

The range of new family arrangements generated by global migration encompasses enormous variety. Upper-middle-class families from places such as Hong Kong and Taiwan send youngsters of middle school and high school age to study abroad—as "astronaut kids" who may live with the mother while the father remains in the homeland[6] or as "parachute kids," living with extended kin while both parents stay at home.[7] There is a long-standing practice of sending immigrant children back to the homeland to be taken care of by grandparents; in some cases, unruly adolescents are sent to be resocialized by their grandparents,[8] but increasingly, infants and toddlers are also cared for by extended family there while parents work around the clock in the new land.[9] In recent years families headed by undocumented immigrants have been wrenched apart by workplace or in-home raids by immigration authorities, leaving citizen children behind in the care of relatives or in foster homes, and sometimes children are forced to return to a country they have never known.[10]

When families separate they expect to reunite soon, but reunifying the family often takes years, especially when complicated by financial hurdles, convoluted immigration regulations, and unauthorized status.[11] When it is time for the children to arrive, they may all come to the new land together, but often they are brought one at a time. Although parents may maintain contact through phone calls, e-mail, the ubiquitous care packages, and when possible visits, these separations and reunifications are difficult psychological experiences for families. The problems arise during the separation phase, and they resurface during the period of reunification.[12] For the children, migrations result in two sets of disruptions in their attachments—first from the parent who goes on ahead, then from the caretakers they became attached to before their own migration.[13]

Once the particular members of immigrant families arrive, they are left to their own devices. The integration policy of the United States is a lack of policy. A faith in the logic of the market and the magic of American culture drives a laissez-faire sensibility to immigrant integration that is both anachronistic and dysfunctional. The only policy framework vaguely supporting immigrants is, amazingly, meant to address the original sin in

America's racial past—the legacy of slavery, de jure segregation, and their transgenerational consequences: the Civil Rights Act.

For immigrant youths schools, for better or worse, become the most important of the new society's institutions. Exactly how do immigration and schooling intersect? A series of reform movements swept the nation just as the largest generation of immigrant-origin students was entering schools. The charter school movement has largely ignored and avoided engaging new immigrant students and their families, thus locking them out of this significant educational opportunity.[14] Further, while the scholarly research suggests that it takes seven years of optimal second-language teaching[15] before immigrant students can reasonably be expected to compete with native-born peers on high-stakes tests, current school policies have them taking these tests within a couple of years of their arrival. Thus the two most ubiquitous educational experiments of the past decade fail to align with the largest-growing population of the nation's new students. Finally, important efforts to focus on parents' involvement have unintended consequences when brought into the immigrant context. In the rest of this essay, we will focus on the latter two issues. As we will show, immigration and schooling at present impose disadvantage on immigrant children.

The Obvious Issue: Language

Public commentary on immigration and education often begins with the subject of language. We ask only the crude question, Should we offer bilingual education? Appropriate policy requires a much clearer understanding of bilingualism.

First, bilingualism is relative.[16] Although a person may be a fluent speaker and writer in her native language, in the second language she may only be able to carry on a simple conversation and be unable to write or read anything but the simplest text. Conversely, a "dormant" bilingual, while capable of political discussions and of writing sophisticated essays in the second language, may understand his native language but have difficulty expressing any but the simplest thoughts in it.[17] Some are best able to express emotions and feelings in their native language but are better able to read, write, and argue in their new language. Still others are "balanced" bilinguals, adept at all levels of communication in more than one language (although this "native-like control over both languages" is a rare accomplishment).[18] Second-language acquisition is dynamic and fluid. It is dependent on previous literacy in the native language and on the contexts in which the new language is acquired and the range of opportunities to use it.

Another distinction is worth noting. "Elite" or "elective" bilinguals already speak the dominant language of the land and choose to acquire a second language for pleasure or to enhance their general profile of skills.[19] By contrast, immigrants who are "folk" or "circumstantial" bilinguals often speak a lower-status language and must acquire the dominant language of their new country as a matter of survival.[20] For such circumstantial bilinguals, the native language may be neglected and can atrophy over time. In fact, immigrants are often discouraged from maintaining it, although it is an important way to communicate with their families and maintain emotional ties. Ironically, then, while the children of the elite are encouraged to study a second language as a marker of status or competence and as a skill for succeeding in the global economy, children who enter the United States adept at using another language are often urged to let go of this ability.

There is also a distinction between the level of language skills necessary to carry on a conversation and carry out the daily transactions of life and those required to be competitive academically. The first dimension of language skill—basic interpersonal communication—can, with adequate exposure, be readily learned within a year or so.[21] Achieving cognitive/academic language, on the other hand, takes an average of seven to ten years of systematic high-quality training and consistent exposure.[22] To get to the point of being able to argue the relative merits of an issue, write a quality essay, read quickly enough to be competitive on a timed test, or detect the subtle differences between multiple-choice items on the SAT in a second language takes extensive time as well as high-quality education.

When we asked students during the first year of a bicoastal study (conducted with four hundred immigrant youths recently arrived from China, the Dominican Republic, various countries in Central America, Haiti, and Mexico, who were recruited from public schools) whether they thought it was important to learn English, fully 99 percent answered yes.[23] During the fourth year of the study, we asked whether they thought English was important for being successful in school—again, the vast majority agreed that it was (94 percent). Further, 93 percent indicated that they liked learning English. But although it has been argued that positive attitudes toward learning a language predict mastery of the new language, we did not find a relation between these positive attitudes and English-language proficiency.[24]

We asked students to complete the sentence, "English is . . ." Nearly half spontaneously answered in a way that demonstrated their clear understanding of how important it is to learn English. Their responses included: "very important to speak [in this country]"; "a language that I have to learn and to know because it is the most important language in the United States"; "very important to get a good job"; "important for the future"; "very important for everything, for opportunities"; "important to succeed"; "important to get ahead." At the same time, many (20 percent) made it clear that they found learning English a challenge: "hard," "very hard," and "difficult" were typical responses.[25]

The second year of the study we asked students, "What do you think are the main obstacles to getting ahead in the United States?" Fifty-six percent spontaneously responded "learning English"—singling out not knowing English as a greater impediment than discrimination, lack of resources, or not being documented. We then listed a number of obstacles that over the years we have learned are concerns for new immigrants. Fully 90 percent of our participants responded that learning English was a challenge they needed to overcome to get ahead. In the last year of the study, we also asked students what they perceived as obstacles to getting to college. Of those who thought they would go to college, 45 percent responded that their English fluency presented a problem. Our respondents were realists: those who were concerned about their fluency scored lower than others on the English-language proficiency test.[26]

We administered a standardized English proficiency test designed to assess the skills of bilingual students.[27] Strikingly, by the fifth year of the study, when our participants on average had been in the country seven years, we found that only 7 percent of the sample scored at or above the normalized mean for native English speakers of the same age on the English-language proficiency subtest (the normalized mean was a score of 100). The mean score for our entire sample was 74.7 (with students' scores ranging from 31 to 156).[28] On average, then, our sample had academic English proficiency scores equivalent to the lowest two percentiles of their native English-speaking peers. The Chinese students scored, on average, nine points higher than the students from the other ethnic groups, but this difference was not statistically significant. More than three-quarters of our participants' scores were more than one standard deviation (15 points) under the mean. Only 22 percent of the total sample fell within one standard deviation of the average native English speaker of the same age.[29]

Why do some students learn English more efficiently than others? We considered several variables: parents' assessment of their own English skills during the first year of the study; how many years the students had been schooled in their country of origin; how many years the students had been in the United States; students' reports of how much English they used in informal situations; measures of the school's poverty and segregation levels; and the percentage of students in the school who were learning English. Understanding this combination of characteristics allowed us to predict nearly half the variance of the last year's English-language proficiency score.[30] Students who attended schools where a higher percentage of the students did well on the state's English language arts exam did significantly better than students who attended a school where a substantial number of its students did not reach proficiency. We surmise that in schools where more of the students performed well on the English language arts exam, the quality of instruction as well as the language models were substantially better than in schools where few students performed well. Likewise, schools with higher daily average attendance rates tend to have better school climates and more effective monitoring of their students than those where fewer students come to school regularly. In such settings, newcomers have a substantially better chance to learn English.

Students' personal backgrounds also mattered. Not surprisingly, parents' literacy was strongly predictive of better performance on the academic English proficiency test, as were the parents' English skills. The number of years the student had been educated in the country of origin (an indicator of general educational level and literacy) contributed to English-language proficiency, as did years in the United States (an indicator of exposure to English). The students who spoke English with others in informal settings had better English proficiency. Many of our students, however, lived in ethnically segregated neighborhoods and either attended segregated schools or were segregated within the school. Thus many had limited opportunities to make friends with native English speakers.

Our data suggest a critical interplay of the skills the students bring with them and the linguistic and educational contexts where they find themselves. The less access newcomers had to rich models of academic English and high-level instruction, the less likely they were to demonstrate strong proficiency in academic English during the last year of the study.

If we expect newcomers to learn English, as they and we would like, our schools need to do a better job of developing educational contexts that will make it happen. While there have been some attempts to address the needs of students coming in at the elementary level, there has been a lamentable absence of efforts to meet the needs of English-language learners arriving at the secondary school level.[31] This gap needs to be addressed if we wish to harness the energies of all of our new students. Language policy for immigrants mimics the much larger disarray in our national immigration policy: it is ad hoc, incoherent, and ultimately self-defeating.

This problem is compounded by the current education fad for standardized tests and high-stakes exams, which most newcomers are unable to pass within a couple of years of arrival as is currently required. Indeed, we, like many others,[32] have become very concerned about the wisdom of using high-stakes tests to assess the progress of new immigrant students. Too many attend segregated and high-poverty schools, where very few of the students—whether native English speakers or immigrants—are adequately prepared to do well on a standardized English test. To be fair to them, we must develop alternative strategies of assessment that are linguistically and culturally appropriate.[33]

The Deeper Issue: Family-School Interactions

To the degree that we consider issues of immigration in the educational context, we tend to focus on bilingualism, and we could do a much better job of understanding the nuances of that topic. Yet there is another fundamental area that we do not address as all. School personnel discussing immigrant students are just as likely to bring up a different issue: the relation between family life and school life. Here is where the problem of the nonalignment between immigration and schooling is most profound.

Perceptive school personnel will often spontaneously bring up family separations and the subsequent reunifications as a challenge faced by immigrant students. For example, a veteran high school counselor in California shared this with us:

> [In many cases] the family has been separated for many years. . . . so when they are reunited sometimes it's a mess in the literal sense of the word. The mother doesn't know the child. . . . Because she knows she's been working, sending money, caring for the child and everything—she's been doing her part. But now it is the child's turn, you know, to show understanding, to show appreciation. . . . Sometimes the mother is in a new relationship. So that kids may be coming to a new family with other siblings and a step-parent.

Likewise, the director of a high school international center in the Boston area talked about his concerns and summed up the challenge:

> I feel like I need to give [students] a great deal of personal and emotional support in the transition they are making. . . . You know, the whole issue of family separations. There are a lot of emotional issues which come into this. . . . We have people here from China, from Brazil, from Haiti, from Central America, and what is interesting is that they are all [talking about] the same issues. "I don't know how to live with my parent."

In our study of recently arrived immigrant students, we found that most had been separated from one or both parents for protracted periods—from six months to ten years. Nearly three-quarters of the youths were separated from one or both of their parents during the migration. We found significant differences between immigrant groups: Chinese families were least likely to be separated over the course of migration (52 percent), while the vast majority of Central American (88 percent) and Haitian children (85 percent) were separated from one or both parents.[34] Approximately 26 percent of children in the sample were separated from both parents, a pattern most often occurring in Central American families (54 percent). Where the child was separated from only one parent, about 26 percent were separated from the mother, while about 20 percent were separated from the father. Separations from mothers occurred most frequently among Dominican families (40 percent), and separations from fathers were most frequent among Mexican families (33 percent).[35] The separation from parents would turn out to be unexpectedly long, with individual students in our sample reporting being separated from one or both parents for nearly their entire childhood. The length of separation varied widely across groups. Of the youths who were separated only from their mothers, 54 percent of Central American children endured separations lasting four years or more, as did approximately a third of both the Dominican and Haitian families. Chinese and Mexican children underwent fewer and shorter separations from their mothers.[36] When separations from the fathers occurred during migration, they were often very lengthy or permanent.[37] For those families that were separated, 28 percent had separations from fathers that lasted over four years. This was the case for 44 percent of Haitian, 42 percent of Central American, and 28 percent of Dominican families.[38]

The act of separation was often described as one of the hardest things about coming to the United States. Jamisa,[39] a fourteen-year-old Dominican girl, said, "The day I left my mother I felt like my heart was staying behind. Because she was the only person I trusted—she was my life. I felt as if a light had [been] extinguished. I still have not been able to get used to living without her." In many cases parents left their children when they were infants and toddlers, speaking with angst of that separation. Carmen, the mother of a thirteen-year-old Central American boy, shared: "It was very hard above all to leave the children when they were so small. I would go into the bathroom of the gas station and milk my breasts that overflowed, crying for my babies. Every time I think of it, it makes me sad." Family intimacy, at or near to the heart of family systems the world over (see Brighouse and Swift, this volume), is the first casualty of immigrant separations.

For many children, especially those who had short-term separations or who had been separated only from one parent while living with the other, described the moment of reunification with the modal word "happy." A thirteen-year-old Guatemalan girl said that on the day she got together with her mother: "[I was] so happy. It was my dream to be with her." Likewise, Yara, a fourteen-year-old Dominican girl, described her family as they got together: "We were so happy. We cried, talked a lot and embraced." Yet for many children enduring protracted separations, the reunification was complicated. In many cases the children recalled that although their parents, mothers in particular, were highly emotional and tearful in welcoming them, for many the parent had become a stranger. Beatriz, a fourteen-year-old new arrival from Guatemala, recalled: "My mother was crying. She hugged me . . . and I felt bad. Like neither my sister nor I knew her." In essence, many youths were migrating twice: to a new land and also to a new family.

In some cases the predominant feeling expressed was simple disorientation. For other adolescents, the extended absence led to a sustained rejection of the parent they perceived as abandoning them. In such cases the damage of the long absence led to rifts that seemed challenging to traverse. Some youths were unforgiving, and by the time parents reentered their lives it was too late. These youths had grown accustomed to living without the missing parent; they were ready to assert greater independence and were unwilling to submit to the parent's authority. A fourteen-year-old Chinese girl, An, confided that after a nine-year absence, "Suddenly I had another creature in my life called 'father' . . . I was too old by then and I could no longer accept him into my life." The autonomy emerging in the context of careful culturally scripted negotiations highlighted by Brighouse and Swift (this volume) is thus altogether different for many children growing up in immigrant families.

Some parents perceived a rupture in trust and intimacy and were willing to do the patient work of bridging the emotional chasm. The mother of a fourteen-year-old Honduran, Felipe, told us: "It was really hard at the beginning because we had been separated for five years. At the beginning he barely trusted me, but now, little by little we are building something." The effects of separations often lingered; and building up the relationship anew was a slow process. But other parents were less patient, hurt and indeed angry that their children did not appreciate the sacrifices made on their behalf. A Haitian father who had worked years to bring over his daughter said through clenched teeth: "She barely looks at me. All she does is complain that she wants to be back with her aunt, and she just treats me like an ATM."

Our data involving newly arrived immigrant youths allowed us to consider two points in time (shortly after migration and five years later) and to measure two psychological outcomes—anxiety and depression.[40] When comparing youths who had not undergone family separations with youths whose families had separated, we found that those who arrived as a family unit were less likely to report symptoms of depression or anxiety. The lowest rates of psychological distress were found among youths who had not been separated from their mothers.[41] We found the greatest distress among youths who had undergone separations of four years or more from their mothers. Many of these children had stayed with their fathers rather than with both grandparents or with aunts and uncles; we learned in our qualitative interviews that two-caretaker homes often afforded more stable care as well as extended family supports.

Immigrant children, then, bring distinct psychological issues into school; their parents, too, an important source of support for their education, bring a different developmental profile than other parents, as we will explore in the next section before turning to how these family effects intersect with school policy.

Immigration and Parental Agency

All societies define parenting according to shared scripts of safety, intimacy, nurture, and emotional care for the children.[42] At the most basic level, parents must provide physical security and a sense of safety. The idea of "home" connotes familiarity and ease, feeling safe, and being cared for in an ethos of intimacy (see Brighouse and Swift, this volume). For immigrant parents this includes finding appropriate housing in a new community where they will feel safe and be able to provide the basic protections for their children. This is not always easily achieved, since many immigrant families find themselves in communities that are deeply troubled and crime-ridden, and where they are unable to achieve the most basic sense of safety and peace even within the walls of their homes.

Providing for the physical safety of their children is only the most basic of parents' responsibilities. Achieving a sense of security involves a range of domains: generating the financial resources needed for feeding and clothing the family as well as meeting the children's health needs and providing schooling. Parents must also access the protections afforded to citizens living as members of the larger community of the nation-state. For many immigrants these basic securities may prove elusive. While migrants are renowned for their work ethic and for struggling to provide for their families, this may not be enough. Poverty among working-class immigrant families remains a protracted problem for newcomers from many countries.[43]

While some immigrant families eventually achieve a semblance of financial security, many face a more formidable threat to their basic security—unauthorized status.[44] The ethos of safety and security essential to healthy family dynamics is unattainable to millions of unauthorized families, who face a pervasive fear driven by the constant threat of being hunted, caught, and deported.

Beyond the basic physical, social, and economic security they should provide, parents have authoritative, socializing, and emotional roles that are essential for optimal child development, autonomy, and well-being.[45] For a variety of reasons, immigrant parents find these core functions systematically compromised by a powerful undertow.

If parents have gone ahead and left their children behind, the normative ideal of intimacy is elusive; transnational contacts give parents only intermittent occasion to intervene with expectations and admonishments about how the children ought to behave. On reunification, the children will experience a new ambiguity. They will need to get to know in new intimate proximity the rhythms, moods, and expectations of parents who are de facto strangers. As for the parents, making ends meet while struggling with a new language and the ways of a new culture drains them of time and energy. Most immigrant parents are mourning the loss of the loved ones left behind. Many, with the best of intentions, find themselves unable to provide the physical presence, time, and energy required to meaningfully parent their children. Further, the cumulative stresses and losses of migrations, while tempered by economic gains, leave many emotionally drained, anxious, depressed, and distracted. They may be physically present but emotionally elsewhere and unavailable to meet their children's day-to-day emotional needs.[46]

Immigration is particularly stressful to parents when they are unable to draw on their usual resources and coping skills at a time when much is at stake for the balance and well-being of the family. Immigration removes parents from many of the supports linked to community ties, jobs, and the main institutions of the new society. Stripped of many of their significant supports (extended family members, best friends, and neighbors), immigrant parents may never fully develop the social maps that help them find their way in a foreign land. Lacking a sense of basic competence, sense of control, and sense of belonging leaves many feeling marginalized. It is difficult to guide children without a compass.

A new paradox slowly unfolds. Even as immigrant parents become more empowered economically, they will experience a keen sense of inadequacy in their ability to parent effectively. At a time when immigrant children and youths need extra guidance, too many immigrant parents find themselves at a loss to provide it.

A loss of parental status comes about, first of all, from the multiple social demotions immigrants experience in the new society. Some take jobs well beneath their qualifications and skills: the doctor from China now working as a nurse; the nurse from El Salvador cleaning houses; the engineer from Ghana driving a taxi. Even a better salary makes these demotions hard to swallow. The child of a Mexican immigrant remembers, "Nothing broke my father except the United States. He couldn't find his footing here. He could not rise again, and he knew it. He tried many jobs—busboy, cannery worker, bakery truck driver. I often think that he settled on bowling alleys because he was the most erudite man there, even if he was a greaser."[47] Many immigrants find themselves toiling in the most stigmatized kinds of dangerous, demanding, and dirty work.

Second, immigration reverses the natural order of authority. Typically parents master the system of engagement in their social sphere. They know the basic rules of socialization and how to guide their children through the moral, social, and cultural maze required for membership and belonging.[48] They can wisely impart the etiquette for how to interact respectfully with others, complete school, and get a job. In a new society, the rules of engagement change, and immigrant parents are no longer masters (or even players) of the game. This is painfully revealed by the eternal complaints of teachers who accuse immigrant parents of not being interested in their children's schooling when in reality they simply don't have the know-how to be "advocate parents" in the new society.

Language is critical here, too. Immigrant children typically come into more intimate contact with the language and culture of the new society than do their parents. Schools will immerse them in the new values and worldviews and, above all, will introduce them to the systematic study of the new language. Teachers typically are members of the majority culture. Other children who may not be immigrants will become the daily interlocutors with whom immigrant youths develop a new linguistic repartee. The children watch television and movies, spend time online, listen to music, and are steeped in the media of their new land. Their parents, on the other hand, may be more removed from these new cultural realities, particularly if, as many do, they work long hours in enclaves with other immigrants who tend to be of the same linguistic, ethnic, and national background. The children's deep immersion in the new culture will make it easier to acquire the new language and will give them the beginnings of a road map to make their way in the new society.

As a result, making a family U-turn, parents now find themselves asking their children for help and guidance on the linguistic and cultural nuances of the new society. Asking children to take on this role will come at a cost. A Vietnamese refugee who arrived to the United States as a child poignantly recalls:

> The dreadful truth was simply this: we were going through life in reverse, and I was the one who would help my mother through the hard scrutiny of hard suburban life. I would have to forgo the luxury of adolescent experiments and temper tantrums, so that I could scoop my mother out of harm's way and give her sanctuary. Now, when we stepped into the exterior world, I was the one who told my mother what was acceptable and unacceptable behavior . . . and even though I hesitated to take on the responsibility I had no choice. It was not a simple process, the manner in which my mother relinquished motherhood. The shift in status occurred not just in the world but in the safety of our home as well, and it became most obvious when we entered the realm of language.[49]

For immigrant parents, relinquishing the parental function is painful. Some do so in helplessness, entrusting their children prematurely with responsibility beyond their years. Some youths cherish this role and feel like responsible and active contributors to the family.[50] Others, however, feel burdened or are left with a "worm that undermines basic certitude." Eva Hoffman writes that her Polish migrant parents "do not try to exercise much influence over me. 'In Poland, I would have known how to bring you up, I would have know what to do,' says my mother, but here she has lost her sureness, her authority."[51] Further, as the children increasingly gain mastery of both the new language and the rules of the game, many feel vague to intense embarrassment as they view their parents bounded by the anachronistic views and sensibilities of the old country.

Some immigrant parents rage against their loss of authority. Hypervigilance, regimented routines, and policing peer influences as well as those of the media become a preoccupation in many immigrant households. But putting in place discipline routines from the Old Country introduces new problems. While withholding a meal, spanking, pulling an ear, or making a child kneel on rice are common practices in many countries, they are dissonant with mainstream ideals of proper discipline in the new land. As parents attempt to discipline their children in ways culturally aligned with their country of origin, many will come to clash with mandated reporters in the new society. A "good spanking" in the Old Country can be a reportable offense in another. Children quickly become wise to the spirit and the letter of the law in the new society and threaten their parents with the sword of Damocles: calling 911.

When immigrant parents have not learned alternative sanctioning mechanisms, they may lose control of their offspring. This may have severe implications for the children's well-being, since it is essential for parents to maintain basic authority within the family.[52] This authority not only is symbolic but is critical for imposing limits around curfew, expectations for doing homework, values concerning respectful behavior toward others, and much more. If parents' authority is undermined, if their voices lose meaning, and if the children lose respect for them, the very foundation of safety and family coherence is compromised.

Many parents thus come to face the paradox of parenting in a promised land. The country that offered them the dream of a better tomorrow and provides the opportunity to give their children greater economic security becomes a battlefield over the children's identity and the coherence and cohesion of the family. A critical question, then, for understanding the intersection of immigration with education policy is how family involvement policies intersect with these features of the immigrant experience.

Engendering Inequity through Family Involvement Policies

The interactions families have with schools can predict the children's academic and behavioral development.[53] Family involvement in schooling has in recent years come to be viewed as critical for educational success, linked to higher academic achievement[54] as well as good adaptive behavior in school.[55] Family involvement is a multidimensional construct that includes a variety of ways a family can be a presence in their children's schooling.[56] Broadly speaking, these dimensions include parenting (attending workshops on topics relevant to their children's development), communication (attending parent-teacher conferences), volunteering (helping out in the classroom or on field trips), learning at home (helping their children with homework), decision making (becoming involved in school decision making), and collaborating with the community (integrating services and resources from the community within the school context).[57]

As teachers and administrators increasingly stress family involvement as a key way to meet children's social and emotional needs, many districts devote significant resources to fostering parents' involvement.[58] Indeed, family involvement was included as one of the six areas of emphasis in the No Child Left Behind Act of 2001, requiring schools to demonstrate that they offer their students' parents opportunities to take part.

Despite the role family involvement appears to play in students' academic and behavioral well-being, parents from certain demographic groups tend to be less involved in schooling. Families from middle-class backgrounds with at least one nonworking parent are advantaged in being able to demonstrate greater presence in schools. Higher levels of education also give parents more flexibility in supporting children academically. But there is also ethnic and cultural variation. Teachers often report that African American,[59] Latino,[60] and Asian American[61] parents are less involved with their children's schooling than white parents. Parents with limited English proficiency have also been found to have lower rates of family involvement.[62] Yet most studies utilize a single-perspective approach, often relying solely on the teacher's perspective[63] or on the parents' point of view.[64] Studies considering racial and ethnic minorities have found that perceptions can differ dramatically between teachers and parents, with teachers tending to underestimate minority parents' involvement in their children's schooling.[65]

Racial and ethnic differences may be partially explained by culturally different beliefs about precisely how a parent "should be" involved.[66] This effect, variably termed patterns[67] of "cultural discontinuity,"[68] "cultural mismatch,"[69] or "cultural incongruence,"[70] may be particularly profound for immigrant families. Mainstream teachers may have strong ideas about what parents' role in their children's education should be—but these teachers' mental models may differ from what parents think.[71]

Thus, family involvement practices may vary from one group to another as a result of vastly different cultural beliefs about parents' appropriate role in education. For example, mainstream teachers tend to define parental involvement as participating in school events, meetings, workshops, and governance activities, working as teacher's aides or tutors, and acting as school advocates within the larger school community. In contrast, Latino parents identified informal activities in the home such as reading and listening to children read, checking homework assignments, obtaining a tutor, providing nurturance, instilling cultural values, talking with children, and sending their children to school well fed, clean, and rested.[72] Studies comparing mainstream American families with Chinese immigrants show that mainstream parents are more likely to volunteer in schools, attend sporting and other extracurricular events, and check homework, while Chinese parents are more likely to do things (out of sight to schools) like purchasing supplemental workbooks or structuring children's after-school time.[73]

In addition to the contrast in minority backgrounds and cultural values and practices, a number of other issues may interfere with immigrant parents' active involvement in schools. Many immigrants originate from non-English-speaking countries. A number of studies have suggested that greater English-language proficiency can also predict more involvement in children's schooling.[74] Parents who are less proficient in English are discouraged from interacting with their children's schools, since English is the primary language spoken at most. Parents who have difficulty understanding school staff and administrators often feel uncomfortable, frustrated, and ashamed, leading them to avoid these contacts.[75]

When families and schools differ in their cultural beliefs about parents' role in their children's schooling, parents' and students' interactions with schools and teachers may be misunderstood and viewed negatively.[76] Teachers who see parents as having value systems similar to their own are less likely to become discouraged or frustrated than those who see them as having different values.[77] When teachers become frustrated with parents, this may be communicated, either directly or indirectly, both to parents and to students, exacerbating the disconnect between schools and families and further removing parents from acting in the ways the school values. Inadequate training on working with immigrant families,[78] coupled with teacher frustration, may cause teachers to misinterpret and consequently underestimate immigrant families' involvement. There is often a vicious cycle: parents who feel unwelcome are less likely to become involved in their children's schooling. Conversely, parents who feel ownership of their children's school are more likely to do so.[79]

In our work across 125 schools, we found that, by and large, teachers reported liking immigrant students because, among other things, they tended to arrive in the United States with behaviors that made classroom management easier.[80] As one teacher put it: "Immigrants have the desire to learn, are more disciplined, and value education," and many other teachers agreed. Teachers also tended to note that immigrant students were more motivated than their native-born peers. As one put it, "The immigrant students are the hungrier ones. They seem to be going for the awards and the academics where some of your mainstream students, or your traditional students, they are just taking their C and fleeing—you know?" Teachers also report, however, that as the newcomers acculturate—as they become more like their native-born peers—their behaviors change for the worse.[81] As another said, "In the beginning, immigrant kids are more respectful, more disciplined because of stricter schools they had in [their] home country. Later, as they become Americanized, which takes between three to four months and a year, they become unruly. Then they become like the American kids—they lack discipline and [do] things to get attention."

Yet the same teachers who were positive about immigrant students were often disdainful of immigrant parents. Teachers time and again reported viewing immigrant parents as uninterested in their children's academic welfare, reporting that they were absent and uninvolved. Judgments about immigrant parents were often harsh: "Part of our problem is that parents don't support their children. . . . Even just to come to school to check and make sure, you know, if they get a poor report card, that they show up, or come even. We have open houses for report cards. We have 1,200 students, and if we have 100 parents, we think it's a good year. So that's what I mean, there isn't that interest there." Another teacher said, "Education may not be the number one priority in their country but it is here. Sometimes I get the sense that it's not important to them."

Teachers frequently complained about the low expectations they thought immigrant parents had for their children. With a sneer, a teacher confided:

> [The best way for parents to support their children] is for them to be a model. You want your children to be educated, you have to educate yourself, so your kids can do the same. The best way is to learn English. Many parents never try

to learn the language. In this community, many of the Mexican immigrants are not educated when they come to the United States. For them coming to the United States is *the* goal. Once they get here, it's "mission accomplished" for them. That was their dream—to come to the United States, but once they get here there are no more dreams. They go from paycheck to paycheck. They don't understand that you have to have goals in order to go places in America.

There is a resounding irony in these views. Children, most would agree, internalize their values—including those about education—largely from their parents. How can teachers reconcile their statements that recently arrived immigrant students "value education" but their parents do not? These misconceptions seem to be born from a lack of meaningful contact and respectful engagement, and from simple cultural misunderstanding. The optimism and drive that teachers see in the eyes of their immigrant students most often result from enormous parental dreams and sacrifices.

When Homework Disadvantages

In a twenty-first-century globalized society, much is required if students are to be prepared to thrive in the new knowledge-intensive economy. Classrooms that foster cognitive engagement—stimulating students to be engaged, curious, and eager to learn—are the sine qua non we have come to expect in good schools. But in schools typically serving new immigrants, most of the teachers did not seem to have this goal. Only in *one case*—among the seventy-five teachers formally interviewed—did a teacher characterize a good student as we would: "Someone who is interested and engages with what is going on . . . and [is] willing to push [herself] to the next level. . . . Kids who are curious." Rather, when we asked teachers to define a good student, we found that intellectual curiosity was almost never mentioned. Instead, most teachers' definitions emphasized compliance and doing homework.[82]

Recent educational reforms have focused on raising students' academic achievement. Schools are held accountable for ensuring that all children make adequate progress toward standards aligned with the general curriculum. In this climate, homework has emerged as a potential vehicle to improve academic achievement. It can provide students with supplemental learning opportunities and encourage them to master material taught in class. Research on homework conducted during the past two decades consistently demonstrates a positive influence of homework on achievement.[83] As many immigrant students strive to improve their grasp on English while seeking to master complex academic content, they stand to gain doubly from the learning opportunities homework provides.

Interestingly, we found that homework was also a primary marker of how teachers graded students. In fact, the strongest correlation between any of our measures and grades was the teacher's report that a child regularly completed homework.[84] Grades (which teachers subjectively assign) were strongly predicted by whether students regularly did their homework.[85] Completing homework, on the other hand, poorly predicted scores on standardized achievement tests.[86]

Hence teachers appeared to be overly reliant on homework to indicate whether a child was a good student. And, regrettably, emphasis on homework places immigrant youths at a disadvantage compared with their middle-class nonimmigrant peers; immigrant students are able to draw on far less homework support from their parents and friends.[87]

Given the links between homework, grades, and attainment, it is important to understand the impediments to completing homework. There are a number of reasons newcomer immigrant students may be at greater risk for failing to turn in their assignments than their mainstream peers. Immigrant students are often unfamiliar with the types of homework assigned in the new context as well as the expectations of teachers in the United States.[88] Furthermore, their academic preparation and English proficiency, especially in the first years after arrival, may not be up to the task of autonomous homework.[89] Students with poor academic preparation or interrupted schooling may not have sufficient academic skills to complete homework independently.[90] Their efforts may also be impeded by challenges associated with poverty: lack of quiet study environments, lack of computers, computer programs, or Internet access, additional responsibilities such as child care, chores, or paid jobs, and limited access to resources such as after-school programs, tutors, or role models.[91] Moreover, immigrant parents maybe be unable to help directly because of limited English proficiency, limited formal education, restricted knowledge of the US educational system, or incompatible work schedules.[92] This is a good example of a situation where the reduction of parental agency experienced by immigrant parents directly intersects with school policies, with negative results for the children. Thus numerous factors, many outside their control, challenge youths' ability to complete homework.[93] Teachers need to adjust expectations and not unfairly penalize immigrant students.

Each homework assignment that is out of reach for immigrant students arguably puts them at a cumulative disadvantage—for failed opportunities to learn, negative teacher perceptions,[94] lower academic self-efficacy,[95] and academic disengagement over time.[96] In other words, the distinctive effects of immigration on children's development—with regard to language and family context in particular—intersect powerfully, and often negatively, with even the most positive or commonsense educational policies. The world of educational policy has yet to take on board in a holistic fashion the relation between the immigrant experience and dominant educational approaches.

Conclusion

Over the past century schooling has emerged as a normative ideal the world over. Schools now define the lives of more children than ever before. In complex democracies, schools ideally socialize emerging citizens for a "shared fate" (Ben-Porath, this volume) as democratic agents in a diverse, fragile, and interconnected world. Schools also prepare future workers and, ideally, enable children and youths to forge the tools and sensibilities they will need to achieve an ideal of flourishing—living well and doing good. In high-income countries marked by structural inequalities, schools both replicate the larger order and paradoxically expect children to learn to be equal (Laden, this volume). As Harris (this volume) shows with elegant evidence, vast inequalities propel disadvantaged parents to want more, not less, from the schools their children attend. For immigrant children, schools have yet another potential: they are the sites for systematic, intimate, and long-term immersion in the new culture and society. Multiple studies have documented the varieties of immigrant optimism, academic engagement, and faith in schools and the future. In its original meaning, *student* meant simply "the eager one." Immigrant youths are doubly eager: as students and as newcomers to the homeland. But by enacting policies and practices noxious to their needs, schools are in too many cases conferring disadvantage, perpetuating parental disempowerment, and revealing a studied indifference to authentically and successfully engaging our newest citizens.

The Myth of Intelligence

Smartness Isn't Like Height

Gregory M. Walton

Introduction

F ormal education is the primary mechanism by which modern societies prepare citizens to take part in civic life and the workforce. Given
the enormous social, political, and economic advantages that arise from
education, how educational opportunities are distributed raises important questions of justice and equal opportunity (e.g., Brighouse and Swift,
this volume; Reich, this volume). Yet the question of how to distribute
educational opportunities depends on assumptions about the nature of
intelligence and its development. Who is educable and how and when?
For instance, if intelligence is assumed to be fixed early in life through
genetics, the state may have a responsibility only to ensure that individuals reach their inborn potential or some minimum level of that potential
and, perhaps additionally, to identify individuals' level of intelligence
and track them into appropriate educational or career paths. If intelligence is thought to be largely the product of early childhood experiences,
the state's responsibility may be to ensure an equal or an adequate educational experience early in life (see Reich, this volume). Drawing on

I thank Carol Dweck, Steve Spencer, and the members of the 2009–10 Spencer Workshop on Education,
Justice, and Democracy at the Institute for Advanced Study, Princeton, New Jersey, especially Danielle
Allen and Rob Reich, for insightful feedback on earlier drafts of this manuscript.

modern social science, I argue in contrast to both assumptions that intelligence is in part *socially situated*—that it is an interaction between persons and situations, between potentials afforded by the individual and how those potentials are elicited or denied in social situations. If this is the case, the demands of justice are larger in scope: they include ensuring that educational situations are structured in ways that allow all people to learn and to perform up to their potential. Moreover, this approach suggests that efforts to assess enduring differences in individuals' intelligence and differential treatment based on these assessments are fundamentally misguided and inappropriate.

When Lewis Terman brought the IQ test to America, he helped create the modern concept of intelligence. An early version of the test had been created by the French psychologist Alfred Binet as a means of identifying the intellectual strengths and weaknesses of poor French schoolchildren. Binet's goal was a hopeful one that emphasized children's malleability and educability. In developing an IQ test, Binet hoped to help schools identify and build on individual students' strengths and identify and address their weaknesses. The approach of Terman, a Stanford psychologist, was radically different. Terman revamped the test, called it the Stanford-Binet Intelligence Scale, and aimed to use it to identify smart people. Terman delivered his test to thousands of California schoolchildren in the 1920s, identified those with the very highest scores, and admitted them to a still-running longitudinal study to track what he anticipated would be their impressive successes in life.

Terman's research institutionalized "IQ" in American culture. Embedded in his approach was a specific conception of intelligence as a stable property of the self, relatively unchanged over the life span, experience, and situations, in which there are broad individual differences that originate largely in inheritance and genetics. Further, Terman suggested, intelligence could be accurately assessed even in childhood using brief standardized tests that would predict important outcomes like educational and career success years later. In short, Terman believed that intelligence is something like height, only more important. It is a fact of who we are: some people are tall, some people are short, and, aside from wearing platform shoes, there is not much we can do about it.

There are those who still endorse a Termanlike conception of intelligence with large, stable individual differences rooted primarily in genetics (e.g., Jensen 1973, 1980; Herrnstein and Murray 1994). Richard Nisbett's (2009) impressive review of social and environmental factors that shape intelligence shows how a strong hereditary view of intelligence persists as well in recent books like Judith Rich Harris's *The Nurture Assumption* (1998), Steven Pinker's *The Blank Slate* (2002), and Steven Levitt and Stephen Dubner's *Freakonomics* (2006). An approach to intelligence that aims primarily at identifying individuals' level of smartness is also evident in the continued use of standardized testing in educational admissions, with tests like the SAT and LSAT shaping admissions decisions in higher education and new tests being used to diagnose the ability of four- and five-year-olds and determine admission to selective kindergarten programs. Some even suggest that society should give up on providing higher educational opportunities to all and restrict these opportunities to people with high intelligence, who are presumably best equipped to take advantage of them (e.g., Herrnstein and Murray 1994).

A view of intelligence as largely stable across much of the life span can also be found in very different quarters, even in research that emphasizes the malleability of intelligence early in life. Scholars of early childhood emphasize the profound importance of early educational experiences in setting children on the right academic track. Such experiences can help children establish the foundation of academic skills and abilities that undergirds later academic and professional success. As a consequence, developmental scholars emphasize the importance and cost effectiveness of early childhood interventions (e.g., high-quality preschool programs) compared with later educational interventions (e.g., job training, adult education) (see Heckman 2006; Diamond et al. 2007). In this approach, just as height is disproportionately shaped by early nutritional experiences, so intelligence is disproportionately shaped by early educational experiences.

There is no doubt that early childhood education lays the critical foundation for academic growth and development. But in some forms this view too can be taken to imply that later in life intelligence is largely fixed, albeit by early experience, not genetics, and relatively immune to local contextual factors. As I will argue in this chapter, modern research from social psychology suggests a different approach. In this approach, intelligence is not like height at all. The problem is not just that our rulers for measuring intelligence are bad—that they are inaccurate—although they often are. The problem is more fundamental: intelligence is not located simply inside an individual. If I am five feet eleven, I am five feet eleven at home and in the office, by myself and with friends. Whether I am "tall" or "short" may depend on whether I am at a jockey convention or in an NBA locker room. But I am always five feet eleven. It may seem common sense that intelligence too is a part of me that does not change in different circumstances; this intuition testifies to the enduring power of Terman's concept of intelligence as a stable property of the self. But modern theorizing of human psychology in general, and research on the impact of situational factors on intellectual performance in particular, suggests a different view.

If intelligence is not like height, what is it like? Consider people's assessments of their own traits and attitudes. Suppose I think I am an assertive person—I speak up and say my mind. Suppose I am a chocoholic—there is nothing I love more than a piece of dark chocolate. These self-perceptions, especially personally important, well-elaborated ones, are things we carry with us from place to place, situation to situation. They are stable aspects of self. And, when asked, we can accurately report on them at will. Right?

In fact, a broad range of research in modern psychology suggests a different view. This research finds that, far more than we commonly believe, our assessment of our own traits and attitudes are constructions of the moment whose expression is the product of situational factors, even subtle ones.

In a classic demonstration, Norbert Schwarz and his colleagues (Schwartz et al. 1991) asked some people to list six examples of situations in which they had behaved assertively and asked other people to list twelve examples. They were interested in the information people glean from the ease or difficulty they experience calling such examples to mind. They predicted that if people pay attention to how difficult it is to list twelve examples of assertiveness, they might infer that perhaps they are not so assertive. This is just what they found: when asked to list twelve examples of their assertiveness, people rated themselves *less* assertive.

Another line of research I conducted with Mahzarin Banaji illustrates how subtle cues shape attitudes. We asked people to list their favorite drink, food, and so forth (Walton and Banaji 2004). Later, under cover of a study on "handwriting," we assigned some people to describe the preferences they had listed using a noun phrase—to write, for instance, "I am a chocolate-eater," a grammatical construction that conveys a strong and enduring preference. Other people were asked to use a weaker verb phrase, for instance, to write "I eat chocolate a lot" (cf. Gelman and Heyman 1999). People were then asked how much they liked chocolate. Would people attend to the linguistic cues embedded in their self-descriptions and thus report stronger attitudes in the noun phrase condition than in the verb phrase condition? They did. People rated their love for chocolate, for example, as stronger and more stable when they had been assigned to write "I am a chocolate-eater" rather than "I eat chocolate a lot."

Perhaps intelligence works something like this: it is a property we commonly see as characteristic or even as defining of the self, as stable in different situations and over time, but one whose quality and expression in fact vary significantly in different social settings. I call this view of intelligence *socially situated*. In this view, intelligence is the product of an interaction between potentials afforded by aspects of the individual and how those potentials are elicited or denied in social situations. This term borrows from scholars who emphasize that intelligence is "situated"—that it depends on context and culture and arises to help people solve the particular problems they face in daily life (e.g., Rogoff and Lave 1984). Complementing this work, the term socially situated emphasizes how common social situations give rise to even subtle psychological processes that affect intelligence and intellectual performance.

Asking how we understand "intelligence" is no mere ivory tower exercise. On the contrary, different understandings of intelligence have profound consequences for educational and social policy and for students and society. A view of intelligence as stable and fixed leads to an emphasis on assessing students' abilities rather than on improving abilities—on testing over teaching and performing over learning. This approach can yield pessimism about the prospects of improving people's academic performance (Nisbett 2009). For instance, a view of intelligence as originating primarily from early childhood experiences can lead to an emphasis on high-quality early school experiences but the neglect of later educational opportunities. If early childhood education is all-important, why improve later educational situations? Further, an understanding of intelligence as fixed can undermine students' effort and motivation in the face of academic setbacks and challenges (Dweck 1999, 2006; Dweck and Leggett 1988). If ability is fixed, setbacks may seem evidence of its lack. If ability is lacking, why try?

In addition, a view of intelligence as stable and fixed implies that grades and standardized test scores can measure a person's inherent intelligence and thus imply that admissions and hiring decisions based on such indicators of merit are fair and just (Bobocel et al. 1998). But what if pervasive situational factors systematically bias these scores for specific groups—for instance, depressing the scores of students from disadvantaged groups and underestimating their ability and potential relative to other students' (Walton and Spencer 2009)? If so, standard selection systems would disadvantage already disadvantaged students and advantage others. Under the auspices of fairness they would launder advantage, turning a psychological edge into an increased chance of admission to a selective educational program and do it in a way that appears fair and just (see Walton, Spencer, and Erman, in press; see also Guinier and Sturm 2001). This system reproduces inequality. With so much at stake, what is the evidence that intellectual performance is socially situated?

Before proceeding, I note that the present analysis is consistent with scholarship exploring the limitations of traditional indicators of intelligence. For instance, such measures may be only weakly predictive of important criterion variables (e.g., school and job performance). They can also be overly narrow and so fail to capture the full range of relevant skills and abilities. Illustrating this approach, Sternberg and colleagues (2006) find that assessing college applicants' practical and creative skills in addition to their SAT scores and high school grades can shrink group differences and raise correlations with college grades (see also Gardner 1999; Oswald et al. 2004; Sedlacek 2004). In examining how performance on even traditional indexes of intelligence is inextricably shaped by social situations, this chapter complements this past work, provides new insights into the nature of intelligence, and draws novel implications for ways to improve educational outcomes and expand equal opportunity.

A Social-Psychological Approach to Understanding Persons and Situations

Since its founding, social psychology has powerfully emphasized how the immediate social and psychological situation affects people's behavior and experience (Ross and Nisbett 1991). Classic studies demonstrate that even brief interactions with strangers can reshape people's very perception of physical reality (e.g., through conformity processes: Asch 1952; Sherif 1935; see also Berns et al. 2005) and cause people to behave in seemingly extraordinary ways, for instance, to harm others as a consequence of obedience to authority (Milgram 1974) or powerful social roles (e.g., as a guard in a mock prison; Haney, Banks, and Zimbardo 1973). Further illustrating the power of social situations is the research described above showing how the subjective ease or difficulty of listing instances of assertiveness affects people's assessment of their own assertiveness.

The social-psychological approach to human nature provides a broad critique of a fixed view of intelligence on two levels. First, in emphasizing the power of situations, it implies that in explaining behavior we give undue weight to persons compared with situations. Lee Ross termed the tendency to explain behavior in terms of the internal attributes and characteristics of others "the fundamental attribution error" (Ross 1977). In a classic study, Ross, Amabile, and Steinmetz (1977) randomly assigned participants to be either the questioner or the contestant in a mock "quiz show." The situational dynamics in this quiz show seem obvious: the questioner can select topics he or she knows something about. Yet when third-party observers are asked at the end of the study to rate the questioner and contestant on their "general knowledge," questioners were consistently rated more highly. Even contestants showed the bias. People did not appropriately weigh even a seemingly obvious feature of the situation—that the questioner got to choose the questions—and as a result they saw questioners as more knowledgeable than contestants.

When we see a student perform well or poorly in school, are we subject to the same fundamental attribution error? Especially when the situational forces at work are far more subtle, do we too readily attribute students' performance to their internal characteristics—their inherent smartness or dumbness—and neglect situational factors that might affect their performance?

Second, the social-psychological approach to human nature challenges the conception of the self implied by a fixed and stable view of intelligence. If pressed, many laypeople view different aspects of people's selves—like their attitudes, beliefs, memories, and personality, as well as their skills and abilities—as basically stable properties that they can access or call forth at will. In contrast to this view is research investigating the effects of context on cognition, self-perceptions, and attitudes (Schwarz et al. 1991; Walton and Banaji 2004; see also Schwarz 2000; Tversky and Kahneman 1981). This research suggests that diverse aspects of self should be thought of as constructions whose content is shaped in part by the context and manner in which they are assessed. In many ways, for instance, memory functions as a reconstruction whose form and content are shaped by the context in which the memory is recalled. This quality gives rise to the possibility of "false memories"—memories that people experience as accurate representations of the past but that are substantially influenced by or even created by subtle suggestions (Loftus 2003).

Consider even personality. Although historically research has examined broad dispositional factors such as individual differences in extraversion or conscientiousness as predictors of behavior, much modern personality research instead emphasizes interactions between people's potentials and how situations elicit those potentials (Mischel and Morf 2003). As an example, a person who has low self-esteem may behave much like a person with high self-esteem in many contexts. But in a relationship, people with low self-esteem may be more apt to doubt their partners' love. Implicitly or explicitly, they think, "I'm not such a great person. How could my partner love me?" As a consequence, they may perceive ambiguous relational events—like a romantic partner's having a friendly conversation with an attractive store clerk of the opposite sex—as evidence of a lack of love and respond by lashing out or withdrawing from the relationship (Murray et al. 2002). Here the behavioral disposition is not automatic or inevitable. It is a potential elicited in specific kinds of situations but not others.

Does intelligence work like this? Is it inextricably bound to social contexts, affected by the manner of assessment, and unstable? Is intelligence socially situated?

Socially Situated Intelligence

In some ways, the notion that intellectual performance is affected by situational factors is obvious and uncontroversial. If a construction crew is taking down a wall outside a classroom, of course students will perform worse. If students enroll in an effective test-prep class and thus take a standardized test with a better understanding of its form and content, they may do better. But these examples seem to be idiosyncratic—sources of random variance in students' performance rather than pervasive factors having broad effects that could systematically disadvantage some groups relative to others and cause us to think differently about the nature of intelligence. Do subtle social situations have large and pervasive effects on the intellectual performance of broad swaths of students? Here I review two examples of such powerful situational factors.

Implicit Theories of Intelligence

One important determinant of intellectual performance is whether students persist and work hard in the face of academic challenges or give up. And whether students persist depends importantly on their implicit theories of intelligence. Some students view intelligence as a fixed quantity that a person either possesses or does not (an "entity" theory). Others view it as a malleable quantity that increases with effort and learning (an "incremental" theory; Dweck 1999, 2006; Dweck and Leggett 1988). Notably, even traditionally measured forms of intelligence are strikingly malleable, with specific kinds of cognitive training programs (e.g., to expand working memory capacity) yielding large improvements on tests of fluid intelligence, a common measure of IQ (Jaeggi et al. 2008).

Here, however, the emphasis is on students' *theories* of intelligence—as fixed or malleable. Students who hold one theory versus the other may be similarly motivated when they feel confident in their abilities or after an academic success. But after an academic failure, their profiles diverge sharply. As shown in diverse laboratory experiments and longitudinal studies, students with a fixed (entity) theory of intelligence tend to perceive academic failure as evidence of their inability—proof that they do not have what it takes to succeed. In response, they tend to withdraw and thus show declines in academic performance over time. By contrast, students with a malleable (incremental) theory of intelligence tend to perceive academic failure as evidence that they have not yet mastered the material. In response, they may increase effort and show improved academic performance over time. For instance, one longitudinal study found that students' implicit theories of intelligence predicted their academic performance over two years in the transition to junior high school (Blackwell, Trzesniewski, and Dweck 2007, study 1). Although students with the fixed and malleable theories entered junior high school with identical past achievement test scores, as the work became harder their math grades diverged. This divergence occurred because students with the two theories reacted differently to challenges and setbacks, with the malleable theory predicting more resilient, effort-based responses.

Where do students learn an entity theory of intelligence? Perhaps indirectly from Terman and others, who advance a fixed concept of intelligence. But an entity theory of intelligence can also be passed on directly to children, for instance through the kind of praise they receive. In one set of studies, Mueller and Dweck (1998) praised fifth-graders for completing a moderately difficult set of logic problems. Some children received entity praise ("That's a really high score, you must be very smart at these problems"). Others received effort praise ("That's a really high score, you must have worked hard at these problems"). A third group received neutral praise ("That's a really high score"). The children were then given a very difficult set of problems, on which they all performed poorly. Finally, children were given a critical second set of moderately difficult problems. The key question involved their resilience—how well would they bounce back after failing very difficult problems?

Children who received neutral praise performed equally well on the first and second sets of moderately difficult problems. But consistent with the effects of implicit theories, children who had received entity praise solved 30 percent fewer problems in the second set. They were also less willing to do more challenging problems in the future—they preferred easy problems on which they could score well. By contrast, students who had received effort praise performed well on the final set—even better than on the first set—and requested more challenging problems in the future—problems they could learn from. Just a single sentence of praise changed the situation and the meaning of failure for students, and shaped their subsequent performance.

If a malleable (or incremental) theory of intelligence predicts more adaptive student behaviors, does teaching students this theory improve academic outcomes? The answer is yes. Before describing the implicit theory of intelligence interventions, I emphasize that this intervention and other social-psychological interventions described below are not silver bullets, even though they can have large and impressive effects (Yeager and Walton 2011). Rather, in testing psychological interventions, researchers necessarily hold constant other important factors, such as the nature of the schooling environment, teachers, and pedagogy, while randomly assigning students to treatment and control conditions. This allows a rigorous test of the causal effect of the tested intervention, but it does so within a particular educational context, which, while not part of the intervention, may be critical to its success. Such studies can demonstrate the potential impact of an intervention in common academic environments, but they do not mean that the intervention will always be effective or that it can compensate for other important factors (such as bad teaching).

This said, in common field settings interventions to a malleable (or incremental) theory of intelligence can significantly raise students' academic achievement. In one experiment, Blackwell and colleagues randomly assigned seventh-grade students to one of two workshops (Blackwell, Trzesniewski, and Dweck 2007, study 2). In the incremental theory workshop, students learned how intelligence can "grow" through effort and learning. They also learned study skills with which to put their malleable theory into practice. In the control workshop, students learned only the study skills. Both groups had shown declining math grades before the workshop, and the control group continued to decline. Although they had learned effective study skills, they were apparently not motivated to put them to work. In contrast, students in the malleable theory workshop condition showed a sharp rebound in their math grades so that they earned significantly higher final grades than students in the control group.

Students who are underrepresented and negatively stereotyped in school may be at heightened risk from the view that intelligence is fixed. The stereotypes that "women are bad at math" and that "black and Latino students are not smart" allege fixed inability. If so, the view that intelligence is malleable may help sustain motivation and achievement among negatively stereotyped students. Consistent with this theorizing, incremental theories interventions have been shown to improve black college students' grades and school attitudes (Aronson, Fried, and Good 2002) and middle school girls' scores on state standardized math tests, eliminating gender differences (Good, Aronson, and Inzlicht 2003).

If seemingly small cues like a sentence of praise or seemingly small situations like participating in a school workshop can substantially affect students' academic engagement and performance over time, it calls into question what we mean by intelligence. Is it just within a student's head? Or is intelligence a quality that emerges as interactions between persons and situations? Are there other examples of subtle situational factors that profoundly shape students' academic performance?

Stereotype Threat

A second example involves stereotype threat (Steele 2010; Steele, Spencer, and Aronson 2002). When African American students perform on intellectual tasks, or when women perform in quantitative fields, they are often aware of negative stereotypes about the ability of their group. This awareness can cause *stereotype threat*—the worry that, should they perform poorly, others could view their poor performance as evidence for the truth of the stereotype. This worry is distracting and causes anxiety; it can prevent students from becoming fully absorbed in the task at hand and thus undermine their performance.

In a classic laboratory study, African American and European American college students took a test composed of difficult verbal problems from the Graduate Record Examinations (Steele and Aronson 1995). When students were told the test was intended to evaluate their verbal reasoning ability—a description that made the negative stereotype about

African Americans' intellectual ability relevant—African Americans performed far worse than European Americans. But when students were told the test was a verbal puzzle task, African American students' performance soared and, in fact, equaled European Americans' (controlling for Scholastic Aptitude Test scores) (Steele and Aronson 1995). Similarly, a study of math performance found that women performed worse than men when students were told that the test investigated gender differences (Spencer, Steele, and Quinn 1999). But when they were told that the test was fair across gender groups, women and men performed equally well.

Notably, negative intellectual stereotypes also affect the performance of students who are not targeted by negative stereotypes, such as whites and men, but here the effect is a positive one. In a meta-analysis (or statistical summary) of forty-three experiments, Geoffrey Cohen and I found that nonstereotyped students experience a performance boost called *stereotype lift* when they perform in situations in which a *different* group is subject to the negative scrutiny and suspicion of a stereotype (Walton and Cohen 2003).

Stereotype threat can also undermine learning—the acquisition of new academic knowledge (Taylor and Walton 2011; see also Rydell et al. 2010). In one study, black and white students were given rare words to learn. For some students the task was described in a way designed to elicit stereotype threat—it was said to evaluate students' ability to learn, thus making negative stereotypes about African Americans relevant. For other students the task was described as investigating "learning styles," which does not evoke the stereotype. A week later, students returned to the laboratory and completed a "warm-up" task in which they were asked to define some of the words they had studied a week earlier. All participants completed the "warm-up" in a nonthreatening, nonevaluative setting, so that performance would reflect how well they had learned the words a week earlier, not psychological threats that could undermine how well they performed. White students performed well regardless of the condition in which they had studied the words. But black students performed far worse when they had studied in the threatening environment than when they had studied in the nonthreatening environment (Taylor and Walton 2011). Those who had studied in the threatening learning environment never fully acquired the academic material. Notably, when students were subsequently asked to define the rest of the words in a threatening situation—a "test" said to evaluate students' verbal ability—even black students who had studied in the nonthreatening environment performed poorly. The results show that

black students experience a form of double jeopardy in academic environments as a consequence of stereotype threat—threat can both prevent
them from fully acquiring academic knowledge and prevent them from
performing well on material they have learned well.

Given the effects of stereotype threat on academic performance in the
laboratory, can interventions to reduce stereotype threat improve academic outcomes in real-world school settings? They can. Here I review
two such interventions.

First, one antidote to stereotype threat involves "self-affirmation." The
self-affirmation intervention is premised on the idea that stereotype threat
can cause students to experience high levels of stress and anxiety in school,
which undermines academic performance (Cohen et al. 2006). To alleviate this stress and anxiety, in the affirmation exercise students are given a
list of important values (e.g., religion, relationships with friends and family, athletics) and asked to select their most important value and write
about why this value is important to them. The theory underlying this
intervention is that when a situation threatens an important identity, reminding people of other valued identities can bolster their feeling of self-
integrity—their perception of themselves as good, efficacious, and
moral—and thereby help people perform at a high level despite threat
(see Sherman and Cohen 2006).

In one randomized field experiment, white and black seventh-graders
in a middle-income school completed an in-class self-affirmation near the
beginning of the school year, soon before a stressful experience (taking a
test) (Cohen et al. 2006). The exercise was presented as an in-class writing
assignment, although, to keep teachers blind to students' condition assignment, teachers passed out materials in sealed envelopes and returned
these to the researchers, never having seen students' essays. In the self-
affirmation condition, students wrote about a value that was personally
important to them. Control students wrote about why a value that was not
important to them might matter to someone else. In total, the affirmation
exercise took fifteen to twenty minutes; it was administered once, twice, or
several times depending on the cohort.

The affirmation had no effect on white students, but it reduced the cognitive accessibility of racial stereotypes among black students and raised
their end-of-term course grades by one-third of a grade point, narrowing
the racial achievement gap by 40 percent. The number of black students
who received a D or an F grade in the course was reduced by half. Long-
term follow-ups with three cohorts of students showed that the boost in

grades for black students extended to their grade-point average (GPA) across all core academic courses and persisted over the last two years of middle school. It appeared to do so by interrupting a negative recursive cycle whereby poor performance begat worse performance over time (Cohen et al. 2009). The affirmation's effects were thus most evident among initially low-performing black students.

A second intervention to address stereotype threat involves bolstering students' sense of social belonging in school. One consequence of stereotype threat is to cause students to question whether others in school will fully include, value, and respect them (Walton and Cohen 2007). The need to belong—to form positive social relationships with others—is fundamental to humans (Baumeister and Leary 1995) and forms a critical basis of motivation and achievement (Walton, Cohen, Cwir, and Spencer 2012). If students feel uncertain of their social belonging in school, they may monitor the school environment for cues that indicate whether they belong. In this state of uncertainty, negative social events—like critical feedback from a teacher or loneliness in class—may seem to be diagnostic of a global lack of belonging in the school. In turn, such global attributions may erode students' engagement in school and academic performance (see Mendoza-Denton et al. 2002).

To prevent such deleterious attributions, the "social-belonging" intervention provides students a nonthreatening explanation for negative social events in school (Walton and Cohen 2007, 2011). The intervention was first tested in a sample of black and white first-year college students. Students read a survey of upper-year students at their school. The survey indicated that negative social events and feelings of not belonging are normal at first in college (e.g., experienced by students of all ethnicities) and dissipate with time. The treatment was designed to lead students to attribute such events and feelings to the difficulty of the transition to college rather than to a lack of belonging on their part or on the part of their racial group (cf. Wilson, Damiani, and Shelton 2002). To encourage students to internalize the treatment message, they were asked to write a speech describing how their own experiences had changed over time in college and to deliver the speech for a video that could be shown to incoming students the following year, ostensibly to ease their transition to college. This procedure takes advantage of the "saying-is-believing" effect—leading people to advocate for a persuasive message to a receptive audience is a potent means of persuasion (Aronson, Fried, and Good 2002). In total, the intervention lasted about an hour. By securing students' sense of social belonging in school, the intervention was designed to change the trajectory of their experience in the school over time—to help them build the positive experiences and social relationships that form the foundation for lasting academic success.

The results suggest that the intervention had this effect. For white students, who have little cause to doubt their belonging in school on account of their race, the treatment had little impact. But for black students it had large and long-lasting benefits. In two cohorts of students, the intervention delivered in the spring of students' freshman year raised black students' GPA from sophomore through senior year compared with multiple randomized control groups. Consistent with the idea that the intervention changed the trajectory of students' experience, the intervention led to a term-by-term rise in African American students' GPA over this three-year period. Overall, from sophomore year through senior year, the intervention reduced the achievement gap between African American and white American students by 52 percent (Walton and Cohen 2011). Moreover, the effects were statistically mediated by measures of the underlying psychological process targeted by the intervention: daily diaries completed in the week after the intervention showed, as predicted, that the intervention made black students' sense of belonging less vulnerable to daily adversity, which no longer seemed to carry a global or symbolic meaning for them. This effect mediated the long-term gain in black students' GPA.

Research on stereotype threat carries an important implication. Insofar as school is a pervasively evaluative environment in which negative stereotypes routinely come to mind, the academic performance of negatively stereotyped students may be systematically depressed by stereotype threat. If this is the case, they would be like runners facing a stiff headwind, whose times underestimate their ability and potential to perform well in a neutral environment. To test this idea, Steve Spencer and I conducted two meta-analyses, one summarizing data from thirty-seven laboratory experiments and the other summarizing data from three field experiments. Together these studies included 18,976 students in five countries (Walton and Spencer 2009). Both meta-analyses compared the performance of negatively stereotyped students (e.g., women, African Americans) in academic environments in which threat had been reduced with the performance of nonstereotyped students (e.g., men, whites). In addition, we compared students who had the same prior level of academic performance—the same prior grades or test scores. If stereotype threat systematically depresses the performances of negatively stereotyped students, these performances should underestimate their performance in settings in which stereotype threat has been removed. If so, in these circumstances, stereotyped students should outperform nonstereotyped students who had the same level of prior academic performance.

This was just what we found. In both meta-analyses, when threat was reduced stereotyped students performed better than nonstereotyped students with the same prior scores. This "latent ability effect" was found for students with all levels of academic performance, and both for women and girls and for ethnic minority students. To illustrate the magnitude of the effect using the SAT as the metric, the size of the observed effect suggests that the SAT Math test underpredicts the math ability of women like those in the surveyed studies by nineteen to twenty-one points and that the SAT Math and Reading tests underpredict the intellectual ability of African and Hispanic Americans by thirty-nine to forty-one points for each group. These differences are substantial and could make the difference between rejection and admission by a selective college or university. Further, they suggest that a broad range of promising stereotyped students have significant academic potential that is hidden by their scores on common performance metrics like grades and test scores.

Implications

This chapter has questioned how useful and valid it is to maintain a view of intelligence as something stable lodged within individuals. The research reviewed here shows that intellectual performance can vary widely depending on how people think about intelligence, on the kind of praise they receive, and on whether subtle cues in school settings trigger concern about negative intellectual stereotypes. At the same time, such stereotypes can positively affect other students not targeted by the stereotype and raise their performance. And, importantly, research finds that even brief interventions—a few school workshops, an in-class writing exercise, or reviewing a survey of older students' experiences in the transition to one's school—can lead to large improvements in students' academic performance, raising grades months and years later (Yeager and Walton 2011).

This research suggests that intellectual performance is not simply lodged within individuals—high test scores and straight As are not owned by a person alone, nor are poor scores or bad grades only the student's responsibility. Rather, intellectual performance is an emergent property of persons and social situations—an interaction between the two. These findings suggest that conceptualizing "intelligence" as a stable property of individuals and a reliable way of distinguishing between them may be inappropriate.

For schools and organizations, understanding intellectual performance as socially situated carries important implications. It suggests that an important task for schools and educators is to sculpt educational environments to eliminate negative social and psychological dynamics that undermine students' experience and performance and contribute to group disparities. The effectiveness of existing psychological interventions suggests the promise of this approach to improve students' outcomes. These psychological strategies may be one way schools, potentially even schools that operate in socially, economically, and racially disadvantaged environments, can effectively raise student outcomes (see Rothstein, this volume).

Insofar as mitigating negative psychological dynamics contributes to the core academic mission of schools, how well schools accomplish this should be an important component of measures of school quality. Determining how to assess school quality is exceedingly difficult, as Ladd and Loeb discuss in this volume. But creating sensitive measures of subtle psychological processes poses further challenges. Although a full discussion of how to assess these processes is beyond the scope of the current chapter, an experimental approach may be of use. For instance, if interventions aimed at reducing stereotype-related threat in a school improved students' outcomes in a randomized field experiment, it would suggest that stereotype threat was present in the school—that it was there to be remedied—and, further, that the school is making progress in mitigating this dynamic. Such evidence would be further strengthened if the intervention was shown to affect important intervening psychological processes.

Relatedly, the socially situated nature of intelligence points to a new mission for the state in general and for selective schools in particular: instead of assessing individuals' intelligence with an eye toward identifying the "best" candidates for admission and promotion, academic environments should be structured to ensure that all students can perform as well as possible. However, when selective schools do decide whom to admit and whom to reject, it is important to consider psychological processes like stereotype threat that can systematically disadvantage members of devalued groups, causing them to perform less well than they are capable of (Walton and Spencer 2009). Insofar as stereotyped students like

African Americans and other ethnic minorities often face other important disadvantages, such as a greater incidence of poverty (Phillips et al. 1998; Rothstein 2004), this compounds disadvantage with disadvantage. When indicators of merit are systematically biased, it is unfair and discriminatory to interpret them at face value (see Walton, Spencer, and Erman, in press). Instead, schools and organizations need to take psychological dynamics into account—to understand intellectual performance as a product of both situations and persons—to interpret indicators of merit and to evaluate candidates fairly and accurately.

CHAPTER 8

Racial Segregation and Black Student Achievement

Richard Rothstein

Introduction

Policymakers typically attempt to address the black-white achievement gap by school reform, notwithstanding consistent research findings that the performance of students in different schools varies less with school quality than with family, community, health, and other socioeconomic inequalities that bring disadvantaged children in general, and African American children in particular, to school less ready to learn, on average, than their middle-class and white peers.

Impediments to learning, including less sophisticated home literacy environments, lack of opportunity for high-quality early childhood care and education, poorer health and greater exposure to allergens and lead, less adequate housing and higher residential mobility, greater economic stress, more exposure to violence and crime, fewer constructive out-of-school activities, and fewer successful adult role models, all are exacerbated when large numbers of disadvantaged children are concentrated in racially isolated low-income neighborhoods with limited opportunities for exit—in short, ghettos.

Children attending ghetto schools less frequently benefit from positive influence from academic peers . They also suffer because of other children's learning impediments: for example, in schools with large proportions of mobile or absent students, the learning of stable and healthy students is also impeded because teachers must repeat material previously taught.

Children attending ghetto schools are less likely to be comfortable with standard English if their verbal interaction outside the classroom is in subcultural dialect; they are then less prepared to participate as adults in the majority culture and economy. They will be excluded from social networks that accelerate access to and success in the broader world of work.[1]

Several school districts have implemented voluntary racial integration programs, usually involving busing black students to schools with predominantly white enrollment. Others attempt to camouflage racial integration policies by mixing students of different family income backgrounds.[2] These integration methods, however, are not practical for the most severely disadvantaged black children, who live in ghettos geographically distant from white communities.

Busing also has negative consequences. It undermines community attachment to neighborhood schools and limits parents' ability to be involved in children's schooling. Teachers and school leaders, especially those serving disadvantaged children, often go to great lengths to encourage parents to volunteer in schools, believing that students' achievement and behavior improves with greater parental attachment to schooling,[3] a belief confirmed by research.[4] Low-income parents in particular have great difficulty becoming involved in schools outside their neighborhoods. They may not have transportation to distant schools, and their work schedules or caring for other children may make involvement difficult in any event, and too difficult when schools are not nearby.

Efforts to organize parents to press school leaders for educational improvements also depend on a community relationship between parents and their children's schools.[5] The exercise of "voice" to effect improvement is inhibited, if not wholly prevented, when schools are far from children's and parents' residences.[6]

Therefore, effective school integration policy requires reducing the residential isolation of low-income black families. Busing can expose children to the positive influence of diversity, but only residential integration can promote this influence along with the positive effects of voice and participation. The benefits of residential integration make it a compelling public interest. But it is less rarely acknowledged that current residential patterns of racial isolation are unconstitutional products of state action. This chapter illustrates that claim.

Courts in the United States are at present unsympathetic to such arguments, and the near-term futility of making them has, unfortunately, dissuaded opponents of residential racial segregation from insisting it is unconstitutional. Instead, civil rights advocates often accept that neighborhoods, and therefore schools, are now segregated de facto, not de jure;

they urge that courts permit racially explicit integration programs only because of their academic benefits to both black and white students, not from constitutional obligation.

However long the hostility of courts to racial integration persists, the legislative and executive branches are also sworn to uphold the Constitution. Awareness of how state action has produced contemporary racial segregation should spur political as well as judicial officials to take remedial action.

In 2007 the Supreme Court found that school integration policies in Louisville, Kentucky, and Seattle, Washington, were unconstitutional because they considered students' race in assigning them to schools. A majority of justices agreed that government has a "compelling" interest in fostering school integration for its academic benefits. But a majority also concluded that the plans could not withstand "strict scrutiny" because they were not designed to remedy specific prior acts of racial discrimination by government.[7]

The Court acknowledged that racially identifiable housing patterns in these cities might result from "societal discrimination," but remedying discrimination "not traceable to [government's] own actions" can never justify racial classifications of students. "The distinction between segregation by state action and racial imbalance caused by other factors has been central to our jurisprudence. . . . 'Where [racial imbalance] is a product not of state action but of private choices, it does not have constitutional implications.'"

In 1974 Justice Potter Stewart asserted that black students were concentrated in Detroit, not spread throughout its suburbs, because of "unknown and perhaps unknowable factors such as in-migration, birth rates, economic changes, or cumulative acts of private racial fears."[8] This is now the consensus view of American jurisprudence, reflected in the Court's Louisville-Seattle opinion.

Yet causes of contemporary segregation are in fact both known and knowable. Schools are segregated mostly because their neighborhoods are segregated, and these neighborhoods have been segregated by a century-long series of federal, state, and local policies to establish a racially segregated nation.

Two years before Justice Stewart's claim of ignorance, President Richard Nixon's annual housing report expressed a more sophisticated view. "Federal housing programs over the years," it said, "have contributed . . . to growing separation of the races, and to the concentration of the poor in decaying urban cities. . . . [Federal housing] programs have contributed to these problems and in many cases intensified them."[9]

In some cases federal, state, and local policies to create and perpetuate segregation have been racially explicit. In other cases racial results were disguised but intended. In others, disparate racial impacts should have been apparent to policymakers, were apparent to some, and should have been avoided. In yet others, unintended racial consequences became apparent after policies were implemented, but not too late to take remedial action.

Over time, federal courts' views have shifted—first in one direction, then another, then back again—regarding whether constitutional violations require racially discriminatory intent, racially disparate impact, or both. But although proof of violations may not meet the narrow standards of contemporary federal justices, policies of the federal, state, and local governments have violated the civil rights of African Americans and in so doing created a segregated society.

In cases where the Court has belatedly banned segregationist policies, these policies did not become unconstitutional only when the Court so decreed. They were unconstitutional from their inception. A finding of unconstitutionality may preclude continuing such policies, but it does not itself undo their ongoing effects. Additional remedial action is constitutionally required, whether by court order or by legislative or executive action.

The courts, Congress, presidential administrations, and scholars have failed to devote serious attention to considering how long the effects of unconstitutional segregationist policies endure. Consider black communities that became rooted in ghettos created by ordinances prohibiting blacks from living elsewhere. Can these neighborhoods be deemed desegregated immediately on repeal of such ordinances? Surely not. Positive government action would be required (for example, by subsidizing only black residents of the affected metropolitan area to purchase homes in previously forbidden neighborhoods). But would such remedial policies continue to be constitutionally required a generation later? Two generations later? There can be no precise answer to such questions, but reasonable answers are possible that take account both of the slow pace with which social change can occur and of the need to place an end limit on public remedies.

In 1883, less than two decades after the abolition of slavery, the Supreme Court ruled that racial discrimination by privately owned theaters, inns, and similar facilities was not unconstitutional because the exclusions of blacks were private acts, not state action regulated by the Fourteenth Amendment. Notwithstanding that these private acts were so pervasive that they effectively constituted a conspiracy to perpetuate the characteristics of slavery, Justice Joseph Bradley wrote for the court:

> When a man has emerged from slavery, and by the aid of beneficent legislation has shaken off the inseparable concomitants of that state, there must be some stage in the progress of his elevation when he takes the rank of a mere citizen, and ceases to be the special favorite of the laws, and when his rights as a citizen, or a man, are to be protected in the ordinary modes by which other men's rights are protected.[10]

In the context of Reconstruction's wane, Justice Bradley's opinion was perverse or naive, but in principle his sentiment was correct. "There must be some stage" when remedial action is no longer justified, and the determination of what that stage should be is a challenge for sociologists and urban planners, who must judge reasonable rates of community change. But when we consider the full panoply of public policies pursued to segregate the nation, and their extensive duration, it seems reasonable to assume that the period needed to undo segregationist policies has, even now, not yet expired.

Judging the time needed to undo segregation, and the policies required, is distinct from the issue of reparations for past injustice, advocated by some. This chapter is concerned with measures needed to undo ongoing effects of segregationist policies—how to provide the next generation of children with the opportunity for integrated education, not how to compensate past generations for the harm of segregated education.

A fear of confusing desegregation with reparations, however, has been one reason the Court and scholars have been reluctant to consider necessary remedies, and it has partially motivated the Court's increasing conservatism in affirmative action cases: the Court has warned, for example, against a "mosaic of shifting preferences based on inherently unmeasurable claims of past wrongs."[11] This appropriate caution can be carried too far. The success of past policies to create racial ghettos in American metropolitan communities may be precisely "unmeasurable," but historians and social scientists can clarify it sufficiently to justify reasonable active policies to undo this success.

Amnesia about the causes of residential racial segregation in American cities, whether deliberate or careless, has permitted the US Supreme Court, as well as policymakers and advocates, to adopt a formalistic and ahistorical interpretation of the equality requirements of the Fourteenth Amendment, whose equal protection language was drafted specifically to complete the effective abolition of African American slavery. While the Thirteenth Amendment abolished slavery itself, the Fourteenth aimed to abolish all middle ground between slavery and full citizenship and participation in American society. Its targets were any government actions that impeded the path to full equality in all walks of American life.

Yet in the hands of contemporary opinion, this constitutional guarantee of a path to equality for African Americans has been perverted into a requirement for "color blindness" that obscures 150 years of such government-sponsored impediments. With government's role obscured, it is easy to conclude that African Americans' failure to achieve equality is attributable either to mysterious demographic and economic forces or to their own choices to self-segregate, perhaps abetted by white private citizens operating entirely independent of the governments they controlled. In such circumstances, "equality" is perversely deemed to demand the absence of government initiative to undo inequality. Yet, in truth, the most powerful enduring actions to ensure that African Americans could not travel the full path from slavery to full equality have been those of government: federal, state, and local.

There is today no widespread acknowledgment of government responsibility for contemporary racial segregation because historians, sociologists, and economists have, with rare exceptions,[12] focused on particular aspects of segregationist policy—either mortgage lending, or public housing construction, or highway routing, or police practices, or discriminatory provision of services, and so on. Government's responsibility for ongoing segregation, however, becomes unavoidably clear only when these policies are considered in combination, as they interact with and reinforce one another to create a state-established system of racial separation.

Racial Zoning

In the nineteenth century, both before and after the Civil War, neighborhoods in the North and South were not as segregated as they later became.[13] Partly this was because many black adults worked as servants in the homes of middle- and upper-class whites, and the propriety of servants' living close to their employers was unquestioned.

Early in the twentieth century, however, as black populations grew and the Jim Crow reaction to Reconstruction accelerated,[14] municipalities, particularly those in border states, adopted zoning laws that restricted blacks to certain blocks or neighborhoods and prohibited them from others. The first such ordinance was adopted in 1910 in Baltimore, followed by Winston-Salem, Birmingham, Atlanta, Richmond, St. Louis, Dallas, and other cities.[15]

In 1917 the Supreme Court overturned the racial zoning ordinance of Louisville, Kentucky.[16] The case illustrates how far neighborhoods were integrated before twentieth-century segregation. Louisville's ordinance was designed to segregate gradually, without a radical uprooting of existing integrated blocks. The ordinance protected the right to remain in integrated neighborhoods of any African Americans who previously lived there, prohibiting only future sales or rentals to blacks on any block where a majority of residents were white. An exception was made for servants, who could continue to move near their employers. The case involved a black man's attempt to move to an integrated block where there were already two black households and eight white ones.

Although the Court found that the ordinance violated the Fourteenth Amendment, enforcement of similar ordinances continued after the decision. In 1927 the Court overturned a New Orleans law that permitted blacks to move to a white neighborhood only if a majority of white residents voted permission.[17] Birmingham continued to enforce its racial zoning ordinance until 1949; the Palm Beach ordinance was still in effect in 1958.[18]

Throughout the nation, many towns and suburbs excluded African Americans entirely by prohibiting their staying overnight. In some, black residents were forcibly expelled (or intimidated into fleeing, often by a lynching) after segregation intensified in the early twentieth century, and then signs were posted warning blacks away. Such signs, typically reading something like, "Nigger, Don't Let the Sun Go Down on You in [Name of Town]" have been documented in over 150 towns and suburbs in thirty-one states. As late as 1998, the central Illinois town of Villa Grove sounded a siren at 6:00 every evening to warn blacks to leave. A sign common in border state towns depicted a black mule, signifying that African Americans must leave before dark. Some such signs remained posted as recently as 2003. Although today the signs themselves are rare, many communities that expelled black residents by force in the early twentieth century, then subsequently prohibited them from remaining overnight, have preserved their acquired all-white status to the present.[19]

Many now do so by zoning ordinances, not explicitly racial, that exclude low-income persons by requiring minimum acreage and square footage or by prohibiting multiunit structures. In 1977 the Supreme Court upheld zoning ordinances that barred low-income housing from communities, ruling that only dispositive racially discriminatory intent, not racially disparate impact, was unconstitutional.[20]

The Court's judgment that disparate impact alone is insufficient to justify a finding of unconstitutionality was reasonable. Virtually any economic legislation will have a disparate impact on blacks. Yet it is often impossible to disentangle racial from nonracial motives when communities attempt to create or preserve an exclusive middle-class environment. In some cases some community activists' racial bias coexists with others' class-based motivation.[21]

Nothing, however, prevents national or state legislatures from requiring inclusionary zoning to remedy the broader pattern of state-sponsored segregation, or simply as a matter of public land use policy.

Restrictive Covenants

More subtle than racial zoning or police-enforced policies to bar African Americans completely were restrictive covenants—private contracts either attached to or independent of land deeds, prohibiting future sales of property to nonwhites. Covenants began to spread about 1917, perhaps to evade the Court's Louisville zoning decision.[22] In 1926 the Supreme Court upheld covenants' legality and enforceability.[23]

Restrictive covenants were actively promoted by the federal government. The Federal Housing Administration's 1938 Underwriting Manual gave these instructions to bank appraisers who hoped to qualify loans for FHA insurance:

> Generally, a high rating should be given only where adequate and enforced zoning regulations exist or where effective restrictive covenants are recorded against the entire tract. . . . [D]eed restrictions should be imposed upon all land in the immediate environment of the subject location. . . . Recommended restrictions should include . . . [p]rohibition of the occupancy of properties except by the race for which they are intended.[24]

Restrictive covenants became commonplace in Chicago, Los Angeles, Washington, Columbus, Detroit, and other cities, attached to sale agreements in new subdivisions. In established areas, neighborhood associations formed to enlist (and pressure) existing residents to sign. By 1944 in Chicago, 175 white neighborhood associations actively enforced covenants that barred sales or rentals to blacks.[25] Between 1943 and 1965, 192 such associations were organized in Detroit.[26]

A 1947 survey of over three hundred housing developments in Queens, Nassau, and Westchester Counties, New York, found that 80 percent of developments of seventy-five units or more, and 48 percent of developments of twenty units or more, had covenants barring black purchasers or renters.[27] Deeds cited the FHA rule as requiring the restriction. Levittown, a 1947 Nassau County development of 17,500 homes, is considered by social historians to be a visionary solution to housing problems of returning war veterans, but developer William Levitt refused sales to blacks, and each contract included a provision prohibiting such resales in the future.[28]

The US Commission on Civil Rights concluded that the FHA had been a "powerful enforcer" of restrictive covenants and that nationwide segregation was "due *in large part* to racially discriminatory FHA policies in effect during the post–World War II housing boom."[29]

In 1948 the Supreme Court, reversing its 1926 decision, ruled that restrictive covenants could not legally be enforced by state or municipal authorities.[30] Compliance was slow. In 1950 the FHA announced it would no longer insure mortgages with new restrictive covenants, but it would continue to insure properties with preexisting covenants. The FHA also continued to insure properties with covenants that were not explicitly racial but that required sale approvals by neighbors or community boards.[31]

Although the 1948 ruling prohibited states from enforcing racially restrictive covenants, not until 1972 did a lower federal court rule that the covenants themselves were illegal and could not be recorded.[32] Suggesting how long it make take for the effects of restrictive covenants to recede, by 2000 Levittown was still only 0.5 percent black, compared with 10 percent for Nassau County as a whole and 20 percent for the adjacent county of Queens.[33]

Public Housing

Federal policy enforced segregation in public housing programs initiated during the Depression, World War II, and the war's aftermath. Harold Ickes, administrator of the New Deal's National Industrial Recovery Act, established a "neighborhood composition rule"—public housing projects could not alter the racial composition of their neighborhoods.[34] In 1944 Ickes's successor as head of the National Housing Agency stated that little could be done to provide housing for black families because no open sites were available in neighborhoods they traditionally occupied.[35]

In 1949 the Senate and House each considered and defeated proposed amendments to the Housing Act that would have prohibited segregation and racial discrimination in federally funded public housing programs.[36]

Local governments administering federal housing funds maintained similar policies. In 1945 Detroit mayor Edward Jeffries's reelection campaign warned white voters that housing projects with black residents would be located in their neighborhoods if his opponent was elected. In 1948–49, the Detroit city council held hearings on twelve proposed public housing projects in outlying (predominantly white) areas. Jeffries's successor, Albert Cobo, vetoed all twelve; only housing in predominantly black areas was approved.[37]

In 1971 construction of 120 low-rise townhouses began in Whitman Park, an all-white neighborhood of Philadelphia. (The neighborhood had once been integrated, but land clearance for the proposed public housing over a decade earlier had displaced all black residents.) A formally organized white neighborhood association, the Whitman Area Improvement Council, demonstrated at the site, blocking construction workers and equipment. Police declined to intervene, and when the company obtained an injunction against the demonstrators, police refused to enforce it. A state judge then barred the construction company from returning to the site, and Philadelphia mayor James Tate ordered the work to cease.

African Americans awaiting public housing then filed suit. As the suit dragged on, a new mayor, Frank Rizzo, stated he would make no compromise because "people in the area felt that black people would be moving into the area if public housing were built." He referred to public housing as "black housing" and vowed he would not permit it in "white neighborhoods."

Meanwhile, the Department of Housing and Urban Development (HUD) rejected requests to pressure Philadelphia by withholding other federal funds. In 1977 a federal appeals court ordered the city to permit construction to resume. The neighborhood association then delayed construction further by demanding new environmental impact studies; the Whitman Park project eventually was completed in 1982, nearly a quarter century after black residents' homes had been demolished to clear the land.[38]

In 1976 the Supreme Court found that the Chicago Housing Authority (CHA), with the complicity of federal housing agencies, had unconstitutionally selected sites to maintain Chicago's segregated pattern.[39] The Court ordered HUD to henceforth locate housing in predominantly white areas of Chicago and its suburbs. The HUD—CHA response was to cease building public housing altogether. No units have been constructed in Chicago since the Court's decision. Instead, the CHA now issues Section 8 housing vouchers, but only a small number have been used to place black families in predominantly white communities.

In the years leading up to the final ruling, the CHA and HUD simply refused to comply with settlement agreements and lower court decisions. In 1971, for example, CHA officials proposed sites for new housing that included some predominantly white areas. Unlike the high-rises it had built to concentrate blacks in the ghetto, these proposals were for low-rise, scattered-site housing. Still Mayor Richard J. Daley rejected them, saying that public housing should go only "where this kind of housing is most needed and accepted."[40]

Faced with similar resistance elsewhere, federal authorities acceded to segregationist demands. In 1970 HUD secretary George Romney proposed public housing units for a Detroit suburb, but the attorney general ordered him to withdraw his initiative. President Nixon stated, "I believe that forced integration of the suburbs is not in the national interest" and issued a formal policy vowing that "this administration will not attempt to impose federally assisted housing upon any community." Later, President Gerald Ford's solicitor general expressed the government's opposition (in the Chicago case) to placing public housing in white communities: "There will be an enormous practical impact on innocent communities who have to bear the burden of the housing, who will have to house a plaintiff class from Chicago, which they wronged in no way."[41] Thus the federal government described nondiscriminatory housing policy as punishment visited on the innocent.

By 1970, public housing authorities had built 250,000 units in the nation's twenty-four largest metropolitan areas. Of these only one project had been constructed outside a central city, a Cincinnati project where seventy-six low-rent units were built in an existing African American suburban enclave.[42] In 1984 a team of investigative reporters visited federally funded public housing projects in forty-seven cities nationwide. The reporters found that the nation's nearly ten million public housing residents were almost always segregated by race and that every predominantly white-occupied project had facilities, amenities, services, and maintenance superior to those of predominantly black-occupied projects.[43]

Home Purchases

Where no restrictive covenants were attached to deeds, the FHA still refused to insure mortgage loans to black applicants for purchase of homes
in white neighborhoods. The FHA's redlining rules made blacks ineligible
for insurance in white areas, made both blacks and whites ineligible in
integrated areas, and permitted insurance of only a very few mortgages to
blacks in predominantly black areas. This FHA policy went beyond other
New Deal housing programs that, as noted above, would place federally
sponsored integrated public housing in neighborhoods that were already
integrated. In Chicago, for example, one federally sponsored public housing project, the Jane Addams Homes, was open to both black and white
tenants because the neighborhood was already integrated.[44]

When the Veterans Administration was authorized by the GI Bill also
to insure mortgages, it adopted the FHA's redlining policies. With most
residential mortgages insured by either the FHA or the VA, these federal
rules are probably more responsible than any other factor for metropolitan segregation, with whites in federally insured homes in the suburbs and
blacks crowded into central cities with few opportunities for escape.

FHA policy not only excluded blacks from suburbs but impoverished
the urban ghetto population. In many cities, black employment rates in
urban industry were high in the 1950s and 1960s, but because African
Americans could not buy homes in the suburbs as did newly secure white
workers, blacks' desire to escape crowded urban conditions spurred their
demand for single-family or duplex homes on the ghetto's outskirts. Because these black middle-class families were a captive market with limited
alternatives, the homes were priced far above their otherwise fair market
values.

Typically, speculators and real estate agents colluded in blockbusting,
a scheme in which speculators purchased homes in borderline black-white
areas, rented or sold the homes to black families, persuaded white families
already living in these areas that their neighborhoods were turning into
black slums and that prices would soon fall precipitously, then purchased
the panicked whites' homes at bargain prices. Typical blockbusters' tactics included hiring black women to push baby carriages through white
neighborhoods, hiring black men to drive cars through white neighborhoods with radios blasting, and making random telephone calls to homes
in white neighborhoods asking to speak to "Johnnie Mae."[45]

Because black families desperate for housing could not qualify for mortgages under FHA policy, the speculators sold these newly acquired properties to blacks at inflated prices, expanding the ghetto. Speculators sold these homes on an installment plan where no equity accumulated from the black purchasers' down payments or monthly payments. These "contract" sales typically provided that ownership would transfer to purchasers after fifteen or twenty years, but if a single monthly payment was late, purchasers could be evicted, having accumulated no equity. The inflated prices made it all the more likely that payments would be late. Owner-speculators could then resell the homes to new contract buyers.

The FHA redlining policy necessitated the contract sale system for black homeowners unable to obtain conventional mortgages, and the system created the conditions for neighborhood deterioration. A contemporary author whose father was a Chicago attorney caught up in the system described it like this:

> Because black contract buyers knew how easily they could lose their homes, they struggled to make their inflated monthly payments. Husbands and wives both worked double shifts. They neglected basic maintenance. They subdivided their apartments, crammed in extra tenants and, when possible, charged their tenants hefty rents. . . .
>
> White people observed that their new black neighbors overcrowded and neglected their properties. Overcrowded neighborhoods meant overcrowded schools; in Chicago, officials responded by "double-shifting" the students (half attending in the morning, half in the afternoon). Children were deprived of a full day of schooling and left to fend for themselves in the after-school hours. These conditions helped fuel the rise of gangs, which in turn terrorized shop owners and residents alike.
>
> In the end, whites fled these neighborhoods, not only because of the influx of black families, but also because they were upset about overcrowding, decaying schools and crime. They also understood that the longer they stayed, the less their property would be worth. But black contract buyers did not have the option of leaving a declining neighborhood before their properties were paid for in full—if they did, they would lose everything they had invested in that property to date. Whites could leave—blacks had to stay.[46]

This contract system was widespread not only in Chicago, but in Baltimore, Cincinnati, Detroit, Washington, DC, and elsewhere. From 1958 to 1961, when Chicago's West Side neighborhood of Lawndale was changing from predominantly white to predominantly black, over half the homes there were purchased on contract, as was approximately 85 percent of all property sold to blacks in Chicago.[47]

The FHA's refusal to insure conventional loans to black home purchasers was thus an important cause not only of racial segregation but of black impoverishment. Federal redlining policy, and the resulting contract system, made it impossible for black families to accumulate wealth—as white families with similar incomes could do—making it all the more difficult for them to break out of isolated ghettos once the FHA abandoned redlining in the mid-1960s.

Licensed Real Estate Agents

Real estate agents have been licensed by state governments since the 1920s. Licenses are difficult to obtain, requiring courses and study to pass an examination. State authorities can, and do, revoke licenses for violations of the extensive regulations that govern agents' behavior. When states license real estate agents whose practices create or maintain segregation, the states effectively sanction these practices.

State-licensed real estate agents have consistently violated black home buyers' rights, as in the blockbusting practices described above that not only exploited white and black buyers alike, but ensured that border areas surrounding black ghettos could not remain integrated.

The 1928 Code of Ethics of the National Association of Realtors stated: "A realtor should never be instrumental in introducing into a neighborhood . . . members of any race or nationality . . . whose presence will clearly be detrimental to property values in that neighborhood." In 1939 the association published a guide for agents illustrating the types of persons to whom homes in white neighborhoods should not be sold, such as "a colored man of means who was giving his children a college education and thought they were entitled to live among whites."[48] Blockbusting, of course, was a clear violation of industry rules, but a violation in support of the rules' underlying segregationist purpose. Realtors' norms were logical applications of the FHA's redlining policy.

The 1968 Fair Housing Act made racial discrimination in housing and the Realtors' rules unlawful (although discrimination was already a violation of constitutional rights when practiced by state-licensed agents). Yet enforcement of the act's prohibitions has been weak. It has mostly fallen to nongovernment civil rights organizations to identify discriminatory practices, usually by sending matched black and white teams of investigators to real estate offices, posing as potential buyers. Testers today continue to identify commonplace segregationist real estate tactics: steering white buyers to homes in predominantly white communities and black buyers to homes in predominantly black communities; failing to show blacks properties that are shown to whites; making disparaging comments to prospective buyers considering purchases in integrated or other-race communities; failing to follow up on phone calls or visits from prospective black purchasers, and similar practices.

Bank Lending and Federal Mortgage Guarantees

As real estate agents are licensed and tightly regulated, banks are even more so. Redlining by both state and federally chartered banks continued long after the VA and FHA ceased requiring it. A study of bank lending procedures done by the Federal Reserve Bank of Boston in 1990 found that area banks discriminated against minority borrowers relative to similarly qualified white borrowers.[49]

Recent discriminatory activity by the federally regulated banking sector has had a devastating economic impact on the black community, increasing its segregation. During the housing bubble that began in the late 1990s and continued through 2007, banks exploited African American home buyers and homeowners by charging them higher interest rates than similarly situated whites and by aggressively marketing exploitative financial products (known as subprime loans) to African Americans who were misled about their costs. The Department of Justice concluded that "the lenders who peddled the most toxic loans targeted [segregated] communities,"[50] but there was little or no effort at enforcement when the practices were ongoing.

The result has been a high rate of foreclosure and home loss in predominantly African American communities, greater than the rate in predominantly white communities. When a community has a high foreclosure rate, the values of all homes in the community decline, largely because foreclosed homes are vacant for extended periods and then poorly maintained by banks, casting a pall over neighboring properties. Empty homes invite vandalism and crime. Each foreclosure causes a decline of about 1 percent in the value of every other home within an eighth of a mile.[51]

When an African American family in a predominantly black community loses its home in foreclosure, its capital accumulation is reversed, and future opportunities to move to a more integrated suburb are lost.[52] A high African American foreclosure rate can reinforce racial stereotypes held by whites and make them less willing to remain in an integrated neighborhood for fear it will deteriorate as well.

Legitimate subprime loans were designed for higher-risk borrowers, with higher interest rates to offset the risk. But when banks marketed these loans to unsophisticated borrowers, they structured them as adjustable rate products, with low initial "teaser" rates and unadvertised much higher rates later, usually after two years. When the higher rates kicked in, borrowers were frequently unable to make payments, and foreclosure followed. Subprime loans also characteristically carried high prepayment penalties to prevent borrowers from refinancing to a prime loan with a lower rate when their financial situation improved or interest rates declined. Some subprime loans also had negative amortization—requirements for initial monthly payments that were lower than needed to cover interest costs, with the difference then added to the outstanding principal.[53]

Banks marketing loans to unsophisticated borrowers also pressured them to refinance unnecessarily, charged excessive closing costs, and ignored traditional underwriting criteria regarding the borrowers' ability to repay. Because of regulators' failure to ensure market transparency, banks had little interest in protecting themselves against borrowers' defaults because they could easily sell the loans on the secondary market. There speculators sold them, in turn, to unsuspecting investors who had no reason to mistrust rating agencies' judgment that the loans' prices on the secondary market reflected their relative safety.

So long as home prices continued to rise, borrowers with subprime loans could continually refinance at new low teaser rates (though with new closing costs) and avoid default. But, as is well known, once the bubble burst, the teaser rates disappeared and the rate of foreclosures climbed.

By 2002, 25 percent of all subprime loans had been made to African Americans, who were about three times as likely to have them as similarly qualified whites.[54] In Buffalo, New York, the most extreme case, three-quarters of all loans to African Americans were subprime; in Chicago, borrowers buying homes in predominantly African American census tracts were four times as likely to have a subprime loan as borrowers in predominantly white census tracts.[55]

Regulatory failure by the Federal Reserve, the Office of the Comptroller of the Currency, and the Department of Housing and Urban Development, as well as the deep involvement of the quasi-public Fannie Mae and Freddie Mac,[56] thus made government complicit in this exacerbation of segregation. By 2008, 55 percent of black mortgage holders nationwide had subprime loans, compared with 17 percent of white mortgage holders.[57] Black borrowers were more likely to have loans with high rates and prepayment penalties than whites with similar characteristics.[58] The disparity was greatest in more segregated communities.[59]

A 2005 survey by the Federal Reserve found that nearly one-quarter of higher-income black borrowers had subprime mortgages, four times the rate of higher-income white borrowers. This is further indirect evidence that federally regulated lenders and brokers specializing in subprime lending probably targeted predominantly black communities.[60]

About 50 percent of all borrowers with subprime loans would have qualified for lower-rate conventional loans.[61] Typically, brokers received a bonus for steering borrowers (disproportionately but not exclusively African American) to subprime loans even when they qualified for conventional rates. The bonus, called a "yield spread premium" (YSP), was based on the difference between the lowest rate a borrower qualified for and the rate actually charged.

The state of Illinois and the cities of Baltimore and Memphis have sued one bank, Wells Fargo, claiming that their jurisdictions lost substantial tax revenues because epidemics of foreclosures resulting from discriminatory subprime lending contributed to the collapse of assessed value in segregated communities. One bank employee testified she was instructed to solicit borrowers in heavily African American zip codes because residents there "aren't so savvy." Another testified that bank officers referred to subprime loans as "ghetto loans."[62]

State-Sanctioned Violence and Discriminatory Policing

State and local governments used force to preserve residential segregation in two ways: by failing to protect black families from violence (or tacitly encouraging such violence) when these families have attempted to move to predominantly white neighborhoods, and by police harassment of black motorists or pedestrians who enter predominantly white neighborhoods.

I noted above that Philadelphia police refused to protect the construction of public housing in a white neighborhood. Most police inaction (or inadequate action) has involved failure to protect black families moving to white neighborhoods from more serious violence—firebombings, shootings, rock throwing, assaults, and vandalism. Such incidents numbered in the thousands. From mid-1944 to mid-1946, there were forty-six firebombings of the homes of blacks in white communities bordering Chicago's African American ghettos.[63] Similar violence took place in Louisville, Atlanta, Cleveland, Cincinnati, Dallas, Miami, Los Angeles, and elsewhere.[64] In Detroit alone there were more than two hundred such incidents in the two decades following World War II.[65]

In 1942 the Federal Works Agency built a Detroit housing project for black workers. Because they felt it was too close to their white neighborhood, two hundred white demonstrators blocked black families from moving in. Police refused to intervene, and a riot ensued. Police made little effort to protect the black movers; of approximately one hundred arrests during the riot, only three were of whites. Of the thirty-eight people hospitalized, only five were white.[66]

In 1964 a white civil rights activist in Chicago mayor Richard J. Daley's home neighborhood rented an apartment to African American college students. A mob gathered and pelted the building with rocks. Police entered the apartment, removed the students' belongings, and told the students on their return from school that they had been evicted.[67]

Leaders of violent anti-integration mobs, often easily identified leaders of neighborhood organizations, were rarely prosecuted. A 1925 mob that threatened to firebomb the home of a black family who had moved into a previously all-white Detroit neighborhood numbered five thousand. Mobs that gathered to prevent blacks from moving into white neighborhoods in Chicago in 1947 and 1951 were equally large.[68]

A US Senate committee report, considering the 1968 Fair Housing Law, noted that local officials frequently failed to prosecute racial violence intended to maintain segregation and concluded that "acts of racial terrorism have sometimes gone unpunished and have too often deterred the free exercise of constitutional and statutory rights."[69]

Move-in violence has continued more recently. In 1991 the Justice Department took jurisdiction in a case involving white cross-burners who attempted to drive black families out of a predominantly white area of Dubuque, Iowa, after state and local prosecutors made only token efforts at prosecution. In 1998 black residents of a housing project in a white neighborhood of Boston sued the city for failing to protect them from racial violence and harassment.[70]

Move-in violence not only has affected black pioneers subjected to such incidents, its chief impact is to intimidate other African Americans from attempting to integrate neighborhoods. Survey data reporting that black respondents prefer to live in predominantly black neighborhoods more likely result from this history than from black preference for self-segregation.

Discriminatory Provision of Municipal Services

Segregation has been exacerbated by municipalities that have provided fewer and less adequate services to neighborhoods where black residents predominate. Those neighborhoods then deteriorate, causing a loss of property value and keeping black families from accumulating equity to move to predominantly white neighborhoods or suburbs. The deterioration is also a disincentive for whites to purchase homes in these neighborhoods and stimulates remaining whites to leave. And the image of a slum neighborhood makes whites fear the effects on their own communities if they permit black families to move in.

Robert Moses, organizer of public services for New York State and New York City in the 1920s and 1930s, refused to build parks in black neighborhoods, asserting that blacks were dirty and would not keep them clean. He built only one playground in all of Harlem, claiming that land there was too expensive, yet he built many in other neighborhoods where land was more expensive. Moses believed African Americans did not like cold water, so to discourage them from using a public swimming pool in a white area only a few blocks from the ghetto, he kept this pool unheated while heating other pools throughout the city. Moses built Riverside Park, along the Hudson River: in its southern section, where few black families lived, he developed the park with tennis courts, promenades, and playgrounds, but similar expenditures were not made in the northern portion adjoining the ghetto. In 1943 a grand jury concluded that lack of recreational facilities, compared with other areas of the city, contributed to a Brooklyn ghetto's high crime rate.[71]

In a 1971 Mississippi case, a Federal Appeals Court found that

> nearly 98% of all homes that front on unpaved streets in Shaw are occupied by blacks [while those fronting on paved streets are occupied by whites]. Ninety-seven percent of the homes not served by sanitary sewers are in black neighborhoods [while those with sanitary sewers are in white neighborhoods]. Further, while the town has acquired a significant number of medium and high intensity mercury vapor street lighting fixtures, every one of them has been installed in

white neighborhoods. The record further discloses that similar statistical evidence of grave disparities in both the level and kinds of services offered regarding surface water drainage, water mains, fire hydrants, and traffic control apparatus was also brought forth and not disputed.[72]

In 2008 a federal jury awarded $11 million in damages to residents of a Zanesville, Ohio, African American neighborhood denied municipal water service for fifty years while white neighborhoods received it. As late as the 1980s, an official of the public regional water authority asserted that "those niggers will never have running water."[73]

Remedies

This chapter has offered accounts from the literature to illustrate the many aspects of government-sponsored segregation. Although it is not yet possible to demonstrate that these accounts reflect systematic practices in many if not most locations, further documentation by scholars would be worthwhile to make a more convincing case. Before memories are lost, interviews with African Americans who experienced residential segregationist policy should be a priority.

Space does not permit me to describe several other federal and state policies whose intent or effect was to create and preserve segregation. Among these are decisions about the location of school district boundaries and school attendance zones; urban renewal policies that reduced the supply of black housing while removing black residents from neighborhoods that white policymakers found desirable for other uses; federal interstate highways whose routes created impermeable barriers between black and white neighborhoods; and public transportation policies that eased the commutes of whites to good jobs in urban centers but not the commutes of blacks to suburban industrial jobs.

Neighborhood racial segregation partly results from the relative poverty of black families, who continue to be consigned to urban ghettos because they cannot afford homes in more affluent white-dominated suburbs. This income inequality has not resulted merely from race-neutral economic forces or private discrimination. Public policy has had the intent and effect of denying African Americans employment that would give them enough income to escape ghettos and upgrade housing to suburbs.

Among these were federal employment policies that barred African Americans from managerial civil service grades;[74] federal certification of the exclusive bargaining rights of labor unions that barred blacks from membership; denial of education and training for nonmenial jobs to qualified black veterans in the administration of the GI Bill;[75] and minimum wage, collective bargaining, and Social Security legislation that purposely excluded from coverage occupations where blacks predominated—agriculture, for example.[76] Such policies are also part of the nexus of interwoven state action that created and perpetuates racial ghettos.

Each of the policies described in this chapter promoted and preserved segregation. In combination, they constitute a system of state-sponsored residential segregation, with school segregation an inevitable consequence.

Although policies to integrate communities and schools should not be restricted to those ordered by courts, neither should judicially ordered remedies be excluded. Judges can, and should, order race-conscious public policies for integration, because they are necessary to undo the lasting effects of state-sponsored segregation.

Effective remedies must be metropolitan in scope, not restricted to a single city or suburb. Many cities, towns, and suburbs, as a direct result of state-sponsored segregation, are racially homogeneous, or nearly so; efforts to undo this segregation require regulations and incentives that result in mixing racial populations across municipal boundaries. Suburbs within metropolitan areas cannot be considered "innocent" of participation in the system of racial segregation, because their residential and economic growth was based on public policies of segregation.

Remedies cannot be effective if limited to a single jurisdiction within a metropolitan area, because such areas are integrated economically, if not racially. Thus, for example, as several jurisdictions have discovered, inclusionary zoning ordinances enacted in a single city or suburb are ineffective, because if there is a demand for housing, developers can easily build elsewhere in the area. If an entire county or even state is covered, however, developers could meet demand only by appropriate inclusionary development.

Many civil rights advocates believe that the Supreme Court's *Milliken* decision made metropolitanwide remedies impossible. There the Court refused to approve a plan that required predominantly white suburbs to accept black students transported from Detroit, on the grounds that because no evidence was produced that any suburb intentionally segregated the schools within its own borders, no suburb could be deemed responsible for segregation and so could not be forced to participate in plans to remedy segregation practiced within the city of Detroit. But this interpretation of *Milliken* does not account for Justice Stewart's observation in his concurrence (in which he deemed the causes of segregation to be "unknown and unknowable"):

> This is not to say, however, that an interdistrict remedy would not be proper, or even necessary, in other factual situations. Were it to be shown, for example, that state officials had contributed to the separation of the races by drawing or redrawing school district lines, by transfer of school units between districts, *or by purposeful, racially discriminatory use of state housing or zoning laws*, then a decree calling for transfer of pupils across district lines or for restructuring of district lines might well be appropriate.[77]

And he added in a footnote:

> The Constitution simply does not allow federal courts to attempt to change that situation [i.e., segregation of Detroit students from students elsewhere in the metropolitan area] unless and until it is shown that the State, or its political subdivisions, have contributed to cause the situation to exist. No record has been made in this case showing that the racial composition of the Detroit school population or that residential patterns within Detroit and in the surrounding areas were in any significant measure caused by governmental activity.[78]

But such a record would have been, and continues to be, easy to make.

In the 1976 Chicago public housing case, Stewart wrote the majority opinion and stressed that the *Milliken* decision did not preclude a metropolitanwide remedy if there was a metropolitanwide constitutional violation. In the Chicago case, civil rights groups proved that HUD and the CHA (authorized to build housing throughout the Chicago metropolitan area) had committed metropolitanwide constitutional violations, and therefore a metropolitanwide remedy was appropriate.

Stewart narrowed the impact of his Chicago ruling by permitting HUD to issue Section 8 housing vouchers in lieu of building suburban public housing. As a result, although vouchers were issued to African Americans living in segregated Chicago public housing, relatively little metropolitan integration resulted.

Curiously, few civil rights cases seem to have been brought in the past thirty-five years to take advantage of Justice Stewart's implicit invitation to prove metropolitanwide violations to support metropolitanwide remedies. Advocates have usually restricted their complaints to school issues, failing to claim that racial imbalance in schools primarily results not from school policy but from state-sponsored residential segregation. But the Court's position is consistent with the necessity of legislative as well as judicial action to craft statewide or national remedies to cure statewide or national violations. Remedies to promote integration could include policies on school district and school attendance boundary setting and pupil assignment; inclusionary residential zoning; public housing and housing subsidy policies; transportation policy; and aggressive regulation of bank, real estate, and fair employment practices.

Summary

The national consensus that school segregation now results only, or primarily, from demographic and economic forces is flawed. Students in both northern and southern communities are now racially isolated substantially as a result of explicit public policy, racially motivated. This public policy has, over the past century, ensured the segregation of residential communities. Notwithstanding the availability of some voluntary school choice, the racial composition of schools necessarily reflects the racial composition of their communities. If neighborhoods have been segregated de jure, it is meaningful to describe a neighborhood-based school system as also segregated de jure.

It follows that not only does racial isolation in schools today reflect poor educational policy, it also reflects unconstitutional segregation. Remedying a constitutional violation is the responsibility of all branches of government, not the judicial branch alone.

Yet for policymakers to consider remedial policies, Americans must confront the widespread lack of appreciation of how far the segregation of American society reflects public policy, and not merely race-blind demographic and economic forces.

PART 3
Strategies

CHAPTER 9

Family Values and School Policy

Shaping Values and Conferring Advantage

Harry Brighouse and Adam Swift

Introduction

Schooling systems in the United Kingdom and the United States, as in many other countries, grant parents a great deal of control over how their children are educated. Parents have the legal right to choose schools that will educate their children in particular value traditions; if such schools are not available within the publicly funded and provided system, parents may choose schools outside that system that do inculcate the values they approve of. If no such school is available, they have the option of homeschooling. In both countries state schools vary greatly in quality, and parents have considerable power to choose among them, through some formal mechanism of school choice or through the housing market. If their children are not admitted to a preferred school, parents may purchase private schooling at whatever price they are willing to pay.

So parents have the legal right to choose a school for their children that will inculcate parental values or help them confer advantage across generations. These two rights are institutionalized quite differently in the two countries. State schools in the United Kingdom are diverse, because

In addition to the sessions at the Institute of Advanced Studies in Princeton, this chapter has benefited from discussion at the American Political Science Association, a Morrell Conference at the University of York, and Oxford University's Centre for the Study of Social Justice.

the government runs many schools in collaboration with representatives of faith communities: Roman Catholic, Church of England, Methodist, Jewish, Hindu, Sikh, and Muslim schools all operate within the state system. Relatively few parents exit for religious reasons. In the United States state schools are much more uniform, and the government does not run any in collaboration with representatives of faith communities: to access schooling with an explicitly spiritual or religious dimension, parents have to resort to private schools or homeschooling. By contrast, the variability of quality (as measured, crudely, by spending) among state schools in the United States is high: schools in wealthy neighborhoods often spend as much as twice as much per student as schools in poor neighborhoods. It is rarely necessary to resort to private schools to confer competitive advantage. Government spending on schools in the United Kingdom, by contrast, tracks need, and to access elite education parents often must resort to private schools.

We recognize that these practices are consistent with popular views of parents' rights, with the demands of international rights human documents, and with the claims of many philosophers that parents have wide-ranging rights over their children. Still, in this chapter we explain why we deny that parents have such extensive fundamental rights to shape their children's values or to confer advantage on them, whether through schooling—public or private—or by other means. We argue that what is valuable about the family—"family values"—can be adequately respected and promoted without granting parents the right either to determine the content of their children's education or to confer advantage on them in ways that undermine fair equality of opportunity.[1] In philosophical terms, the state's duty to respect parents' rights and parent-child relationships does not imply a duty to permit schools that allow such determination and conferral, or a duty to let parents opt out of schooling on such grounds. So, for example, elite private schools are not protected by parents' rights, nor are religious schools, nor is some general policy of parental choice concerning schooling.

Our analysis of family values and parents' rights is conducted at an avowedly theoretical and "ideal" level of abstraction. Unlike philosophers, who can (and do) simply imagine better forms of society, policymakers and politicians are subject to practical conflicts and feasibility limitations. Constitutional law, democratic public opinion, entirely predictable responses by social actors to changing incentive structures, and many other factors come between philosophers' ideal scenarios and the real world. Family relationships and parents' interests, furthermore, are not the only values at stake, and other values might, in some circumstances, count in favor of allowing elite private and religious schools. Given our understanding of the effective political and social constraints, how might schools (or, more grandly, the school system) be reformed to promote a properly weighted balance of family values and other desirable goals?

First, we elaborate an account of the role of philosophy in evaluating education policy. Second, we summarize our theory of what is valuable about the family, introducing the idea of "familial relationship goods," which yields an account, outlined in the third section, of the kind of rights parents have with respect to their children. Subsequent sections set out the implications of our view specifically with respect to parents' rights to shape their children's values and to confer advantage on them. We emphasize the limits of those rights while also considering how policymakers might best promote an optimal balance of values—including "family values"—in circumstances where many believe those rights are extensive.[2]

How to Evaluate (Education) Policy

Political philosophers try to get as clear as possible about what values are valuable and how valuable they are relative to one another. They attempt to sort these values into principles that can guide the design of institutions. Actual political agents, of course, are never in a position to redesign institutions directly, but the values and principles philosophers articulate and defend give us a basis for judging how well or badly a given set of existing institutions realizes our ideals and guide us in designing reforms aimed at improving those institutions. So the distinctive contribution of philosophy to the process of evaluation and design is in identifying the relevant values. What should evaluators and designers do with the information provided by this contribution? Here is an ideal-typical sketch of how we think the interaction between philosophy and social science most usefully takes place. We describe the stages as if the procedure were linear, but in reality it is recursive—there are interactions between the stages.

The procedure would start by working out all the values in play, informed by the best political philosophy at our disposal—the "ingredients" in the recipe, as G. A. Cohen puts it[3]—together with an account of their weight relative to one another. These values must include not only those immediately pertinent to the area of policymaking under scrutiny but also those relating to other areas of social life where policy changes may have collateral effects. While the work of establishing the values is philosophical, conjectures about collateral effects themselves must be informed by social science; even at this stage of the procedure philosophers will find it easier to inform decision making if they have an understanding of institutions and the relevant social science. These values must also include those relevant to the assessment of the means or procedures by which outcomes may be brought about. For example, policymakers who are unaccountable may lack democratic authority even if their actions promote social justice, just as policymakers may be acting legitimately even if their policies are unjust.[4]

The next stage involves looking at the world, assessing how well it realizes the values at stake and exactly how it falls short of realizing each of them. It is impossible to do this without knowing what values are at stake, but we also need extensive social scientific evidence that is sensitive to precisely those values.

The third stage is assessing what changes are feasible in the circumstances. Identifying the feasible set requires both careful description of existing states of affairs—to judge well where we can realistically hope to get to from here, we need to know precisely where we are—and predictions—with probabilities and timescales—about the likely effects of any things we might do to change them, which itself presupposes adequate understanding of social mechanisms and causal processes.

At the fourth and final stage we establish, among the feasible set of reforms, which would constitute the best improvement, all things considered. Given that only in the most fortunate circumstances will one option, or consistent package of options, create improvements with respect to all values, this requires judgment about which are more urgent in the given situation.

A good deal easier said than done: we might think of this multistage procedure as itself an "ideal theory" of how to get from philosophy to policy. Every stage is difficult, and the difficulties compound. At the first, even the best philosophers are significantly less skilled at giving persuasive reasons for making judgments of relative weight than at identifying relevant values in appropriate detail, even when they can get agreement on precisely what those values are. At the second, nobody ever has a full and accurate description of the state of the world, or even of the state of the part of the world they are particularly interested in. Not only do we lack some of the details, but we lack certainty about the details we do have. And even if we had agreement about the relative weight of all the values in play, our lacking full information about the state of the world means we are going to have at best partial information about the ways those values fail to be realized optimally.

The third and fourth stages are harder still. By "an adequate understanding of the social mechanisms and causal processes" we may well have to mean something very weak, with uncertain probabilities and short timescales. The social world is full of complexity and unintended consequences, and often we will have to make and act on judgments about what to do when, despite the best efforts of social scientists, we can rely on no more than informed guesses about what will happen if we do it. We have to make judgments about what actors actually have the capacity to do in the circumstances we are creating by introducing the reform and to consider, even if they do have the capacity, whether the incentives are well calibrated to get them to act as we want and whether the resources are available for them to respond effectively to the incentives. Even if we hold some policies to be feasible in the longer term, we cannot directly access our most preferred states of affairs, so we have to attend carefully to the dynamics those actions are likely to set in motion. This is likely to involve hard judgments about how much to aim for when, how to balance more likely short-term gain against lower probability long-term gain, how to weigh small but more robust progress against bigger but more easily reversed progress, and so on. These uncertainties, of course, create plenty of room for disagreement about what should be done even between those who would evaluate concrete outcomes, and the means of achieving them, in the same way.

In the context of this volume, one aspect of our method is worth emphasis. To act effectively, governments have to divide up their work, so policy is pursued in distinct sectors. But, as Jonathan Wolff and Avner De-Shalit observe, an approach that focuses exclusively on a particular sector is problematic because "there is often leakage between areas of decision-making."[5] Health policy decisions can affect education—elementary schools in the United States, for example, face problems with students whose vision and hearing problems go undiagnosed and untreated because the health system is not designed to identify and treat them in children from low-income families. In most states, housing and education policy are administered, and to a large extent made, at the local level, but by separate bodies elected by distinct electorates. Almost everywhere housing policy encourages neighborhoods to be segregated by socioeconomic status, but those making education policy have incentives to create integrated schools, which is politically difficult and financially costly when neighborhoods are segregated. Some of the leakage is relatively easy to identify before the fact, and at the macro level attentive decision makers can coordinate with other agencies. But some is very hard even for imaginative observers to see and, even when seen, lower-level agencies can find it impossible to cooperate efficiently because they answer to different regulations. It is natural, then, for much debate to be carried out within conventionally defined policy sectors. But, *pace* Michael Walzer, "educational goods," "health goods," "familial goods," "economic goods," and "transportation goods" are not distinct spheres in the sense that we should aim to promote and distribute them according to some rule that governs *just those goods*.[6] Rather, goods contribute in different ways to people's well-being. Some support others (some kinds of ill health undermine our use of education, some educational outcomes underpin our ability to have successful family lives and derive well-being from economic goods); some can substitute for others (education can enhance someone's well-being enough to substitute for lower income); and some make contributions to well-being only through effects on the others (transportation). It is important to analyze particular goods and their distribution quite narrowly, but all-things-considered judgments will take into account the relation between their distribution and that of other goods.

What's Valuable about the Family?

We call our particular account of what justifies the family the "familial relationship goods" account.[7] It is a variant of what Simon Keller calls a "special goods" justification: the family is justified because it helps realize very valuable goods that cannot be produced, or cannot as reliably be produced, under other arrangements.[8] We believe the family is justified because it provides an institution in which children's interests can be well met, and in which adults' interest in having a parental relationship with a child, which makes a distinctive and important contribution to adult flourishing, can be well realized.

Here, briefly, are some of the goods the family distinctively realizes for both children and adults:

• Children enjoy the loving attention of, and bond with, a particular adult, a relationship that is widely regarded as essential for their emotional development but is also valuable in other ways.

- Children enjoy the security provided by the presence of someone with a special duty of care for them and are assigned to someone who will, more or less reliably, see to it that their interests in cognitive, physical, emotional, and moral development are met.
- Adults enjoy a distinctively valuable relationship with the children they parent that differs from all other relationships in its qualities and its contribution to their ability to flourish in life.

The first two goods accrue to children. The family may not be the only arrangement that could fulfill these interests adequately, but we believe that any alternative institution would have to ensure the construction of a parentlike bond between some adults and each child; its successful establishment and maintenance would raise the same issues as those that animate us here.

The third good accrues to adults. The institution of the family allows them to have a relationship of a kind that cannot be replaced by relationships with other adults, for example. The child is spontaneously loving and intimate with the parent and is transparent to the parent in way that is not symmetrical. The parent has a special duty to protect and promote the child's interests including the interest most children have in becoming someone who no longer needs a parent's special duty of care. The idea that parents have fiduciary duties toward their children is familiar from Locke (though the precise content of those duties is widely disputed).[9] Our additional claim is that adults have a nonfiduciary interest in playing the fiduciary role; it is valuable for their children that they play it well, but is also a distinctive source of their own flourishing. To provide this good for adults, the institution for child rearing needs to be the family, or something that mimics the family very closely.

Familial relationship goods are, we think, great goods. Measures adopted in pursuit of equality of opportunity, or even full distributive justice, would be deeply problematic if they jeopardized their realization. But recognition of, or respect for, "the family" is not all or nothing. We can assess case by case whether the appeal to "family values" justifies the mechanisms by which parents shape their children's values, or confer advantage on them, by looking at the role those mechanisms play in realizing familial relationship goods. Roughly, the value of the family gives us strong reason to protect activities essential for creating and sustaining the loving, intimate relationship that is essential for meeting children's interests and is also valuable for the parent, but not for the protection of other things that parents do to, with, and for their children.

What Rights Do Parents Have and What Rights Don't They Have?

The core right that parents have is the right to an intimate relationship of a certain kind with their children. From this we can derive a series of associational rights required to protect that relationship. As Rob Reich explains, "Raising a child is never merely a service rendered to another person but is the collective sharing of a life."[10] This has implications for the character of the permissions parents must have to share aspects of their lives with their children. The most obvious is that they must have the right to live with their children and spend a substantial part of the day with them—without this they cannot get to know them, nor can the children get to know their parents, in the ways necessary for intimacy. Beyond that, they must be permitted to share many of their enthusiasms with their children, including their particular cultural and religious heritage. Consider two paradigm cases: reading bedtime stories and bringing children to a place of worship.

Reading a bedtime story does several things simultaneously. Parents are intimately sharing physical space with their children, providing background for future discussions, preparing them for sleep, and, if they are young, calming them and reinforcing their identification one with another. They are giving children exclusive attention at a particularly important time of day. They are free to select stories that take children to faraway places or that take them both back to the parent's childhood or, in some families, to grandparents' and great-grandparents' childhoods. Even if the children select a favorite story, their love of the story is often not unrelated to their parent's feelings about it.

Bringing children to a place of worship, similarly, does several things simultaneously. Parents are exposing them to stories about the past, inducting them into a community of faith, giving them the opportunity to be self-consciously spiritual in the particular way encouraged by that community, and laying the groundwork for understanding the specific guidance for living given by the faith tradition in question. Parents are also supplying the basis for a shared language and shared understanding that provide the background for disagreements and convergences about how children should live their lives when they have matured enough to make judgments for which they must bear some responsibility.

To sustain intimate relationships with others, it is not enough to spend a good deal of time with them; one must be free to be oneself in their presence—to express spontaneous enthusiasm for things one cares about and to denigrate things one abhors. When raising children, a good deal of self-monitoring is surely appropriate, but too much undermines intimacy. Spontaneous enthusiasm and denigration will surely shape children's values, even where that is not their aim. But beyond this, some deliberate attempts to create shared values may also be required. One can readily imagine intimacy despite people's having different religious beliefs or different intellectual interests or different aesthetic or sporting tastes, but without *some* overlap in interests and values it is hard for intimacy to have a basis. Without substantial opportunity to share themselves intimately with their children, in ways that reflect their own judgments about what is valuable, parents' ability to forge and maintain an intimate relationship is in jeopardy. Both parents and children lose out and the loss goes to the core of what is valuable about the relationship. If parents were barred from engaging in these or relevantly similar activities, it would be impossible for them to realize the relationship goods that justify the family.

Children have an interest in continuing an intimate relationship with their parents into adulthood. In the earliest years the enthusiasms, values, and experiences being shared can only come from the parents because there is no alternative in which the parents are genuinely sharing themselves with their children. Later, and not much later, children will come to have their own enthusiasms and values, and in any healthy intimate relationship there is give and take. Parents might have no liking at all for hip-hop music but succeed in fostering some sympathy when a child becomes a hip-hop enthusiast. They might watch their children play soccer only under duress but really try to learn about, and come to share, a fascination with tortoises or fashion. Parents are acting both in their own interests and in their children's when they do so, and they have an obligation to try to overcome the common reluctance to developing new enthusiasms as part of maintaining a connection with a growing child.

Note that these rights of parents are not connected to or derived from their separate interests in freedom of religion, association, or expression, or from their expressive interests more generally.[11] They derive from the interest, shared by children and adults, in having *a relationship of a certain kind*. In current circumstances, for some parents, that relationship will confer competitive advantage on some children, advantaging them over others in myriad ways. But where the effect is to deprive others of fair equality of opportunity, our account of why parents must be permitted to enjoy that kind of relationship does not imply the permission to achieve that outcome. If measures were taken to reduce the conferring of

advantage—for example, by equalizing wage rates or by increasing investment in the human capital development of other children—parents would
have no grounds for complaint about their rights with respect to their children. In the absence of those measures, parents may find themselves conferring competitive advantage, which they have no moral right to do, simply by
interacting with their children in ways that are indeed protected by
rights.

Shaping Values and Schooling

So parents have a right to a relationship with their children that will inevitably lead to some shaping of children's values and a derivative right to
shape those values as necessary to sustain a healthy relationship. Does this
give them a right to demand that the state either provide, or allow them
to resort to, schools in which their children will be educated in strict accordance with their values? We believe not.

Other values are at stake. Two obvious ones are the interest both
their children and other people have in the children's becoming competent citizens and the interest their children have in developing the capacity to make independent and reason-responsive judgments on matters
fundamental to how they will live their lives. We'll focus on the second.[12]
Children have an interest in developing their capacity for considered and
reflective judgment, for self-knowledge, and for adopting and developing
the ability to revise what Rawls refers to as a "conception of the good"—a
more or less cohesive set of action-guiding values. This interest, which for
simplicity's sake we'll call an interest in autonomy, stands in the way of
allowing parents the level of control over children's values that they have
over the revision of their own. The right to parent a child is conditional on
parents' discharging their fiduciary duties, and parents' rights over their
children do not extend beyond those required for them to do that. The
duty to do what they can to enable their children to develop the capacity
for autonomy is a key part of the job description.

Why do children have an interest in becoming autonomous? The arguments fall into two broad camps. Some emphasize the role that making
and acting on one's own informed judgments plays in individual well-
being. Joseph Raz, for example, argues that in modern societies, in which
one has considerable freedom and in which one's environment is constantly changing, autonomy is an important tool for negotiating unavoid-

able choices.[13] Another argument points out that people vary considerably in their personal constitutions: ways of life that would indeed contribute to the flourishing of some people raised in them do not contribute to that of others, so self-knowledge and the ability to make independent critical judgments are vital if the latter are to live good lives from the inside. A homosexual who experiences his homosexuality as unchangeable simply cannot live well in a heterosexual marriage. Trapped, he will be alienated from it and from himself; there is nothing wrong with the way of life, but if he cannot endorse it as good for him, he cannot flourish within it. Similarly, some women's lives cannot go well while abiding by the particular demands—modesty, sexual fidelity—of a religion they may have been raised in. Different ways of life elevate different virtues, and some children are ill constituted to develop those their parents affirm.

Other arguments focus instead on the dignity of the individual. Even if the judgments I make for myself do not make my life go any better than had I unthinkingly complied with the demands or expectations of others—indeed even if my judgments make it go worse—there is value in being the author of my own life. And I am truly its author only if I live my life at least partly as a response to the reasons there are for living it, knowing some alternatives. The heteronomy of conforming unreflectively to one's parents' expectations no more confers dignity than does the heteronomy of simply following one's animal passions. Though we cannot argue for it in the space available here, we believe that both strands of argument for autonomy have considerable force.

It will be obvious how parents' freedom to choose the school their children attend might frustrate the development of the capacity for autonomy. There is an extensive literature on the issues attending famous US court cases such as *Wisconsin v. Yoder* (in which Amish parents argued that their right to free exercise of religion meant their children should be exempt from a law requiring that all children attend school to age sixteen) and *Mozert v. Hawkins* (in which a group of "fundamentalist" Christian parents argued that their children should be exempt from a civics curriculum containing textbook material they objected to).[14] Our view on these familiar issues is that, whatever the constitutional or legal situation, parents' rights over their children extend only to those compatible with meeting their fiduciary duties, which include the duty to enable the development of the child's capacity for autonomy.

Much discussion of this issue focuses on the rights of religious parents, or on their violations of their children's rights. But secular parents too can compromise their children's prospective autonomy. Think of those who go to such lengths to shield their children from exposure to religious traditions, commitments, and practices that the children cannot adopt any of them. Some who accuse religious parents of indoctrination or compromising autonomy may well be doing the same thing themselves. Some social environments cooperate quite well with parents who, while they value their children's making independent judgments within a secular range, want to shield them from religious traditions; with such cooperation it is easy not to notice that one is breaking faith with one's commitment to their prospective autonomy. For children to have a chance of adopting a religious or spiritual way of life—or of reflecting on, and perhaps adjusting, their parents' secular worldview in a way that is informed by an understanding of what such a way of life has to offer—they must usually have real contact with those who live such lives. Reading books, watching documentaries, and visiting places of worship are not enough. They must encounter spiritual practices and religious faith in the reality of people's lives, articulated in real lived experience, for which they need close extended contact with sincere religious practitioners. For that to happen they have to be in environments populated in part by such people, and those environments must be structured to make close interaction likely.

In our society the most promising such environment is, in fact, the school. But insofar as parents choose schools (whether state or private) to shape their children's values to match their own, we can anticipate that children from secular and faith backgrounds will be less likely to encounter one another. In many parts of the United States, for example, children from evangelical Christian families are (ironically) dramatically underrepresented within public schools because they congregate in lightly regulated private Christian schools. Not only is *their* prospective autonomy compromised by this practice—so is the prospective autonomy of those children from secular families whose parents make no independent effort to ensure that they have close and continuing interaction with children from religious backgrounds.

This last observation helps explain why our view about the importance of autonomy does not imply a general hostility to religious schooling, or schooling with a spiritual dimension, at the policy level. Putting aside for a moment that policymakers rightly have several aims for education, of which safeguarding children's prospective autonomy is only one, whether religious schools should be prohibited, permitted, funded, or integrated into the public system turns on which of those policies best serves the overall goal of ensuring that all children have an education that adequately serves their interest in becoming autonomous without excessively threatening healthy parent-child relationships. Some discussions of these issues assume that nonreligious schools serve an interest in becoming autonomous better than religious schools do. But many nonreligious schools inhibit the development of autonomy by promoting unreflective acceptance of the values and norms that prevail in the mainstream society their students already inhabit.

In any case, the effectiveness of particular kinds of school should not be the central issue for policymakers. For safeguarding autonomy, as for educational aims more generally, policymakers should be interested not in what kind of school best advances the aims, but in which of the feasible arrangements for the school system as a whole best serve the aims in the circumstances.

Consider the following case. Should the UK government selectively fund and collaborate in the governance of willing Muslim schools? Let us suppose, for the sake of argument, that Muslim schools serve the autonomy of children who attend them less well than other schools. In the United Kingdom it is almost certainly illegal to prohibit children's attending Muslim schools, and many Muslim parents can afford Muslim private schooling. So policymakers have a choice: leave all Muslim schools out of the public system, in which case parents will continue to use them but they will be entirely separate from other schools, or fund and collaborate in governing selected schools that will to some extent be integrated into the public system. The policymaker should take a strategic stance, considering the middle- and longer-term effects of each option on educational aims, including personal autonomy, and take into account such factors as how many children will attend Muslim schools under each regime, what those schools will be like, and how the design of the regime will affect the integration of Muslims into the surrounding social environment. Relevant information will be gathered by wide consultation, which should not be exclusively with self-styled "representatives" of the community in question, and policymakers must understand that respect for values of democratic legitimacy will sometimes restrict them from actions that would otherwise be justified. Our view, based on observation and some knowledge of the situation rather than on rigorous examination of the evidence, is that the wise option in these circumstances is the second—which policymakers have, in fact, taken.

Of course, in the United States, where the Supreme Court forbids governments to collaborate with religious organizations in governing schools, this kind of policy is simply not available. And it might be that in the different political and cultural environment of the United States such a policy would not have the desired effects even if it were.

Suppose that, as in the United States and the United Kingdom, religious schools are legally accessible. What should policymakers aim for within nonreligious schools? We have suggested that autonomy requires that children from religious families come into contact with other ways of life that make them meaningfully available, and the same for nonreligious children. Secular schools should be inviting to religious parents and their children, not only to serve those children's capacity for autonomy by inducing them to attend the schools, but to create an environment in which nonreligious children can become autonomous.

As we have said, educators rightly have several aims for children, and safeguarding their prospective autonomy, albeit important, is just one.[15] Policymakers should promote these goals as best they can, understanding that trade-offs will have to be made. So, for example, a policy that best safeguards the prospective autonomy of the most children may be worse than some other policy with respect to fair equality of opportunity or the production of competent democratic citizens. The hope is that educational aims are congruent in the circumstances and that some feasible policy does very well with respect to them all, but there are no guarantees. When there are conflicts, policymakers must manage the trade-offs, weighing the goods at stake as best they can.

We have not asked what stance the government should take toward religious schooling in ideal circumstances. Rather, we have factored in certain feasibility constraints that reflect the particular circumstances of the countries in question: in particular the constraint that religious schooling must be permitted. One might think, for example, that in principle religious schools should be prohibited, and that doing so would be consistent with fully respecting familial relationship goods, while still holding that, as long as religious schooling is not prohibited, the stance of the government to religious schools should be open and welcoming.

We say that parents have no right to choose schools in which their children will be educated in strict accordance with their values. Does this mean they should have no say at all over the ethos or values of the schools their children attend? One might think they have ample opportunity to influence the formation of their children's values within the home and that, since schools are an obvious way to institutionalize children's interest in being exposed to additional and sometimes contradictory influences, parents have no right at all to a say over schools. We do not have a full account

of how far parents should be able to use schooling to influence their children's values, but we do believe there is an important "family value" that
should be factored into judgments about how schools treat students and
what they teach them. While serving the educational interests of children
broadly conceived, the school should do what it can to avoid jeopardizing
or interfering with healthy parent-child relationships.

Schools in Nazi Germany and the Soviet Union obviously failed in this
respect when they encouraged children to disclose their parents' disloyalty
to the state. Efforts by the US government to educate Native Americans
were similarly pernicious.[16] But some failures are less obvious. Consider
that some religious parents in the United States fear that the public school
their child might attend will hold their religious practices, values, and
faith in contempt. They worry that the child will be both disdained and
turned against them. Yet many such parents have healthy relationships
with their children. And while their fears may in many cases be exagger-
ated, grounded as they often are in false beliefs promoted by religious and
political entrepreneurs, sometimes they are well founded. In some public schools many, and sometimes most, of the authoritative adults scorn
evangelical or fundamentalist versions of Christianity, or of Islam, often
in considerable ignorance of the relevant beliefs and practices. It is not
unreasonable for parents to fear that, in these schools, teachers will be
exasperated with students from such families, and sometimes intolerant,
even where their values and commitments are as well grounded, thought
out, and defended as those of others whose beliefs teachers tolerate and
sometimes embrace. Nor is it unreasonable to worry that this situation
may harm healthy parent-child relationships without contributing to the
child's autonomy (quite apart from any collateral effects on the level of
alienation religious communities feel from public institutions). School districts frequently train teachers to be sensitive to cultural and racial diversity, but they rarely train them in religious sensitivity. Yet it can be just as
damaging to a parent-child relationship to express or imply contempt for
religious commitments as for cultural commitments or racial heritage.[17]

Conferring Advantage and Schooling

School systems in both the United States and the United Kingdom afford
advantaged parents ways to choose schools that will confer advantage on
their children. The detailed mechanisms, and the role of government, are

importantly different in the two countries, which in turn makes a difference to all things considered optimal policy proposals. When discussing
the philosophical issues, however, we can treat them together, which we
will do by talking about "elite" schools—understanding "elite" rather
loosely as a shorthand term for "advantaged schools that enable advantaged parents to confer advantages on their children." Such schools may
be in the public or the private sector, and of course "eliteness" in this
sense admits of degree. There are two interesting questions here. The first
is about policy: Do familial relationship goods require governments to
design the education system in a way that permits advantaged parents to
use it to confer advantage on their children? The second is about parents:
Given the way education systems are in fact designed, in what circumstances, if any, do familial relationship goods justify parents' using the
opportunities for conferring advantage that it creates?[18]

Some would argue that elite schooling compromises the interests of the
child so schooled: just as direct observation of religious children is needed
for informed choice about the ways to live a life, so, perhaps, the autonomy
of privileged children depends on their awareness of how those in different
socioeconomic groups live. Others would point rather to the democratic
case for socially integrated schools: citizens' political judgments should be
informed by the perspectives of all members of one's political community
and by an understanding of how decisions affect their lives. We will focus
instead on the fact that elite private schooling jeopardizes an important
component of social justice—the principle of equal opportunity according to which social background, as manifested, for example, in parental
income and wealth, should not influence one's prospects.[19] If elite private
schooling enhances the prospects of those who receive it, then it conflicts
with equal opportunity. But so, by hypothesis, does reading bedtime stories, a practice we have argued must not be prohibited. Is there a relevant
difference?

There is. Recall our description of what is going on when a parent
reads to a child at bedtime—it amounts to an intimate sharing of the self.
Of course, reading bedtime stories is not the only way of doing this. Different families may realize familial relationship goods by telling stories
rather than reading them, by dancing, singing, playing, cooking, or eating
together, or in many other ways. What we dispute is that these kinds of
goods are normally produced by sending a child to an elite school. This is
a different kind of activity, concerned with which other adults and children
will interact with one's child and in what ways.

We said "normally." Two kinds of exception are worth mentioning. One is when the child's interests will not adequately be served unless the parent exercises a particular choice. Imagine a child who is being severely bullied in a regular school, or whom serious emotional difficulties put at risk of depression and other consequences in a regular setting. Parents may reasonably believe that exercising a choice of school is necessary, in this case, to meet their fiduciary duties to the child. This exception would not, though, be a reason to protect elite schools as we have defined them. It may, in current circumstances, justify parents' opting out of the state school system, and it may give governments reason to provide adequately for children with special needs of this kind, but there is no justification here for protecting parents' opportunity to confer advantage on their children. The other kind of exception is more interesting. Sometimes parents send their children to elite private schools not so they can gain competitive advantage over others, but because they want them to have access to, enjoy, and participate in certain experiences that will connect them to one another. Perhaps they are sending their children to the school they themselves attended, or the same kind of school in a different location; or perhaps they judge that only at this school, or a school of this kind, will students acquire a love of Latin or science that parent and child will share or, if they are immigrants, become appropriately connected to the culture of their parents' country of origin.

We have a couple of observations about such cases. The first concerns the alternative means by which parents and children can realize familial relationship goods. That a particular interaction is a vehicle for their realization is insufficient to establish that parents should be permitted to engage in that interaction, since there may be other ways families can do as well, or well enough, in terms of "family values" but that are less disruptive of equal opportunity. Parents do not have a right to just that set of options realizing familial relationship goods that they prefer, and where their preferred options undermine equal opportunity (or other values) in very great ways, it is not unreasonable to expect them to seek their realization by other means. Does the relationship really depend on a shared love of Latin? If so, couldn't parents teach it themselves?

The second observation concerns the relation between familial relationship goods, on the one hand, and the other benefits that may—but need not—accrue to those who receive them. Even where the freedom to engage in a particular interaction is essential for realizing such goods, and granting that freedom is indeed required, all things considered in the circumstances, we should be clear that that consideration yields no protection for the receipt of other incidental or extrinsic benefits. And insofar as the education itself should be conceived as a kind of advantage, it yields no reason not to adopt other measures to equalize prospects for well-being between children who do and do not receive it by, for example, taxing the benefit. Suppose state school systems cannot offer all families what they really do need to enjoy the kind of relationships we have been talking about. It may then be that those parents should be permitted to opt out of the system and provide for themselves, privately. But in that case the government would be doing no wrong if it attempted to undermine the capacity of those schools to confer advantage. Which is to say that defending private schooling by an appeal to family values is not a defense of the freedom to send one's children to an *elite* school.

Many will think our emphasis on the goods of intimate relationships misses the simple truth that part of what it means to love others is to wish them to be better-off. Parents prevented from acting on their loving motivation to promote their children's well-being—by means that would include sending them to elite schools—are being denied a good that is distinctively made available by parent-child relationships. We do not dispute that claim. What we do deny is that *that* good is weighty enough to warrant the state's being required to permit parents to engage in those interactions or transmissions if they conflict with other children's interest in equal opportunity. As long as there is ample space for parents to realize the really important familial relationship goods, those that yield our primary account of the family's value, parents have no claim to the further freedoms needed for them to act on their loving motivation generally to further their children's interests, where granting those freedoms would undermine equal opportunity.

What might a policymaker do with these observations? We won't attempt to provide a framework for an entirely just education system. Instead we want to sketch how our observations might inform quite specific decisions about issues that frequently face those who make policy in real-world circumstances.

We should begin by noting that nothing in our argument warrants the conclusion that governments should, indeed, abolish elite schools or even mitigate all their effects that produce inequality of opportunity. We have argued only that claims about parents' rights and family values do not justify their protection.[20] Other reasons might support maintaining such schools, and the inequalities of opportunity they tend to produce, in some circumstances. To take just one example, what if it turned out that, once deprived of the ability to confer advantage on their children, relatively advantaged parents expended their resources in a less socially productive manner, for example, on excessive private consumption? Then one might think that, despite the negative effects on equal opportunity, it is better to give them avenues to invest in their children's human capital: if, for example, some principle of benefiting the less advantaged is prior to a principle of equal opportunity, and if we have reason to believe that the marginal increase in the human capital of the unfairly advantaged children will be turned to the benefit of the less advantaged.[21]

But consider two more specific policy proposals. The first, discussed in Richard Rothstein's contribution to this volume, is inclusionary zoning: requiring new housing developments to be mixed race and mixed income. One of Rothstein's several rationales for measures like this is to achieve a mix within local school populations, without which, he suspects, it is next to impossible to provide equitable educational experiences to disadvantaged children. The second proposal is to supplement the spending on disadvantaged children either through "weighted student funding" (United States) or a "pupil premium" (United Kingdom). The purpose of this widely used measure is to channel more funding and, presumably, better educational experiences to disadvantaged children.[22] Depending on the facts, equal opportunity might recommend such measures in particular circumstances. Neither, of course, is in itself likely to make a large difference to the inequalities within the system: both at best provide conditions making it more possible for committed policymakers and administrators to tackle serious educational disadvantage.

How might the proposals raise issues concerning the value of the family? Think first about inclusionary zoning. Some may complain that this is an attack on the family because the zoning measures, if widely in place, would inhibit parents' ability to raise their children as they see fit. Since by our account there is no right to raise one's child as one sees fit, this complaint has no weight. If choosing the community where one raises one's children were like reading bedtime stories, there might be a case. But there are two problems with this line of reasoning. First, *all* zoning ordinances affect how far parents can choose the community where they raise their children. Since exclusionary zoning is now rare in the United States, consider by contrast the common practice of "large lot" zoning— setting large minimum size requirements on both lots and the houses built on them in particular new developments. Large lot zoning restricts poor parents' ability to live in communities where their children will come into regular contact with more advantaged children. It also restricts the ability of affluent parents to choose communities where their children will inter- act regularly with others from the full socioeconomic spectrum. Parents who seek to raise their children within a socioeconomically homogeneous community are no more inhibited by inclusionary zoning than parents who seek to raise their children in mixed communities are inhibited by "large lot" and other zoning practices. Second, choosing to raise one's child in a homogeneous socioeconomic community just does not seem relevantly like reading bedtime stories. Except, perhaps, in very special cases, the choice of exactly where to live, and who else lives in one's neighborhood, does not have implications for the kind of relationship we think of as being at the core of what is valuable about the family.

A different objection would claim that parents realize familial relation- ship goods whenever they act on their loving motivation to promote their children's interests, and that inclusionary zoning restricts some parents' capacity to do that. We agree with both claims, but neither makes the ob- jection a good one. First, as we argued above, that particular relationship good is simply not weighty enough to warrant respect when that would un- dermine equal opportunity. Second, advancing that good against propos- als for inclusionary zoning is beside the point, because there is no default zoning regime. Any change in regime will make it easier for some parents, and harder for others, to advance their children's interests relative to the status quo. Large lot zoning gives wealthy parents even more ability to advance their children's interests; inclusionary zoning reduces their abil- ity but enhances the same ability of less advantaged parents. We think of familial relationship goods as among the goods whose distribution should concern a theory of justice. Different zoning regimes distribute those goods differently.

Similar points could be made against attempts to claim that the pupil premium or weighted student funding undermines familial relationship goods. It is true that these must be paid for out of taxes, reducing the ability of taxed parents to advance their children's interests. And it is true that estate or inheritance taxes are often experienced as attacks on the family in a more direct or immediate way, where the property so taxed is conceived as earned for, and belonging to, the family rather than the individual.[23] But again, all-things-considered judgments would surely re- gard children's interest in equality of opportunity as more weighty than wealthy parents' interest in conferring advantage on their children (and children's interest in receiving that advantage), even while conceding that some loving familial interactions would thereby be prevented. Remember that where the advantage is competitive, each family's ability to confer it is bought at the expense of another family's. And second, if the premium is large enough to affect the quality of the schooling disadvantaged children receive, it increases disadvantaged parents' ability to advance *their* children's interests. In fact, because a pupil premium, if large enough and implemented within the right kind of management structure, could substantially change the quality of schooling such children receive, for some parents it may make the difference between being unable and able to meet their children's fundamental interests, thus considerably enhancing the realization of familial relationship goods relative to the status quo.

It is worth noting that policymakers attempting to promote equal opportunity through schooling in a society that accords parents a good deal of freedom always face the problem that advantaged parents have a good deal of scope to secure competitive advantage for their children by acting outside the school system and the school day. We make no claim that regulating schooling is the only, or even the most efficient, way of making opportunities more equal.

Conclusion

So parents have a right to a certain kind of relationship with their children, one that will inevitably and justifiably lead to their shaping their children's values to some extent. Schools and school policy should try not to undermine this relationship, but parents' rights over their children extend only to those compatible with meeting their fiduciary duties, which include enabling their children to develop autonomy: the interests of the child in developing the faculties, traits, and knowledge needed to make reason-responsive judgments must carry a great deal of weight in the decisions schools and policymakers make, and in their negotiations with parents. Parents have no right at all to use the school system to advantage their own children in ways that undermine equality of opportunity, and schools and policymakers should resist their attempts to do so while understanding that other important values (such as benefiting less advantaged members of society) might sometimes count in favor of focusing additional resources on talented or well-placed children.

School policymakers have to consider the full range of values at stake, weighing them against each other and using the best information available about both how those values are realized on the ground and how proposed feasible changes will affect their realization. We have tried to illustrate this by outlining a somewhat precise account of what constitutes family values and asking how they should guide and constrain policymakers in shaping policies concerning religious schooling and promoting equal opportunity. Many readers doubtless will reject our conclusions. That might be because they disagree about what fundamental values are at stake, about how they should be weighed against each other, about what is feasible, or about the likely actual effects of different policies (or about more than one of these possible sources of disagreement). If we have not persuaded our readers, we hope we at least have helped them identify why not.

CHAPTER 10

The Federal Role in Educational Equity

The Two Narratives of School Reform and the Debate over Accountability

Patrick McGuinn

The fundamental lesson of the last seven years, it seems to me, is that education investment without accountability can be a real waste of money. But accountability without investment can be a real waste of effort. Neither will work without the other. If we want our students to learn more we should do both. — President William J. Clinton (2000)

Introduction

This chapter is meant to demonstrate how the philosophical debates about education, democracy, and justice described in this volume translate into the politics and policymaking of school reform at the federal level. Two crucial facts drive the school reform debate in America today: the enormous impact of poverty on educational opportunity and student achievement, and the inability to date of our public schools to compensate for the educational disadvantages stemming from poverty. While most observers agree that there is both a socioeconomic dimension and a schooling dimension to America's educational problems, there is considerable disagreement about which is more important and should form the starting point for policymaking. For some, poverty is the decisive issue, and it is misguided and unreasonable to expect schools to generate substantial improvement in educational outcomes without broader efforts to address socioeconomic gaps. Others, however, believe that schools can have a major impact on their own if reforms alter the way they are financed, governed, staffed, and held accountable for results.

The history of school reform in the United States over the past half century has in many ways been a struggle between proponents of these two views. For much of the 1960s through 1990s, adherents of the "external to schools" view predominated, and state and federal policy focused primarily on integration and on bringing additional resources to the education of disadvantaged students that could compensate for educational deficits in the home. Because the nation's educational problems were largely attributed to poverty and to deficits in school resources, dysfunctional school policies that perpetuated educational inequalities went largely unaddressed. This philosophical debate over the role of schools was further complicated by an ideological divide over the proper role of the federal government in education. The result was little federal effort around creating accountability for student achievement or promoting innovative strategies for improving underperforming schools. Over the past two decades, however, the pendulum has swung back, and the "internal to schools" view has come to dominate the national discourse. The passage of No Child Left Behind (NCLB) in 2001, a watershed moment in American educational history, did not merely expand the federal role in education but also transformed it by adding a new focus on assessment and accountability to the traditional federal emphasis on resources. While so far NCLB's impact on student performance is ambiguous at best, it is clear that the law has radically upended and reshaped the politics of education in America, blurring traditional partisan and ideological markers.

This new political moment has created an opening for new alliances and new policies in the pursuit of educational equity. Nowhere are the new politics of education clearer than inside the Democratic Party, where a contentious debate has raged over President Barack Obama's Race to the Top school reform grant competition, School Improvement Grant program, and blueprint for revising NCLB. This chapter uses the "policy-centered approach" to social analysis developed by political scientists Joe Soss, Jacob Hacker, and Suzanne Mettler to explore how new federal policies have created new politics in education, particularly in the area of teacher accountability.[1] The central questions of the current political debate are whether improved democratic governance (through an expansion of federal power in the face of the blockages of local politics) can improve education performance and, more specifically, whether we should expect new patterns of democratic governance to achieve educational improvements mainly through more equitable allocations of school and family resources or through providing a decision-making context for schools themselves that pushes them to maximize their pedagogic capacity.

NCLB, Race to the Top, and the New World of School Reform: From Policy to Politics

Early federal education policy—most prominently the Elementary and Secondary Education Act (ESEA) of 1965—focused on addressing the resource gaps in schools created by districts' reliance on local property taxes. Education was part of the Great Society's broader War on Poverty and linked to integration and a variety of expanded social welfare programs. For thirty years after the passage of the ESEA, Democratic elites were largely united behind a resource equity paradigm of using state courts and federal programs to provide supplemental educational resources to high-poverty districts. By the 1990s, however, both the War on Poverty and efforts to create racially integrated schools had stalled in the face of public opposition and legal challenges. The persistence of achievement gaps despite large increases in education spending led many observers to question whether resources alone could generate educational improvement without other school reforms. Many Republicans had long held this view, and they were now joined by the centrist Democratic Leadership Council and by some antipoverty and civil rights groups like the Education Trust and the Citizens' Commission on Civil Rights. This shift created a powerful bipartisan political coalition and helped bring about the 1994 Improving America's Schools Act (IASA) and the 2001 No Child Left Behind, which moved the focus of federal policy from school inputs (resources) to school outputs (achievement).[2]

The big increases in funding, considerable statutory discretion given to states, and soft federal implementation under IASA initially helped smooth over lingering differences within the Democratic Party regarding this new federal emphasis on accountability. But the more intrusive and punitive mandates of NCLB, as well as its tough implementation by the Bush administration, brought the Democratic Party's divide on education roaring back. As Tom Loveless has observed, NCLB has a very "peculiar politics," since it combines both liberal and conservative approaches to school reform. NCLB, Loveless writes, "consists of conservative ideas—

testing, accountability, and incentives—wrapped in liberal clothing—a big federal program that seeks, as its primary objective, the equalization not only of educational opportunity, but also of educational outcomes."[3]

NCLB requires states to create academic standards, test children in reading and math annually in grades three through eight (and once in high school), and hold them accountable for the results. States must determine which students are proficient, identify schools where too few students are proficient, ensure that specified measures are taken with regards to schools that fail to make "adequately yearly progress" (AYP), and set targets that ensure that 100 percent of children are proficient in reading and math by 2014. One of the most important mandates in the law is that school report cards must disaggregate student test scores for subgroups based on race or ethnicity, economically disadvantaged status, limited proficiency in English, and need for special education. Crucially and controversially, a school that does not meet the proficiency target for *any one of these groups* is classified as "in need of improvement," and states are required to undertake an escalating series of interventions (including offering public school choice, tutoring, technical assistance, and restructuring) with schools and districts that persistently fail to meet AYP targets.

The scope, specificity, and ambition of the law's mandates signaled something akin to a revolution in federal education policy. With NCLB the federal government for the first time pressured states in a sustained way to undertake systemic change in their education systems and held them accountable for students' academic performance. NCLB's requirement that states conduct annual testing and report student scores has forced them to build new systems for data gathering and dissemination and produced greater transparency in public education than ever before. Parents, advocacy groups, the media, and policymakers now have access to a wealth of disaggregated student performance data that they have used to shine light on previously dark corners of neglect in the educational system. School report cards, demands that schools make escalating progress toward closing achievement gaps, and a corrective action and restructuring process that specifies the steps persistently underperforming schools must take to improve have all directed unprecedented attention and resources to turning around failing schools. By holding states clearly accountable for the performance of their public schools, NCLB has also prodded state departments of education to expand their capacity to monitor local districts, provide technical assistance, and intervene where necessary.[4]

The pressure to produce rapid gains in student achievement has also pushed states to innovate at an unprecedented rate. Phyllis McClure, a longtime member of the Title I Independent Review Panel, has observed: "NCLB has grabbed the education community's attention like no previous ESEA reauthorization. It has really upset the status quo in state and local offices. . . . For the first time, district and school officials are actually being required to take serious and urgent action in return for federal dollars."[5] Though the pace and extent of innovation vary widely across individual states, nationwide the number and variety of alternative schools (charters, magnets, virtual schools), alternative routes for licensing teachers and administrators, and new approaches to instruction have grown dramatically in the wake of NCLB. For example, nationwide the number of charter schools—which tend to serve low-income and minority students—has grown from 1,297 in 1999 to 5,043 in 2009.[6]

Most Democrats agree that the active engagement of the federal government in the pursuit of greater educational equity is a good thing, as is the requirement that states be held accountable in some way for improving the academic performance of their disadvantaged students. At the same time, however, a variety of concerns have been raised about the design and implementation of the test-based accountability system at the heart of NCLB and the ways it has fallen short of its goals and produced unintended negative consequences in American classrooms. As David Cohen and Susan Moffitt have observed, the federal government's ambitious goals in education have not been matched by sufficient attention to how teachers and administrators can realize these goals; there has been a large disconnect between policy and practice. NCLB in particular, they argue, has been hampered because its "aims far outstripped capability and instruments," and "it is unlikely to become more effective educationally or sustainable politically unless its aims, instruments, and capability can be made more commensurate."[7] Paul Manna has highlighted how NCLB created perverse incentives that led schools and states to adopt counterproductive compliance behaviors such as teaching to the test, narrowing the curriculum, focusing on "bubble kids" rather than student growth, and lowering standards, which undermined NCLB's ultimate goals.[8]

The election of Obama as president in 2008—combined with Democratic control of Congress—gave the Democratic Party an opportunity to assert a new vision of education reform. Many observers initially assumed this would lead to a move away from school accountability and a reassertion of the traditional liberal focus on school resources, integration, and social welfare programs. But Obama seems to have accepted two fundamental premises of the Bush administration—and of the accountability movement. First, that many of the problems in education have political roots and that the federal government should focus not only on providing additional resources but on overcoming the powerful forces of the status quo in public education to foster policy change and experimentation. And second, that schools and teachers should be held responsible for improving the academic performance of all students, even (and especially) those whose educational prospects are hampered by poverty. In the ESEA, President Obama has called for continuing annual testing, for expanding federal efforts to restructure the worst-performing schools, and for a new focus on innovation and charter schools.

The centerpiece of the Obama education agenda has been the $4.35 billion Race to the Top (RTT), $3 billion School Improvement Grant (SIG), and $650 million Investing in Innovation (I3) funds. Historically almost all federal education funds have been distributed through categorical grant programs that allocated money to districts according to need-based formulas. States and districts in this traditional model received funding automatically, regardless of the performance of their schools or the promise of their particular school reform policies. While there has always been variation across states and districts in the federal funds received, this variance was due to differences in state educational needs (the number of poor, English as a second language, or special education students, for example) rather than differences in school policies. The RTT, SIG, and I3 funds, by contrast, were distributed through a competitive grant process in which states and districts were rewarded only for developing reform proposals aligned with five administration priorities: developing common standards and assessments; improving teacher training, evaluation, and retention policies; developing better data systems; adopting preferred school turnaround strategies; and building stakeholder support for reform.

The programs spurred states to enact a wide variety of education policy changes[9] to meet the federal conditions for eligibility and to increase their chances of winning, and the *Washington Post* declared that RTT "helped transform the national discussion on education."[10] RTT represents a new and potentially transformative role for the federal government in American education as a driver of reform and innovation. It also stirred the school reform pot politically in states as never before, by forcing interest groups to publicly stake out their positions on the various reform components of RTT in the debate over whether to apply and under what conditions.[11]

Together NCLB and RTT have dramatically exposed the tension between the visions of school reform that exist within the country—and especially within the Democratic Party—over how best to advance the cause of educational equity for poor and minority children.[12] Teachers unions in particular have vocally opposed the new focus on teacher accountability, and in July 2010 delegates at the National Education Association (NEA) convention gave RTT a vote of no confidence and called for US secretary of education Arne Duncan's resignation. A few weeks later, seven leading civil rights groups, including the National Association for the Advancement of Colored People (NAACP) and the National Urban League called on Obama to change core elements of his education agenda—including the emphasis on charters, competitive grants, and school restructuring—saying they were detrimental to the interests of low-income and minority students.[13] In a subsequent speech to the National Urban League, Secretary Duncan challenged the civil rights community to "be bold and ambitious in our thinking. . . . We have a moral obligation to change these outcomes and it won't happen unless we start doing things differently."[14] Duncan promised to pursue more funding for federal formula programs like Title I and to use the Department of Education to push for more equitable distribution of school resources, enforce civil rights laws, and create an Equity and Excellence Commission. But he also defended the administration's emphasis on accountability and the reforms pushed by Race to the Top, arguing that it "has done so much to dismantle the barriers to education reform with less than 1 percent of what we spend on K–12 education." He declared that the "suggestion that charters are bad for low-income and minority students is absolutely wrong" and that competitive grant programs "unleash creativity and innovation . . . and target . . . high needs schools."

As states have struggled to meet NCLB's ambitious goals and chafed at the reforms rewarded by RTT, some of the initial philosophical reservations within both parties about the new federal emphasis on accountability have come storming back. Many Republicans resent the coerciveness of the new federal role, while many Democrats are concerned about the impact of standardized testing on instruction and the focus on schools over broader economic and social change. But the contemporary debate over NCLB and RTT also has revealed that the politics of education have changed significantly over the past decade in ways likely to have lasting influence on efforts to bring about educational equity. The current political moment makes it particularly worthwhile to focus on changes in the politics of education within the Democratic Party. Better understanding the debate among Democrats over school reform can teach us a great deal about the ways the ideals of education, democracy, and justice are discussed and pursued in contemporary American politics, as well as how the current politics of education create both opportunities and constraints for federal policymakers.

Divided Democrats: The Two Narratives of School Reform

As Helen Ladd and Susanna Loeb note in this volume, equity can be conceptualized quite broadly in terms of equal educational opportunity or more narrowly as access to equal quality schools. These different ways of conceptualizing equity have led to disparate policy approaches, with some arguing for enhancing the conditions external to the school that affect learning and others favoring a school-centered approach. Harry Brighouse and Gina Schouten point out that while "the dichotomous classification of interventions to ameliorate educational disadvantage into 'external-to-school' and 'internal-to-school' reforms is commonplace," it is problematic because many policy advocates and policy interventions do not fit neatly into these categories.[15] It is certainly true, for example, that many "external to schools" adherents support some forms of accountability and attention to school improvement and that many "internal to schools" folks support addressing the roots of educational inequality that stem from poverty. However, while the approaches need not be mutually exclusive, the strong emphasis on teacher and school accountability in NCLB and RTT has increasingly put them at odds, particularly over recent proposals for teacher evaluation and school restructuring. For if "external to school" factors are thought to be paramount—and teachers and schools unable to make a significant impact on achievement on their own—then it makes little sense for policymakers to focus on holding them accountable.

The two sides disagree not only about the contribution schools can make to reducing achievement gaps but also about whether schools—or districts or states—are likely to take politically unpopular steps to address educational inequities without federal pressure. As Helen Ladd's recent research on New Zealand has emphasized, the orientation of a nation's accountability system fundamentally comes down to trust.[16] When policymakers have trust in teachers and school administrators, they are likely to design a low-stakes accountability system, but in the absence of trust the system will attach high stakes to student performance. More specifically, the degree of trust in educators will have three implications: for type of assessment (qualitative versus quantitative), degree of centralization (state versus federal control), and prescriptiveness of policy interventions (flexibility versus standardization). Over the past two decades, the United States has moved from a high-trust, low-stakes accountability system to a low-trust, high-stakes one, precipitated by shifts in educational politics that have themselves accelerated this move.

As a result, two competing narratives of school reform have emerged: one focused on providing additional resources to schools and families to enhance educational opportunity and another focused on using test-based accountability reforms to equalize school quality. These different narratives are largely captured in the platforms of two school reform advocacy organizations, the Broader, Bolder Approach to Education (BBA) and the Education Equality Project (EEP), respectively.[17] While advocates of the BBA and EEP share similar goals in terms of advancing educational equity, they have different visions of the obstacles that stand in the way and the policies the federal government should adopt to pursue their goals. More specifically, the two sides disagree over standardized testing, school choice, the importance of resources, teacher accountability, schools' power to overcome the effects of poverty, and the public school system's ability to regenerate itself without external pressure. It is interesting that membership in the groups does not map onto partisan or ideological divisions and that the leaders of both groups are Democrats. As Dana Goldstein observed in 2009, "The major fight on education policy isn't between Republicans and unions, or even between Republicans and Democrats, but rather within the Democratic coalition."[18]

One way to observe the difference between the two narratives of school reform is to listen to the debate over whether the nation is facing an educational "crisis" or, more specifically, whether the crisis in education is a schooling crisis or a poverty crisis with educational implications. This debate began with the release of the "A Nation at Risk" report in 1983 but continues today. That report emphasized the failures of the public school system and called for reform but was criticized in books such as David Berliner and Bruce Biddle's *The Manufactured Crisis: Myths, Fraud, and the Attack on America's Public Schools* (1995). The debate over whether our schools are in crisis is not mere semantics but has enormous substantive and political importance. This is true not just in terms of the impact on political discourse around education reform, but also because if there is a schooling crisis then it inclines one toward more rapid and "radical" school reforms. If there is a crisis in schools, then innovation-experimentation and accountability are essential, and there is a greater willingness to accept the possible negative consequences of these approaches.

The first narrative attributes racial and socioeconomic achievement gaps primarily to poverty and segregation. Since in this view schools cannot be expected to remedy educational deficits that have social or economic roots, NCLB and the standardized testing and accountability movement more generally are at best a waste of time and at worst dangerously counterproductive. This view emphasizes that researchers have long documented the high correlation between socioeconomic status and student achievement. Writing in the 1960s, James Coleman concluded that poverty was the primary explanation for the achievement gap and that differences in school demographics—rather than school quality—largely accounted for variation in student achievement.[19] And as Richard Rothstein notes in this volume, American neighborhoods and schools today remain strikingly segregated by race and class.[20] This concentrated poverty— often compounded, as Carola and Marcelo Suárez-Orozco show (this volume), by the cultural and linguistic challenges of immigrants—produces concentrated educational disadvantage that some observers believe is impossible to rectify without a major effort to expand home and community resources that can enhance the "opportunity to learn."

Diane Ravitch and Linda Darling-Hammond are widely considered the spokespersons for this movement, and their recent books *The Death and Life of the Great American School System* and *The Flat World and Education* (respectively) roundly criticize test-based accountability of the sort contained in NCLB and RTT. Darling-Hammond argues that "we need to create systems that routinely guarantee all the elements of educational investment to all children." These elements include, she says, health care; housing and food security; high-quality preschool; equitably funded schools; effective teachers in every community; schools equipped to deal with students' social needs; and standards, curriculums, and assessments focused on "twenty-first century skills." Darling-Hammond notes: "While the administration's blueprint for reauthorizing ESEA carries some hints of such strategies, its framework still envisions competition and sanctions as the primary drivers of reform rather than capacity building and strategic investments. If this remains the primary frame for federal and state policy, it is unlikely that we will rebuild good schools in every community."[21]

Darling-Hammond and Ravitch joined with the Economic Policy Institute to form a new group, the Broader, Bolder Approach to Education, to highlight the failings of NCLB and advocate on behalf of this alternative, progressive vision of school reform. The group has individual signatories from across K–12 and higher education, including the presidents of the two teachers unions (the National Education Association [NEA] and American Federation of Teachers [AFT]), Michael Rebell of the Campaign for Fiscal Equity, Susan Neuman, the former Bush administration assistant secretary for elementary and secondary education, and a variety of school leaders and academics (many from schools of education). The BBA mission statement declares that "the potential effectiveness of NCLB has been seriously undermined by its acceptance of the popular assumptions that bad schools are the major reason for low achievement, and that an academic program revolving around standards, testing, teacher training, and accountability can, in and of itself, offset the full impact of low socioeconomic status on achievement."[22]

The BBA rejects the annual standardized testing of all children called for in NCLB and in Obama's ESEA blueprint and instead urges a shift to qualitative assessments backstopped by National Assessment of Educational Progress (NAEP) testing of a small sample of students in each state. Similarly, it also opposes federally mandated school improvement plans, instead calling for more locally based school inspection and restructuring teams to ensure accountability. While the BBA calls for continuing school improvement efforts, it emphasizes pedagogical interventions (such as reduced class size and professional development for teachers) rather than governance reforms. On RTT, the BBA objects to "the heavy emphasis in the regulations on using student test scores for the formal evaluation of teachers and school principals."[23]

The "equalize educational opportunity" narrative and the focus on "external to school" factors have long been dominant in the Democratic Party and continue to appeal to a considerable segment of its members. However, for perhaps the first time since the Great Society, that approach no longer commands the undivided loyalty of Democrats. A competing narrative—and an alternative reform agenda—has developed around testing, accountability, and choice and has attracted the support of a growing number of party members, including many urban school superintendents, mayors, governors, and civil rights groups. The second narrative of school reform sees the status quo in American education as untenable and believes it is unlikely to change without strong reform pressure from Washington that holds states and schools accountable for improving student performance. Based in part on the success of charter schools such as those operated by the Knowledge is Power Program (KIPP), it believes that schools, in particular and in contrast to other institutions, can generate dramatically improved results for poor and minority students.[24]

In this view, centralized testing and accountability policies are essential to changing the political dynamics around education reform—to breaking a status quo that has prevented schools from taking action to close racial and socioeconomic achievement gaps despite a large increase in federal and state education spending over the past forty years. The political power of teachers unions and upper- and middle-class families is seen as preventing states and localities from adopting policies on behalf of poor children, and ossified bureaucratic school systems are deemed unable or unwilling to address their own problems. The system is seen as broken in many ways, particularly in urban areas, and the purpose of the federal role is considered to be fostering or requiring policy change and innovation and ensuring that school leaders and teachers have meaningful consequences attached to their efforts to close achievement gaps.

The test-based accountability coalition is made up of a diverse array of groups from across the political spectrum. It includes conservative business groups like the Business Roundtable and Chamber of Commerce that are concerned about education's impact on economic competiveness, centrist Democratic Party groups like the Progressive Policy Institute and Democrats for Education Reform, think tanks like the Education Sector and the Center for American Progress, civil rights organizations like the National Council of La Raza, and antipoverty groups like the Education Trust. Members of these groups have joined to create organizations like the Achievement Alliance, the Policy Innovators in Education (PIE) Network, and the Education Equality Project to advocate publicly and lobby privately on behalf of accountability-based school reform.[25] The Gates, Broad, and Walton Foundations have spent considerable funds advancing this mission.

The chairs of the Education Equality Project are former New York City Schools chancellor (and former Clinton administration official) Joel Klein; Michael Lomax, president of the United Negro College Fund; and Janet Murguia, president of the National Council of La Raza. In an op-ed for the *Washington Post* they wrote:

> In the debate over how to fix American public education, many believe that schools alone cannot overcome the impact that economic disadvantage has on a child, that life outcomes are fixed by poverty and family circumstances, and that education doesn't work until other problems are solved. This theory is, in some ways, comforting for educators. After all, if schools only make a marginal difference, we can stop faulting ourselves for failing to make them work well for millions of children. . . . Problem is, the theory is wrong. It's hard to know

how wrong—because we haven't yet tried to make the changes that would tell us—but plenty of evidence demonstrates that schools can make an enormous difference despite the challenges presented by poverty and family background.

Joel Klein, Michael Lomax, and Janet Murguia highlight the large achievement gaps between students of similar socioeconomic backgrounds in different urban districts to argue that districts that have embraced teacher reforms (like Boston, Charlotte, New York, and Houston) are serving poor children much better than districts (like Detroit, Milwaukee, and Los Angeles) that have not. They conclude by arguing: "Apologists for our educational failure say that we will never fix education in America until we eradicate poverty. They have it exactly backward: We will never eradicate poverty until we fix education. The question is whether we have the political courage to take on those who defend a status quo that serves many adults but fails many children."[26] Pro-accountability Democrats generally do not oppose increasing resources for education per se; rather, they believe that this has been the focus of federal policy for the past forty years, that school spending has quadrupled, and that the results have cast doubt on the efficaciousness of increased resources—lacking other reforms—to close achievement gaps. They also have major concerns about the dysfunction of local school systems and their ability to spend increased resources effectively without improved governance or increased external pressure to be accountable for results.

The support of many civil rights groups for test-based accountability is a crucial political development that places them fundamentally at odds with another of the most important Democratic Party constituencies, the teachers unions.[27] Jesse Rhodes, for example, has argued that "contrary to the conventional wisdom, certain civil rights organizations, not conservative forces, provided much of the impetus for federal standards, testing, and accountability reforms."[28] This dynamic has led civil rights groups into some unusual political confrontations in recent years, such as over the Connecticut lawsuit against NCLB in 2006. Connecticut had filed suit against the US Department of Education, objecting to the federal government's denial of waivers that would allow it to test students in every other grade rather than in grades three through eight, and alleging that the federal government was underfunding the law by about $50 million. The NAACP decided to side with the Bush administration on the grounds that "Connecticut is failing its most disempowered children" and that states do not have the right to ignore federal legislation aimed at helping minorities. Victor L. Goode, the NAACP's assistant general counsel, cited the importance of federal protections: "One can't help but remember back in the Dixiecrat period when certain Southern states asserted that they were not required to comply with certain federal civil rights laws designed to protect people's rights."[29]

Another moment emblematic of the divide occurred in June 2008, when a measure called the "Graves-Walz No Child Left Behind Recess until Reauthorization Act," backed by the teachers unions, was introduced in Congress. As the title implies, the act would have suspended the accountability provisions of NCLB—and sanctions for failing schools—until the law was reauthorized. However, the Leadership Conference on Civil Rights—the nation's largest coalition of civil rights organizations—sent a strongly worded letter urging members of Congress to oppose the act. The letter stated:

> LCCR believes that NCLB is a civil rights law, and that some of the requirements of NCLB constitute, in essence, the rights of children to obtain a quality education. The NCLB Recess until Reauthorization Act calls itself a "temporary suspension" of those same requirements. Even a temporary suspension of a civil rights law, and therefore of the civil rights of our children, is unconscionable.[30]

But the civil rights community is by no means completely united in its support of test-based accountability, and many would like to see both more resources *and* more accountability. As a result, some civil rights groups have joined forces with organizations that emphasize resources and oppose test-based accountability, such as the Broader, Bolder Approach and the Forum on Educational Accountability.[31] The cross-membership of some groups in organizations that appear to embrace conflicting goals has further muddled a complicated story.

While it is not possible to fit every group neatly into one or the other of these camps, the two narratives identify a broad divide today within the school reform debate—and particularly inside the Democratic Party.[32] These broad philosophical differences have important substantive consequences for matters of policy. In particular, potent disagreements have emerged over several bright-line issues, and how these disagreements are resolved will have a major impact on the pursuit of equity in education (and the Democratic education agenda) going forward. These bright-line issues include standardized tests, teacher evaluation and accountability, charter schools, school choice, innovation, restructuring, and competitive grants. I will focus here just on one—teacher evaluation and tenure—to provide a summary picture of how these two narratives lead to different positions on educational reform.

Teacher Accountability

Perhaps no single issue highlights the potential and the pitfalls of the new political moment in education more than teacher evaluation and tenure reform. Research has long documented the ways existing state teacher evaluation, tenure, and dismissal policies are dysfunctional and have impeded efforts to improve teacher quality and student achievement.[33] Tenure was created during the early twentieth century to establish guidelines to protect teachers from the arbitrary, unfair, and often discriminatory dismissal practices that were common in local schools. While due process protections remain necessary today, their expansion over time has made it so difficult and costly for districts to dismiss tenured teachers that they rarely attempt to do so, even when serious concerns arise about a teacher's effectiveness. The norm across the country is for teachers to be given tenure automatically after three years in the classroom, with no meaningful evaluation of their teaching effectiveness, and they are extremely unlikely to be fired during their career no matter how ineffective they are.[34]

In 2008 the National Council on Teacher Quality gave forty-one states failing grades for their tenure policies, and nine states were given a grade of D. By its definition, not a single state in the country had even "partly" met the goal of developing a "meaningful" process for making tenure decisions. To effectively weed out poorly performing teachers, both granting tenure and revoking it ultimately depend on the underlying district teacher evaluation systems, but these were also deeply flawed.[35] In "The Widget Effect" (2009), for example, the New Teacher Project lamented "our pervasive and longstanding failure to recognize and respond to variations in the effectiveness of our teachers."[36] And because our least effective teachers are concentrated in our poorest schools, the cost of leaving them in the classroom has been borne disproportionately by our most disadvantaged students.

Yet despite the abundant evidence that major evaluation and tenure reform was necessary, virtually no state had made a serious sustained effort before Race to the Top.[37] Politically, evaluation and tenure had long been considered the third rail of education politics because unions vigorously fought efforts to weaken job protections for teachers, which in any event were buried in local collective bargaining contracts that were seen as beyond the appropriate reach of federal policy. Obama and Duncan changed the politics around teacher accountability by repeatedly highlighting the dysfunction in our teacher evaluation and tenure systems, shining light on an issue that had long received inadequate attention.[38] Their use of the bully pulpit, combined with the high-profile debates in state legislatures over tenure reform, has brought much greater media coverage to the issue than ever before.

This rhetorical push combined with the financial incentives of RTT prompted an unprecedented wave of teacher evaluation and tenure reforms at the state level.[39] RTT pushed states to improve their capacity to evaluate teachers better and to adopt policies to ensure that student achievement data were incorporated into tenure and dismissal decisions. Teacher effectiveness reforms constituted the single biggest category of possible points (28 percent) in the RTT competition, and to be eligible to apply, states could not have any law creating a "firewall" that prohibited using such data in teacher evaluations.[40] An additional requirement for states that received stimulus funds was that all districts publish teacher and principal evaluation information online; the availability of such information caused a firestorm in Los Angeles and has the potential to keep teacher accountability on the agenda for a long time.[41]

But the changes the Obama administration is demanding have long been passionately opposed by the teachers unions and put the administration at odds with Democrats who dislike test-based accountability and prefer that federal policy focus on factors external to schools. BBA, for example, argues that "neither schools nor teachers should be held accountable based primarily on test scores of students. Such accountability can lead to gross misidentification of failing schools and creates incentives to teach to the test, narrow the curriculum, and substitute drill for education."[42]

The debate over teacher accountability had a touchstone moment in March 2010 when a Rhode Island school district superintendent decided to fire the entire teaching staff at Central Falls High School. The school was in the poorest district in the state, had a large immigrant population, and was chronically low performing—only 7 percent of eleventh-graders passed state math tests, and the school had failed to make adequate yearly progress for seven consecutive years. Although teachers unions criticized the firings, President Obama called the move appropriate and necessary to bring about reform and accountability for closing racial and socioeconomic achievement gaps. The Central Falls incident received tremendous national media attention and highlights two crucial questions related to the quest for greater equity in education. How can the resources and authority of the federal government be deployed most effectively to drive state and district school improvement efforts? And how can the federal desire to spur accountability and innovation be balanced with respect for states rights and local control in education as well as with maintaining reasonable employment conditions for teachers?

The situation at Central Falls High School is emblematic of the equity challenge in American public schools at the beginning of the twenty-first century, and it also casts into stark relief the two competing narratives of school reform. The district is poor—the poorest in the state—and has long had low test scores, failing for seven years to make adequate yearly progress under NCLB. The state superintendent, Deborah Gist, identified the school, along with five others in Providence, as candidates for turnaround under Obama's School Improvement Grant program and ordered their leaders to adopt one of the program's models. The federal SIG program allocates $3.5 billion to turning around chronically failing schools. Similar federal programs in the past have given states wide discretion in spending the money but have yielded few innovative approaches and have been largely ineffective. As a result, SIG is highly prescriptive, requiring states to choose from one of four federally sanctioned turnaround models: transformation, turnaround, closure, or charter conversion.

The district superintendent, Frances Gallo, initially chose a transformation model that entailed replacing the principal but retaining most staff. The model called for an extended school day, common planning time for teachers, after-school tutoring, and third-party evaluation of the school's teaching staff. But after a dispute arose with the local union over the additional requirements and how much teachers would be paid for them, Gallo (backed by the school board) decided to fire the entire staff. Obama publicly supported the move, stating that "if a school continues to fail its students year after year after year, and it doesn't show signs of improvement, then there's got to be a sense of accountability. And that's what happened in Rhode Island last week."[43] Secretary Duncan called the move courageous. AFT president Randi Weingarten responded that "firing all of the teachers is a failed approach and will not result in the kinds of changes necessary to improve instruction and learning." The *New York Times* noted that "officials at the two unions, the National Education

Association and the American Federation of Teachers, were so angry in the hours after Mr. Obama first endorsed the firings that an irreconcilable break with the administration seemed possible."[44] In the end, under prodding from the Obama administration and the national AFT leadership, both sides returned to the bargaining table and reached a compromise in which teachers agreed to the superintendent's reform proposals and layoffs were avoided.

The new federal focus on teacher accountability has also changed the political dynamics around the issue, with governors and state legislators advancing policy changes in many states. Colorado, Illinois, Tennessee, Delaware, Indiana, Idaho, and Florida enacted major reforms to their teacher evaluation and tenure statutes, and a number of other states (such as Michigan and New Jersey) have initiated efforts to do so.[45] These developments have paved the way for important shifts in the position of the AFT and NEA and a more reform-oriented approach to collective bargaining contracts. AFT president Randi Weingarten acknowledged in an important January 2010 speech that "our system of evaluating teachers has never been adequate." She called for replacing brief teacher observations by principals (which she called a "perfunctory waste of time") with "constructive and robust teacher evaluation" and for "the creation of a system that would inform tenure, employment decisions, and due process proceedings." "We recognize," she added, "that too often due process can become a glacial process. We intend to change that." Weingarten hailed the contract negotiated by the New Haven chapter of the AFT in October 2009, which limits job protections for teachers in failing schools and includes provisions for performance pay and teacher evaluation based in part on student growth. More recently, the AFT agreed to major changes in evaluation and tenure policies in contracts in Washington, DC, and New York City and endorsed a major overhaul in Colorado. In July 2011, after years of intense opposition, the NEA also endorsed the use of standardized test scores, along with other measures, in teacher evaluations.[46]

In a sign of the more comprehensive approach being taken to teacher assessment, the DC Impact evaluation system utilizes a sophisticated statistical model that includes a variety of nonteacher factors that could affect gains, including student mobility, test error, family background, English-language proficiency, and special education status. A national conference on labor-management collaboration recently announced by US secretary of education Arne Duncan, AFT president Randi Weingarten, and NEA president Dennis Van Roekel is another promising example of progress,

since it is intended to "highlight examples of progressive collective bargaining agreements across the country and promote opportunities for
management and labor to forge reforms at the state and district level."[47]
The political pressures and policy incentives created by federal programs
like RTT and SIG thus appear to have forced teachers, administrators,
and policymakers to address long-standing obstacles to developing a high-
quality teaching force, which many researchers believe is the single most
important school factor for improving student achievement.[48]

The debate over reforming teacher evaluation and tenure demonstrates both how much the politics of education have shifted inside the
Democratic Party—where a Democratic president leading on this issue
would have been unthinkable a decade ago—but also the considerable
remaining disagreements over the best approach for pursuing educational
equity in America. The pending reauthorization of the ESEA represents
a crucial fork in the road for American education policy: Do we continue
to pursue centralized test-based accountability for teachers and schools?
Or do we shift the focus to enhancing social welfare programs and entrust
states and localities with more discretion in their school improvement
efforts?

Adherents of the "external to schools" and "internal to schools" narratives tend to interpret the shortcomings of NCLB in ways that are strikingly different and that support their own general visions of reform. So for
the "external to schools" position, NCLB's inability to close achievement
gaps (along with its many negative unintended consequences) demonstrates conclusively the folly of standardized testing and centralized accountability systems, as well as the need to return to a more decentralized,
professionally driven education system buttressed by additional resources
for families and teachers. In this view, the "failure" of NCLB is evidence
that a heavy-handed approach can't work and that the federal government
should back away from an aggressive role in using test-based accountability to drive school reform.

Adherents of the "internal to schools" view, meanwhile, tend to adopt
a "mend it, don't end it" approach to NCLB and test-based accountability.
They believe one of the biggest problems was that the law left too much
discretion in the hands of states and districts (since it let them set their
own policies on standards, tests, proficiency cut scores, school restructuring, supplemental education services and choice, and highly qualified
teachers), enabling the politics of the status quo to undermine major reform. The answer in this view is national standards and tests that prevent

gaming the system, along with more meaningful federal teacher evaluation and school turnaround mandates. For example, while NCLB has been
widely criticized for the "dumbing down" of state standards and tests and
the lowering of proficiency bars to meet AYP, accountability advocates
believe this action by states only reinforces the need for the federal government to hold states' feet to the fire by moving to a system of national
standards and assessments like those being developed by the Common
Core initiative of the National Governors Association and the Council of
Chief State School Officers.

Since the Clinton era, Democratic leaders have struggled to reconcile the competing demands of the "internal to schools" and "external
to schools" wings of the party. They have typically done so by proposing
a "grand bargain" in education—increased federal funding for schools
in exchange for accepting increased accountability for improving student
performance. For the reasons described above, earlier iterations of the
grand bargain (in the form of IASA and NCLB) have left advocates
of both views unsatisfied. Developments in the wake of NCLB and
RTT have in some ways broadened and hardened the divisions between
the two camps, simultaneously increasing the number and influence of
accountability-oriented Democrats and also increasing the resistance to
NCLB-type reforms among many others in the party. The divide within
the Democratic Party has also been on display in the divergent reactions
to the departure of Washington, DC, schools chancellor Michelle Rhee
and the release of the education documentary "Waiting for Superman"
in the fall of 2010. But the shifting politics of education have also forced
the issue of educational inequality into the spotlight as never before and
encouraged policymakers to look for new solutions to old problems.

Conclusion

This chapter has traced the shifts in federal education policy over the past
half-century, as well as a growing debate inside the Democratic Party over
the place of accountability reforms in bringing greater educational equity. The "equalize schooling" and "equalize educational opportunity"
narratives differ fundamentally in how they view school reform. Advocates of test-based accountability see school reform as being as much a
political problem as an educational one, and they believe that a federal
focus on standardized, comparable measures of student achievement is

necessary to bring about systemic improvement. Other Democrats focus on the need for greater attention to the disadvantages students bring with them to school and on the negative consequences of testing. It is important to recognize that the accountability movement has changed the political discourse around education in fundamental ways over the past decade. While the first round of federal test-based accountability policies have clearly had some unintended consequences, the spotlight they have shone on education injustice has engendered a more comprehensive and fruitful conversation in a way few other things could have done.

Scholars of the politics of education have tended to focus on interparty struggles and how Republicans and Democrats have fought to advance their competing visions of school reform. The significant and growing divisions within the Democratic Party, however, have received less attention despite their enormous import for the future direction of education policy in this country. In one view the growing split within the Democratic Party over school reform is disheartening, since it disrupts what for many years had been a powerful and united coalition on behalf of equity. In another view, however, given the persistence of educational inequities during that period of intraparty unity, perhaps the disagreements will force difficult conversations and alternative approaches that will ultimately advance the cause of educational equity in the United States. Either way, it is clear that we must more fully understand the dynamics that have led to the development of two dramatically different visions of school reform inside the Democratic Party—and in American politics more generally—if we are to develop more effective responses to the considerable challenge of educational inequity that remains before us.

The pursuit of expanded educational opportunity in the United States stands at a fascinating and crucial moment as the country contemplates the future direction of school reform policies in the era following No Child Left Behind. The persistence of large racial and socioeconomic achievement gaps is undermining the realization of America's democratic promise. Assessment and accountability—properly designed—are essential to advancing educational equity for low-income and minority children in the United States. Regardless of the particular definition of "educational equity" one embraces, it is unlikely to be achieved without efforts to measure and motivate progress toward reaching it. The crucial task for the White House (and policymakers more generally) is to improve on the initial versions of these reforms—to learn from the earlier mistakes of policy design and implementation and, in particular, to improve teacher quality and expand states' capacity to improve chronically underperforming schools. It is increasingly clear that neither a focus on factors external to schools nor a focus on accountability alone will deliver necessary school improvement. Major political shifts and a newly aggressive federal role in education have created an unprecedented opportunity to integrate the various elements of the competing narratives—to create a more comprehensive, more systemic, and ultimately more effective approach to school reform that includes new resources for schools and enhanced social welfare supports for families, as well as greater innovation and accountability for school results.[49]

There is a sense, then, in which the heated political infighting and impassioned debates over the future direction of federal education policy inside the Democratic Party are a positive development for the cause of equity. The test-based accountability movement—for all its pitfalls—has forced the country's political leaders to focus in an unprecedented way on closing racial and socioeconomic achievement gaps, to undertake long overdue conversations about the kinds of resources and policies needed to bring about this goal, and to engage the country's public schools in a sustained era of experimentation. It has forced people to consider whether our institutions of democratic governance give schools a foundation that allows them to maximize their pedagogic capacity. The expansion of the federal role in education, and the new focus of federal engagement on accountability, rests on the philosophical view that improved democratic governance will expand educational opportunity not merely by promoting more equitable allocation of resources but by itself making schools stronger institutions, better fitted to fulfill their fundamental mission. While considerable disagreement remains on the nature of the federal role, and in particular on issues such as standardized tests, charter schools, and teacher accountability, the new politics of education are spurring changes in our educational discourse and policymaking that are far past due and that are essential to the pursuit of educational equity.

CHAPTER II

Reading Thurgood Marshall as a Liberal Democratic Theorist

Race, School Finance, and the Courts

Anna Marie Smith

Introduction

Imagine an account of education, justice, and democracy written from the perspective of the civil rights movement. This story would grant a prominent place to the Supreme Court's 1954 decision, *Brown v. Board of Education.*[1] To be sure, the current trends toward resegregation, racially biased tracking into dead-end special education classes, and the exposure of black and Latino schoolchildren to arbitrary expulsions remain serious concerns. The promise of *Brown* has yet to be fully realized. In this chapter I want to set aside that important point. I will instead identify the political theory of education rights that lies at the center of Thurgood Marshall's conception of justice.

In this theory, education rights are defined as an entitlement to a unique public good, insofar as securing access to an adequate and publicly funded education for the least advantaged children places them on the path to equal citizenship. Indeed, for children from very low income families and traditionally excluded social groups, the right to decent publicly

I thank Rosanna and Charles Jaffin and the Institute for Advanced Study for supporting my political theory and legal research on education rights. I benefited enormously from the contributors' constructive criticism; my thanks especially to Danielle Allen, Rob Reich, and Pat McGuinn. I am very grateful that Michael Rebell generously consented to participate in personal interviews with me, and graciously permitted me to audit his course at Columbia Law School. Alice Bennett and Lucia Rafanelli provided expert editing advice.

funded instruction—which, at a minimum, incorporates a rigorous, rich, and stimulating high school curriculum and guarantees exposure to highly qualified teachers—may represent the only key to equal citizenship that lies within their grasp. Although it is this theory that animates the *Brown* decision,[2] at least in part, the legal architecture of *Brown* is such that it is relatively easy to overlook its presence. I want to argue that, against the grain of the Court's subsequent abandonment of racial integration in the schools and its recent decision against voluntary integration school assignment plans in *Parents Involved*,[3] the spirit of that political theory has survived, albeit in weakened and fragmentary forms. We can see its oppositional expression in Justice Thurgood Marshall's dissenting opinions in cases like *Milliken*[4] and *Rodriguez*,[5] and we can find its affirmation in a recent state school finance case, *Campaign for Fiscal Equity (CFE)*.[6] The linkage between Marshall's dissents and the *Campaign for Fiscal Equity* decision consists in their shared identification of the pupil as a future citizen and their conception of the rising generation's education entitlement as the indispensable human rights cornerstone in a liberal democratic society.

Let me quickly sketch, first, the "*Milliken*" democratic theory before turning back to the dissenting "Marshallian" perspective. From the *Milliken* Court's perspective, the *Brown* Court's intervention into education policy was legitimate only because Jim Crow laws and policies represented such a sharp departure from the American norm. However, the majority reasoned in *Milliken*, that deviation from mainstream American values was corrected once and for all when the Supreme Court ordered the desegregation of the schools in *Brown* and President Lyndon Johnson signed the Civil Rights Act and the Voting Rights Act into law in the mid-1960s.

Within the terms of the *Milliken* Court's implicit theory of democracy, individual African Americans have been liberated from the shackles of Jim Crow racism, and the federal government has basically exhausted its interventionary obligations on behalf of the most vulnerable. In other words, we have decisively entered a postracist world. Further, we can all count on our society's just background: the essentially fair structure of the free market has been correctly reestablished as our primary social sorting machine. The *Milliken* democratic theory firmly holds that, properly left to its own devices, the free market ensures that individual talent and effort are justly rewarded. Where "big government" programs, such as Johnson's War on Poverty, may have made some sense during the final days of the Jim Crow era, it is now time to embrace a stripped-down sense of collective responsibility and government obligation. The *Milliken* discourse has, if anything, become even more authoritative in the legal, social, intellectual, and political realms since the early 1970s. Indeed, in the midst of the current recession, when Congress could be offering the states extensive fiscal support to maintain services, create new jobs, and dramatically improve their school systems, the Obama administration has managed to garner its approval only for an overly modest recovery package. From a *Milliken*-oriented perspective, it now appears that the political rights of the disempowered have been fully restored; as such, every individual who seeks changes to our existing educational policies should look exclusively to the legislative and executive branches for relief. Aggrieved parties should bring their claims to their elected representatives; the electoral process offers an adequate venue for the pursuit of legitimate demands for distributive justice. Consequently, the *Milliken* democratic theory regards the moment when the judiciary could legitimately intervene in the terrain of educational equity as belonging in the distant past.

Marshall firmly rejects this implicit political theory in his *Milliken* dissent. In Marshall's jurisprudence, the Fourteenth Amendment guaranteeing the equal protection of the law essentially offers individuals who belong to traditionally disempowered minorities constitutional protection against racial domination. If educational reforms merely ushered in color-blind policies and left massive and systemic racial inequalities basically intact, then they would not go far enough in removing the vestiges of Jim Crow segregation and would therefore fail to meet the constitutional threshold. Marshall also wrote a dissenting opinion in *Rodriguez,* the key public school funding case that was decided the year before, in 1973. He argued in his *Rodriguez* dissent that because there is a close nexus between educational opportunity and federally protected rights that are central to the individual's participation in the democratic process, such as the right to free speech, the right of association, and the right to vote, the federal courts should recognize, protect, and promote the individual's constitutional right to a public school education. From Marshall's perspective, the federal courts should intervene where the states are discriminating against racial minorities and where the states' school funding schemes are so inadequate that they deprive disadvantaged children of an adequate education.

In this chapter I will examine several court decisions pertaining to distributive justice and the school system in order to present a fuller portrait of the "*Milliken*" and "Marshallian" theories of democracy. I will discuss, in particular, two types of cases. First, I will interpret the cases involving race, especially segregation and voluntary pupil assignment, as confrontations between these two theories of democracy. Second, I will give a somewhat briefer treatment to the cases that arise out of the challenges to the states' public school funding schemes on behalf of low-income students.

I do not intend to offer a comprehensive discussion of the legitimacy of judicial review for the entire field of education law. When we move to other axes of educational justice, such as the controversies about students' free speech rights, the accommodation of religious minorities, and the collective bargaining rights of teachers, the Marshallian versus *Milliken* distinction being offered here may become less salient. Moreover, I will not attempt to capture the entire range of positions on judicial review where race and school funding are concerned. Some progressives, like Jonathan Kozol,[7] are sharply critical of the *Milliken* paradigm yet remain skeptical about the political value of litigation on public school funding. By the same token, two of the Supreme Court justices who heard the *Brown* case, Felix Frankfurter and Robert Jackson, abhorred segregation but worried that a decision overturning a settled law like *Plessy* would constitute illegitimate judicial activism.[8]

I nevertheless contend that we can learn a great deal about education equity and the very meaning of the term democracy by studying these major perspectives on education and the courts, appreciating the deep contrasts between them, and understanding how they remain relevant today. By underlining the centrality of educational entitlement to the preparation of the individual pupil for civic participation, and to the recognition of individuals who belong to traditionally excluded social groups as fully qualified participants in political deliberation, the Marshallian discourse that we can find in Marshall's own dissents and in *CFE* remains faithful to the most promising dimensions of the *Brown* decision.

Before we turn, then, to the more detailed analysis of the *Milliken* and Marshallian theories of democracy, we need to return to *Brown* to identify the framework it established for educational equity jurisprudence.

Brown and the Liberal Democratic Political Theory of Equal Citizenship

In the NAACP's segregation cases, the plaintiffs challenged educational systems in which blacks received an inferior education[9] and those in which black children benefited from educational inputs substantially equal to those of their white counterparts but were nevertheless harmed by racial segregation.[10] As long as the 1896 *Plessy v. Ferguson*[11] precedent remained intact, the Jim Crow laws establishing "separate but equal" facilities would be upheld as constitutional.

Working closely with local affiliates in Kansas, South Carolina, Virginia, Delaware, and Washington, DC, the NAACP advised selected teams of black parents to attempt to enroll their children in schools that had been officially designated for whites only. When they were turned away, Marshall and his colleagues represented them and their children as they brought their claims before the courts. In 1954, the Supreme Court handed down the unanimous *Brown* decision, holding that when students are segregated by race, their right to equal protection under the Fourteenth Amendment is violated, even where the school district provides equal tangible inputs to both parts of the racially segregated school system. Reversing *Plessy* in the area of schooling, the *Brown* Court held that "to separate [African American] children from others of similar age and qualifications solely because of their race generates a feeling of inferiority as to their status in the community that may affect their hearts and minds in a way unlikely ever to be undone."[12]

For our purposes, it should also be emphasized that the *Brown* decision's attack on white supremacy revolved around the right to educational equity for the rising generation of a historically and systematically subordinated people. In abstract terms, *Plessy* could have been reversed in the context of many forms and sites of racial discrimination, ranging from segregation in interstate transportation, public accommodation, urban planning, and the collusion of the federal government in residential segregation.[13] As the *Brown* decision itself states, the right to education is immediately central to the formation of a democratic people, since the least advantaged can gain inclusion within the polity as equal citizens only insofar as they obtain the instruction required to master complex information pertaining to public affairs and develop key faculties such as critical thought and self-expression.

Moreover, since social inclusion in a market society often turns on the individual's ability to earn a living wage, the least advantaged pupils also depend on the education entitlement to prepare them for entry into citizenship through an indirect yet equally important second route: successful competition in the labor market. Genuine equality of opportunity requires much more than the formal prohibition of discrimination; it must create the conditions in which equally talented pupils can enjoy roughly the same life chances regardless of the income, wealth, and social status of their parents.[14] Ideally, the education entitlements of the least advantaged children will permit them to become self-supporting wage earners in their adult lives and to garner the dignity and recognition that the market society ideally reserves for the hardworking and law-abiding participants in the social contract, regardless of their race, ethnicity, religion, gender, or sexual orientation.[15]

Assuming, for the moment at least, that the economic structure actually does generate an adequate number of living wage employment opportunities for all high school graduates, and that the public school system actually furnishes the least advantaged with a high-quality education that adequately prepares its graduates for these positions, the education entitlement endows the least advantaged with a meaningful opportunity to perform well enough in the labor market and to thereby earn the respect of their more advantaged counterparts. In this ideal scenario, the least advantaged who possess an adequate level of talent at birth[16] will be able to situate themselves as hardworking and self-supporting taxpayers and thereby demand recognition as equal citizens and as valued participants in any political deliberation. Our public sphere would be all the richer and more democratic as a result, since it is highly likely that young adults from the least advantaged families would be able to bring to light social problems that are specific to the low-income sector of the population. It is only by ensuring that the testimonies of the least advantaged are given adequate attention in our deliberations that we can hope to progress toward fulfilling our liberal democratic ideals.[17]

As the *Brown* decision itself states,

> Today, education is perhaps the most important function of state and local governments. Compulsory school attendance laws and the great expenditures for education both demonstrate our recognition of the importance of education to our democratic society. It is required in the performance of our most basic public responsibilities, even service in the armed forces. It is the very foundation of good citizenship. Today it is a principal instrument in awakening the child to cultural values, in preparing him for later professional training, and in helping him to adjust normally to his environment. In these days, it is doubtful that any child may reasonably be expected to succeed in life if he is denied the opportunity of an education. Such an opportunity, where the state has undertaken to provide it, is a right which must be made available to all on equal terms.[18]

The limits of constitutional law are nevertheless evident even here, in one of the Supreme Court's finest moments. This particular passage has the status of a dictum; in the technical terms of constitutional doctrine, these ringing words of national redemption have no binding powers in any subsequent case. Moreover, Chief Justice Earl Warren, the author of the decision, was obliged to acknowledge the relative weakness of the federal government; the primacy of the states where education is concerned is disturbed only to an extent by the *Brown* Court. When American citizens advance a claim for educational opportunity, de novo, the state government retains the primary jurisdiction. Congress federalized the entitlement to old age pensions under the 1935 Social Security Act, but as of 1954, it had not yet introduced the federal government as a significant actor in K–12 education. Working in the context of the 1950s, that is, before any substantial congressional and presidential interventions in primary and secondary school policy, Warren refuses to place the judicial branch in a position dramatically ahead of the other branches. Given this situation, the analogy with old age pensions has no place in *Brown*. The federal government can insist on equity in the distribution of only those particular educational assets that the state has, on its own authority and initiative, chosen to provide. It cannot direct the state to establish a common school system or to guarantee that its schools are meeting a given standard of excellence.

Milliken and the Abandonment of *Brown*

It quickly became clear to Marshall and the NAACP that the Court could not overcome the resistance of state and local governments.[19] Congress bolstered *Brown* somewhat when it adopted the Elementary and Secondary Education Act (ESEA) in 1965. Under Title I of the ESEA, the federal government provided aid to public schools in an attempt to improve the education of children from poor families. Although the ESEA targeted low-income white and black schoolchildren alike, the huge overrepresentation of African Americans among the poor meant it had a profound potential to correct racial inequities. However, Title I's influence remained very limited. The states zealously guarded their authority over the curriculum and educational standards. To win enough votes in Congress, the drafters of the ESEA had to make sure that federal allocations were spread out to school districts far and wide, thereby blunting the law's redistributive impact.

First and foremost, however, the potential of Title I was limited because the education policies of the local and state governments had been deliberately designed to reflect and perpetuate race and class hierarchies. David Cohen and Susan Moffitt offer a sobering portrait of the barriers that prevented the Johnson administration from making much progress toward the achievement of its Title I objectives:

> In 1965, the Southern states were operating racially dual school systems, in which "Negro" schools were poorly funded, were often in bad physical condition, and lacked decent books, let alone libraries and laboratories. In many rural districts, both black and white schools were educationally weak. Schools in the North, especially the urban North, spent more, on average, than their Southern counterparts, but schools in black or poor neighborhoods typically had less money and worse facilities than schools in more privileged parts of the same cities; out-of-date books if, indeed, there were books at all; crowded conditions; and weak teachers.[20]

The barriers to racial equality in the distribution of school-based educational opportunities are particularly formidable in the United States. Moreover, these inequalities are prominent nationwide. At the time of the *Brown* decision, they were pronounced both in the South, where segregation was given explicit expression in the law, and in the North and West as well. In the North and West, racial hierarchies were systematically perpetuated by de facto discriminatory policies relating to residential zoning, school assignment policies, the design of the public school tax system, and so on. Although low-income whites were also being left behind as a result, the backlash against the civil rights movement that arose in the 1950s and 1960s made constructing a progressive cross-racial alliance in favor of education equity extremely difficult. Indeed, Presidents Richard Nixon and Ronald Reagan enjoyed significant success in recruiting working-class whites for the Republican Party as a result of their demonization of the civil rights movement and their attacks on school desegregation, busing, alleged welfare cheats, and affirmative action. The targeted federal programs designed to channel aid to low-income school districts and to address childhood poverty were reduced or eliminated under President Reagan in the 1980s. The impact of this fiscal turn away from the egalitarian Great Society policies of President Johnson was exacerbated by the adoption of a "high-stakes testing without investing" approach. As a result, the black-white achievement gap began to grow again in the late 1980s.[21]

The trends in the judicial branch, meanwhile, were not conducive to realizing *Brown*'s promise. With President Nixon's judicial appointments, the Supreme Court's composition changed dramatically. The decisions of the Warren Court had often reflected, in whole or in part, the position of the civil rights attorneys. The majorities on the Burger and Rehnquist Courts, by contrast, often handed down decisions that were deeply influenced by ideas about democracy closely resembling the *Milliken* ideal type outlined above. Although the Supreme Court upheld busing children to aid desegregation in its 1971 decision, *Swann v. Charlotte-Mecklenburg Board of Education*,[22] the majority also signaled its willingness to rein in the federal judiciary where racial inequality in the schools was the product of ostensibly race-neutral policies and the plaintiffs had not proved that the local or state governments deliberately intended to discriminate against racial minorities.

The Court's abandonment of *Brown* became clear when it handed down its *Milliken v. Bradley*[23] decision in 1974, in which it decided that the federal courts could not impose a remedy involving students from multiple school districts unless the plaintiffs had proved that the boundaries between the districts had been intentionally drawn to promote school segregation or that every district included in the remedy had itself deliberately adopted segregationist policies. At the conclusion of the original trial, the district court found that the inner-city Detroit school board had engaged in deliberate racial segregation. In his *Milliken* dissent, Justice Byron White further argued that the record contained ample evidence that the state of Michigan had systematically colluded with segregationist real estate interests in drawing up plans for separate suburban residential areas. Intended for middle-class and well-to-do whites, Detroit's suburbs were protected from multiracial encroachment by exclusionary state-sanctioned housing policies. Each suburban entity was endowed with its own geographically distinct school board, the authority to raise school taxes based on the local housing stock, a strictly defined school catchment area, and the power to ignore the needs of the inner city. Given the concentration of the black population in the inner city and that of the white population in the surrounding suburbs, any remedy that focused exclusively on the inner-city district would fail to bring about racial integration in its schools. The district court imposed a multidistrict remedy in its decision. Using various techniques, including busing, the remedy was designed to integrate the majority black inner-city student bodies with their majority white counterparts in the suburbs. Such a plan was ambitious, but for the four *Milliken* dissenters the district court was nevertheless operating well within its powers to provide equitable relief to the plaintiffs.

Justice Warren Burger, writing for the *Milliken* majority, actually conceded that residential segregation in the greater Detroit area had been extensively supported by federal agencies and that Michigan's policies had further contributed to school segregation.[24] In the end, however, the Court found that the plaintiffs had failed to demonstrate that the segregationist patterns in the greater Detroit area had been substantially caused by policies intentionally adopted by the state of Michigan and the various suburban districts to discriminate against black schoolchildren. As such, Justice Burger reasoned, the multidistrict remedy could not be permitted.

At this juncture, Justice Burger gives direct expression to the majority's otherwise implicit theory of democracy. By setting aside the boundaries between the fifty-three white majority suburban districts and Detroit's black majority inner-city district, Burger writes, the district court had failed to give adequate weight to the principle of local control: "[No] single tradition in public education is more deeply rooted than local control over the operation of the schools; local autonomy has long been thought essential both to the maintenance of community concern and support for public schools and to quality of the educational process."[25]

If the district court judge assumed administrative authority for the consolidated "superdistrict" comprising all fifty-four original districts, such a remedy *"would deprive the people of control of schools through their elected representatives."*[26] As for the black students residing within the boundaries of the Detroit inner city that had been virtually left to fend for itself, the Constitution afforded them very little effective protection. "The constitutional right of the Negro respondents residing in Detroit is to attend a unitary school system *in that district.*"[27] True, the inner-city school board had a duty to dismantle its own segregated system and to stop discriminating against its black students. However, the white majority suburban districts had absolutely no enforceable duties where the education of inner-city black schoolchildren was concerned.

For the *Milliken* majority, then, educational democracy places an extremely minimal obligation on the state concerning recognition of a bona fide political subject, the self-governing local school district. The state need only ensure that the group of homeowners, taxpayers, and parents residing in a contiguous geographical space has a rudimentary capacity to conduct reasonably fair elections based on the principle of one person, one vote. The first-order questions about the moral, legal, and political legitimacy of this subject and its fundamentally exclusionary principles are thereby suppressed. Despite the massive historical evidence that over-whelmingly demonstrates that residential patterns in the United States have never been the fruit of fair political deliberations but have grown out of the tyranny of the most advantaged, biased public and private institutions and the distorting effects of cultural racism on the formation of con-sumers' housing preferences,[28] the *Milliken* theory of democracy requires the state to certify as a fully fledged polity any collectivity that meets these basic conditions, regardless of its arbitrary and exclusionary constitutive principles. The *Milliken* majority's democratic theory ideologically ne-gates the fact that this apparently natural and innocent entity, the local school district, is actually an artifact whose basic design reflects powerful and deeply entrenched race- and class-oriented interests.[29]

In his *Milliken* dissent, Justice Marshall argued that the majority's deci-sion amounted to a betrayal of the *Brown* decision:

> After twenty years of small, often difficult steps toward that great end, the Court today takes a giant step backwards. Notwithstanding a record showing wide-spread and pervasive racial segregation in the educational system provided by the State of Michigan for children in Detroit, this Court holds that the District Court was powerless to require the State to remedy its constitutional violation in any meaningful fashion.[30]

For Marshall, the theory of democracy invoked by the majority was little more than a fig leaf that it deployed to conceal the profound injustice of its decision:

> Ironically purporting to base its result on the principle that the scope of the remedy in a desegregation case should be determined by the nature and the extent of the constitutional violation, the Court's answer is to provide no rem-edy at all for the violation proved in this case, thereby guaranteeing that Negro children in Detroit will receive the same separate and inherently unequal edu-cation in the future as they have been unconstitutionally afforded in the past. I cannot subscribe to this emasculation of our constitutional guarantee of equal protection of the laws and must respectfully dissent.[31]

Justice Marshall also raised the possibility that the majority's decision would exacerbate an already unjust configuration of race, wealth, political power, and educational opportunity. He suggested that in the aftermath of

Milliken, black children would continue to view their schools as segregated and inferior institutions, while the relatively few white parents residing in the inner city would move to the white majority suburbs to enhance their children's opportunities. "By limiting the District Court to a Detroit-only remedy and allowing that flight to the suburbs to succeed, the Court today allows the State to profit from its own wrong and to perpetuate for years to come the separation of the races it achieved in the past by purposeful state action."[32]

The Rehnquist Court largely continued the Burger Court's retreat from *Brown*. In *Board of Education of Oklahoma City Public Schools v. Dowell*,[33] the Court addressed the status of the school boards seeking relief from desegregation orders. These cases involve boards that had been brought before the federal courts by minority plaintiffs and had been found to have operated a dual school system. In the decisions handed down against them, the remedy often entailed being placed under the supervision of the federal court, through the vehicle of the desegregation order. *Dowell* relaxed the standards for the conditions under which the boards could obtain the dissolution of that order. Once again, the *Dowell* majority invoked purportedly democratic concepts as it curtailed the federal courts' authority to intervene. *Dowell* reminded the trial court that the "federal supervision of local school systems was intended as a temporary measure to remedy past discrimination."[34] The virtue of local control, the decision continued, is that it "allows citizens to participate in decision-making, and allows innovation so that school programs can fit local needs."[35] To "condemn a school district . . . to judicial tutelage for the indefinite future" would be a "Draconian result."[36]

In his *Dowell* dissent, Justice Marshall argues that in adopting weakened rules, the majority "fails to recognize explicitly the threatened reemergence of one-race schools as a relevant 'vestige' of *de jure* segregation."[37] He documents in great detail the resistance by the Oklahoma City school board to the federal courts' attempts to integrate the school system after *Brown* was handed down, and he notes that over half of the elementary schools in the district in the mid-1980s had virtually single-race student bodies. Since *Brown* held that racially separate educational facilities are inherently unequal, the perpetuation of single-race schools in districts with a history of de jure segregation conveys a message of inferiority to black children and therefore perpetrates a violative stigmatic injury. Quoting the Court's own precedents, Marshall reasons that the purpose of a federal court's imposing a desegregation decree on a school district

with a proven record of de jure segregation is to *"eliminate* racially identifiable schools."[38] Consequently, Justice Marshall argues that the *Dowell*
majority should have erected a much stricter test for the dissolution of the
desegregation court orders:

> I believe a desegregation decree cannot be lifted so long as conditions likely to
> inflict the stigmatic injury condemned in *Brown I* persist and there remain feasi-
> ble methods of eliminating such conditions. Because the record here shows, and
> the Court of Appeals found, that feasible steps could be taken to avoid one-race
> schools, it is clear that the purposes of the decree have not yet been achieved
> and the Court of Appeals' reinstatement of the decree should be affirmed.[39]

After Marshall: *Freeman, Jenkins, Grutter,* and Seattle *Parents Involved*

After Justice Marshall retired in 1991, the Court remained closely divided
on school segregation and affirmative action. Majorities on the Court nevertheless continued to rally behind decisions that gave further expression
to the *Milliken* democratic theory. Much of the Court's holdings in its 1992
Freeman v. Pitts[40] decision about the De Kalb County schools in Atlanta,
Georgia, concerned technical questions about the authority of the district
court to relinquish partial supervision and control over a school district
where it had achieved unitary status in one of several policy areas. For our
purposes, the *Freeman* holdings pertaining to the causes of racial segregation in the schools and their implications for the school board's remedial
duties are particularly significant.

   In De Kalb County, 50 percent of the black students were attending
schools whose student bodies were more than 90 percent black at the time
of the trial, while 59 percent of white students attended schools that were
over 90 percent white. The *Freeman* Court describes the demographic
changes that took place within the district—especially the increase in the
proportion of black students in the De Kalb schools from 5.6 percent in
1969 to 47 percent in 1986—as the fruit of "private choices" of home buyers and parents.[41] The Court's finding that government action did not lie
behind the formation of racially segregated student bodies like the ones
in De Kalb County is extremely important. A school district cannot be
held responsible for demographic patterns that are primarily caused by

the cumulative effect of "private choices." In *Freeman,* the Court held that "where resegregation is a product not of state action but of private choices, it does not have constitutional implications."[42]

Justices Harry Blackmun, John Paul Stevens, and Sandra Day O'Connor concurred in the *Freeman* judgment but stated in a separate opinion, written by Justice Blackmun, that they disagreed with the majority on its holdings regarding the origins of residential segregation and the single-race-oriented student bodies in the county. They reasoned that the federal courts had to consider the possibility that the school board's proven de jure segregation policies had themselves given rise to racially skewed residential patterns. For example, white parents shopping for a new home might skip over a neighborhood if its local school is informally regarded, thanks to the legacy of segregation, as a "black" institution. Indeed, Justice Blackmun argued that where a school board has engaged in de jure segregation in the past and is the subject of a consent decree, it should not be able to assert that racial imbalances in its schools' student bodies have been primarily caused by the decisions of private actors such as home buyers and therefore have no constitutional significance. Instead, the school board in this position ought to bear the burden of proving that its own policies have not caused those imbalances.[43] Echoing Justice Marshall, Blackmun insisted that a school district under a desegregation order should be expected to pursue remedial policies for a significant time and that it could not be relieved of a court order simply because compliance was becoming more difficult to achieve.[44]

In *Missouri v. Jenkins,*[45] the state of Missouri was seeking relief from a district court's remedial order. The district court had directed the state to pay for a substantial enrichment program designed to enhance the black majority inner-city school district in Kansas City. The purpose of the program was twofold: to create attractive schools in the inner city that would entice voluntary enrollments from the white families living in the nearby suburbs and to compensate the black inner-city students who were being assigned to schools that lacked racial diversity. Ultimately, the Court decided in the state's favor. In his *Jenkins* dissent, which was joined by Justices Ruth Bader Ginsburg and Stephen Breyer, Justice David Souter distinguished *Milliken.* He pointed out that the district court was not ordering mandatory student reassignments, and that it was well within the limits of its equitable powers when it directed the state to finance several special initiatives for the inner-city schools, including a capital improvement program, hikes in teacher salaries, the establishment of a high-quality "magnet school," a reduction in class size, a full-day kindergarten, summer school, after-school tutoring, and an early childhood development program.[46]

The *Jenkins* majority conceded that the greater metropolitan area had experienced a dramatic trend toward "white flight" and that many of the district's inner-city schools had student bodies that were more than 90 percent black. It nevertheless held that the state could not be required to bear the financial burden for the Kansas City, Missouri, enrichment program. The plaintiffs had proved only that the inner-city school district had engaged in deliberate segregation within its own boundaries. The state, being legally responsible for the conduct of its local governments, could be required to fund programs designed to dismantle segregation within the inner city itself. However, the district court erred when it ordered the state to pay for special compensatory programs for the inner-city schools and to assist them in attracting voluntary enrollments from the surrounding suburban areas. Since the plaintiffs had not demonstrated that the state and its local governments had deliberately set out to produce the multidistrict racial segregation pattern for the entire metropolitan area, the trial court could not saddle the state with these additional costs.

In her concurrence, Justice O'Connor invoked *Milliken* to argue that when the original segregation case involved a single district, the federal district court is committing "territorial transgression"[47] by imposing a multidistrict remedy. Although "white flight" to the suburbs may be "troubling," the district court had overstepped its authority.[48] There are, she wrote, "myriad factors of human existence which can cause discrimination in a multitude of ways on racial, religious, or ethnic grounds."[49] As such, it was reasonable that reformers would seek remedies that had an impact beyond the boundaries of the inner-city school district. However, Justice O'Connor counseled them to look to the political process, rather than the federal courts, for relief.[50]

In 2007 the Supreme Court handed down its *Parents Involved in Community Schools v. Seattle School District No. 1*[51] decision, in which it prohibited the voluntary adoption by a school board of a desegregative student assignment plan. The Court had recently upheld affirmative action in higher education in *Grutter v. Bollinger.*[52] The *Parents Involved* decision nevertheless distinguished *Grutter* on the grounds that the school boards were looking only at the race of each student, while colleges and universities were considering race as one of many diversity factors. Further, the universities have a legitimate interest in fostering freedom of speech and thought; while the public schools obviously have a similar interest, the majority reasoned, it had to be assigned a much more modest weight, given the relative youth of their students. Chief Justice John Roberts mustered five votes in support of striking down the voluntary school assignment policies as unconstitutional, with one each from Justices Samuel Alito, Anthony Kennedy, Antonin Scalia, and Clarence Thomas. The chief justice was abandoned by the swing voter, Justice Kennedy, but retained the support of Justices Alito, Scalia, and Thomas on several other holdings. The plurality of four signed the passage in which Roberts stated that all forms of racial classification deployed by government entities, including the classifications necessary to implement remedial programs, were "odious to a free people,"[53] "divid[e] us by race,"[54] "reinforce the belief . . . that individuals should be judged by the color of their skin,"[55] and "demea[n] the dignity and worth of a person."[56] Casting severe doubt on the prospect that any race-conscious remedial policy would ever survive judicial scrutiny, the plurality of four concluded, "The way to stop discrimination on the basis of race is to stop discriminating on the basis of race."[57]

School Funding Litigation: *Rodriguez* and *Campaign for Fiscal Equity*

The Marshallian democratic paradigm favors judicial intervention to safeguard the Fourteenth Amendment right of the disadvantaged to relief from domination. Where socioeconomic hierarchies have become pronounced and deeply entrenched, historically excluded minorities cannot compete successfully in the political contests that determine the policies of the executive and legislative branches. From Marshall's perspective, the judicial branch should subject laws to a higher level of scrutiny where they have a deleterious impact on the members of minority groups that cannot muster enough political power to defend their own interests through the electoral process. Marshall further believed that low-income Americans—as well as African Americans and Latinos—often deserve the Court's special protection in this regard, especially where laws deploying income-based classifications effectively block them from exercising the rights that are particularly cherished in the American legal tradition.

The Burger Court handed down its landmark federal school funding decision, *San Antonio v. Rodriguez*,[58] sixteen months before it did so in *Milliken*. Whereas Justice Powell wrote the *Rodriguez* decision on behalf of the majority, Chief Justice Burger authored *Milliken*. However, the makeup of the Court, the 5/4 division, and the membership in the two voting blocs were exactly the same in both instances: Chief Justice Burger and Justices Powell, Stewart, Blackmun, and Rehnquist voted to reject the plaintiffs' request for the federal courts' intervention in state educational policy to promote the rights of the disadvantaged, while Justices Brennan, White, Douglas, and Marshall dissented. The continuities between the political theories that are implicit in each majority decision are striking.

Under our current school funding system, property-poor districts, and the inner-city school districts in large metropolitan areas that must compete with other local government agencies for their shares of the general tax revenues, can end up with grossly insufficient revenue streams, especially where the state fails to provide enough compensatory subsidies. From a legal point of view, it is important to keep in mind that local governments fall under the jurisdiction of their respective states. In 2007, about 42.8 percent of public school revenues came from local sources, and 49.4 percent came from the states. Federal allocations made up only 7.8 percent of public school funds nationwide.[59] In other words, the states are legally responsible for approximately 92 percent of school spending. To make matters even worse, the greatest inequitable variations are interstate in nature rather than intrastate.[60] The federal courts have nevertheless refused to recognize massively inegalitarian state school funding schemes as unconstitutional. In its 1973 *Rodriguez* decision, the majority held that individual pupils residing in a property-poor district do not enjoy a fundamental due process right to education under the federal constitution,[61] and that the great inequities in Texas's school funding system did not constitute a violation of their equal protection rights.[62]

In his *Rodriguez* dissent, Marshall argued that there was no "substantial justification for a scheme which arbitrarily channels educational resources in accordance with the fortuity of the amount of taxable wealth within each district."[63] He sharply criticized the majority for holding that the state's system promoted democratic values by allowing local taxpayers to determine their neighborhood schools' budgets to reflect their particular support for public education.[64] He noted that the plaintiffs resided in a low-income inner-city district, Edgewood, where taxpayers had evidently expressed their staunch support for school spending. They had elected slates of school board representatives who had, in turn, imposed on Edgewood's taxpayers one of the state's highest school property tax rates. However, the district's taxable property base was modest. As a result, the local

contribution was thirteen times less than that of Alamo Heights, a wealthier district also in the San Antonio area. Even after Edgewood collected
a strongly redistributive share from the federal government, it ended up
with a per pupil school allocation of $356, a figure 1.7 times smaller than
Alamo Heights' $594.[65]

Marshall further argued that the federal constitution implicitly protects
the individual's right to an education insofar as the exercise of federally
guaranteed rights, such as the right to vote, the right of association, and
the right to free speech closely depend on access to educational opportunities.[66] He reasoned that the Texas school finance scheme was discriminatory, given its inequitable impact on the pupils who live in property-poor
districts, and that the state had not demonstrated that it served a legitimate government purpose. The scheme could not actually promote local
control, since taxpayers who highly valued K–12 education but resided in
property-poor districts could not ensure that their local schools would be
equitably funded. The strong pro-education preferences of the Edgewood
taxpayers could not be translated into robust public investments in the
schools, and thus their local graduates would not be able to compete effectively with their counterparts from property-rich districts.

Marshall concluded that "the right of every American to an equal start
in life, so far as the provision of a state service as important as education
is concerned, is far too vital to permit state discrimination on grounds as
tenuous as those presented by this record."[67] Marshall argued that education is indispensable for the individual flourishing that makes a democratic
society possible:

> No other state function is so uniformly recognized as an essential element of
> our society's well-being. In large measure, the explanation for the special im-
> portance attached to education must rest . . . on the facts that "some degree of
> education is necessary to prepare citizens to participate effectively and intelli-
> gently in our open political system . . . ," and that "education prepares individu-
> als to be self-reliant and self-sufficient participants in society."[68]

Marshall further commented that the Court's decision meant the plaintiffs could seek relief only through the political branches. Looking back
at the history of the case, Marshall noted that the district court had postponed its decision for two years to give the state legislature a chance to
introduce adequate reforms. It was only after the legislature had failed to
act during its 1971 session that the district court had rendered its decision

that the Texas school finance system violated the equal protection clause
of the Fourteenth Amendment. For Marshall, the state legislature's failure
to correct the gross disparities was hardly surprising: "The strong vested
interest of property-rich districts in the existing property tax scheme poses
a substantial barrier to self-initiated legislative reform in educational financing."[69] The Court, he reasoned, was shirking its duty by effectively
remitting the plaintiffs to "the vagaries of the political process which, contrary to the majority's suggestion, has proved singularly unsuited to the
task of providing a remedy for this discrimination."[70]

The *Rodriguez* majority entirely rejected Marshall's position, and in
doing so it prefigured the *Milliken* democratic theory. The Court conceded
that the Texas school funding scheme could cause the pupils who reside in
property-poor districts and cannot afford to attend private schools to receive a lower-quality education than that received by their counterparts in
wealthier districts. It further acknowledged that the children in property-
poor districts like Edgewood might end up being less capable of expressing themselves persuasively or casting intelligent votes in their adult years.
The state of Texas was nevertheless ensuring that all children enjoyed the
opportunity to "acquire the basic minimal skills necessary for the enjoyment of rights of speech and of full participation in the political process."[71]
Even with all its flaws, the Texas system survived the Court's rational basis
test because the state was ensuring that every child received a basic education, and its school funding scheme preserved and promoted the "local
sharing of responsibility for public education."[72] From the perspective of
the *Rodriguez* majority, none of the political decisions that had led to such
an enormous gap between the rich and the poor, the formation of severely
class-segregated neighborhoods, and the establishment of a school funding system strongly biased against low-income families was constitutionally violative. Taking the state at its word, the majority held that the school
finance scheme served a legitimate government purpose: promoting local
control. "To the extent that the Texas system of school financing results in
unequal expenditures between children who happen to reside in different
districts, we cannot say that such disparities are the product of a system
that is so irrational as to be invidiously discriminatory."[73]

Since *Rodriguez* was handed down in 1973, advocates for low-income
children have challenged the state school funding schemes in the state
courts. To date, forty-five of the fifty states have seen these lawsuits; since
1989, the low-income plaintiffs have won in about two-thirds of these
cases.[74] Although the legal foundations for their complaints are distinct

from those advanced by the plaintiffs in the federal segregation and school funding cases, the spirit of Marshall's theory of democracy lives on in these cases.

In the landmark New York case *Campaign for Fiscal Equity,*[75] for example, the precise terms the state court used to define the right to education guaranteed under the state constitution's education clause are highly significant. Echoing Marshall's argument about the close nexus between access to education and the individual's democratic capacity, the *CFE* court established a standard oriented toward civic functioning. Young New Yorkers would have received an adequate education from the state's public school system if, at the time of their graduation, they could participate effectively in the civic affairs of their community as effective and knowledgeable voters and jurors. A sound basic education should offer instruction in "the basic literacy, calculating, and verbal skills necessary to enable children to eventually function productively as civic participants capable of voting and serving on a jury."[76] Later, New York's highest court further noted that its definition of a threshold educational opportunity implicitly included access to the instruction necessary for finding and holding a job that pays more than the minimum wage.[77] Even with this clarification, however, civic functioning remains the New York court's lodestar.

Critics of the *CFE* court might balk at its civic functioning standard on the grounds that it is ill suited to the procedures and capacities of the judicial branch. *CFE* actually represents a breakthrough in this regard. Of all the state courts' school finance cases, it alone explicitly defines educational adequacy with reference to competent jury service, for example.[78] Moreover, the *CFE* standard proved quite amenable to the fact-finding work performed by the trial court. In the subsequent rounds of litigation, the lawyers for the plaintiffs called various expert witnesses and entered into evidence hundreds of exhibits meant to establish that, at a minimum, competent jurors and voters needed the linguistic and mathematical skills corresponding to the state's own grade twelve curriculum, but that the public schools in New York City could not deliver that level of educational opportunity to their pupils because of their state-sanctioned underfunding. For its part, the state put up a strong defense. It argued that the state constitution's education clause was meant to be only hortatory, and that if Article XI actually did constitute an enforceable entitlement, the standard ought to be pegged at the amount of education a graduate needed to find and hold a minimum wage job. The public interest was adequately served as long as the typical graduate had the capacity to be economically self-sufficient, not needing to turn to the state's poverty programs for subsistence.[79] To cover all the bases, however, the defendants also addressed the plaintiffs' civic functioning arguments; they claimed that competent jury service and voting required merely an eighth-grade education. The state's expert on educational psychology testified, for example, that newspaper articles about elections and jury instructions "typically feature vocabulary and sentence length comparable to those of texts eighth-graders are expected to be able to read."[80]

In the end the plaintiffs prevailed, and the *CFE* decision effectively endorsed Marshall's theory of democracy. The *CFE* court maintained the civic functioning standard, determined that New York's Article XI required the state to deliver a high level of educational opportunity to its public school pupils roughly equivalent to the state's own grade twelve curriculum, and held that the state's existing finance scheme was unconstitutional insofar as it had caused the New York City public schools to fall below the standard. Just as the district court in *Rodriguez* had given the Texas legislature a chance to adopt remedial legislation, the *CFE* court set a deadline for New York's compliance. After the legislature failed to act, the *CFE* court handed down a decision requiring the state to ensure that the city schools received $1.93 billion in additional core operating funds each year and to implement a $9.4 billion capital improvement project.[81]

Conclusion

In his democratic theory, Marshall offers a robust defense of the coequal status of the judicial branch. Although we can identify many types of democracy according to their various institutional features, "the people" in a genuinely democratic society have access to effective opportunities for holding the ruling elite accountable and for consistently exercising their sovereignty.[82] However, Marshall would reject the overvaluing of electoralism and majoritarianism. Even if we had perfectly free and fair elections that were not marred by gerrymandering, minority voter suppression, and campaign finance bias, and even if we introduced significant electoral reforms that promoted the voices of the traditionally excluded, allowed voters to signal the intensities and rank order of their preferences, and encouraged the formation of cross-race and cross-class alliances,[83] democratic thinkers like Marshall would still regard them as inadequate. Not only are elections intermittent, but by their very nature they channel popular sovereign energies into a tightly constrained framework. In the voting booth, the citizen must choose between the "highly aggregated alternatives offered by the political parties."[84] In addition to holding free and fair elections, a healthy democratic society would feature a vibrant civil society, and it would provide its members with a broad menu of institutional opportunities to hold the rulers accountable between elections. During these interstitial periods, members of a democratic society might express their claims in the public sphere in a wide variety of ways, such as by mobilizing interest groups to directly lobby the legislative and executive branches, organizing media campaigns that enhance the salience of given issues and provide valuable forms of public education and opportunities for engagement, or staging mass protests in support of key social movements. For Marshall, public interest litigation makes up a vital element of the multimodal and multi-institutional array of opportunities for expressing popular sovereignty that are characteristic of any democratic society. Marshall would argue that a judiciary fluent in the best moral arguments that the American people have historically offered would interpret the principle of equal protection as an antidomination value rather than a formal color blindness rule.[85] As long as the judicial branch is properly guided by this interpretive orientation toward the Fourteenth Amendment, he would argue that judicial review would be indispensable in democratizing American society.

There is a particularly close "nexus," Marshall argued in his 1973 *Rodriguez* dissent, between individuals' right to educational opportunity and their liberal democratic political rights. Without an adequate education, individuals cannot effectively exercise their right to vote, and they cannot make the most of their right to free speech. For this reason, Marshall's argument for judicial intervention in education policy constitutes a contribution to democratic theory in several senses. He is addressing a particular problem within the whole field of distributive justice, namely individuals' access to educational opportunity. With his conception of stigmatic injury, Marshall is capturing the argument that an inequitable education system automatically communicates a powerful political message: since the state has officially marked a whole class of students as not deserving a decent education, the other members of the polity are permitted to treat them with disrespect and to dismiss their claims out of hand. Educational inequity is a kind of hidden curriculum, as it were. For Marshall, individuals' entitlement to education is a special case of a socioeconomic right—more than, say, the right to adequate housing or a subsistence income, individu-

als' access to a decent education is a condition of possibility for any meaningful exercise of their political rights. The democratic theorist takes an
especially deep interest in distributive justice when educational goods,
such as primary and secondary schooling, are on the table. In a genuinely
democratic society, we would have equitable social policies—goods and
resources would be fairly distributed, for example—and in addition our
policies would be the product of inclusive democratic deliberations.[86] Marshall reminds us that both dimensions matter a great deal: we need to
achieve a social justice outcome, and we need to follow democratic procedures in pursuing that ideal.

Even the most optimistic review of the Court's response to the civil
rights plaintiffs' claims for racial equity in the schools would have to con-
cede that since the days of the Warren Court, the tide has fundamentally
turned against the Marshallian social justice paradigm, and the Court has
been much more favorably disposed toward the approach to democracy
that animates *Rodriguez* and *Milliken*. Technically, *Brown* remains the
law of the land; no school district may engage in explicit and intentional
racial discrimination. From the Marshallian perspective, however, much
remains to be done, many gains have been lost, and new forms of inequity are now emerging. After some progress toward unitary systems, the
schools have been resegregating since the early 1990s, not only due to the
reduction of federal judicial intervention, state-aided district design, and
residential segregation. Resegregation has also been caused by the use of
racially biased tracking and the limitation of minority students' access to
education through the discriminatory use of special education referrals,
dead-end programs for English language learners, and punitive disciplinary regimes.[87]

Further, the political system remains profoundly shaped by class and
race hierarchies. Congress made some attempt to address the systemic
educational inequalities by adopting the ESEA and launching the Title
I allocations, but their redistributive potential was limited from the start
by an insufficient federal infrastructure and the legislative necessity of
pursuing a very weak form of redistribution. Once school districts began
to receive federal funds under Title I, the Justice Department and later
the Department of Education gained some leverage that allowed them to
enforce federal laws against racial discrimination. Under the Republican
administrations of Presidents Ronald Reagan, George H. W. Bush, and
George W. Bush, however, this vector of civil rights enforcement was severely curtailed. While it is true that No Child Left Behind (NCLB), the

current version of the ESEA, at least opens up some potential for new civil rights gains insofar as it requires collecting race-specific test scores, the long-term implications of its accountability system for educational equality and racial justice remain to be seen.[88]

Under these conditions, Marshall would want to ensure that low-income African Americans and Latinos continue to have access to the federal and state courts. Significant progress has been made in reducing the budgetary gaps between the various districts within each state;[89] research suggests that where the state courts have handed down decisions in the plaintiffs' favor in the school finance lawsuits, school spending patterns have become more egalitarian.[90] Resegregation and the inequitable distribution of key educational resources such as highly qualified and effective teachers nevertheless remain pressing problems.[91] The particularly acute educational needs of students from low-income families, African American and Latino students, and immigrant pupils who are struggling to learn English are all too often neglected. Marshall has been essentially proved correct: where socioeconomic hierarchies are particularly pronounced and entrenched, advocates for the disempowered may well find it necessary to prod the political branches to adopt adequate remedies for educational disparities, and that prodding may well be aided by public interest lawsuits.

Given that the composition of the courts is such a salient factor in the outcome in education equity cases,[92] it is impossible to make a simple prediction about the value of public interest litigation for the politically excluded. And under all conditions, effective social change will come about only as the result of mass organizing and the renewal of radical democratic social movements.[93] Indeed, the success Marshall enjoyed depended in no small part on the contributions of unsung African Americans from all walks of life, including those who helped to build the historically black colleges, sent in their subscriptions to W. E. B. Du Bois's NAACP newspaper the *Crisis*, and risked their lives to march in the streets against segregation. The difficult work of building radical democratic social movements that can inform and support public interest advocacy remains essential. Even when the advocates ultimately prevail in court, further public pressure is needed to ensure that the political branches comply with the decision. From Marshall's perspective, however, strategically chosen public interest lawsuits remain an indispensable tool in the political resource kits of social justice advocates and the disempowered.

CHAPTER 12

Sharing Knowledge, Practicing Democracy

A Vision for the Twenty-First-Century University

Seth Moglen

Universities and Democracy

Although democracy is a foundational value in our society, we live at a moment of widespread pessimism about its effective, meaningful practice in the United States. As voter turnout indicates, faith in the electoral process is disturbingly low: only half of American adults vote in presidential elections, about a third vote in midterm congressional races, and the numbers for state and local offices are even more dispiriting.[1] And even as ordinary people doubt their ability to influence Congress or state legislatures or city councils in ways that will improve their lives, their opportunities for more direct forms of democracy are still more limited. Most Americans have little experience with actively deliberating and participating in collective decision making about issues that immediately affect them where they live or work or learn.

A generation ago, cultural critic and political thinker Raymond Williams described democracy as a "long revolution" in Western societies. He insisted that in the second half of the twentieth century we were still at an early stage in learning the practices and procedures of democracy, and he argued that one of the most urgent tasks of our societies was to invent and cultivate such practices. That task is more urgent today than ever, in the United States as elsewhere.[2]

Universities have an important role to play in this process, if they choose to embrace it. Universities have, of course, long been precious resources for democratic societies. They produce, preserve, and disseminate knowledge about our most pressing challenges. And they have unmatched expertise in conducting substantive, sustained conversation about difficult problems in ways that are nonreductive, open to competing viewpoints, respectful of difference, and capable of drawing on diverse sources of knowledge. Thus, by their very nature and in fulfillment of their central research and teaching mission, universities foster essential practices on which democracy rests.

But universities constrain their democratic potential, and the most elite universities are in some respects the most constrained of all. Their democratic potential is limited, in particular, by intellectual segregation. By this I mean that much of the valuable knowledge created in universities circulates only within the academic world and is not widely shared outside it—and also that, at our current stage of democratic development, many important kinds of knowledge never find their way into universities at all. Intellectual segregation has at least two principal causes today. The first has to do with the nature of advanced research itself. In most disciplines, researchers work in technical vocabularies, and they have an increasing tendency to share their knowledge only with other specialists, often through dispersed international networks. There are good reasons for working in this way—and such practices are indeed necessary for some kinds and stages of research—but these dynamics also lead to intellectual ghettos. Second, elite research universities in the United States remain class-bound institutions, and this means they are also, given the nature of American society, racially unrepresentative. Students admitted to them continue to come disproportionately from wealthy families: the poorer students are, the less likely they are to attend. This is especially true of the most expensive private universities, but—distressingly—it is increasingly true of public research institutions as well. The class dynamics evident in admissions practices are compounded by the tendency of elite research universities, especially private ones, to segregate themselves from the economically disadvantaged and racially diverse communities near which they are located. Taken together, these dynamics constrain the social circulation of knowledge produced in universities and reduce the richness of that knowledge by narrowing the range of social perspectives contributing to its production.

I propose that universities today should expand their democratic mission: they should become engines of democracy. In the era of trivializing sound-bites and talk radio demagoguery, universities can disseminate more widely the complex forms of knowledge necessary for democratic decision making. They can, moreover, play a larger role in promoting informed, open, nonreductive conversations about difficult problems. They can widen the public sphere, bringing people together to deliberate—not merely students and teachers, but people throughout their wider communities. Universities have the stature and the resources, for example, to bring public officials together with those who have elected them, to bring corporate decision makers together with those whose communities will be transformed by their choices, and to create democratic spaces in which atomized and often deeply divided populations can enter into fuller dialogue. Universities might, in short, help us become more answerable to one another.[3]

But if universities want to promote democracy, in this broader sense, they will need to commit themselves to intellectual desegregation. In part, of course, this means they must intensify their efforts to diversify their student bodies. But they should also enhance their relationships with the towns, cities, and regions they are part of. Universities should, as a matter of course, focus more of their intellectual resources on their communities and, in particular, on those portions of them most adversely affected by unjust social arrangements. Research faculty should be encouraged to consider, at some moment in their careers, how their expertise might be brought to bear on the problems facing the towns and cities they live in. Universities should cultivate settings where faculty, students, staff, and those outside the university come together to share knowledge about their communities, to address current problems, to take stock of their histories, and to deliberate about possible futures. Such settings can enable those within the university to share specialized forms of knowledge that are often unavailable to their neighbors—and they can also help those within gain access to local knowledge of which they are often ignorant. By focusing on the shared problems of their own communities, in short, universities can foster intellectual desegregation and can enhance their democratic role in our complex and troubled societies.[4]

This essay will describe one effort to pursue this kind of democratic university-community collaboration. In fall 2007, Lehigh University launched the South Side Initiative, an enterprise that has sought to shift the relationship between a wealthy private research institution and the ethnically diverse, predominantly working-class South Side neighborhoods of the postindustrial city of Bethlehem, Pennsylvania, where the university is located. As the codirector of this initiative, I am not in a position to offer a neutral, objective assessment. I offer instead a report from the field, an attempt to take stock of early efforts and challenges. The dream of the democratic university is not, of course, a new one. It has been revived by successive generations of university citizens for more than a century—and many related experiments are under way on other campuses.[5] I offer these reflections, then, as a contribution to an ongoing conversation, an unfolding collaboration.

History Matters

Every university is located in a particular place, with its own distinctive history, its own configurations of power, its own patterns of privilege and disadvantage, its own experience of democracy and its inhibition. A university cannot function as an engine of democracy unless its members are conscious of the history of their community and of the university's place in that history. What faculty and administrators do not know about the ways their institutions have exercised power and pursued their own interests will come between them and their neighbors. In fact, it already has: those within the university are often the last to know. We found this out the hard way in Bethlehem, as I will explain below. But let me begin with an overview of the history of our city and of Lehigh's role within it. Our recent efforts can be properly understood only in this context.

Bethlehem was founded in 1741 as a utopian religious community by the Moravians, a pietist Protestant sect originating in central Europe. Bethlehem was, in several respects, one of the most egalitarian places in eighteenth-century North America. The Moravians created a communal economy in which everyone worked for the community and received on equal terms not only food, shelter, and clothing but also access to a free system of education, child care, health care, and care for the elderly. Remarkably, in Bethlehem in the 1750s no one feared individual poverty or destitution in old age or illness. There was exceptional gender symmetry in Moravian Bethlehem: women were freed from the burden of privatized child care and domestic labor, enabling them to assume leadership in the community, both spiritual and social. It was a surprisingly integrated multiracial town in which Africans, Native Americans, and Europeans speaking at least sixteen languages lived, worked, worshipped, and learned together. Everyone in this eighteenth-century immigrant enclave—male and female, across all racial groups—was taught to read. In contrast to the usual story of failed utopias, this egalitarian community was economically successful and indeed was one of the most technologically advanced places in European North America. A population growing from seventeen to seven hundred people in the mid-eighteenth century sustained fifty crafts and industries, many of them water-powered, and constructed one of the first systems of municipal running water in North America.

But the egalitarianism of this community was compromised and under-mined in emblematically American ways from the outset. It was a slavehold-ing society: most of those literate Africans, living in conditions of relative material equality with their European coreligionists, were also held as chat-tel by the church. It was a town built on land that had been stolen from the native people, the Lenape, in an especially cynical manner by those who sold it to the Moravians. And despite its prosperity and economic success, the communal economy was dismantled after one generation by church leaders in Germany, and the ensuing privatization of social and economic life led swiftly to the collapse of both economic and gender equality.[6]

A hundred years later, in the late nineteenth century, Bethlehem be-came one of the iconic steel towns of industrial America. It was home to Bethlehem Steel, one of the world's largest steel companies and one of the wealthiest corporations in US history. Bethlehem Steel played an especially important role in the development of the structural steel (most famously the wide-flanged I-beam) that made possible the skyscrapers, suspension bridges, and battleships of twentieth-century America.

For a century, every aspect of life in the city revolved around the mas-sive Bethlehem Steel plant (referred to by everyone in the city, with a mixture of affection and awe, simply as "the Steel"). Most families in the city owed their livelihoods to the Steel, directly or indirectly. It created extraordinary wealth for its owners and for its large managerial class: Bethlehem Steel executives were among the wealthiest Americans, and they built their mansions on the north side of the city. The Steel also cre-ated jobs for thousands of working-class immigrants from many nations, who poured into South Bethlehem to work in the plant. These immigrants built tight-knit, intergenerationally sustained ethnic neighborhoods. Many houses in South Bethlehem were built by groups of immigrants collectively with their neighbors—first one family's home, then another's. Some people today are still living in the houses they were born in eighty or ninety years ago.

In the late nineteenth and early twentieth centuries, there was intense economic exploitation in Bethlehem. Many steelworkers were maimed or killed on the job. They worked long hours for low wages. (If you ask elderly people in the city today, they will tell you, without hesitation, that their fathers earned ninety-six cents for a twelve-hour shift.) There was, in response, a long history of labor organizing at the Steel—and of fierce antiunion violence. During periods of labor agitation, the steel company brought in state militia and private armies to break strikes and to intimidate workers and their families. The Steel was finally unionized in 1941, on the eve of America's entrance into World War II, in the wake of an especially violent strike and the subsequent intervention of the Roosevelt administration. As a result of workers' successful organizing, for fifty years there were good union jobs at the Steel, which brought higher wages, improved safety, paid vacations, good health care plans, and pensions. The union transformed Bethlehem into a model of postwar working-class prosperity. For the first time, steelworkers began sending their children to college in significant numbers.

Starting in the late 1970s, the US steel industry underwent an intensifying crisis as a result of rising competition from foreign steel producers and from nonunion domestic "minimills." This crisis resulted in the gradual scaling back of the steel plant in Bethlehem and its ultimate closure in 1995. In 2001 the entire Bethlehem Steel Corporation went bankrupt, and it pursued a bankruptcy strategy that has become the norm for major American corporations: the company's lawyers persuaded the courts to allow them to sell off assets to other companies while shedding pension and health care obligations to retirees. As a result, thousands of former Bethlehem Steel employees lost the retirement and medical security for which they had given lifetimes of work.[7]

The Steel's closing ultimately led to the loss of thousands of jobs, but Bethlehem did not endure the sudden, catastrophic unemployment experienced in places like Flint or Detroit. Layoffs took place gradually over a decade, and there was a shift to low-paid, nonunion work. As a result, poverty grew once more in the city. Today more than a quarter of residents and the great majority of children on the South Side live in poverty.[8] A disproportionate number of these are the newest migrants, now from Puerto Rico and the Dominican Republic, who are replacing predecessors who had come from Hungary and Slovakia, Poland and Portugal. South Bethlehem suffers from many of the social problems that accompany poverty in the United States, including failing public schools and serious public health problems. The former Bethlehem Steel site is the largest urban brownfield in the United States: its massive ruins and tainted soil cover hundreds of acres at the heart of the city.

Lehigh University is located in the middle of South Bethlehem, and it has had a complex and paradoxical historical relationship with the South Side. Founded in the 1860s, Lehigh developed in close collaboration with Bethlehem Steel. Its early strength was in engineering: it supplied both the engineers and the technical knowledge that made Bethlehem Steel one of the most profitable steel producers in the world. While Lehigh played a significant role in creating massive profits for the Steel, the company also gave the university large sums of money (from its founding gift onward). Steel executives dominated the board of trustees from the time of the university's founding until late in the twentieth century. The building of an elite private research university also played a symbolic role for the Steel's managerial class, as a way of accumulating and displaying cultural capital—a story echoed in the founding of other late nineteenth- and early twentieth-century US research universities, including Stanford, Duke, and Carnegie Mellon.[9]

Even as the university was intimately tied to Bethlehem Steel, it largely closed its doors to the working people of South Bethlehem, who rarely had the financial or educational resources to gain admission. These dynamics led to a long history of town-gown class segregation. This kind of segregation is common to many US university towns and cities, though these dynamics had a special intimacy and geographical visibility in Bethlehem, where a wealthy private university serving a regional East Coast elite was located in the middle of an ethnically diverse, heavily immigrant working-class community. The blast furnaces are visible from the university campus, and the university's spires are visible from the workers' houses. Although Lehigh does not have locked gates to exclude outsiders like many private urban universities in the United States, the border between the university and the city has been policed with vigilance for generations. My elderly South Side neighbors tell stories about being questioned by the police seventy years ago if they set foot on the university grounds in their midst. My younger neighbors, especially African American and Latino men, are today routinely stopped by police at night if they walk on campus or even on adjacent public streets.[10]

An important episode in university-community relations began in the 1960s as Lehigh expanded its campus. Like many other private urban universities around the country (the University of Chicago is a parallel case, for example, as Danielle Allen has shown), Lehigh sought to solve its space constraints by working closely with city government to employ eminent domain powers in the interest of "urban renewal." With the university's active participation, the city declared portions of an adjacent working-class neighborhood "blighted" and forced residents to sell their homes, sometimes against their will. Lehigh purchased the land, razed the houses, and built a new section of its campus where its neighbors had been living. One of my neighbors had the misfortune of having two successive family homes seized: one to make way for university expansion and the other for building a scenic road that takes students and their parents directly from the highway to campus, bypassing working-class neighborhoods that might unsettle the image of an elite university.[11]

Over the past two decades, Lehigh has taken steps to develop more positive relations with its urban neighbors. These efforts have mirrored those widely pursued at other institutions. They have been well intentioned and have produced some positive results, but they have also been haunted by the history of segregation they have sought to address and they have been weakened by inadequate attention to persistent underlying power relations. A newly arrived president, for example, invested in decorative streetlights to improve the appearance of the downtown, but neighbors noted that they petered out within a few blocks from campus. When the university built new dormitories on the edge of campus (on the very blocks seized through eminent domain proceedings some years earlier), the project included space for a modest plaza with restaurants, advertised as a "gateway" to campus that would encourage university-community interaction. Many neighbors, including some of those whose family homes had once been on the site, perceived the architecture as constituting a new defensive wall between the university and the city. The university established regular appeals for charity. Most important, Lehigh opened a Community Service Office that coordinates thousands of hours of student volunteer activity each year. The Community Service Office has fostered much valuable work, especially undergraduates' sharing knowledge with local schoolchildren in homework clubs and tutoring programs. Strikingly, however, the university's positive gestures of assistance have consistently reinforced the hierarchical relations between campus and community. Like other wealthy universities—and indeed like most wealthy sectors of American society—Lehigh has tended to oscillate between viewing poor people as a potential danger to be policed or, in less threatening moods, as the beneficiaries of charity. Rarely has the university been able to recognize its neighbors as partners in education and democracy.

This was the state of affairs in 2004, when the city of Bethlehem arrived at a momentous turning point. After a decade of abandonment, the core of the Steel site—a hundred acres at the heart of the city—was purchased by a New York–based real estate developer. Within days of the purchase, it was revealed that the major stakeholder was in fact the Las Vegas Sands Corporation, one of the largest casino enterprises in the United States, which was filing for a license to open a casino. The state of Pennsylvania had just legalized casino gambling, officially as a strategy for postindustrial urban and regional redevelopment. Presuming that their citizens were unwilling to raise taxes to pay for common needs, Pennsylvania's legislators, like those in dozens of states around the country, turned to skimming casino profits as a last resort for generating public revenue. The Las Vegas Sands Corporation secured the license and built a casino in the middle of the Steel site, at the center of a toxic brownfield.

Back in 2005, though, before the casino had been built, people across the city recognized that Bethlehem was at a crossroads. The redevelopment of hundreds of acres at the heart of the city appeared to be entirely in private hands (a casino corporation now replacing Bethlehem Steel), as were many decisions about the future of the city. Competing positive and negative scenarios circulated. City officials and Sands executives asserted that the casino had the resources to develop the site, would generate tax revenue, would create jobs, and would become an anchor for healthy urban redevelopment. Critics asserted that the casino would bring crime and gambling addiction to the most desperate members of the community; that the city would be overrun by traffic; that the casino would create urban blight and the collapse of retail districts and neighborhoods, including those a few blocks from Lehigh's campus. Bethlehem residents, predictably enough, had mixed responses: some were hopeful, others alarmed. But there was, at least in my experience, a widespread sense of powerlessness: people felt they would have no voice in decisions about the future of the steel site (which many of their lives had revolved around for generations) or about the future of the city more generally.

South Side Initiative

It was in this context that we launched the South Side Initiative (SSI) in fall 2007. A group of Lehigh faculty—mostly in the humanities and social sciences, but some from the natural sciences, business, education, and engineering—began to meet with university staff and with community leaders and residents to determine what role the university might most productively play at this moment of extraordinary change in the city. In the course of the first year, we cast our net wide, meeting with politicians and public officials, with business leaders and journalists, and with community groups of many kinds (including immigrant aid and direct service providers, teachers and public health workers, local arts and historical organizations, church groups and environmental organizations, union members and small business owners, economic development organizations and senior citizens groups). Through these conversations we sought to understand, first, what kinds of knowledge people in Bethlehem needed in order to make sense of what was taking place in the city and what role a research university could play in helping them to produce, disseminate, and gain access to that knowledge. Second, we wanted to know how the university might help to create more space for active democratic deliberation and decision making at this moment of transformation.

In response to what we learned, and through trial and error, SSI developed a range of activities and programs. These were in many respects familiar to the usual functioning of a university. We brought in visiting speakers, held public events, organized classes, and set up working groups. All these activities, though, focused on topics of pressing concern in the city, and each was organized to foster opportunities for faculty and students to come together with community members to exchange different forms of knowledge and to deliberate on local challenges. Visiting speakers, for example, were invited to give conventional academic talks in the specialized languages of their disciplines (where appropriate), but they were also asked to participate in public forums where they could share knowledge through dialogue with residents, public officials, and journalists. SSI courses focused Lehigh faculty expertise and students' attention on important issues in the life of the city. Although some faculty already had substantial bases of local knowledge, others were bringing developed expertise to bear on local issues for the first time. SSI classrooms thus provided spaces where teachers and students alike were often crossing for the first time the intellectual barriers segregating elite knowledge from local circumstances. We rapidly recognized the importance of having these courses team taught by Lehigh faculty and community members (we call these community partnership courses) and of opening classes to community participation so that courses do not replicate the familiar dynamic that casts students and scholars as privileged observers and community members as objects of study. Working groups have similarly brought faculty and students together with community members to engage in sustained multiyear work on particular issues to which we could bring both academic expertise and local knowledge and investment.

Three illustrations will reveal how these activities work together in practice. Because of the urgency of the topic, during SSI's first year we brought to Bethlehem leading experts on casinos, who shared the results of their research on the effects of casino development in towns and communities across the United States. At one public forum, for example, attended by many community members, the leading historian of Atlantic City, Bryant Simon, explained in detail how and why the casinos that had been brought in to revive that city had actually destroyed the urban core. He described the specific dynamics of land speculation that led to inflated house prices and rents and then led, unexpectedly, to laying waste whole neighborhoods. He explained the economic processes by which restaurants, bars, movie theaters, and grocery stores were driven out of business. He explained, too, why Atlantic City's municipal government had less revenue to spend on social services in 2007 than before casinos arrived, despite the impressive-sounding "host fees" and taxes the casinos pay to the city.[12] Local public officials, including the director of planning for the city of Bethlehem, attended the forum, participating in the conversation, raising questions, and responding to questions and concerns from members of the audience along with local business owners and union members. Local journalists were present, and they not only reported on the dialogue but have also followed up on practical policy issues that emerged from the conversation, including real estate speculation, the protection of local business, and local hiring practices at the casino.

This last issue offers an interesting demonstration of the democratic potential of university-led intellectual desegregation. SSI visiting experts mentioned in passing that, despite federal civil rights protections, casinos in predominantly African American and Latino communities around the country have in practice often ended up with mainly white (and often nonlocal) staff, especially in better paid, public casino floor positions. This issue became salient in our conversations only when African American and Latino residents of Bethlehem, who had lived in Atlantic City and experienced discrimination in casino hiring there, emphasized the significance of the issue for our own city and for South Side residents in particular. SSI brought the issue to the attention of a local economic development group, which agreed to organize a series of public information sessions about casino hiring (with the active participation of casino representatives). We wanted these sessions to provide detailed information to demystify the security screening process, which has been the main mechanism for reducing minority job applications, especially in communities with substantial immigrant populations and with disproportionately high incarceration rates resulting from the "war on drugs." These sessions were conducted bilingually to accommodate Bethlehem's large Spanish-speaking population, and they were attended by hundreds of South Side residents. This group also set up computer banks, staffed in part by Lehigh students, to enable residents without computer skills or access to complete the online-only applications for jobs, since in many working-class communities these applications have been another obstacle to successful job seeking. By sharing scholarly expertise and local knowledge, the university was thus able to collaborate with a local nonprofit to maximize opportunities for local employment. In the years ahead, I hope this circuit of knowledge sharing will be further extended by follow-up research on the actual percentage of South Side residents hired by the casino, and their racial and ethnic composition. That research could be transparently shared with the casino, local officials, and journalists and in turn provide material for future SSI classes and published scholarship. Such practices of intellectual desegregation enhance the ability of faculty, students, residents, elected officials, journalists, and the developers themselves to attend to issues of social justice in the practical affairs of the city.

SSI and its community partners felt that equally important work could focus on environmental questions, given the evident challenges and dangers of redeveloping the nation's largest urban brownfield. We invited scientist and philosopher Kristin Schrader-Frechette to speak to a mixed university-community gathering on environmental contamination and environmental justice in a global frame.[13] During her visit she noted that, in her view, the most pressing environmental danger raised by the Steel site redevelopment might well be posed by the two million additional automobiles that the Sands Corporation estimated would bring customers to the casino each year, passing through densely populated working-class neighborhoods. Especially in a valley ringed by hills, Schrader-Frechette said she would expect to see dramatically increased air pollution and a consequent spike in asthma. This was a source of particular concern to us, since South Side residents and local health practitioners had already identified epidemic levels of asthma as a top public health problem. Before the casino opening, 40 percent of children attending the South Side's elementary school had already been diagnosed with chronic asthma. SSI formed a working group on traffic, air pollution, and asthma that is drawing on faculty expertise across the social and natural sciences and is creating a coalition of faculty, students, South Side residents, community health practitioners, and public officials to monitor air pollution and asthma levels and develop strategies for remediation. SSI community partnership classes have focused faculty, student, and community expertise on the environmental, political, regulatory, and economic issues surrounding this major urban development and public health challenge. A Lehigh graduate student was recently honored for her original research in this field. Meanwhile, local journalists have reported on this story, and public officials have acknowledged the urgency of the issue. In this domain, intellectual desegregation has enriched the university's central research and teaching mission, has fostered public awareness and political responsibility where it would not otherwise exist, and most important, has begun to expand a democratic public sphere in which the university's South Side neighbors will be able to make stronger claims to the clean air we are all entitled to.

Finally, the redevelopment of the Steel site is a matter not merely of economic opportunities and environmental challenges, but also of memory and identity. For thousands of people in Bethlehem, the Steel was the economic magnet that brought their immigrant families to the city—and, for good and ill, it was the center of work and of an entire way of life. People throughout the city have a keen desire for that history to be told, and they want to participate in the interpretation of its evolving and contradictory meanings. They are afraid that it will vanish without a trace or that its meanings will be trivialized or fixed by others. From the outset, SSI was aware that the university had particularly valuable resources to share in this area—and an exceptional amount to learn from its neighbors, not merely about the city of Bethlehem but about the United States, about the lived experience of global capitalism and the bewildering migrations it has unleashed, about the accomplishments and catastrophes of industrialization, about the evolving character of working-class communities, about patterns of racism and of ethnic competition and cooperation, about transformations in gender roles, sexuality and family life, and so on.

Because people in the city were deeply concerned with these questions, we brought in experts to talk about strategies other postindustrial communities used to interpret their histories. At one well-attended university-community gathering, for example, anthropologist Cathy Stanton described the accomplishments and limitations of the celebrated museum in Lowell, Massachusetts that commemorates that city's now-vanished textile industry. Drawing on her research, Stanton emphasized a paradox: that the Lowell museum, and other institutions devoted to industrial history, tend to attract professional-class visitors from outside the community who are seeking to make sense of the working-class lives of parents or grand-parents, but that such institutions commonly exclude current working-class residents of the city itself, many of them recent immigrants who do not identify with a vanished industry whose commemoration does not appear to be engaged with the urgent present challenges of their lives.[14] The implications of this argument for our own city were evident to all, and those implications have been actively discussed at SSI public history events ever since, as multigeneration steelworker families and newly arrived immigrants discuss with Lehigh faculty and students and with local history and arts groups the forms of historical interpretation we need in Bethlehem, as well as the importance of creating vibrant institutions to enable South Siders to explore the lived experiences of the city today.

Public history, public humanities, and public art lie at the heart of SSI's collaborative work. Through classes, Lehigh students and faculty join their neighbors in exploring the city's past, in conducting interviews and making documentary films, in creating fiction, poetry, and visual art that explores the complex realities of Bethlehem. An expert in medieval literature asks students to consider how studying medieval representations of poverty may help them understand and respond ethically to the contradictory experience of meeting Lehigh University employees at a local soup kitchen because their wages are inadequate to cover their basic needs.[15] Other professors teach courses on social movements and practical democracy, asking students to collaborate with their neighbors in creating feasible democratic strategies to improve life in the city. Through citywide public art projects, community members, students, faculty, and staff create maps of the city we have inherited and of the city we would like to live in. Ambitious plans are being developed to create a center for interpreting the history of working-class life on the South Side and for enabling the widest possible processes of community self-expression. In these enterprises we seek not to supplant but to support the work of existing, but chronically underfunded, local arts and historical organizations. Through creative and cultural desegregation, we seek to expand the public sphere in the city, to enable people of all kinds to share knowledge, and to invent democratic practices to meet our common needs.

Perhaps the most surprising thing about SSI is the excitement with which it has been embraced by members of the university community and by people throughout the city. Distrust remains strong, but the desire to overcome a century and a half of university-community segregation is also powerful, and participation has exceeded our expectations. In its first three years, SSI sponsored dozens of classes across the humanities, social sciences, and natural sciences focused on the city of Bethlehem. Thousands of people, at Lehigh and throughout the city, have participated in our activities.

But there are serious challenges to the work of intellectual desegregation. We face them in Bethlehem, as colleagues do all over the country (and around the world) who are trying to help universities realize their democratic potential. We face practical problems, of course, including the struggle for time and resources. If faculty and staff pursue this work as an overload, on top of their usual research, teaching, and service, it will be poorly executed and it will, in the long run, fail. Such failures will fulfill negative expectations and complacent presumptions about the necessity of separating research and teaching from the problems of our communities in order to meet appropriate standards of excellence in our disciplines. If we want universities to function as engines of democracy, and if we want to pursue intellectual desegregation, these goals must be included in the strategic plans of our institutions, and we need to pursue this work as a direct extension of our central research and teaching mission. Faculty will need time and resources, for example, to develop courses and to foster research agendas that bring their full scholarly expertise to bear on local problems. If significant numbers elect to pursue this kind of work, it will have an effect on curriculum, and departments will need to embrace such curricular changes as enhancements in the sophistication and power of the education provided to students. The work of intellectual desegregation cannot be successfully pursued by scholars in their spare time as a hobby or under the guise of charity. It must be embraced as a precious and challenging democratic practice among equals, to which scholars and teachers devote themselves as an integral aspect of their professional lives. In recent decades the status of the "public intellectual" has grown considerably, but institutions have not yet committed themselves to creating the conditions that enable public intellectuals to flourish.

The problems of time and resources are, of course, even more formidable for many community members who wish to participate in this work. Especially in relatively poor communities where many are working multiple jobs, it is exceptionally difficult for people to find time to take part in public forums, to attend lectures or classes, to collaborate on public art projects, or to participate in working groups, even if the questions at issue are important to them. The double shift, the speedup of our work lives, and the ever-lengthening workweek (which affects people across the class spectrum) are among the most powerful forces eroding the democratic public sphere in the United States today. If people must choose between going to work and voting, or between seeing their children and deliberating, then there is not, in the end, much choice at all. In such circumstances, the democratic public sphere becomes a privileged domain accessible only to those with substantial incomes and contained workweeks. If universities want to cultivate the public sphere and enhance opportunities for informed deliberation, they will need to think carefully and act creatively to maximize people's ability to participate. Obvious practices like providing child care for public events ought, today, to be a matter of course. But universities will rapidly find themselves up against still deeper institutional obstacles—including, for example, policies that prevent neighbors from attending classes without paying prohibitive fees or from being paid for sharing their expertise as instructors in community partnership courses. If universities, private and public alike, believe that fulfilling their democratic mission requires that faculty and students share knowledge with those outside the university and have opportunities to learn from them, then they must act vigorously to break the material constraints that impede the free circulation of ideas.

Other challenges have to do with the conventions of academic knowledge production and with institutionalized structures of prestige and reward that discourage intellectual desegregation. As long as research on local problems remains a low-status activity—with concomitant effects on publication, tenure, promotion, and prestige—scholars will continue to avoid it. As long as scholars believe that only specialized technical vocabularies will command respect, they will continue to employ them exclusively. If they remain convinced that addressing national and international conferences of experts will confer prestige, but addressing town hall meetings will not, then we know where we will continue to find one another. I must emphasize in this context that I believe strongly in the value of specialized technical vocabularies and of international gatherings of narrowly focused experts: my own scholarly practice has drawn me persistently and beneficially to both. But if we know *only* how to do speak in these vocabularies and are comfortable *only* in these settings, then our intellectual lives and our practices of citizenship have become badly truncated.

Some will say that, in the era of globalization, focusing research and teaching energies on local problems is an invitation to provincialism. I disagree. Globalization does not happen elsewhere. The movement of global capital and its attendant social, political, and cultural effects are as evident in our own communities as anywhere on earth. They remade Bethlehem in the era of eighteenth-century European empire and the transatlantic slave trade as surely as they did in they heyday of Bethlehem Steel, and as surely as they do today in the postmodern moment of the transnational casino economy. Elite research universities must ask themselves why they are willing to invest large sums to send students on study-abroad programs in Latin America but will not encourage them to meet their Latino and Latina neighbors down the street. They should also ask why so many of our institutions contain experts on clean water technology, the history of feminism, and the rise of religious intolerance in the West who have never asked their students to consider how we might address tainted water supplies, sexual violence, or religious conflict in our own communities. We do, indeed, need to reduce US provincialism, and this will require more international literacy and contact. But intellectual cosmopolitanism does not require that we ignore the problems of our own communities. Global practices of solidarity cannot be cultivated by perpetuating segregation as the dominant habit of mind among educated elites or as a structuring principle of our universities and our cities.

Although many other obstacles stand in the way of the democratic university, I will end by returning to the problem of trust. We cannot foster the trust that democratic deliberation rests on if we are unwilling to attend to the histories of power, privilege, inequality, and discrimination that cast their shadow over university-community relations where we live and work. There is no comfortable way to learn this lesson. When we launched the South Side Initiative in Bethlehem in the fall of 2007, at our very first meeting with local residents and community leaders we began to receive our own education. We introduced ourselves and briefly described our democratic and collaborative aims, and then we asked those assembled to introduce themselves. After a few minutes, an elderly woman who has lived and worked on the South Side her entire life explained eloquently that before she was willing to enter into a new partnership, she wanted acknowledgment that the university had torn down the house in which she had been born and which her family had lovingly maintained for decades. After making her statement, she noted drily that she thought it was time to eat.

That was the end of the meeting, or so I thought. Our agenda seemed to be a shambles. For months afterward, we were irritated every time we thought of the gathering and of the frustration of our organizational efforts that day. But that was the day my codirector and I learned for the first time about the university's supplanting its neighbors using the city's eminent domain powers. Only long afterward—after many successful collaborations and after the making of an SSI-sponsored documentary about university expansion on the South Side—did I come to see the event in a different light, as a transformative occasion. I came to see that my neighbor had, with considerable diplomacy and restraint, offered to teach us something we needed to learn. I also came to realize that she had not sabotaged the meeting or ended the conversation, as I had mistakenly imagined. Rather, she had generously proposed that we break bread together. Despite a long and often painful history, and in the face of real losses, she was suggesting that we sit down to eat and begin to get to know one another. It was time to begin the conversation.

Notes

Introduction

1. For data on public education expenditures, see the annual report from the US Census Bureau, *Public Education Finances: 2009* (Washington, DC: US Census Bureau 2011), xii; see also the National Association of State Budget Officers (NASBO) State Expenditure Report, Fiscal Year 2010, 13–20, http://nasbo.org/Publications/StateExpenditureReport/tabid/79/Default.aspx. For the citation from *Brown v. Board of Education*, see *Brown v. Board of Education* 347 US 483 (1954).

2. Ngai 2004, 18.

3. Ngai 2004, 18.

4. Schlesinger 1998.

Chapter 1

1. The size of the decline between 1972 and 2000 depends on the measure of variation. The Gini coefficient declined by 20 percent, and the coefficient of variation (defined as the standard deviation across districts divided by the mean) declined by 24 percent (Corcoran and Evans 2008, table 19.2).

2. *Rose v. Council for Better Education*, 790 S.W. 186 60 Ed. Law Rep. 1289 (1989), defined adequacy in terms of seven learning goals: (1) sufficient oral and written communication skills to enable students to function in a complex and rapidly changing civilization; (2) sufficient knowledge of economic, social, and political systems to enable the student to make informed choices; (3) sufficient understanding of governmental processes to enable the student to understand the issues that affect his or her community, state, and nation; (4) sufficient self-knowledge and knowledge of his or her mental and physical wellness; (5) sufficient grounding in the arts to enable each student to appreciate his or her cultural and historical heritage; (6) sufficient training or preparation for advanced training in either academic or vocational fields so as to enable each child to choose and pursue life work

intelligently; and (7) sufficient levels of academic or vocational skills to enable public school students to compete favorably with their counterparts in surrounding states, in academics or in the job market (http://www.schoolfunding.info/states/ky/lit_ky.php3).

Chapter 2

1. Public expenditures on K–12 public schooling flow from every important governing unit in the United States: cities, counties, states, and federal government, a stream of resources that combined exceeded $550 billion in 2007. K–12 public schooling is the single largest outlay in most local and state budgets. See US Census Bureau 2009, xi.

2. See Converse 1972, 324, referring to the effect of education on political participation.

3. Minorini and Sugarman 1999, 206.

4. Ryan and Heise 2002.

5. For a detailed account of this shift across a variety of educational policy domains, see Koski and Reich 2007.

6. 20 U.S.C. § 6316(b)(1).

7. See Ryan's (2004) analysis.

8. See, e.g., John Rawls, *A Theory of Justice* (1971); Larry Temkin, *Inequality* (1993); Frankfurt 1987; Temkin 2001; Parfit 1997; Anderson 1999, 287; Dworkin 2000. For discussion of the relevance of these ideals to education, see also Anderson 2007; Satz 2007; Brighouse and Swift 2008; and Liu 2006.

9. For a representative formulation along these lines, see Temkin 2003. Because sufficiency applies a uniform standard to all, one might claim that it should be understood as a kind of egalitarian argument. Indeed, any champion of sufficiency will claim that it possesses two features routinely associated with egalitarianism. First, sufficiency should be universal among the relevant group; second, and following from the first, sufficiency should be impartial and treat people equally. In practice, this means no discrimination should be made among people based on arbitrary characteristics such as race and sex. Universality and impartiality are part and parcel of the sufficiency paradigm, and in this respect it overlaps with the equality paradigm.

10. This historical and dynamic view of sufficiency is critical to Satz's (2007) analysis.

11. Parfit 1997, 211.

12. This is precisely what many believe happened in California, which went from atop the list of states in school spending to nearly the bottom of the list in the wake of the *Serrano* decision.

13. Glazer 2006.

14. See Hanushek 2011.

15. A further illustration of this point can be found in the chapter by Helen Ladd and Susanna Loeb in this volume, which discusses two egalitarian principles—equal access to equal quality schools and equal educational opportunity—and one adequacy principle of educational distribution.

16. It bears noting, however, that it is questionable to make inferences about the distribution of opportunities from the distribution of outcomes. In practice, unequal outcomes by group (e.g., the black-white test gap) surely flow from unequal opportunities. But in a strict conceptual mapping, there has to be space for some agents' not taking advantage of the opportunities available to them (though whether we should hold them responsible for not doing so when they are children is of course a further question). I thank Adam Swift for clarification on this matter.

17. Anderson 1999, 2004.

18. Anderson 2004, 106.

19. Anderson 1999, 317–18.

20. Satz 2007.

21. Satz 2007.

22. From a litigation and policy perspective, however, this is more than a mere quibble. To the extent that policymakers must craft educational finance or standards-based reform policy according to an adequacy framework tied to a notion of democratic citizenship, we need a clear understanding of what level of education will produce the type of citizens we seek.

23. These costs are determined in a number of ways: various "costing-out" methods whose calculations can be performed only with sophisticated statistical models, professional judgment panels whose task is to decide what constitutes resources sufficient to generate equal opportunities at the specified outcomes, and "best practice" analyses to determine what cost-effective strategies improve the achievement of disadvantaged students.

24. One might object that it is impossible to insulate public institutions such as publicly funded schools from being deployed by citizens in unequal ways for private gain. Parents, after all, routinely use public schools as a vehicle for private advantage when they sort themselves into residential areas, and therefore school districts, based on wealth. As a practical matter, it may well be impossible to prevent unequal private returns from being extracted from public institutions that are supposed to be provided equally. But the point is not that it is wrong for unequal private returns to be generated from publicly provided institutions, but that it is wrong for public institutions to be subject to manipulation by individuals to produce private returns. So long as the threshold of educational adequacy is met, the sufficiency advocate appears to have no principled reason to object to using public schools to deliver private advantages far above the threshold of adequacy. Put differently, assuming that threshold is met, the adequacy framework cannot register any moral difference between educational inequalities that are the product of private or family behavior (e.g., paying for a private tutor) and those that arise from

private and family behavior channeled through the state's own institutions, such as private contributions to public schools.

25. Hirsch 1976.

26. Hirsch 1976, 5.

27. Brighouse and Swift 2008, 478.

28. Barry 2005, 176–77.

29. This is the place to register the obligatory remark that the value of education is not *only* positional. Obviously, education is also intrinsically valuable. Those who receive an education gain skills and capabilities, they can develop their talents, and they are better able to pursue their life goals and use their freedom. The reasons offered in favor of a liberal education (at least those worth taking seriously) consist in increasing the likelihood that a person will flourish, not in conferring a positional advantage. It would be foolish to deny the nonpositional value of education, a fact that quite properly ought to play a role in guiding the distribution of education. My claim is that while education matters absolutely, relative standing in the distribution of education, within one's rough age cohort, matters a great deal too.

30. As Brighouse and Swift rightly note, however, one strategy for dealing with the unequal distribution of a good with strong positional aspects is to attempt to reduce or eliminate the positional aspects of the good itself. The goal would be to mitigate the instrumental value of the good in question for success in some competitive arena. Thus, in dealing with the positional aspects of education, they consider the option of "eliminat[ing] the causal link between relative education and absolute income by equalizing wage rates" or reducing the causal link between relative education and absolute chances of getting interesting and responsible jobs by "reducing the stigma attached to nepotism, by allocating jobs by lottery, or by reforming the job structure to make jobs more equally interesting and responsible" (Brighouse and Swift 2008, 488–89). For scholars whose work discusses actual policy reform, it seems to me unduly utopian to contemplate allocating jobs by lottery or to wish for a world in which all work was equally interesting and responsible. A better strategy would be to draw on Lesley Jacobs's notion of "stakes fairness" and reduce the stakes that attach to success in certain competitions causally linked in the current environment to educational attainment. It is not the positionality of education itself that is objectionable, it is the amazingly high stakes that attach, for instance, to failing to earn a high school diploma or to winning entry into an elite university. This strategy concedes that education will never shed its positional aspects completely but seeks to limit the sort of winner-takes-all competitions in which education is so instrumentally valuable. See Jacobs 2004, 37ff. I thank Eamonn Callan for helpful discussion on this point.

Chapter 3

1. See, e.g., Levine 2007 and Callan 1997a.

2. Forst 2009.

3. Relatively clear examples of prominent philosophers who hold this first picture of justice are those called luck egalitarians, such as Brian Barry, Jeremy Waldron, Ronald Dworkin, and G. A. Cohen, as well as those who talk of justice in terms of capabilities, such as Amartya Sen and Martha Nussbaum. Debates in education about equality versus adequacy also adopt this picture. See, for instance, Ladd and Loeb (this volume) and Reich (this volume), as well as Satz 2007, Koski and Reich 2007, and Brighouse and Swift 2006a.

4. Young 1990, 2007; Forst 2007, 2009; and Anderson 1999. Though Young places John Rawls within this distributive picture, Forst and Anderson do not, and neither would I.

5. These aspects of education are discussed by those concerned with the art of teaching rather than questions of educational policy and distribution.

6. Forst 2011.

7. For further elaboration of the critera of rejection mattering for deliberation to be reasonable, see Laden 2000 and, more generally, Laden 2012.

8. On the robustness of relational equality, see Anderson 1999 and Cohen 1989b.

9. The chapter as a whole is meant to exemplify this approach, so I won't say more about it here. It differs, however, from the position outlined by Brighouse and Swift (this volume).

10. On the importance of this initial capacity for seeing others as objects of our moral regard, see Gaita 2000.

11. For a somewhat different path to a similar set of conclusions about equality as a matter of our civic practices and habits, see Allen 2004.

12. The generation of trust in hierarchical authority relations deserves at least a whole other essay. Although I think being reasonable is one way to generate trust, I am not claiming it is the only or even the most important way.

13. For a much fuller discussion of this picture of reasoning, see Laden 2012. The picture of reasoning developed there makes reasoning a much more capacious category than standard pictures do. In particular, it does not exclude certain forms of interaction that depend on affect or emotion, and by focusing on the place of reasoning in being and becoming equal I do not mean to exclude such activities. I am also grateful to Maggie Schein for discussion on this point.

14. See, e.g., Schapiro 1999. As Schapiro points out, being fully reasonable is not merely a matter of natural development. Many adults are also not capable of being fully reasonable, but in their case it is generally a result of a bad education (understood broadly), not a limited psyche. But see Pritchard 1996 and Nucci 2001.

15. I note only to leave aside here the possibility of developing an argument based on what has been said to this point for the kind of democratic education that involves seeing schools not as sites of teaching but as "learning communities." See, for instance, Dewey 1916; Apple and Beane 2007; Meier 2002; and Power, Higgins, and Kohlberg 1989.

16. Danielle Allen (unpublished manuscript) makes a similar move in discusssing civic education.

17. Let me mention two alternatives that I think overlap with the suggestions below, KIPP and just community schools. While KIPP schools are hierarchical and tightly regulated and just community schools grew out of the free school movement of the 1960s and were loose and democratic in a way that it is hard to imagine thirty-five years later, both share a commitment to an ideal of answerability. Making good this claim is unfortunately beyond the scope of this chapter. See Power, Higgins, and Kohlberg 1989 and Matthews 2009.

18. The general idea of a basic right to justification is central to Forst's own approach to justice. See Forst 2002.

19. Note that here lies the basis for a different kind of argument for the value of establishing certain sets of student's rights within schools than those that merely try to extend more general arguments for rights into the special circumstances of the schools. For some illuminating discussions of the issues involved here as they are generally approached, see Brighouse and Swift (this volume).

20. See, for one detailed example, Schein 2008.

21. Matthews 2009, which relates the development of KIPP schools, and Meier 2002.

22. For a wonderful example of this dynamic outside the context of a school, see the end of Moglen's chapter in this volume.

23. Lareau 2003.

24. Here we come to grounds that might be developed into an argument for the importance of integration of classrooms and schools by class, race, and any other systemic social division. For a version of such an argument, see Anderson 2007.

25. In *Work Hard. Be Nice*, Matthews (2009) describes a number of such trust-building measures taken by the founding teachers of KIPP in their early days as teachers, from going to visit the parents of their students to living in the neighborhoods where they taught.

26. I take up the distinction between reasoning as a means to reaching agreement and reasoning as being responsive to others in a great deal more detail in *Reasoning* (Laden 2012, esp. chap. 6).

Chapter 4

1. Holmes 1995; White 1996; Gutmann 1987; Callan 1997a; Levine 2007.

2. Dagger 1997.

3. See a liberal multicultural view in Kymlicka 2001 and a distinct one in Parekh 2002.

4. Williams 2003 offers a helpful exploration of citizenship as shared fate. The current view of shared fate broadens Williams's focus on actions as the core dimension that binds us together as well as on the educational implications of shared

fate. While her work is more Rawlsian than mine and relies more on deliberative accounts of justification and mutual effect, there are still many points we agree on, and I am indebted to her work on the topic. I offer a more detailed discussion of Williams's work on shared fate in Ben-Porath 2006, esp. chap. 1.

5. I use the term citizenship education or education for citizenship rather than civic education because my discussion constructs citizenship broadly rather than focusing on the more skills-oriented vision that the term civic education denotes.

6. Spiro 2007. And see historical discussion on the concept of citizenship, culminating as well in recognizing the importance of visions of shared fate, in Williams 2009.

7. Arendt and Jaspers 1992.

8. This question is similar in structure and intent to the one Brighouse and Swift pose at the start of their chapter on the family in this volume: As an institution, what values or interests does it serve that other institutions could not serve as effectively? While the nation and the nation-state are less intimately connected to widespread dimensions of the human psyche, they are still significant institutional phenomena in the past few centuries and therefore merit a similar analysis, which I try to briefly provide here. Like Brighouse and Swift's, my analysis is not meant to justify or support a specific structure or instance of the nation-state (just as they do not aim to justify a specific family structure or practice). And just as they find the family to be an important institution to satisfy specific human aspirations, mostly those related to child rearing and intimacy, I suggest that the nation-state as an institution and the nation as a context for membership and affiliation respond to certain social and political aims and that, in the contemporary world, the nation-state is uniquely positioned to satisfy these aims.

9. This account clarifies some of what makes the nation-state a valuable institution (there are other values promoted by this structure that I do not discuss here; I offer further discussion in Ben-Porath 2007), but note that it leaves open the possibility of competing and additional values, and it does not give up the possibility of criticizing any particular nation-state or its actions.

10. Galston 1995.

11. Galston 1991, 245.

12. Brubaker, n.d.

13. Macedo 2000, 3.

14. See discussion in Shachar 2009. Although in summer 2010 this debate was mostly generated by those who oppose the birthright citizenship of children of undocumented immigrants, the discussion on birthright need not be exclusionary in nature and intent, as Shachar's egalitarian approach exemplifies.

15. Honohan 2006; Goodin 2007.

16. Shared fate citizenship is somewhat comparable to instrumental (or Roman rather than Greek) visions of civic republican citizenship, particularly ones that acknowledge and accept deep diversity as a constant in contemporary democratic

societies. According to one common distinction, Arendtian views of civic republicanism, which rely on Greek roots, portray participation as the most fully human activity. Roman views such as Philip Pettit's regard participation as instrumental to preserving freedom, which for both is the essential legitimating reason for the state. See Pettit 1999.

17. Williams 2003, 231.

18. Smith 2003.

19. Williams 2003, 231.

20. Reich 2007, 711. As I argued in the previous section, identity should not be the sole focus of this endeavor, but I nonetheless agree with Reich's analysis of the capacity of the common school to provide a rich context for developing desirable forms of democratic citizenship.

21. Calhoun 2007; Brubaker 1996, 2004.

22. This vision refers back to the notion of "ascriptive Americanism" that Rogers Smith criticizes.

23. Callan 1997a,76; see also Callan 2010.

24. Schools' capacity to pursue these goals is also affected by their makeup: today's patterns of de facto segregation mean that many children meet mostly those who are like them in class, race, language, country of origin, and political ideology. As Rothstein says in his chapter in this volume, much of this de facto segregation has resulted from decisions and practices based on the rejection of shared fate as a guideline in policymaking and regulation, as well as in personal choices.

25. One challenge to shared fate citizenship that is beyond the scope of this chapter is the exclusive (and sometimes bigoted) notions of citizenship that evolve in times of hardship. I discuss the challenges to shared visions of citizenship in Ben-Porath 2006. Prolonged economic hardship can increase social phenomena like suspicion toward immigrants and other groups that are portrayed by some as "taking away jobs" or "not paying their dues." Learning to envision citizenship as a form of shared fate can offer a partial answer to this matter, as I elaborate in the next section.

26. See Kymlicka and Norman 1994.

27. Galston 1991, 243.

28. Kymlicka and Patten 2003; Suárez-Orozco and Suárez-Orozco (this volume); Aspachs-Bracons et al. 2008.

29. See, for example, Réaume 2000; See also Kymlicka (2001b, 80), for example: "*La survivance* in Quebec has depended on a number of these very basic conditions: French-language education, not only in childhood, but through to higher education; the right to use one's language, not only when interacting with government, but also in one's day to day job, whether in the public service or private employment; the right not only to exempt francophone immigrants from the requirement to learn English to gain citizenship . . . [and] the right to self-government, as embodied in a federal subunit which has the power to make decisions with respect to education, employment, and immigration."

30. Callan 2004, 80.

31. Callan 1997a; see also Ackerman 1980.

32. This is true about groups that affiliate with other national groups, including First Nations and Native Americans, but also immigrant groups that continue their affiliation with their nation of origin in addition to their adopted national home. There need not be a tension in multiple national affiliations, but certain contexts generate such tensions nonetheless. For example, the "war on terror" has had a significant adverse effect not only on American Muslims in general and their sense of shared fate, but also on certain subgroups like Palestinian Americans. See a careful study of these effects in the context of schooling in Abu el-Haj 2010.

33. See Reich 2002, esp. chap. 4.

34. See Levine 2007; Levinson 2007.

35. Some of the reasons for the sense of disengagement and lack of efficacy can be traced to class-based practices such as those documented in Lareau 2003; others have to do with institutions and practices that treat children and adults of different classes differently. The difference in schooling experiences and educational opportunities can be assumed to affect poorer children's low sense of efficacy (see discussion in Levine 2007).

36. Levinson 2007; Kahne and Middaugh 2008.

37. See Wilkenfeld 2009. Also see Blyth and Milner 2007.

38. Deal and Peterson 2009; Wiggins and McTighe 2007. On the importance of trust among the adults in the school for providing effective education to children, see Payne 2008.

39. Some studies have indicated a correlation between civic education in schools, outside the context of the civic curriculum, and the development of civic attitudes. Informal aspects of civic education in schools seem to be more effective than a formal, content-based curriculum in fostering civic understanding and practice. See Conover and Searing 2000.

40. I am grateful to a reviewer for the University of Chicago Press for emphasizing this point.

Chapter 5

1. See appendix A for a detailed description of the analytic plan for all analyses conducted in this study, and appendix B for a description of the measures employed in this research.

2. The finding in figure 1 that black parents report experiencing more discrimination over their lifetimes than their white counterparts might be an underestimate of the actual racial difference. The racial gap on the experience of discriminatory treatment may be wider than groups report owing to underreporting by blacks (and overreporting by whites). Consistent with the current study, Coleman, Darity, and Sharpe (2008) found that black male and female workers are far more likely than whites to report experiencing racial discrimination at work, even when a host

of human capital and labor market factors are controlled. However, when they compared reports of wage discrimination against independent measures of wage discrimination, they found that black respondents significantly underreported their exposure to discrimination and white respondents significantly overreported theirs. Their analysis produced statistical evidence of wage discrimination—racial wage gap net of human capital and labor market factors—for 87 percent of black workers (both male and female) who reported having experienced discrimination on the job in the MCSUI survey. In contrast, their results displayed no statistical evidence of wage discrimination for the overwhelming majority of white females (97 percent) and males (89 percent) who reported having been exposed to racial discrimination. Their findings extend to reports of discrimination in raises and promotions, which led them to conclude that reports of job discrimination or discrimination in wages and promotions are generally coupled with a real wage penalty for blacks, but not for whites.

3. The standard error is useful in illustrating the size of uncertainty in the estimate. Since the statistics are based on a sample of students drawn from a population, they are estimates of the "true" value that would be observed if the entire population was surveyed. Therefore, estimates have a margin of error, which in statistics is referred to as the standard error because it represents the average discrepancy of the means that would be obtained among all possible samples (of a given size) drawn from the population and the real population mean. Given the assumption of normality (that the values in the population are distributed in a manner that can be described by a bell-shaped curve), an estimate is significant only if it is twice the standard error. This means that in the case of a positive estimate (say 0.3), the standard error (say 0.1) could be subtracted from the estimate twice and the estimate will still remain above zero, suggesting that we could be 95 percent confident that the true value in the population is greater than zero—or simply "significant." However, since subtracting a standard error of 0.2 from an estimate of 0.3 twice would equal -0.1, we could not be 95 percent certain that the population value we are estimating is greater than zero. In this case the estimate would be described as not significant (NS).

Chapter 6

1. Congressional Budget Office 2006, vii.
2. Hondagneu-Sotelo and Avila 2001.
3. United Nations Development Programme 2009.
4. Hondagneu-Sotelo and Avila 1997.
5. Bernhard, Landolt, and Goldring 2006; Foner 2003.
6. Ong 1999; Waters 2002.
7. Ong 1999; Zhou 2009, 21–46.
8. Foner 2003; Smith 2006.

9. Bohr, Whitfield, and Chan 2009; Gaytán, Xue, and Yoshikawa 2006.

10. Capps et al. 2007; Chaudry et al. 2010.

11. Bernhard, Landolt, and Goldring 2006; Foner 2003; Menjívar 2006; Menjívar and Abrego 2009, 160–89.

12. Falicov 2007; Suárez-Orozco, Todorova, and Louie 2002; Suárez-Orozco, Bang, and Kim 2011, 222–57.

13. Ambert and Krull 2006; Bernhard, Landolt, and Goldring 2006; Dreby 2009; Suárez-Orozco, Todorova, and Louie 2002; Wong 2006.

14. Sattin-Bajaj and Suárez-Orozco 2010.

15. Cummins 1991, 161–75; Snow 1993, 392–416.

16. Butler and Hakuta 2005.

17. Grosjean 1999.

18. Peal and Lambert 1962; Hakuta 1987.

19. Valdés and Figueroa 1994.

20. Valdés and Figueroa 1994.

21. Cummins 1991, 161–75.

22. Cummins (1991) bases his five to seven years to acquire academic English skills on an optimal, well-funded Canadian context, while Collier (1995 reports that ten years is a more realistic time frame. Previous literacy in native language, quality of language instruction, opportunities to use and develop language, as well as other factors serve to ease or impede second language development.

23. This study utilized a subset of data from the Longitudinal Student Immigrant Adaptation Study, a five-year study using interdisciplinary and comparative approaches, triangulating data to document patterns of adaptation among recently arrived immigrant youths from five sending origins arriving at two receiving centers in the United States (Suárez-Orozco, Suárez-Orozco, and Todorova 2008). Here we make use of both quantitative data from structured interviews conducted with individual students in the first and fifth years of the study and qualitative data gathered through semistructured interviews with youths, their parents, and personnel in their schools. For more information about the sample and the methodology, see Suárez-Orozco, Suárez-Orozco, and Todorova 2008.

Participants. Students in the study were recruited from over fifty schools in the Boston and San Francisco metropolitan areas densely populated by immigrants. The schools were located across seven school districts representing typical contexts of reception for newcomers from each of the groups of origin (US Census Bureau 2000). By the last year of the study, 74 percent of our students were attending high school. Most participants (65 percent) attended large schools with more than a thousand students, and 22 percent attended schools with between five hundred and a thousand students. Most of our students' schools were also racially and economically segregated, characterized by high percentages of students living in poverty, with an average of 48.5 percent (SD = 23.6 percent) of students receiving free or reduced-cost lunches. The minority representation rate at the schools our students attended was, on average, 78.0 percent (SD = 23.7 percent). (See Suárez-Orozco, Suárez-Orozco, and Todorova 2008 for detailed description of school contexts.) A diverse sample (N = 407; 53 percent female) of recently arrived immigrant students from Central America, China, the Dominican Republic, Haiti, and Mexico was initially recruited. Participants ranged in age from nine to fourteen at the beginning of the study (M = 11.7 years of age), though Haitians were on average a year younger than Dominicans and Chinese. All participants had been in the United States no more than a third of their lives (M = 1.93 years). By year 5, the final sample included 309 students (Chinese = 72; Dominican = 60; Central American = 57; Haitian = 50; Mexican = 70), representing an attrition rate of 5 percent annually. In this essay, we report on the 282 students for whom we had available the anxiety and depression outcome data for both year 1 and year 5.

24. Suárez-Orozco, Suárez-Orozco, and Todorova 2008.

25. Suárez-Orozco, Suárez-Orozco, and Todorova 2008.

26. Suárez-Orozco, Suárez-Orozco, and Todorova 2008.

27. Muñoz-Sandoval et al. 1998; Suárez-Orozco, Suárez-Orozco, and Todorova 2008.

28. Suárez-Orozco, Suárez-Orozco, and Todorova 2008.

29. Suárez-Orozco, Suárez-Orozco, and Todorova 2008.

30. Predicting English-language proficiency: Multiple regression analysis explaining English-language proficiency (ELP year 5) with parents' literacy in native Language, parents' English-language skills, student's years of schooling in the country of origin, time in the United States, percentage of time student speaks English in informal settings, school attendance rate, and percentage of school population reaching proficiency or above on English Language Arts (ELA) exam.

Independent Variable	β	SE	t	p
Intercept	−23.57	17.93	−1.31	ns
ELA Exam	0.26	0.04	6.98	***
English Use in Informal Settings	4.63	1.00	4.76	***
Parents' English Proficiency	1.31	0.40	3.32	***
Prior Schooling	−1.41	0.51	−2.74	**
Parents' Literacy	2.25	0.67	3.34	**
School Daily Avg. Attendance Rate	0.60	0.18	3.32	**
Time in US	0.16	0.06	2.54	*

$R^2 = .48$, $F(8, 249) = 33.01$, ***

31. Faltis 1999; Ruiz-de-Valasco, Fix, and Clewell 2001.

32. Valdés and Figueroa 1994.

33. American Psychological Association 2012.

34. Suárez-Orozco, Bang, and Kim 2011.

35. Suárez-Orozco, Bang, and Kim 2011.

36. Suárez-Orozco, Bang, and Kim 2011.

37. Suárez-Orozco, Bang, and Kim 2011.

38. Suárez-Orozco, Bang, and Kim 2011.

39. All names used throughout this chapter are pseudonyms to protect the identity of our participants.

40. Suárez-Orozco, Bang, and Kim 2011.

41. Likewise, youths who had undergone separations of less than two years reported less anxiety and depression.

42. LeVine 2003.

43. Hernandez, Denton, and Macartney 2007; Urban Institute 2005.

44. Suárez-Orozco et al., 2011.

45. Maccoby 1992.

46. Suárez-Orozco and Suárez-Orozco 2001.

47. Urrea 1998, 41.

48. Maccoby 1992.

49. Cao 1997, 32.

50. Orellana 2009.

51. Hoffman 1989, 145.

52. Maccoby 1992.

53. Bronfenbrenner 1986.

54. Fan and Chen 2001; Henderson and Mapp 2002; Hong and Ho 2005; Izzo et al. 1999.

55. Ferguson et al. 2008.

56. Epstein 1995; Fantuzzo, Tigh, and Childs 2000.

57. Epstein 1995.

58. Sheldon 2002.

59. Griffith 1998.

60. Griffith 1998; Scribner, Young, and Pedroza 1999.

61. Chao 2000; Griffith 1998; Mau 1997; Sy and Schulenberg 2005.

62. García Coll and Magnuson 2000; Peña 2000; Suárez-Orozco, Suárez-Orozco, and Todorova 2008.

63. Hughes, Gleason, and Zhang 2005; Izzo et al. 1999.

64. Huntsinger and Jose 2009; Sy and Schulenberg 2005.

65. Kohl et al. 2000; Rice 2010.

66. Rice 2010.

67. Rice 2010.

68. Delpit 1995; Ogbu 1993.

69. Garcia Coll et al. 2002; Ladson-Billings 1995.

70. Sirin, Ryce, and Mir 2009.

71. Trumbull, Rothstein-Fisch, and Hernandez 2003.

72. Scribner, Young, and Pedroza 1999.

73. Chao 2000; Huntsinger and Jose 2009.

74. Delgado-Gaitin 1991; García Coll et al. 2002; Kuperminc, Darnell, and Alvarez-Jimenez 2008; Suárez-Orozco, Suárez-Orozco, and Todorova 2008.

75. Louie, 2012.

76. Delpit 1995; Okagaki and Sternberg 1993.

77. Lasky 2000.

78. Theilheimer 2001.

79. Mapp 2003; Patrikakou and Weissberg 2000; Delgado-Gaitin 1991.

80. Suárez-Orozco, Suárez-Orozco, and Todorova 2008.

81. Suárez-Orozco and Suárez-Orozco 1995.

82. Suárez-Orozco, Suárez-Orozco, and Todorova 2008.

83. Cooper, Robinson, and Patall 2006.

84. Suárez-Orozco, Suárez-Orozco, and Todorova 2008. In a regression analysis including mother's education, father's work, classroom engagement, English proficiency, and homework proficiency with GPA as the outcome, whether students completed their homework was the single strongest predictor of grades at the end of the year. Bang et al. 2009.

85. Wendel and Anderson 1994.

86. Suárez-Orozco, Suarez-Orozco, and Todorova 2008.

87. Bang et al. 2009.

88. Suárez-Orozco, Suárez-Orozco, and Todorova 2008.

89. Suárez-Orozco, Suárez-Orozco, and Todorova 2008.

90. Hakuta, Butler, and Witt 2000; Suárez-Orozco, Suárez-Orozco, and Todorova 2008.

91. Suárez-Orozco et al. 2010.

92. Suárez-Orozco, Suárez-Orozco, and Todorova 2008.

93. Bang et al. 2009.

94. Weinstein 2002.

95. Schunk 1991.

96. Goslin 2003; Suárez-Orozco, Suárez-Orozco, and Todorova 2008.

Chapter 8

1. For a full discussion of the relation of nonschool factors to school success, see Rothstein 2004, 2008; Massey and Denton 1993, especially chap. 6; and Wilson 1987. For illustrations of the workings of race and informal networks, see Eaton 2001.

2. Kahlenberg 2006.

3. Benveniste, Carnoy, and Rothstein 2003, 71–85.

4. Wilder 2008, 3; McNeal 1999.

5. Warren 2001; Shirley 1997; Ferguson 2005; Fruchter and Gray 2006.

6. Hirschman 1970.

7. *Parents Involved in Community Schools v. Seattle School District No. 1, et al.*, No. 05–908, 2007. Anthony Kennedy participated in both majorities—one finding that integration is a compelling government interest, and the other that the districts' policies to address this interest could not withstand strict scrutiny.

8. *Milliken v. Bradley*, 418 U.S. 717, 1974.

9. Quoted in Polikoff 2006, 114.

10. Civil Rights Cases 1883.

11. *City of Richmond v. J. A. Croson Co.*, No. 87–998, 1989.

12. Comprehensive summaries include Weaver 1948; Kushner 1979; and to a considerable extent, Massey and Denton 1993.

13. See references in Kushner 1979, 552.

14. For the classic history, see Woodward 1955. Also see Lemann 2006.

15. NAACP 1917.

16. *Buchanan v. Warley*, 245 U.S. 60, 1917.

17. *Harmon v. Tyler*, 273 U.S. 68, 1927.

18. Kushner 1979.

19. Loewen 2005.

20. *Village of Arlington Heights v. Metropolitan Housing Development Corp.* 429 U.S. 252, 1977.

21. See, for example, Kirp, Dwyer, and Rosenthal 1995.

22. Kushner 1979.

23. *Corrigan v. Buckley*, 271 U.S. 323, 1926.

24. Excerpts cited in Polikoff 2006, 113; Weaver 1948, 72.

25. Weaver 1948.

26. Sugrue 1995.

27. Dean 1947.

28. Cohen 2003; Williamson 2005.

29. Cited in Polikoff 2006, 113; emphasis added.

30. *Shelley v. Kraemer*, 334 U.S. 1 (1948).

31. Polikoff 2006.

32. *Mayers v. Ridley*, 465 F.2d 630 (D.C. Cir. 1972).

33. AreaConnect Online, n.d.

34. Hirsch 1998, 14.

35. Weaver 1948.

36. Julian and Daniel 1989, 668–69.

37. Sugrue 1995, 564, 568–69.

38. Davidson 1978; *Resident Advisory Board v. Rizzo*, U.S. Third Circuit Court of Appeals. 564 F.2d 126 (1977).

39. *Hills v. Gautreaux* 425 U.S. 284, 1976.

40. Polikoff 2006.

41. Polikoff 2006, 91, 92, 148.

42. Murasky 1971.

43. Flournoy and Rodrigue 1985.

44. Hirsch 1983, 14.

45. McPherson 1972.

46. Satter 2009, 2, 8.

47. McPherson 1972.

48. Kushner 1979, 599. In 1928 the organization's name was the National Association of Real Estate Boards.

49. Munnell et al. 1996; Ladd 1998.

50. Powell 2010.

51. Relman 2008; Immergluck and Smith 2006.

52. Relman 2008.

53. Atlas, Dreier, and Squires 2008.

54. Atlas, Dreier, and Squires 2008, n. 21; Bradford 2002, vii–viii.

55. Bradford 2002. A "predominantly African-American (or white) census tract" is one where 75 percent or more of the residents were African American (or white).

56. Ross and Yinger 2002.

57. Rivera et al. 2008.

58. Bocian, Ernst, and Li 2006.

59. Furman Center for Real Estate and Urban Policy 2009.

60. Andrews 2005.

61. Warren 2007.

62. Powell 2009, 2010.

63. Weaver 1948.

64. Rubinowitz and Perry 2002.

65. Sugrue 1995.

66. Weaver 1948.

67. Rubinowitz and Perry 2002.

68. Rubinowitz and Perry 2002; Bell 2008.

69. Bell 2008.

70. Rubinowitz and Perry 2002.

71. Caro 1975, 490, 494, 512, 514, 532–33, 557–58.

72. *Hawkins v. Town of Shaw, Mississippi*, U.S. Court of Appeals, 437 F.2d 1286, 5th Cir., 1971.

73. Colfax 2009; Zanesville 2007.

74. See, for example, King 1995.

75. See, for example, Katznelson 2005; Herbold 1994-95; Onkst 1998; Turner and Bound 2002.

76. See, for example, Katznelson 2005.

77. *Milliken v. Bradley*, 418 U.S. 717, 1974; emphasis added.

78. *Milliken v. Bradley*, 418 U.S. 717, 1974; emphasis added.

Chapter 9

1. "The family" is, of course, hotly contested ideological terrain. We use the term specifically to refer to the parent-child dyad. That the adults realizing our

"family values" can be single parents or same-sex parents and need have no biological connection to those they parent makes our view an intervention in that ideological debate. We attempt to explain what is really valuable about parent-child relationships in a way that rescues "family values" from some of their conventional connotations.

2. We use the term values in two distinct ways. When we say that familial relationship goods are values we mean they are objectively good. But when we talk about shaping children's values we are referring to children's attitudes—their subjective beliefs about what is good.

3. Cohen 2013, 146.

4. For fuller discussion of different ways of conceptualizing justice and its relation to deliberative legitimacy, see Anthony Laden's contribution to this volume.

5. Wolff and De-Shalit 2007, 90.

6. Walzer 1983.

7. This and much else in the chapter summarizes views set out more fully in Brighouse and Swift 2006b and 2009b and to be set out yet more fully in our forthcoming *Family Values*.

8. Keller 2007.

9. Locke 1996.

10. Reich 2002, 149.

11. For the view that parents' interest in expressive liberty yields extensive rights to determine the content of their children's education, see Galston 2002.

12. For discussions of the first, see Gutmann 1987, Morse 2001, and Ben-Porath (this volume).

13. Raz 1986, 369–70.

14. *Wisconsin v. Yoder*, 406 U.S. 205 (1972); *Mozert v. Hawkins County Board of Education*, 827 F.2d 1058 (6th Cir. 1987). See, for example, Reich 2002 and Dwyer 1999.

15. See Brighouse 2006 for elaboration of others.

16. See Adams 1997.

17. Damage to parent-child relationships is perhaps particularly likely, and sensitivity to the potential for that damage particularly important, in circumstances such as those of immigrant parents described by Carola and Marcelo Suárez-Orozco (this volume), where parents' authority has already been undermined by the inversion of healthy dependency relationships.

18. For fuller discussion, see Brighouse and Swift 2009b and Adam Swift 2003.

19. For discussion of this—meritocratic—specification of the principle of equal opportunity and its relation to others, see Brighouse and Swift 2008.

20. We thus disagree with Nathan Glazer, for whom the main obstacle to integration and equalization is "the value of freedom from state imposition when it affects matters so personal as the future of one's children." Even if states did equalize funding, Glazer thinks a commitment to individual freedom means that politicians

could not "prevent well-to-do or knowledgeable parents from adding more on their own, or from leaving the state system entirely." He is right, of course, that such prevention would compromise the freedom of those so prevented. Our claim is that parents have no right to that freedom.

21. See Brighouse and Swift 2008.

22. But see Grubb 2008 and Cohen and Moffitt 2009 for explanations of why this presumption is often mistaken.

23. See Graetz and Shapiro 2005.

Chapter 10

1. In this perspective, "policy serves as the focal point for a broader analysis of how political forces shape governance and how government actions reshape the society and polity. . . . policies are not just products of politics, but also active forces in the political transaction itself." Soss, Hacker, and Mettler 2007, 14.

2. For more on the history of educational politics and policymaking in the United States, see McGuinn 2006.

3. Loveless 2006, 24.

4. Hess and Finn 2007.

5. McClure 2004.

6. Center for Education Reform 2009.

7. Cohen and Moffitt 2009, 43.

8. Manna 2011.

9. Data from a 2011 Center on Education Policy survey of state education officials revealed that "nearly all of the dozens of ARRA-related reform strategies included in our survey are being acted on by a majority—often a large majority of the responding states." Center on Education Policy 2011, 3.

10. "Race to the Top Itself Needs Some Reform" 2010.

11. For more on RTT, see McGuinn 2010a.

12. For a lengthy treatment of these debates, see Brill 2011.

13. A major launch event for the framework was indefinitely postponed, however, when the groups' leaders were called to the White House to meet with the president's education advisers. The meeting led the civil rights leaders in attendance to announce afterward that there were "broad areas of agreement" with the administration on education. McNeill 2010.

14. Duncan 2010.

15. Brighouse and Schouten 2011.

16. Ladd 2010.

17. The BBA was convened by the Economic Policy Institute, and its leadership includes two contributors to this volume: Helen Ladd and Richard Rothstein. In 2011, the Education Equality project merged with Stand for Children. Today the EEP message of accountability and reform is perhaps most prominently articu-

lated by the Policy Innovators in Education Network (PieNet), of which Stand for Children is a member.

18. Goldstein 2009; see also Colvin 2009.

19. Coleman 1966.

20. Rothstein 2004 offers a more detailed study of economic segregation and its effects on schools.

21. Darling-Hammond 2010b.

22. Broader, Bolder Approach to Education 2009.

23. Broader, Bolder Approach to Education 2009.

24. See, for example, Chenoweth 2007, 2009.

25. For more on the rise and activities of a new wave of education reform advocacy organizations, see McGuinn 2012.

26. Klein, Lomax, and Murguia 2010.

27. On teachers unions' political opposition to school accountability reforms, see Hartney and Flavin 2011 and Moe 2011. See also Taylor and Rosario 2009.

28. Rhodes 2011.

29. Salzman 2006.

30. "Oppose the No Child Left Behind Recess until Reauthorization Act" 2008.

31. Note that there are tensions—some exposed and some latent—within the accountability coalition. While there is agreement on the need to drive systemic reform in state school systems, there is some disagreement on what particular reforms and student populations should be emphasized. Business groups tend to be less concerned about equity and more focused on excellence, and more concerned with reform than with providing additional resources to schools. Civil rights and antipoverty groups, meanwhile, focus on equity, want more resources alongside more reform, and tend to support targeted means-tested voucher programs while opposing more universal voucher or tax credit proposals.

32. For a detailed exchange between leaders of the BBA and EEP, see Williams and Noguera 2010.

33. A 2006 Brookings Institution report, for example, concluded that "schools could substantially increase student achievement by denying tenure to the least effective teachers." Gordon, Kane, and Staiger 2006, 13.

34. Data from the US Department of Education's 2007–8 Schools and Staffing Survey reveal that on average each year school districts dismiss or decline to renew only 2.1 percent of teachers (tenured and nontenured) for poor performance. McGuinn 2010b.

35. National Center on Teacher Quality 2008.

36. Weisberg et al. 2009.

37. Sandi Jacobs of the National Center for Teacher Quality reported that "no state has really done anything to ensure that tenure is meaningful. A handful of states have longer than average probationary periods before tenure is awarded, but

none of those has any sort of meaningful criteria—just a longer timeline. We've found just two states—Iowa and New Mexico—that have some rudimentary requirements, but these are just first steps toward connecting tenure to effectiveness." Personal correspondence with the author, August 12, 2009. Barbara Thompson, the project leader for teaching quality at the Education Commission of the States, agreed with this assessment, noting that she saw efforts to link tenure to teaching effectiveness "getting shot down all the time." Telephone interview with the author, August 12, 2009.

38. Sawchuk 2009.

39. Sawchuk 2010b.

40. Six states removed such firewalls in response to RTT, including California, Indiana, and Wisconsin. Eleven states have gone further and enacted legislation that requires student achievement data to be used in teacher evaluation or tenure decisions. For more on RTT, see McGuinn 2010a.

41. Brody 2010; Felch, Song, and Smith 2010.

42. Broader, Bolder Approach to Education 2010.

43. Greenhouse and Dillon 2010.

44. Greenhouse and Dillon 2010.

45. Heiten 2011.

46. *Carey v. Population Services*, Int'l, 431 U.S. 678, 2011.

47. US Department of Education 2010.

48. For a promising example, see Hamill 2011.

49. The school finance movement, for example, is beginning to build on and integrate with the accountability movement in interesting ways. As Anna Marie Smith notes in this volume, school finance lawyers are increasingly using test score data to make a case for the need for additional resources, to provide an outcome measure for equity (or adequacy), and to monitor district and state progress toward equity and adequacy goals.

Chapter 11

1. *Brown v. Board of Education of Topeka*, 347 U.S. 483 (1954).

2. See Derrick Bell's (2005) radical critique of *Brown* as the product of Cold War biracial "interest convergence."

3. *Parents Involved in Community Schools v. Seattle School District No. 1, et al.*, 551 U.S. 701 (2007).

4. *Milliken v. Bradley*, 418 U.S. 717 (1974).

5. *San Antonio School District v. Rodriguez*, 411 U.S. 1 (1973).

6. *Campaign for Fiscal Equity v. State of New York*, 295 A.D. 2d 1 (2003).

7. Kozol 2005.

8. Sunstein 2004.

9. See, for example, *Sweatt v. Painter*, 339 U.S. 629 (1950).

10. See, for example, *Brown v. Board of Education of Topeka*, 347 U.S. 483 (1954).

11. *Plessy v. Ferguson*, 163 U.S. 537 (1896).

12. *Brown v. Board of Education of Topeka*, 347 U.S. 483 (1954), at 494.

13. "Brown is commonly thought to have been a case about racial discrimination. It is even said to have established a constitutional norm of 'colorblindness.' But to the participants in the case, and to the Court at the time, the case was fundamentally about education." Sunstein 1992.

14. See Rawls 1999.

15. "The dignity of work and of personal achievement, and the contempt for aristocratic idleness, were from colonial times onward at the very heart of American civic self-identification. The opportunity to work and to be paid an earned reward for one's labor was a social right, because it was a primary source of public respect. It was seen as such, however, not only because it was a defiant cultural and moral departure from the corrupt European past, but also because paid labor separated the free man from the slave.... [Individuals excluded from the American polity] have regarded voting and earning not as just the ability to promote their interests and to make money. They have seen them as the attributes of an American citizen. And people who are not granted these marks of civic dignity feel dishonored, not just powerless and poor. They are also scorned by their fellow citizens." Shklar 1998, 387–88.

16. Even in this ideal scenario, which is intended to reproduce several features of Rawls's notion of fair equality of opportunity (Rawls 1999), the possibility of failing to attend adequately to the needs of the least talented remains a serious problem. See Arneson 1999; Brighouse and Swift 2009a; and Brighouse and Swift 2006a. However, Rawls at least anticipates this problem in several passages in *A Theory of Justice*; see, for example, sec. 17, pp. 86–87, 88–89, 90. "Resources for education are not to be allotted solely or necessarily mainly according to their return as estimated in productive trained abilities, but also according to their worth in enriching the personal and social life of citizens, including here the less favored. As a society progresses the latter consideration becomes increasingly important." Rawls 1999, 90.

17. Young 1990.

18. *Brown v. Board of Education of Topeka*, 347 U.S. 483 (1954), at 493.

19. Klarman 2004.

20. Cohen and Moffitt 2009, 6.

21. Darling-Hammond 2010b, 18–21.

22. *Swann v. Charlotte-Mecklenburg Board of Education*, 402 U.S. 1 (1971).

23. *Milliken v. Bradley*, 418 U.S. 717 (1974), at 717 ff.

24. On the salience of official action on the part of federal, state, and local governments where the promotion of the geographic isolation of low-income black families is concerned, see Rothstein (this volume).

25. *Milliken v. Bradley*, 418 U.S. 717 (1974), at 741–42.

26. *Milliken v. Bradley*, 418 U.S. 717 (1974), at 744; emphasis added.

27. *Milliken v. Bradley*, 418 U.S. 717 (1974), at 746; emphasis added.

28. See, for example, Massey and Denton 1993; Self 2005; Sugrue 2005; Oliver and Shapiro 2006; Krysan 2002; Logan, Stults, and Farley 2004; Williams, Nesiba, and McConnell 2005; and Wyly and Hammel 2004.

29. A comprehensive critical analysis of the political conditions being invoked by the *Milliken* majority would, of course, tackle further questions. After probing the legitimacy of the exclusionary constitution of "the people," it would investigate the quality of the collective decision-making process through which the education policy for the schools was determined. Under Rawlsian or Habermasian standards, for example, we would attempt to discover how well that process conformed to the deliberative ideal—that is, how far legislators sincerely defend their proposed laws based on their contribution to the common good, the political liberties of the participants are given a fair value, and equality is manifested. If we found that the political process primarily consisted of market-oriented relationships, such as between interest groups who engage in bargaining to advance their own particular interests without regard for the common good, it would be clear that democracy's threshold conditions had not been established. See Cohen 2006. See also Anthony Laden (this volume) on the centrality of public justification to the reasoning that is adequate to a democratic society.

30. *Milliken v. Bradley*, 418 U.S. 717 (1974), at 782.

31. *Milliken v. Bradley*, 418 U.S. 717 (1974), at 782.

32. *Milliken v. Bradley*, 418 U.S. 717 (1974), at 806.

33. *Board of Education v. Dowell*, 498 U.S. 237 (1991).

34. *Board of Education v. Dowell*, 498 U.S. 237 (1991), at 247.

35. *Board of Education v. Dowell*, 498 U.S. 237 (1991), at 248.

36. *Board of Education v. Dowell*, 498 U.S. 237 (1991), at 249.

37. *Board of Education v. Dowell*, 498 U.S. 237 (1991), at 251.

38. *Board of Education v. Dowell*, 498 U.S. 237 (1991), at 252; emphasis in the original.

39. *Board of Education v. Dowell*, 498 U.S. 237 (1991).

40. *Freeman v. Pitts*, 503 U.S. 467 (1992).

41. *Freeman v. Pittss*, 503 U.S. 467 (1992), at 495.

42. *Freeman v. Pitts*, 503 U.S. 467 (1992), at 495.

43. *Freeman v. Pitts*, 503 U.S. 467 (1992), at 512.

44. *Freeman v. Pitts*, 503 U.S. 467 (1992), at 518.

45. *Missouri v. Jenkins*, 515 U.S. 70 (1995).

46. *Missouri v. Jenkins*, 515 U.S. 70 (1995), at 168–69.

47. *Missouri v. Jenkins*, 515 U.S. 70 (1995), at 106.

48. *Missouri v. Jenkins*, 515 U.S. 70 (1995), at 111.

49. *Missouri v. Jenkins*, 515 U.S. 70 (1995), at 112.

50. *Missouri v. Jenkins*, 515 U.S. 70 (1995), at 112.

51. *Parents Involved in Community Schools v. Seattle School District No. 1, et al.*, 551 U.S. 701 (2007), 701 ff.

52. *Grutter v. Bollinger*, 539 U.S. 306 (2003).

53. *Parents Involved in Community Schools v. Seattle School District No. 1, et al.*, 551 U.S. 701 (2007), at 746 (internal citation suppressed).

54. *Parents Involved in Community Schools v. Seattle School District No. 1, et al.*, 551 U.S. 701 (2007), at 746.

55. *Parents Involved in Community Schools v. Seattle School District No. 1, et al.*, 551 U.S. 701 (2007), at 746 (internal citation suppressed).

56. *Parents Involved in Community Schools v. Seattle School District No. 1, et al.*, 551 U.S. 701 (2007), at 746 (internal citation suppressed).

57. *Parents Involved in Community Schools v. Seattle School District No. 1, et al.*, 551 U.S. 701 (2007), at 748. Advocates for voluntary school assignment policies deliberately designed to promote racial diversity may take some comfort that Justice Kennedy was clearly not prepared to go this far; however, it could also be argued that the approach he maps out in his concurrence relies on several illogical assumptions. It is not at all certain that Justice Kennedy has proposed a workable solution that would survive further constitutional challenges. See *Parents Involved in Community Schools v. Seattle School District No. 1, et al.*, 551 U.S. 701 (2007), at 782–98.

58. *San Antonio School District v. Rodriguez*, 411 U.S. 1 (1973), at 1 ff. There is, of course, a great deal of debate about the relation between education spending and the quality of educational opportunity. On the difficulty of measuring educational quality, see Ladd and Loeb (this volume). I will assume, for the sake of the argument, that properly targeted and managed increases in school spending, at equitable levels reflecting actual student need, would constitute a necessary element in any effective program designed to improve the educational opportunities for the low-income pupils who are currently attending underperforming schools.

59. Gee, Daniel, and Goldstein 2008, 10.

60. See Ladd and Loeb (this volume).

61. *San Antonio School District v. Rodriguez*, 411 U.S. 1 (1973), at 35.

62. *San Antonio School District v. Rodriguez*, 411 U.S. 1 (1973), at 24.

63. *San Antonio School District v. Rodriguez*, 411 U.S. 1 (1973), at 71.

64. *San Antonio School District v. Rodriguez*, 411 U.S. 1 (1973), at 75.

65. *San Antonio School District v. Rodriguez*, 411 U.S. 1 (1973), at 11–13. Note that none of these figures are weighted for actual student need; it is highly likely that the disparities would be much greater if these figures were adjusted for this.

66. *San Antonio School District v. Rodriguez*, 411 U.S. 1 (1973), at 102–3.

67. *San Antonio School District v. Rodriguez*, 411 U.S. 1 (1973), at 71.

68. *San Antonio School District v. Rodriguez*, 411 U.S. 1 (1973), at 112 (internal citation suppressed).

69. *San Antonio School District v. Rodriguez*, 411 U.S. 1 (1973), at 72, n. 2.

70. *San Antonio School District v. Rodriguez*, 411 U.S. 1 (1973), at 71.

71. *San Antonio School District v. Rodriguez*, 411 U.S. 1 (1973), at 37.

72. *San Antonio School District v. Rodriguez*, 411 U.S. 1 (1973), at 49.

73. *San Antonio School District v. Rodriguez*, 411 U.S. 1 (1973), at 54–55.

74. Rebell 2009, 2–3.

75. *Campaign for Fiscal Equity v. State of New York*, 8 N.Y. 3d 14 (2006) (known as *CFE* III).

76. *Campaign for Fiscal Equity v. State of New York*, 86 N.Y. 2d 307 (1995) (known as *CFE* I), at 316.

77. *Campaign for Fiscal Equity v. State of New York*, 100 N.Y. 2d 893 (2003) (known as *CFE* II), at 905.

78. Michael Rebell, interview with author, 2010.

79. *Campaign for Fiscal Equity v. State of New York*, 295 A.D. 2d 1 (2002) (*CFE* II, appellate court decision), at 8.

80. *CFE* II, at 906.

81. *CFE* III.

82. Schmitter and Karl 1991, 76.

83. Guinier 1994.

84. Schmitter and Karl 1991, 78.

85. See Justice Marshall, *Regents of the University of California v. Bakke*, 438 U.S. 265 (1978) (concurring in part and dissenting in part). See also Schnapper 1985.

86. Cohen 2006.

87. Noguera 2010.

88. Ladd 2009.

89. See Ladd and Loeb (this volume).

90. See Reich (this volume).

91. Darling-Hammond 2010b, 18–65.

92. Reed 2001.

93. Compare Rosenberg 1991 and McCann 1994.

Chapter 12

1. Between 1988 and 2008, the percentage of voting-age Americans casting ballots in presidential elections has ranged from a low of 49.1 percent (1996) to a high of 56.8 percent (2008), while turnout for midterm congressional elections has varied from 36.4 percent (1998) to 37.1 percent (2006). Data drawn from Congressional Research Service reports, Election Data Services Inc., and State Election Offices. Summarized at "National Voter Turnout in Federal Elections: 1960–2008," Infoplease, last modified 2008, http://www.infoplease.com/ipa/A0781453.html.

2. Williams 1984. For an overview of Williams's thinking on these matters, see Moglen 1993.

3. For a related vision of the democratic university, which has influenced my own thinking, see Allen 2004, 161–86. On the broader ways educational institutions can foster a democratic ethos in which we can become more answerable to one another, see Laden (this volume).

4. Practices of intellectual desegregation of the kind I am describing would be enriched by—and might be seen as a practical effort to foster—a version of the "shared fate citizenship" education Ben-Porath calls for in this volume.

5. Early twentieth-century visionaries of the democratic university include, of course, W. E. B. Du Bois and John Dewey. Successive waves of democratic movement building, in the Progressive Era, the 1910s, the 1930s, and again in the 1960s and 1970s, each produced new visions of the socially engaged modern university. In recent years "civic engagement" has emerged as a widespread goal of US colleges and universities—though the actual meaning of this goal varies a great deal in practice, encompassing everything from traditional models of charity and student volunteerism that support established social hierarchies to ambitious experiments in democratic institution building. The scale of this development can be registered, in part, by the extensive membership of colleges and universities in large national networks such as Campus Compact and Imagining America.

6. This account of Moravian Bethlehem, and the succeeding account of the city's later history, is based on research for my book in progress, *Bethlehem: American Utopia, American Tragedy*. For useful overviews of Moravian Bethlehem, see Smaby 1988 and Engel 2009.

7. For a lively journalistic overview of Bethlehem Steel's relation to the city, see Strohmeyer 1986. On the Bethlehem Steel Corporation's bankruptcy, see Reutter 2004, 443–62.

8. According to the 2000 census, 25.7 percent of South Side residents were living below the official poverty line. See *Bethlehem, Pennsylvania: General Population and Housing Characteristics from the 2000 US Census*, Bureau of Planning and Zoning. http://www.bethlehem-pa.gov/pdf/BethCensusReport2000.pdf.10. In conversation with me, Principal Ed Docalovich reported that in 2010, 91 percent of students at the South Side's public junior high school, Broughal Middle School, qualified for free or reduced-cost lunches.

9. For official accounts of the university's history, written by the daughter of a former Lehigh president and by a history department faculty member, respectively, see Bowen 1924 and Yates 1992.

10. The class segregation of US colleges and universities, and of their communities, is of course part of a broader history of residential and educational segregation (by class and often by race and ethnicity) that continues to shape the entire system of US education from preschool to graduate school. For other aspects of this broader history of segregation, see chapters in this volume by Rothstein and Smith—and for efforts to conceptualize and address the inequitable effects of this history, see chapters by Harris, Suárez-Orozco and Suárez-Orozco, McGuinn, Reich, Brighouse and Swift, and Ladd and Loeb.

11. On the city's use of eminent domain to seize blocks of houses north of Packer Avenue, and on the university's role in this process, see the SSI-sponsored documentary film by Jeff Remling, *Urban Renewal in the South Side*. For a discussion of the University of Chicago case, see Allen 2004, 176–80.

12. See Simon 2004.

13. For her views on these issues, see Shrader-Frechette 2007.

14. See Stanton 2006.

15. For this professor's reflections on the pedagogical method of the course, see Crassons 2009. For a demonstration of the power of this kind of socially engaged teaching to transform a scholar's understanding of her own area of research expertise (in this case medieval allegory), see Crassons 2011.

References

Abrego, L. 2009. "Economic Well-Being in Salvadoran Transnational Families: How Gender Affects Remittance Practices." *Journal of Marriage and Family* 71:1070–85.

Abu el-Haj, Thea Renda. 2010. " 'The Beauty of America': Nationalism, Education, and the War on Terror." *Harvard Education Review* 80, (2): 242–75.

Ackerman, Bruce. 1980. *Social Justice in the Liberal State.* New Haven, CT: Yale University Press.

ACLU (American Civil Liberties Union). 1999. "ACLU Victorious in Texas Black Arm Band Case." August 30. http://www.aclu.org/free-speech/aclu-victorious-texas-black-arm-band-case.

Adams, David Wallace. 1997. *Education for Extinction: American Indians and the Boarding School Experience, 1875–1928.* Lawrence: University Press of Kansas.

Allen, Danielle S. 2004. *Talking to Strangers: Anxieties of Citizenship since* Brown v. Board of Education. Chicago: University of Chicago Press.

———. n.d. "On Democratic Education: Three Principles." Unpublished manuscript.

Ambert, Anne Marie, and Catherine Krull. 2006. *Changing Families: Relationships in Context.* Upper Saddle River, NJ: Pearson.

American Psychological Association. 2012. *Meeting the Challenges Associated with Immigration: A Psychological Perspective—Report of the Presidential Task Force on Immigration.* Washington, DC: American Psychological Association.

Ameson, Richard. 1999. "Against Rawlsian Equality of Opportunity." *Philosophical Studies* 93 (1): 77–112.

Anderson, Deborah, and David Shapiro. 1996. "Racial Differences in Access to High-Paying Jobs and the Wage Gap between Black and White Women." *Industrial and Labor Relations Review* 49:273–86.

Anderson, Elizabeth. 1999. "What Is the Point of Equality?" *Ethics* 109 (2): 287–337.

———. 2004. "Rethinking Equality of Opportunity: Comment on Adam Swift's *How Not to Be a Hypocrite.*" *Theory and Research in Education* 2 (2): 99–110.

————. 2007. "Fair Opportunity in Education: A Democratic Equality Perspective." *Ethics* 117 (4): 595–622.

Andrews, Edmund L. 2005. "Blacks Hit Hardest by Costlier Mortgages." *New York Times*, September 14.

Apple, Michael, and James Beane, eds. 2007. *Democratic Schools: Lessons in Powerful Education*, 2nd ed. Portsmouth, NH: Heinemann.

AreaConnect. n.d. "Levittown Population and Demographics." http://levittownny.areaconnect.com/statistics.html.

Arendt, Hannah, and Karl Jaspers. 1992. *Correspondence, 1926–1969.* New York: Harcourt Brace Jovanovich.

Arneson, Richard. 1999. "Against Rawlsian Equality of Opportunity." *Philosophical Studies* 93 (1): 77–112.

Aronson, J., C. B. Fried, and C. Good. 2002. "Reducing the Effect of Stereotype Threat on African American College Students by Shaping Theories of Intelligence." *Journal of Experimental Social Psychology* 38:113–25.

Asch, Solomon E. 1952. *Social Psychology*. Englewood Cliffs, NJ: Prentice-Hall.

Aspachs-Bracons, Oriol, Irma Clots-Figueras, Joan Costa-Font, and Paolo Masella. 2008. "Compulsory Language Educational Policies and Identity Formation." *Journal of the European Economic Association* 6 (2–3): 434–44.

Atlas, John, Peter Dreier, and Gregory D. Squires. 2008. "Foreclosing on the Free Market: How to Remedy the Subprime Catastrophe." *New Labor Forum* 17 (3): 18–29.

Baker, Gladys L. 1939. *The County Agent*. Chicago: University of Chicago Press.

Baldi, Stéphane, and Debra Branch McBrier. 1997. "Do the Determinants of Promotion Differ for Blacks and Whites?" *Work and Occupations* 24:478–97.

Bang, H. J., C. E. Suárez-Orozco, J. Pakes, and E. O'Connor. 2009. "The Importance of Homework in Determining Immigrant Students' Grades in Schools in the USA Context." *Educational Research* 51 (1): 1–25.

Barry, Brian. 2005. *Why Social Justice Matters.* Cambridge: Polity Press.

Baumeister, R., and M. Leary. 1995. "The Need to Belong: Desire for Interpersonal Attachments as a Fundamental Human Motivation." *Psychological Bulletin* 117:497–529.

Bell, Derrick. 2005. *Silent Covenants:* Brown v. Board of Education *and the Unfulfilled Hopes for Racial Reform.* Oxford: Oxford University Press.

Bell, Jeannine. 2008. "The Fair Housing Act and Extralegal Terror." *Indiana Law Review* 41 (3): 537–53.

Ben-Porath Sigal. 2006. *Citizenship under Fire: Democratic Education in Times of Conflict.* Princeton, NJ: Princeton University Press.

————. 2007. "Civic Virtue out of Necessity: Patriotism and Democratic Education." *Theory and Research in Education* 5 (1): 41–59.

————. 2010. "Exit Rights and Entrance Paths: Accommodating Cultural Diversity in a Democracy." *Perspectives on Politics* 8 (4): 1021–33.

Benveniste, Luis, Martin Carnoy, and Richard Rothstein. 2003. *All Else Equal: Are Public and Private Schools Different?* New York: RoutledgeFalmer.

Bernhard, J. K., P. Landolt, and L. Goldring. 2006. "Transnational, Multi-local Motherhood: Experiences of Separation and Reunification among Latin American Families in Canada." *CERIS, Policy Matters 24.* http://ceris.metropolis.net /PolicyMatter/2006/PolicyMatters24.pdf.

Berns, G. S., J. Chappelow, C. F. Zink, G. Pagnoni, M. E. Martin-Skurski, and J. Richards. 2005. "Neurobiological Correlates of Social Conformity and Independence during Mental Rotation." *Biological Psychiatry* 58:245–53.

Bickel, Alexander M. 1962. *The Least Dangerous Branch: The Supreme Court at the Bar of Politics.* Indianapolis: Bobbs-Merrill.

Bird, John, A. Shebani, and Dianne Francombe. 1992. *Ethnic Monitoring and Admissions to Higher Education.* Bristol, UK: Bristol University, Employment Department.

Blackwell, L. S., K. H. Trzesniewski, and C. S. Dweck. 2007. "Implicit Theories of Intelligence Predict Achievement across an Adolescent Transition: A Longitudinal Study and an Intervention." *Child Development* 78:246–63.

Blyth, Eric, and Judith Milner. 2007. "Exclusion from School: A First Step in Exclusion from Society?" *Children and Society* 7 (3): 255–68.

Bobocel, D. R., L. S. Son Hing, L. M. Davey, D. J. Stanley, and M. P. Zanna. 1998. "Justice-Based Opposition to Social Policies: Is It Genuine?" *Journal of Personality and Social Psychology* 75:653–69.

Bocian, Debbie Gruenstein, Keith S. Ernst, and Wei Li. 2006. *Unfair Lending: The Effect of Race and Ethnicity on the Price of Subprime Mortgages.* Center for Responsible Lending. May 31. http://www.responsiblelending.org/mortgage-lending/tools-resources/rr011-Unfair_Lending-0506.pdf.

Bohr, Y., N. T. Whitfield, and J. L. Chan. 2009. "Transnational Parenting: A New Context for Attachment and the Need for Better Models: Socio-ecological and Contextual Paradigms." Presented at the meeting of the Society for Research in Child Development, Denver.

Boss, Pauline. 1999. *Ambiguous Loss: Learning to Live with Unresolved Grief.* Cambridge, MA: Harvard University Press.

Bowen, Catherine Drinker. 1924. *A History of Lehigh University.* South Bethlehem, PA: Lehigh Alumni Bulletin.

Bowman, Philip, and Cleopatra Howard. 1985. "Race-Related Socialization, Motivation, and Academic Achievement: A Study of Black Youths in Three-Generation Families." *Journal of the American Academy of Child Psychiatry* 24:134–41.

Boyd, Donald, Hamilton Lankford, Susanna Loeb, Matthew Ronfeldt, and James Wyckoff. 2011. "The Role of Teacher Quality in Retention and Hiring: Using Applications-to-Transfer to Uncover Preferences of Teachers and Schools." *Journal of Policy Analysis and Management* 30 (1): 88–110.

Bradford, Calvin. 2002. *Risk or Race? Racial Disparities and the Subprime Refinance*

Market. Center for Community Change, May. http://www.cccfiles.org/shared
/publications/downloads/Risk_or_Race_5–02.pdf.

Breyer, Stephen. 2005. *Active Liberty: Interpreting Our Democratic Constitution.*
New York: Vintage Books.

Brickman, P., and D. T. Campbell. 1971. "Hedonic Relativism and Planning the
Good Society." In *Adaptation-Level Theory,* edited by M. H. Appley. New
York: Academic Press.

Brighouse, Harry. 2006. *On Education.* New York: Routledge.

Brighouse, Harry, and Gina Schouten. 2011. *Understanding the Context for Existing
Reform and Research Proposals.* Washington, DC: Brookings Institution Press.

Brighouse, Harry, and Adam Swift. 2006a. "Equality, Priority, and Positional
Goods." *Ethics* 116 (3): 471–97.

———. 2006b. "Parents' Rights and the Value of the Family." *Ethics* 117 (1):
80–108.

———. 2008. "Putting Educational Equality in Its Place." *Education Finance and
Policy* 3 (4): 444–66.

———. 2009a. "Educational Equality versus Educational Adequacy: A Critique of
Anderson and Satz." *Journal of Applied Philosophy* 26 (2): 117–28.

———. 2009b. "Legitimate Parental Partiality." *Philosophy and Public Affairs* 37
(1): 43–80.

———. n.d. *Family Values.* Princeton, NJ: Princeton University Press. Forthcoming.

Brill, Steven. 2011. *Class Warfare: Inside the Fight to Fix America's Schools.* New
York: Simon and Schuster.

British National Statistics. 2001. *Census 2001: Key Statistics for Local Authorities in
England and Wales.* South Wales: Office of National Statistics.

A Broader, Bolder Approach to Education. 2009a. "A Broader, Bolder Approach
to Education." http://www.boldapproach.org/index.php?id=2.

———. 2009b. "Comments to the Department of Education on the Proposed
Regulation for Race to the Top Education Stimulus Fund." http://www.bold
approach.org/bba_ladd_doe_aug_2009.pdf.

———. 2010. "Key Points regarding ESEA Reauthorization." May 18. http://www
.boldapproach.org/20100512_bba_key_points_esea_reauthorization.pdf.

Brody, Leslie. 2010. "Districts to Disclose Teacher Ratings." *Newark Star Ledger,*
September 23.

Bronfenbrenner, U. 1986. "Ecology of the Family as a Context for Human Development: Research Perspectives." *Developmental Psychology* 22 (6): 723–42.

Brubaker, Rogers. 1996. *Nationalism Reframed.* Oxford: Oxford University Press.

———. 2004. *Ethnicity without Groups.* Cambridge, MA: Harvard University
Press.

———. n.d. "The Everyday Workings of Ethnicity in an Ethnopolitically Charged
Setting: Categories, Languages, Institutions." Paper delivered at the University
of Pennsylvania's Program for Democracy, Citizenship and Constitutionalism,
September 23, 2010.

Bryceson, D., and U. Vuorela. 2002. "The Transnational Families in the Twenty-First Century." In *The Transnational Family: New European Frontiers and Global Networks*, edited by D. Bryceson and U. Vuorela. Oxford: Berg.

Butler, Y. G., and K. Hakuta. 2005. "Bilingualism and Second Language Acquisition." In *The Handbook of Bilingualism,* edited by T. K. Bhatia and W. C. Ritchie, 114–44. London: Blackwell.

Calhoun, Craig. 2007. *Nations Matter: Culture, History and the Cosmopolitan Dream.* New York: Routledge.

Callan, Eamonn. 1997a. *Creating Citizens: Political Education and Liberal Democracy.* Oxford: Oxford University Press.

———. 1997b. "The Great Sphere: Education against Servility." *Journal of Philosophy of Education* 31 (2): 221–32.

———. 2004. "Citizenship and Education." *Annual Review of Political Science* 7:71–90.

———. 2010. "Better Angels of Our Nature: Dirty Hands and Patriotism." *Journal of Political Philosophy* 18:3.

Cao, Lan. 1997. *Monkey Bridge.* New York: Penguin Books.

Capps, R. M., R. M. Castañeda, A. Chaudry, and R. Santos. 2007. *The Impact of Immigration Raids on America's Children.* Washington, DC: Urban Institute.

Card, David. 2001. "Estimating the Return to Schooling: Progress on Some Persistent Econometric Problems." *Econometrica* 69 (5): 1127–60.

Carey, Kevin. 2011. "An Admirable Move for the Country's Biggest Teachers' Union." *New Republic*, July 11.

Caro, Robert. 1975. *The Power Broker: Robert Moses and the Fall of New York.* New York: Vintage Books.

Center for Education Reform. 2009. "National Charter School and Enrollment Statistics 2009." http://www.edreform.com/_upload/CER_charter_numbers.pdf.

Center on Education Policy. 2011. "More to Do, but Less Capacity to Do It." *States' Progress in Implementing the Recovery Act Education Reforms.* February.

Chao, R. K. 2000. "Cultural Explanations for the Role of Parenting in the School Success of Asian American Children." In *Resilience across Contexts: Family, Work Culture, and Community*, edited by R. W. Taylor and M. C. Wang, 333–63. Mahwah, NJ: Lawrence Erlbaum.

Charnley, H. 2000. "Children Separated from Their Families in the Mozambique War." In *Abandoned Children*, edited by Catherine Panter-Brick and Malcolm T. Smith. Cambridge: Cambridge University Press.

Chaudry, A., J. Pedroza, R. M. Castañeda, R. Santos, and M. M. Scott. 2010. *Facing Our Future: Children in the Aftermath of Immigration Enforcement.* Washington, DC: Urban Institute.

Chenoweth, Karin. 2007. *It's Being Done: Academic Success in Unexpected Schools.* Boston: Harvard Education Press.

———. 2009. *How It's Being Done: Urgent Lessons from Unexpected Schools.* Boston: Harvard Education Press.

Circle Schools. v. Phillips, 381 F.3d 172 (3d Cir. 2004).

"Cites Science Ties Unbroken by War." 1943. *New York Times*, February 28.

Civil Rights Cases. 1883. *United States v. Stanley, etc.*, 109 U.S. 3 (1883).

Clinton, William J. 2000. Speech to the Education Writers Association, April 14. http://archives.clintonpresidentialcenter.org/?u=041400-speech-by-president-to-education-writers-association.htm.

Clotfelter, Charles T., Helen F. Ladd, and Jacob L. Vigdor. 2007. "High Poverty Schools and the Distribution of Teachers and Principals." *North Carolina Law Review* 85 (5): 1345–79.

———. 2011. "Teacher Mobility, School Segregation, and Pay-Based Policies to Level the Playing Field." *Association for Education Finance and Policy* 6 (3): 399–438.

Coard, Bernard. 1971. *How the West Indian Child Is Made Educationally Subnormal in the British School System: The Scandal of the Black Child in Schools in Britain.* London: New Beacon Books.

Coard, Stephanie, Scyatta Wallace, Howard Stevenson, and Lori Brotman, 2004. "Towards Culturally Relevant Preventive Interventions: The Consideration of Racial Socialization in Parent Training with African-American Families." *Journal of Child and Family Studies* 13:277–93.

Cohen, David, and Susan Moffitt. 2009. *The Ordeal of Equality: Did Federal Regulation Fix the Schools?* Cambridge, MA: Harvard University Press.

Cohen, G. A. 2013. "Rescuing Conservatism: A Defense of Existing Value." In *Finding Oneself in the Other*, ed, Michael Otsuka, 143–74. Princeton, NJ: Princeton University Press.

Cohen, G. L., J. Garcia, N. Apfel, and A. Master. 2006. "Reducing the Racial Achievement Gap: A Social-Psychological Intervention." *Science* 313:1307–10.

Cohen, G. L., J. Garcia, V. Purdie-Vaughns, N. Apfel, and P. Brzustoski. 2009. "Recursive Processes in Self-Affirmation: Intervening to Close the Minority Achievement Gap." *Science* 324:400–403.

Cohen, Joshua. 1989a. "Deliberation and Democratic Legitimacy." In *The Good Polity: Normative Analysis of the State*, edited by Alan Hamlin and Philip Pettit. New York: Blackwell.

———. 1989b. "Democratic Equality." *Ethics* 99 (4): 727–51.

———. 2006. "Deliberation and Democratic Legitimacy." In *Contemporary Political Philosophy: An Anthology*, edited by Robert Goodin and Philip Pettit, 159–68. New York: Blackwell.

Cohen, Lizabeth. 2003. *A Consumers' Republic.* New York: Vintage Books.

Coleman, James. 1966. "Equality of Educational Opportunity Study." United States Department of Health, Education and Welfare. http://www.icpsr.umich.edu/icpsrweb/ICPSR/studies/6389.

Coleman, Major G., William A. Darity, and Rhonda V. Sharpe. 2008. "Are Reports of Discrimination Valid? Considering the Moral Hazard Effect." *American Journal of Economics and Sociology* 67:149–75.

Colfax, Reed N. 2009. "*Kennedy v. City of Zanesville*: Making the Case for Water." *Human Rights* 36 (4): 18–19. http://www.abanet.org/irr/hr/fall09/colfax_fall09.htm.

Collier, Virginia. 1995. *Acquiring a Second Language for School.* Directions in Language and Education, vol. 1, no. 4. Washington, DC: National Clearinghouse for Bilingual Education.

Colvin, Richard. 2009. "Straddling the Democratic Divide." *Education Next* 9 (2): 10–17.

Common Core State Standards Initiative. 2010. "Common Standards." http://www.corestandards.org.

Congressional Budget Office. 2006. "Immigration Policy in the United States." http://www.cbo.gov/ftpdocs/70xx/doc7051/02-28-Immigration.pdf.

Conover, P. J., and D. A. Searing. 2000. "A Political Socialization Perspective." In *Rediscovering the Democratic Purpose of Education,* edited by Lorraine M. McDonnell, Michael Timpane, and Roger Benjamin. Lawrence: University Press of Kansas.

Converse, Philip. 1972. "Change in the American Electorate." In *The Human Meaning of Social Change*, edited by Angus Campbell and Philip Converse. New York: Russell Sage Foundation.

Cook, Philip J., and Jens Ludwig. 1997. "Weighing the 'Burden of Acting White': Are There Race Differences in Attitudes toward Education?" *Journal of Policy Analysis and Management* 16:256–78.

Cooper, H., J. C. Robinson, and E. A. Patall. 2006. "Does Homework Improve Academic Achievement? A Synthesis of Research, 1987–2003." *Review of Educational Research* 76 (1): 1–62.

Corcoran, Sean P., and William N. Evans. 2008. "Equity, Adequacy and the Evolving State Role in Education Finance." In *Handbook of Research in Education Finance and Policy*, edited by Helen F. Ladd and Edward B. Fiske. New York: Routledge, Taylor and Francis.

Crassons, Kate. 2009. "Poverty, Representation, and the Expanded English Classroom." *English Language Notes* 47 (2): 95–104.

———. 2011. "Going Forth in the World: *Piers Plowman* and Service Learning." In *Approaches to Teaching Langland's "Piers Plowman."* New York: Modern Language Association.

Cross, William E., Thomas A. Parham, and Janet E. Helms. 1991. "The Stages of Black Identity Development: Nigrescence Models." In *Black Psychology,* edited by Reginald Jones, 319–38. Berkeley, CA: Cobb and Henry.

Culver, John C., and John Hyde. 2000. *American Dreamer: The Life and Times of Henry A. Wallace.* New York: Norton.

Cummins, J. 1991. "Language Development and Academic Learning." In *Language, Culture, and Cognition,* edited by L. M. Malavé and G. Duquette. Clevedon, UK: Multilingual Matters.

Dagger, Richard. 1997. *Civic Virtues: Rights, Citizenship, and Republican Liberalism*. Oxford: Oxford University Press.

Darling-Hammond, Linda. 2010a. "Restoring Our Schools." *Nation*, May 27.

———. 2010b. *The Flat World and Education: How America's Commitment to Equity Will Determine Our Future*. New York: Teachers College Press.

Davidson, Joe. 1978. "Troubled Ground in Philadelphia." *Black Enterprise* 9 (1): 14–15.

Deal, Terrence E., and Kent D. Peterson. 2009. *Shaping School Culture: Pitfall, Paradoxes, and Promises*. 2nd ed. San Francisco: Jossey-Bass.

Dean, John P. 1947. "Only Caucasian: A Study of Race Covenants." *Journal of Land and Public Utility Economics* 23 (4): 428–32.

Dee, Thomas. 2004. "Are There Civic Returns to Education?" *Journal of Public Economics* 88 (9–10): 1697–1720.

Delgado-Gaitin, C. 1991. "Involving Parents in the Schools: A Process of Empowerment." *American Journal of Education* 100 (1): 20–46.

Delpit, Lisa. 1995. *Other People's Children: Cultural Conflict in the Classroom*. New York: New Press.

Dewey, John. 1916. *Democracy and Education*. New York: Macmillan.

Diamond, A., W. S. Barnett, J. Thomas, and S. Munro. 2007. "Preschool Program Improves Cognitive Control." *Science* 318:1387–88.

"Dr. Carl Taeusch, Ex-Professor, 72." 1961. *New York Times*, September 23.

"Dr. Pitkin Runs Model Farm." 1934. *Washington Post*, July 31.

Dreby, J. 2009. "Honor and Virtue: Mexican Parenting in the Transnational Context." *Gender and Society* 20 (1): 32–59.

"Drop Backer of U.N. Flag for Schools." 1953. *Chicago Daily Tribune*, January 23.

Duncan, Arne. 2010. Remarks at the National Urban League Centennial Conference. July 27. http://www.ed.gov/news/speeches/secretary-arne-duncans-remarks-national-urban-league-centennial-conference.

Dweck, Carol. S. 1999. *Self-Theories: Their Role in Motivation, Personality, and Development*. Philadelphia: Psychology Press.

———. 2006. *Mindset: The New Psychology of Success*. New York: Random House.

Dweck, C. S., and E. L. Leggett. 1988. "A Social-Cognitive Approach to Motivation and Personality." *Psychological Review* 95:256–73.

Dworkin, Ronald. 1977. *Taking Rights Seriously*. Cambridge, MA: Harvard University Press.

———. 2000. *Sovereign Virtue: The Theory and Practice of Equality*. Cambridge, MA: Harvard University Press.

Dwyer, James. 1999. *Religious Schools versus Children's Rights*. Ithaca, NY: Cornell University Press.

Eaton, Susan E. 2001. *The Other Boston Busing Story: What's Won and Lost across the Boundary Line*. New Haven, CT: Yale University Press.

Edwards, Audrey, and Craig K. Polite. 1992. *Children of the Dream.* New York: Doubleday.

Elliott, James R., and Ryan A. Smith. 2004. "Race, Gender, and Workplace Power." *American Sociological Review* 69:365–86.

Engel, Katherine Carte. 2009. *Religion and Profit: Moravians in Early America.* Philadelphia: University of Pennsylvania Press.

Epstein, J. L. 1995. "School/Family/Community Partnerships: Caring for the Children We Share." *Phi Delta Kappan* 76 (9): 701–12.

Falicov, C. J. 2007. "Working with Transnational Immigrants: Expanding Meanings of Family, Community, and Culture." *Family Process* 46 (2): 157–71.

Faltis, C. J. 1999. "Creating a New History." In *So Much to Say: Adolescents, Bilingualism, and ESL in Secondary Schools*, edited by C. J. Faltis and P. M. Wolfe, 1–9. New York: Teachers College Press.

Fan, X., and M. Chen. 2001. "Parental Involvement and Students' Academic Achievement: A Meta-analysis." *Educational Psychology Review* 13 (1): 1–22.

Fantuzzo, J., E. Tigh, and S. Childs. 2000. "Family Involvement Questionnaire: A Multivariate Assessment of Family Participation in Early Childhood Education." *Journal of Educational Psychology* 92 (2): 367–76.

Felch, Jason, Jason Song, and Doug Smith. 2010. "Grading the Teachers." *Los Angeles Times*, August 14. http://www.latimes.com/news/local/la-me-teachers-value-20100815,0,2695044.story.

Ferguson, Ann Arnett. 2000. *Bad Boys: Public Schools in the Making of Black Masculinity.* Ann Arbor: University of Michigan Press.

Ferguson, C., M. Ramos, Z. Rudo, and L. Wood. 2008. "The School Family Connection: Looking at the Larger Picture; a Review of Current Literature." National Center for Family and Community Connections with School. http://www.sedl.org/pubs/free_community.html.

Ferguson, Ronald F. 2005. "Toward Skilled Parenting and Transformed Schools inside a National Movement for Excellence with Equity." Prepared for the Achievement Gap Initiative (AGI) and O'Connor Project at Harvard University and the First Educational Equity Symposium of the Campaign for Educational Equity, at Teachers College, Columbia University, October 24–25. http://www.agi.harvard.edu/Search/SearchAllPapers.php.

"Fifth International Congress for the Unity of Science." 1940. *Erkenntnis* 9 (5): 369–71.

First Amendment Center. 2009. "State of the First Amendment 2009." http://www.firstamendmentcenter.org/pdf/SOFA2009.analysis.tables.pdf.

Flournoy, Craig, and George Rodrigue. 1985. "Separate and Unequal: Illegal Segregation Pervades Nation's Subsidized Housing." *Dallas Morning News*, February 10.

Foner, Nancy. 2003. "Intergenerational Relations." In *Hearts Apart: Migration in the Eyes of Filipino Children.* Quezon City, Philippines: Scalabrini Migration Center.

————. 2009. "Introduction: Intergenerational Relations in Immigrant Families." In *Across Generations: Immigrant Families in America,* edited by Nancy Foner. New York: New York University Press.

Fordham, Signithia, and John U. Ogbu. 1986. "Black Students' School Success: Coping with the Burden of 'Acting White.' " *Urban Review* 18:176–206.

Forst, Rainer. 2002. "The Basic Right to Justification: Towards a Constructivist Conception of Human Rights." *Constellations* 6 (1): 35–60.

————. 2007. "First Things First: Redistribution, Recognition and Justification." *European Journal of Political Philosophy* 6:291–304.

————. 2009. "Zwei Bilder der Gerechtigkeit." In *Sozialphilosophie und Kritik,* 205–28. Frankfurt-am-Main: Suhrkamp.

————. 2011. "Political Liberty: Integrating Five Conceptions of Autonomy." In *The Right to Justification*, translated by Jeffrey Flynn. New York: Columbia University Press.

Fortin, Jane. 2009. *Children's Rights and the Developing Law*, 3rd ed. Cambridge: Cambridge University Press.

Frankfurt, Harry. 1987. "Equality as a Moral Ideal." *Ethics* 98 (1): 21–43.

Fruchter, Norm, and Richard Gray. 2006. "Community Engagement: Mobilizing Constituents to Demand and Support Educational Improvement." *Voices in Urban Education,* no. 13, 5–13.

Furman Center for Real Estate and Urban Policy. 2009. "The High Cost of Segregation: Exploring the Relationship between Racial Segregation and Subprime Lending." Policy Brief, November, New York University.

Gaita, Raimond. 2000. *A Common Humanity*. New York: Routledge.

Galston, William, 1991. *Liberal Purposes*. Cambridge: Cambridge University Press.

————. 1995. "Two Concepts of Liberalism." *Ethics* 105 (3): 516–34.

————. 2002. *Liberal Pluralism*. Cambridge: Cambridge University Press.

————. 2004. "Civic Education and Political Participation: The Current Condition of Civic Engagement." *PS: Political Science and Politics*, April, 263–66. http://www.apsanet.org/imgtest/CivicEdPoliticalParticipation.pdf.

García Coll, C., D. Akiba, N. Palacios, B. Bailey, R. Silver, L. DiMartino, and C. Chin. 2002. "Parental Involvement in Children's Education: Lessons from Three Immigrant Groups." *Parenting* 2 (3): 303–24.

García Coll, C. T., and K. Magnuson. 2000. "Cultural Differences as Sources of Developmental Vulnerabilities and Resources: A View from Developmental Research." In *Handbook of Early Childhood Intervention,* edited by S. J. Meisels and J. P. Shonkoff, 94–111. Cambridge: Cambridge University Press.

Gardner, H. 1999. *Intelligence Reframed: Multiple Intelligences for the 21st Century*. New York: Basic Books.

Gaytán, F. X., Q. Xue, and H. Yoshikawa. 2006. "Transnational Babies: Patterns and Predictors of Early Childhood Travel to Immigrant Mothers' Native Countries." Presented at the annual National Head Start Research Conference, Washington, DC.

Gee, E. Gordon, Philip T. K. Daniel, and Stephen R. Goldstein. 2008. *Law and Public Education: Cases and Materials.* Newark, NJ: Lexis Nexis.

Gelman, S. A., and G. D. Heyman. 1999. "Carrot-Eaters and Creature-Believers: The Effects of Lexicalization on Children's Inferences about Social Categories." *Psychological Science* 10:489–93.

Gindling, T. H., and S. Poggio. 2009. "Family Separation and the Educational Success of Immigrant Children." Policy Brief, University of Maryland, Baltimore.

Glazer, Nathan. 2006. " 'The Shame of the Nation': Separate and Unequal." *New York Times*, September 25.

Goldin, Claudia, and Lawrence Katz. 2008. *The Race between Education and Technology.* Cambridge, MA: Belknap Press of Harvard University Press.

Goldstein, Dana. 2009. "The Education Wars." *American Prospect*, March 23.

Good, C., J. Aronson, and M. Inzlicht. 2003. "Improving Adolescents' Standardized Test Performance: An Intervention to Reduce the Effects of Stereotype Threat." *Journal of Applied Developmental Psychology* 24:645–62.

Goodin, Robert. 2007. "Enfranchising All Affected Interests, and Its Alternatives." *Philosophy and Public Affairs* 35.1:40–68.

Goodin, Robert, and Philip Pettit. 2006. *Contemporary Political Philosophy: An Anthology.* New York: Blackwell.

Goodnough, Abby. 2010. "Rethinking District Plan on Condoms in School." *New York Times*, June 24. http://www.nytimes.com/2010/06/25/us/25condoms.html.

Gordon, Robert, Thomas Kane, and Douglas Staiger. 2006. "Identifying Effective Teachers Using Performance on the Job." Brookings Institution, Washington, DC.

Goslin, David A. 2003. *Engaging Minds: Motivation and Learning in America's Schools.* Lanham, MD: Scarecrow Press.

Graetz, Michael J., and Ian Shapiro. 2005. *Death by a Thousand Cuts: The Fight over Taxing Inherited Wealth.* Princeton, NJ: Princeton University Press.

Gratton, B. 2007. "Ecuadorians in the United States and Spain: History, Gender and Niche Formation." *Journal of Ethnic and Migration Studies* 33 (4): 581–99.

Graubard, Mark. 1946. "Scientific Hypotheses and the Culture Matrix." In *Approaches to Group Understanding: Sixth Symposium.* New York: Conference on Science, Philosophy and Religion in Their Relation to the Democratic Way of Life.

Greenhouse, Steven, and Sam Dillon. 2010. "School's Shake-Up Is Embraced by the President." *New York Times*, March 6.

Griffith, J. 1998. "The Relation of School Structure and Social Environment to Family Involvement in Elementary Schools." *Elementary School Journal* 99:53–80.

Grosjean, F. 1999. "Individual Bilingualism." In *Concise Encyclopedia of Educational Linguistics*, edited by B. Spolsky, 284–90. London: Elsevier.

Grossman, Pam, Susanna Loeb, Julia Cohen, Karen Hammerness, James Wyckoff, Don Boyd, and Hamp Lankford. 2010. "Measure for Measure: The Relationship between Measures of Instructional Practice in Middle School English

Language Arts and Teachers' Value-Added Scores." Working Paper 16015, National Bureau of Economic Research.

Grubb, Norton. 2008. *The Money Myth*. New York: Russell Sage Foundation.

Guiles v. Marineau, 461 F.3d 320 (2d Cir. 2006).

Guinier, Lani. 1994. *The Tyranny of the Majority: Fundamental Fairness in Representative Democracy*. New York: Free Press.

Guinier, Lani, and Susan Sturm. 2001. *Who's Qualified? A New Democracy Forum on Creating Equal Opportunity in School and Jobs*. Boston: Beacon Press.

Gutmann, Amy. 1987. *Democratic Education*. Princeton, NJ: Princeton University Press.

Hakuta, K., Y. Goto Butler, and D. Witt. 2000. "How Long Does It Take English Learners to Attain Proficiency?" Policy Report 2000–1, University of California Linguistic Minority Research Institute.

Hakuta, Kenki. 1987. *The Mirror of Language: The Debate on Bilingualism*. New York: Basic Books.

Hamill, Sean. 2011. "Forging a New Partnership: The Story of Teacher Union and School District Collaboration in Pittsburgh." Aspen Institute, June.

Hamilton, David E. 1990. "Building the Associative State: The Department of Agriculture and American State-Building." *Agricultural History* 64 (2): 207–18.

Haney, C., W. C. Banks, and P. G. Zimbardo. 1973. "Study of Prisoners and Guards in a Simulated Prison." *Naval Research Reviews* 9:1–17.

Hanushek, Eric. 2011. "Education Production Functions." In *The New Palgrave Dictionary of Economics*, 2nd ed., edited by Steven N. Durlauf and Lawrence E. Blume. London: Palgrave Macmillan. 200.*The New Palgrave Dictionary of Economics Online*. Palgrave Macmillan. 8 October. http://www.dictionaryofeconomics.com /article?id=pde2008_E000238&edition=current&q=hanushek&topicid=&result _number=4#citations.

Harris, Angel L. 2006. "I (Don't) Hate School: Revisiting 'Oppositional Culture' Theory of Blacks' Resistance to Schooling." *Social Forces* 85:797–834.

Harris, Angel L., and Keith Robinson. 2007. "Schooling Behaviors or Prior Skills? A Cautionary Tale of Omitted Variable Bias within the Oppositional Culture Theory." *Sociology of Education* 80:139–57.

Harris, Judith Rich. 1998. *The Nurture Assumption: Why Children Turn Out the Way They Do*. New York: Touchstone.

Hartney, Michael, and Patrick Flavin. 2011. "From the Schoolhouse to the Statehouse: Teacher Union Political Activism and U.S. State Education Reform Policy." *State Politics and Policy Quarterly 11 (3): 251–68*.

Haveman, Robert H., and Barbara Wolfe. 1984. "Schooling and Economic Well-Being: The Role of Non-market Effects." *Journal of Human Resources* 19 (3): 377–407.

Hawley, Ellis W. 1974. "Herbert Hoover, the Commerce Secretariat, and the Vision of an 'Associative State,' 1921–1928." *Journal of American History* 61 (1): 116–40.

Headey, B., and A. Wearing. 1989. "Personality, Life Events, and Subjective Well-Being: Toward a Dynamic Equilibrium Model." *Journal of Personality and Social Psychology* 57:731–39.

Heckman, J. J. 2006. "Skill Formation and the Economics of Investing in Disadvantaged Children." *Science* 312:1900–1902.

Heiten, Liana. 2011. "States Continue Push to Toughen Teacher Policies." *Education Week*, July 12.

Henderson, A. T., and K. L. Mapp. 2002. "A New Wave of Evidence: The Impact of School, Family, and Community Connections on Student Achievement." National Center for Community and Connections with Schools. http://www.sedl.org/connections/resources/evidence.pdf.

Herbold, Hilary. 1994–95. "Never a Level Playing Field: Blacks and the GI Bill." *Journal of Blacks in Higher Education* 6:104–8.

Hernandez, Donald J., Nancy A. Denton, and Suzanne E. Macartney. 2007. *Family Circumstances of Children in Immigrant Families: Looking to the Future of America*. New York: Guilford Press.

Herrnstein, Richard J., and Charles Murray. 1994. *The Bell Curve: Intelligence and Class Structure in American Life*. New York: Free Press.

Hess, Frederick, and Checker Finn, eds. 2007. *No Remedy Left Behind*. Washington, DC: AEI Press.

Hirsch, Arnold R. 1983. *Making the Second Ghetto: Race and Housing in Chicago, 1940–1960*. Chicago: University of Chicago Press.

———. 1998. *Making the Second Ghetto: Race and Housing in Chicago, 1940–1960*. Reissued with a new foreword. Chicago: University of Chicago Press.

Hirsch, Fred. 1976. *Social Limits to Growth*. Cambridge, MA: Harvard University Press.

Hirschman, Albert O. 1970. *Exit, Voice, and Loyalty: Response to Decline in Firms, Organizations, and States*. Cambridge, MA: Harvard University Press.

Hoffman, Eva. 1989. *Lost in Translation: A Life in a New Language*. New York: Penguin.

Holmes, Steven. 1995. *Passions and Constraints: On the Theory of Liberal Democracy*. Chicago: University of Chicago Press.

Hondagneu-Sotelo, Pierrette, ed. 2003. *Gender and U.S. Immigration: Contemporary Trends*. Berkeley: University of California Press.

Hondagneu-Sotelo, Pierrette, and Ernestine Avila. 1997. "'I'm Here, but I'm There': The Meanings of Latina Transnational Motherhood." *Gender and Society* 11 (5): 548–71.

Hong, S., and H. Ho. 2005. "Direct and Indirect Longitudinal Effects of Parental Involvement on Student Achievement: Second-Order Latent Growth Modeling across Ethnic Groups." *Journal of Educational Psychology* 97 (1): 32–42.

Honohan, Iseult. 2006. "Educating Citizens: Nation-Building and Its Republican Limits." In *Civic Republicanism in Theory and Practice*, edited by Iseult Honohan and Jeremy Jennings, 199–213. New York: Routledge.

Hughes, Diane. 2003. "Correlates of African American and Latino Parents' Messages to Children about Ethnicity and Race: A Comparative Study of Racial Socialization." *American Journal of Community Psychology* 31:15–32.

Hughes, Diane, and Lisa Chen. 1997. "When and What Parents Tell Children about Race: An Examination of Race-Related Socialization among African American Families." *Applied Developmental Science* 1:200–214.

Hughes, J. N., K. A. Gleason, and D. Zhang. 2005. "Relationship Influences on Teachers' Perceptions of Academic Competence in Academically At-Risk Minority and Majority First Grade Students." *Journal of School Psychology* 43:303–20.

Huntsinger, C. S., and P. E. Jose. 2009. "Parental Involvement in Children's Schooling: Different Meanings in Different Cultures." *Early Childhood Research Quarterly* 24 (4): 398–410.

Immergluck, Dan, and Geoff Smith. 2006. "The External Costs of Foreclosure: The Impact of Single-Family Mortgage Foreclosures on Property Values." *Housing Policy Debate* 17:57–79.

Immerwahr, Daniel. 2010. "Agrarian Intellectuals at Home and Abroad: Decentralism in U.S. Thought and Policy, 1935–1955." Presented at the US Intellectual History Conference, New York, October 22.

Infoplease. 2008. "National Voter Turnout in Federal Elections: 1960–2008." http://www.infoplease.com/ipa/A0781453.html.

Izzo, C., R. P. Weisberg, W. J. Kasprow, and M. Fendrich. 1999. "A Longitudinal Assessment of Teacher Perceptions of Family Involvement in Children's Education and School Performance." *American Journal of Community Psychology* 27 (6): 817–39.

Jackson, C. Kirabo. 2009. "Student Demographics, Teacher Sorting, and Teacher Quality: Evidence from the End of School Desegregation." *Journal of Labor Economics* 27 (2): 213–56.

Jackson, Philip. 1968. *Life in Classrooms*. New York: Holt, Rinehart and Winston.

Jacobs, Lesley. 2004. *Pursuing Equal Opportunities*. Cambridge: Cambridge University Press.

Jaeggi, S. M., M. Buschkuehl, J. Jonides, and W. J. Perrig. 2008. "Improving Fluid Intelligence with Training on Working Memory." *Proceedings of the National Academy of Sciences* 10:14931–36.

Jensen, Arthur Robert. 1973. *Educability and Group Differences*. London: Methuen.

———. 1980. *Bias in Mental Testing*. New York: Free Press.

Johnson, W. R., and D. Neal. 1998. "Basic Skills and the Black-White Earnings Gap." In *The Black-White Test Score Gap*, edited by Christopher Jenks and Meredith Phillips. Washington, DC: Brookings Institution.

Jones-Taylor, V., and G. M. Walton. 2011. "Stereotype Threat Undermines Academic Learning." *Personality and Social Psychology Bulletin* 37 (8): 1055–67.

Julian, Elizabeth K., and Michael M. Daniel. 1989. "Separate and Unequal—the

Root and Branch of Public Housing Segregation." *Clearinghouse Review* 23:666–76.

Kahlenberg, Richard D. 2006. *A New Way on School Integration.* Century Foundation. http://www.tcf.org/publications/education/schoolintegration.pdf.

Kahne, Joseph, and Ellen Middaugh. 2008. "Democracy for Some—the Civic Opportunity Gap in High School." Circle Working Paper 59. *CIRCLE*, civicyouth .org.

Kane, Thomas, Eric Taylor, John Tyler, and Amy Wooten. 2010. "Identifying Effective Classroom Practices Using Student Achievement Data." Working Paper 15803, National Bureau of Economic Research.

Katznelson, Ira. 2005. *When Affirmative Action Was White.* New York: W. W. Norton.

Kaufman, Paul, ed. 1938. *Understanding Ourselves: A Survey of Psychology Today.* Washington, DC: Graduate School of the US Department of Agriculture.

———. 1939. *The Adjustment of Personality.* Washington, DC: Graduate School of the US Department of Agriculture.

Keller, Simon. 2007. *The Limits of Loyalty.* Cambridge: Cambridge University Press.

Kellog, Charles E. 1966. *The College of Agriculture: Science in the Public Service.* New York: McGraw-Hill.

Kerckhoff, Alan C. 2000. "Transition from School to Work in Comparative Perspective." In *Handbook of the Sociology of Education,* edited by Maureen T. Hallinan, 453–74. New York: Kluwer Academic/Plenum.

———. 2003. "From Student to Worker." In *Handbook of the Life Course,* edited by Jeylen T. Mortimer and Michael J. Shanahan, 251–67. New York: Kluwer Academic/Plenum.

King, Desmond. 1995. *Separate and Unequal: Black Americans and the U.S. Federal Government.* Oxford: Clarendon Press.

Kirp, David L., John P. Dwyer, and Larry A Rosenthal. 1995. *Our Town: Race, Housing, and the Soul of Suburbia.* New Brunswick, NJ: Rutgers University Press.

Klarman, Michael J. 2004. *From Jim Crow to Civil Rights: The Supreme Court and the Struggle for Racial Equality.* New York: Oxford University Press.

Klein, Joel, Michael Lomax, and Janet Murguia. 2010. "Why Great Teachers Matter to Low Income Students." *Washington Post,* April 9, A19.

Kogan, M., and M. Maden. 1999. "An Evaluation of Evaluators: The Ofsted System of School Inspection." In *An Inspector Calls: Ofsted and Its Effect on School Standards,* edited by Cedric Cullingworth, 9–31. London: Kogan.

Kohl, G. O., L. J. Lengua, R. J. McMahon, and the Conduct Problems Prevention Research Group. 2000. "Family Involvement in School: Conceptualizing Multiple Dimensions and Their Relations with Family and Demographic Risk Factors." *Journal of School Psychology* 38:501–23.

Kohlberg, Lawrence. 1970. "The Moral Atmosphere of the School." In *The Unstudied Curriculum: Its Impact on Children,* edited by Norman V. Overly, 104–239.

Washington, DC: Association for Supervision and Curriculum Development, National Education Association.

Koski, William S., and Jesse Hahnel. 2008. "The Past, Present and Possible Futures of Educational Finance Reform Litigation." In *Handbook of Research in Education Finance and Policy*, edited by Helen F. Ladd and Edward B. Fiske. New York: Routledge, Taylor and Francis.

Koski, William S., and Rob Reich. 2007. "When 'Adequate' Isn't: The Retreat from Equity in Educational Law and Policy and Why It Matters." *Emory Law Review* 56 (3): 545–618.

Kozol, Jonathan. 2005. *The Shame of the Nation: The Restoration of Apartheid Schooling in America.* New York: Crown.

Krysan, Maria. 2002. "Community Undesirability in Black and White: Examining Racial Residential Preferences through Community Perceptions." *Social Problems* 49:521–43.

Kuperminc, G. P., A. J. Darnell, and A. Alvarez-Jimenez. 2008. "Family Involvement in the Academic Adjustment of Latino Middle and High School Youth: Teacher Expectations and School Belonging as Mediators." *Journal of Adolescence* 31:469–83.

Kushner, James A. 1979. "Apartheid in America: An Historical and Legal Analysis of Contemporary Racial Segregation in the United States." *Howard Law Journal* 22:547–685.

Kymlicka, Will. 1995. *Multicultural Citizenship.* Oxford: Oxford University Press.

———. 2001a. *Contemporary Political Philosophy.* Oxford: Oxford University Press.

———. 2001b. *Politics in the Vernacular: Nationalism, Multiculturalism, and Citizenship.* Oxford: Oxford University Press.

Kymlicka, Will, and Wayne Norman. 1994. "Return of the Citizen: A Survey of Recent Work on Citizenship Theory." *Ethics* 104 (2): 352–81.

Kymlicka, Will, and Alan Patten. 2003. *Language Rights and Political Theory.* Oxford: Oxford University Press.

Ladd, Helen F. 1998. "Evidence on Discrimination in Mortgage Lending." *Journal of Economic Perspectives* 12 (2): 41–62.

———. 2009. "School Improvement Efforts." http://www.boldapproach.org /statement.html.

———. 2010. "Education Inspectorate Systems in New Zealand and the Netherlands." *Education Finance and Policy* 5 (3): 378–92.

Ladd, Helen F., and Edward B. Fiske, eds. 2008. *Handbook of Research in Education Finance and Policy.* New York: Routledge.

———. 2009. "Weighted Student Funding for Primary Schools: An Analysis of the Dutch Experience." Sanford School Working Paper, Duke University.

Ladd, Helen F., and Janet Hansen, eds. 1999. *Making Money Matter: Financing America's Schools.* Final report of the National Academy of Sciences Committee on Education Finance. Washington DC: National Academy of Sciences Press.

Laden, Anthony Simon. 2000. "Outline of a Theory of Reasonable Deliberation." *Canadian Journal of Philosophy* 30:551–80.

———. 2001. *Reasonably Radical: Deliberative Liberalism and the Politics of Identity*. Ithaca, NY: Cornell University Press.

———. 2012. *Reasoning: A Social Picture*. Oxford: Oxford University Press.

Ladson-Billings, G. 1995. "Toward a Theory of Culturally Relevant Pedagogy." *American Educational Research Journal* 32 (3): 465–91.

Lankford, Hamp, Susanna Loeb, and James Wyckoff. 2002. "Teacher Sorting and the Plight of Urban Schools: A Descriptive Analysis." *Education Evaluation and Policy Analysis* 24 (1): 37–62.

Lareau, Annette. 2003. *Unequal Childhoods: Class, Race and Family Life*. Berkeley: University of California Press.

Lasky, S. 2000. "The Cultural and Emotional Politics of Teacher–Parent Interactions." *Teaching and Teacher Education* 16:843–60.

Lemann, Nicholas. 2006. *Redemption: The Last Battle of the Civil War*. New York: Farrar, Straus, and Giroux.

Levine, Peter. 2007. *The Future of Democracy*. Lebanon, NH: Tufts University Press.

LeVine, Robert. 2003. *Childhood Socialization: Comparative Studies of Parenting, Learning and Educational Change*. Hong Kong: Hong Kong University Press.

Levinson, Meira. 2007. "The Civic Achievement Gap." Circle Working Paper 51. *CIRCLE*. civicyouth.org.

Levitt, Steven D., and Dunber, Stephen J. 2006. *Freakonomics: A Rogue Economist Explores the Hidden Side of Everything*. New York: William Morrow.

Lewis, Amanda E. 2003. *Race in the Schoolyard: Reproducing the Color Line in School*. New Brunswick, NJ: Rutgers University Press.

Liu, Goodwin. 2006. "Education, Equality, and National Citizenship." *Yale Law Journal* 116 (2): 330–411.

Locke, John. 1996. *Some Thoughts concerning Education and of the Content of the Understanding*. Edited by Ruth W. Grant and Nathan Tarcov. Indianapolis: Hackett.

Loewen, James. 2005. *Sundown Towns*. New York: New Press.

Loftus, E. F. 2003. "Make-Believe Memories." *American Psychologist* 58:867–73.

Logan, John, Bryan Stults, and Reynolds Farley. 2004. "Segregation of Minorities in the Metropolis: Two Decades of Change." *Demography* 41:1–22.

Lord, Russell. 1942. "Food, Farmers, and the Future." *Survey Graphic* 31 (January): 26–30.

Louie, Vivian. 2012. *Keeping the Immigrant Bargain: The Costs and Rewards of Success in America*. New York; Russell Sage Foundation.

Loveless, Tom. 2006. "The Peculiar Politics of No Child Left Behind." Presented at "Will Standards-Based Reform in Education Help Close the Poverty Gap?"

Conference, University of Wisconsin–Madison, February 23–24. http://www
.brookings.edu/papers/2006/08k12education_loveless.aspx.

Lubick, George M. 1985. "Restoring the American Dream: The Agrarian-Decentralist
Movement, 1930–1946." *South Atlantic Quarterly* 84 (1): 63–80.

Lucas, R. E., A. E. Clark, Y. Georgellis, and E. Diener. 2003. "Reexamining Adaptation and the Set Point Model of Happiness: Reactions to Changes in Marital
Status." *Journal of Personality and Social Psychology* 84 (3): 527–39.

Luthar, S. S., and D. Cicchetti. 2000. "The Construct of Resilience: Implications
for Interventions and Social Policy." *Development and Psychopathology* 12:
857–85.

Maccoby, E. E. 1992. "The Role of Parents in the Socialization of Children: An
Historical Overview." *Developmental Psychology* 26 (8): 1006–17.

Macedo, Stephen. 2000. *Diversity and Distrust: Civic Education in a Multicultural
Democracy*. Cambridge, MA: Harvard University Press.

Mahalingam, R., B. Sundari, and K. M. Molina. 2009. "Transnational Intersec-
tionality: A Critical Framework for Theorizing Motherhood." In *Handbook
of Feminist Family Studies,* edited by S. A. Lloyd, A. L. Few, and L. R. Allen.
London: Sage.

Manna, Paul. 2011. *Collision Course: Federal Education Policy Meets State and Local Realities*. Washington, DC: CQ Press.

Mapp, K. L. 2003. "Having Their Say: Parents Describe Why and How They Are Engaged in Their Children's Learning." *School Community Journal* 13 (1): 35–64.

Mason, Patrick L. 1997. "Race, Culture and Skills: Interracial Wage Differentials
among African Americans, Latinos and Whites." *Review of Black Political
Economy* 25:5–39.

———. 2007. "Intergenerational Mobility and Interracial Inequality: The Return
to Family Values." *Industrial Relations* 46:51–80.

Massey, Douglas S., and Nancy A. Denton. 1993. *American Apartheid: Segregation
and the Making of the Underclass*. Cambridge, MA: Harvard University Press.

Mathews, Jay. 2009. *Work Hard. Be Nice.* Chapel Hill, NC: Algonquin Books.

Mau, W. 1997. "Parental Influences on the High School Students' Academic
Achievement: A Comparison of Asian Immigrants, Asian Americans, and
White Americans." *Psychology in the Schools* 34 (3): 267–77.

McCann, Michael. 1994. *Rights at Work: Pay Equity Reform and the Politics of
Legal Mobilization*. Chicago: University of Chicago Press.

McClure, Phyllis. 2004. "Grassroots Resistance to NCLB." *Education Gadfly* 4
(11). http://www.edexcellence.net/gadfly/index.cfm?issue=140#a1723.

McCumber, John. 2001. *Time in the Ditch: American Philosophy and the McCarthy
Era*. Evanston, IL: Northwestern University Press.

McGuinn, Patrick. 2006. *No Child Left Behind and the Transformation of Federal
Education Policy, 1965–2005*. Kansas: University Press of Kansas.

———. 2010a. "Creating Cover and Constructing Capacity: Assessing the Origins,

Evolution, and Impact of Race to the Top." American Enterprise Institute, December.

———. 2010b. "Ringing the Bell for K–12 Teacher Tenure Reform." Center for American Progress, February. http://www.americanprogress.org/issues/2010/02/teacher_tenure_reform.html.

———. 2012. "Fight Club: How New School Reform Advocacy Groups Are Changing the Politics of Education." *Education Next* (May).

McNeal, Ralph B., Jr. 1999. "Parental Involvement as Social Capital: Differential Effectiveness on Science Achievement, Truancy, and Dropping Out." *Social Forces* 78 (1): 117–44.

McNeill, Michele. 2010. "Duncan Deflects Civil Rights Groups' Criticism: You're 'Wrong.'" *Education Week,* July 29.

McPherson, James Alan. 1972. "'In My Father's House There Are Many Mansions—and I'm Going to Get Me Some of Them Too': The Story of the Contract Buyers League." *Atlantic Monthly*, April, 52–82.

Meier, Deboarah. 2002. *The Power of Their Ideas: Lessons from a Small School in Harlem.* Boston: Beacon Press.

Mendoza-Denton, R., G. Downey, V. J. Purdie, A. Davis, and J. Pietrzak. 2002. "Sensitivity to Status-Based Rejection: Implications for African American Students' College Experience." *Journal of Personality and Social Psychology* 83:896–918.

Menjívar, C. 2006. "Family Reorganization in the Context of Legal Uncertainty: Guatemalan and Salvadoran Immigrants in the United States." *International Journal of Sociology of the Family* 32 (2): 223–45.

Menjívar, C., and L. Abrego. 2009. "Parents and Children across Borders: Legal Instability and Intergenerational Relations in Guatemalan and Salvadoran Families." In *Across Generations: Immigrant Families in America,* edited by Nancy Foner. New York: New York University Press.

Mickelson, Roslyn Arlin. 1990. "The Attitude-Achievement Paradox among Black Adolescents." *Sociology of Education* 63:44–61.

Milgram, Stanley. 1974. *Obedience to Authority: An Experimental View.* New York: Harper and Row.

Miller v. California, 413 U.S. 15 (1973).

Miller, Joshua Rhett. 2010. "California Students Sent Home for Wearing U.S. Flags on Cinco de Mayo." Foxnews.com, May 6. http://www.foxnews.com/us/2010/05/06/california-students-sent-home-wearing-flags-cinco-mayo.

Minorini, Paul, and Steven Sugarman. 1999. "Educational Adequacy and the Courts: The Promise and Problems of Moving to a New Paradigm." In *Equity and Adequacy Issues in Educational Finance*, edited by H. F. Ladd, R. Chalk, and J. S. Hansen. Washington, DC: National Academy Press.

Mischel, W., and C. C. Morf. 2003. "The Self as a Psycho-social Dynamic Processing System: A Meta-perspective on a Century of the Self in Psychology." In

Handbook of Self and Identity, edited by Mark R. Leary and June Price Tang-
ney, 15–46. New York: Guilford Press.

Modood, Tariq. 1993. "The Number of Ethnic Minority Students in British Higher
Education: Some Grounds for Optimism." *Oxford Review of Education* 19:
167–82.

Moe, Terry. 2011. *Special Interest: Teachers Unions and America's Public Schools.*
Washington, DC: Brookings Institution Press.

Moglen, Seth. 1993. "Contributions to the Long Revolution: Raymond Williams
and the Politics of the Postwar New Left." In *Raymond Williams: Politics, Education, Letters*, edited by W. John Morgan and Peter Preston, 65–87. New York:
St. Martin's Press.

Morris, Edward W. 2005. "'Tuck in That Shirt!' Race, Class, Gender, and Discipline in an Urban School." *Sociological Perspectives* 48:25–48.

Morse, Jennifer Roback. 2001. *Love and Economics.* Dallas, TX: Spence.

Mortimore, Peter, Pam Sammons, Louise Stoll, David Lewis, and Russell J. Ecob.
1988. *School Matters: The Junior Years.* London: Open Books.

Mueller, C. M., and C. S. Dweck. 1998. "Intelligence Praise Can Undermine Motivation and Performance." *Journal of Personality and Social Psychology* 75:
33–52.

Munnell, Alicia H., Geoffrey M. B. Tootell, Lynn E. Browne, and James McEne-
aney. 1996. "Mortgage Lending in Boston: Interpreting HMDA Data." *American Economic Review* 86 (1): 25–53.

Muñoz-Sandoval, A. F., J. Cummins, C. G. Alvarado, and M. L. Ruef. 1998. *Bilingual Verbal Ability Tests: Comprehensive Manual.* Itasca, IL: Riverside.

Murasky, Donna M. 1971. "*James v. Valtierra*: Housing Discrimination by Referen-
dum?" *University of Chicago Law Review* 39 (1): 115–42.

Murnane, Richard J., John B. Willett, and Frank Levy. 1995. "The Growing Importance of Cognitive Skills in Wage Determination." *Review of Economics and
Statistics* 77 (2): 251–66.

Murray, S. L., P. Rose, G. M. Bellavia, J. G. Holmes, and A. G. Kusche. 2002.
"When Rejection Stings: How Self-Esteem Constrains Relationship Enhance-
ment Processes." *Journal of Personality and Social Psychology* 83:556–73.

NAACP (National Association for the Advancement of Colored People). 1917.
"Segregation." *Crisis* 15 (2): 69–73.

NASBO (National Association of State Budget Officers). 2010. State Expenditure
Report, Fiscal Year 2010, 13–20. http://nasbo.org/Publications/StateExpenditure
Report/tabid/79/Default.aspx.

National Center on Teacher Quality. 2008. "2008 State Teacher Policy Yearbook."
http://www.nctq.org/stpy08.

Ngai, M. 2004. *Impossible Subjects: Illegal Aliens and the Making of Modern America.* Princeton, NJ: Princeton University Press.

Nisbett, Richard E. 2009. *Intelligence and How to Get It: Why Schools and Cultures
Count.* New York: W. W. Norton.

Noguera, Pedro. 2010. "A New Vision for School Reform: The Change We Need in Education Policy." *Nation*, June 14, 12.

Nucci, Larry. 2001. *Education in the Moral Domain*. Cambridge: Cambridge University Press.

Oettinger, Gerald S. 1996. "Statistical Discrimination and the Early Career Evolution of the Black-White Wage Gap." *Journal of Labor Economics* 14:52–78.

Ogbu, John U. 1978. *Minority Education and Caste: The American System in Cross-Cultural Perspective*. New York: Academic Press.

———. 1991. Minority Responses and School Experiences." *Journal of Psychohistory* 18:433–56.

———. 1993. "Variability in Minority School Performance: A Problem in Search of an Explanation." In *Minority Education: Anthropological Perspectives*, edited by E. Jacob and C. Jordan, 83–111. Norwood, NJ: Ablex.

———. 2003. *Black American Students in an Affluent Suburb: A Study of Academic Disengagement*. Mahwah, NJ: Lawrence Erlbaum.

Okagaki, L., and R. J. Sternberg. 1993. "Parental Beliefs and Children's School Performance." *Child Development* 64:36–56.

Oliver, Melvin, and Thomas Shapiro. 2006. *Black Wealth/White Wealth: A New Perspective on Racial Inequality*. New York: Routledge.

Olsen, Laurie. 1997. *Made in America: Immigrant Students in Our Public Schools*. New York: New Press.

O'Neill, Onora. 1992. "Children's Rights and Children's Lives." *International Journal of Law, Policy and the Family* 6 (1): 24–42.

Ong, Aihwa. 1999. *Flexible Citizenship: The Cultural Logics of Transnationality*. Durham, NC: Duke University Press.

Onkst, David H. 1998. " 'First a Negro . . . Incidentally a Veteran': Black World War Two Veterans and the G.I. Bill of Rights in the Deep South, 1944–1948." *Journal of Social History* 31 (3): 517–43.

"Oppose the No Child Left Behind Recess until Reauthorization Act." 2008. Letter dated June 18. http://www.civilrights.org/advocacy/letters/2008/nclb-recess.html.

Orellana, M. F. 2009. *Translating Childhoods: Immigrant Youth, Language, and Culture*. Piscataway, NJ: Rutgers University Press.

Orellana, M. F., B. Thorne, A. E. Chee, and W. S. E. Lam. 2001. "Transnational Childhoods: The Participation of Children in Processes of Family Migration." *Social Problems* 48 (4): 572–91.

Orfield, G., and C. Lee. 2006. *Racial Transformation an the Changing Nature of Segregation*. Cambridge, MA: Civil Rights Project at Harvard University.

Oswald, F. L., N. Schmitt, B. H. Kim, L. J. Ramsay, and M. A. Gillespie. 2004. "Developing a Biodata Measure and Situational Judgment Inventory as Predictors of College Student Performance." *Journal of Applied Psychology* 89:187–207.

Oyserman, Daphna, Markus Kemmelmeier, Stephanie Fryberg, Hezi Brosh, and Tamera Hart-Johnson. 2003. "Racial-Ethnic Self-Schemas." *Social Psychology Quarterly* 66:333–47.

Parekh, Bhikhu. 2002. *Rethinking Multiculturalism: Cultural Diversity and Political Theory.* Cambridge, MA: Harvard University Press.

Parents United for Better Schools, Inc. v. School District of Philadelphia Board of Education, 148 F.3d 260. (3d Cir. 1998).

Parfit, Derek. 1997. "Equality and Priority." *Ratio* 10:202–21.

Parliamentary Select Committee. 1973. *Parliamentary Select Committee on Immigration and Race Relations.* Session 1972–73, *Education*, vol. 1. London: Her Majesty's Stationery Office.

Patrikakou, E. N., and R. P. Weissberg. 2000. "Parents' Perceptions of Teacher Outreach and Parent Involvement in Children's Education." *Journal of Prevention and Intervention in the Community* 20 (1/2): 103–19.

Payne, Charles. 2008. *So Much Reform, So Little Change: The Persistence of Failure in Urban Education.* Cambridge, MA: Harvard Education Press.

Peal, E., and W. E. Lambert. 1962. "The Relationship of Bilingualism to Intelligence." *Psychological Monographs* 76 (546): 1–23.

Peña, D. C. 2000. "Family Involvement: Influencing Factors and Implications." *Journal of Educational Research* 94 (1): 42–54.

Pettit, Philip. 1999. *Republicanism: A Theory of Freedom and Government.* Oxford: Oxford University Press.

Phillips, M., J. Brooks-Gunn, G. J. Duncan, P. Klebanov, and J. Crane. 1998. "Family Background, Parenting Practices, and the Black-White Test Score Gap." In *The Black–White Test Score Gap*, edited by Christopher Jencks and Meredith Phillips, 103–48. Washington, DC: Brookings Institution.

Pianta, R., J. Belsky, R. Houts, F. Morrison, and the NICHD ECCRN. 2007. "Opportunities to Learn in America's Elementary Classrooms." *Science* 315: 1795–96.

Pianta, R. C., K. M. LaParo, and M. Stuhlman, 2004. "The Classroom Assessment Scoring System: Findings from the Prekindergarten Year." *Elementary School Journal* 104:409–26.

Pinker, Steven. 2002. *The Blank Slate: The Modern Denial of Human Nature.* New York: Viking.

Polikoff, Alexander. 2006. *Waiting for Gautreaux.* Evanston, IL: Northwestern University Press.

Powell, Michael. 2009. "Memphis Accuses Wells Fargo of Discriminating against Blacks." *New York Times*, December 31.

———. 2010. "Blacks in Memphis Lose Decades of Economic Gains." *New York Times*, May 31. http://www.nytimes.com/2010/05/31/business/economy/31memphis.html.

Power, F. Clark, Ann Higgins, and Lawrence Kohlberg. 1989. *Lawrence Kohlberg's Approach to Moral Education.* New York: Columbia University Press.

Pritchard, Michael S. 1996. *Reasonable Children: Moral Education and Moral Learning.* Lawrence: University Press of Kansas.

Public Agenda. 2000. "Great Expectations: How the Public and Parents—White, African American and Hispanic—View Higher Education." Report 00–2. Washington, DC: National Center for Public Policy and Higher Education.

"Race to the Top Itself Needs Some Reform." 2010. *Washington Post*, August 27.

Ratha, D. 2009. "Outlook for Remittance Flows—2009–2011." Migration and Development Brief 10. Washington, DC: World Bank.

Ravitch, Diane. 2008. *The Death and Life of the Great American School System: How Testing and Choice Are Undermining Education*. New York: Basic Books.

Rawls, John. 1971. *A Theory of Justice*. Cambridge, MA: Harvard University Press.

———. 1999. *A Theory of Justice*. Rev. ed. Cambridge, MA: Harvard University Press.

———. 2001. *Justice as Fairness: A Restatement*, edited by Erin Kelly. Cambridge, MA: Belknap Press of Harvard University Press.

Raz, Joseph. 1986. *The Morality of Freedom*. Oxford: Oxford University Press.

Réaume, D. G. 2000. "Official Language Rights: Intrinsic Value and the Protection of Difference," In *Citizenship in Diverse Societies*, edited by Will Kymlicka and Wayne Norman, 254–72. Oxford: Oxford University Press.

Rebell, Michael A. 2009. *Courts and Kids: Pursuing Educational Equity through the State Courts*. Chicago: University of Chicago Press.

Reed, Douglas S. 2001. *On Equal Terms: The Constitutional Politics of Educational Opportunity*. Princeton, NJ: Princeton University Press.

Reich, Rob. 2002. *Bridging Liberalism and Multiculturalism in American Education*. Chicago: University of Chicago Press.

———. 2006. "The Uneasy Relation between Philanthropy and Equality." In *Taking Philanthropy Seriously: Beyond Noble Intentions to Responsible Giving*, edited by William Damon and Susan Verducci. Bloomington: Indiana University Press.

———. 2007. "How and Why to Support Common Schooling and Educational Choice at the Same Time," *Journal of Philosophy of Education* 41 (4): 709–25.

Relman, John P. 2008. "Foreclosures, Integration, and the Future of the Fair Housing Act." *Indiana Law Review* 41 (3): 629–52.

Remling, Jeff. "Urban Renewal in the South Side." http://digital.lib.lehigh.edu /cdm4/beyond_viewer.php?DMTHUMB=1&DMTEXT=documentary&search works=searchdocumentary_0&ptr=015831.

Reuben, Julie A. 1996. *The Making of the Modern University: Intellectual Transformation and the Marginalization of Morality*. Chicago: University of Chicago Press.

Reutter, Mark. 2004. *Making Steel: Sparrows Point and the Rise and Ruin of American Industrial Might*. Urbana: University of Illinois Press.

Rhodes, Jesse. 2011. "Progressive Policymaking in a Conservative Age? Civil Rights and the Politics of Federal Education Standards, Testing, and Accountability." *Perspectives on Politics* 9 (3): 519.

Rice, Patryce. 2010. "Family Involvement and Academic and Behavioral Outcomes for Children of Immigrants." PhD diss., New York University.

Rivera, Amaad, Brenda Cotto-Escalera, Anisha Desai, Jeannette Huezo, and Dedrick Muhammad. 2008. "Foreclosed: State of the Dream 2008." *United for a Fair Economy*, January 15. http://www.faireconomy.org/files/StateOfDream_01_16_08_Web.pdf.

Roemer, John E. 1998. *Equality of Opportunity.* Cambridge, MA: Harvard University Press.

Rogoff, B., and J. Lave. 1984. *Everyday Cognition: Its Development in Social Context.* Cambridge, MA: Harvard University Press.

Rosenberg, Gerald. 1991. *The Hollow Hope: Can Courts Bring about Social Change?* Chicago: University of Chicago Press.

Ross, Catherine J. 1996. "From Vulnerability to Voice: Appointing Counsel for Children in Civil Litigation." *Fordham Law Review* 64:1571.

———. 1999. "An Emerging Right for Mature Minors to Receive Information." *University of Pennsylvania Journal of Constitutional Law* 2:223.

———. 2000. "Anything Goes: Examining the State's Interest in Protecting Children from Controversial Speech." *Vanderbilt Law Review* 15:427–93.

———. 2008. "Legal Constraints on Child-Saving: The Strange Case of the Fundamentalist Latter-Day Saints at Yearning for Zion Ranch." *Capital University Law* Review 37:361.

———. 2010. "Fundamentalist Challenges to Core Democratic Values: Exit and Homeschooling." *William and Mary Bill of Rights Journal* 18:991–1010.

Ross, Lee. 1977. "The Intuitive Psychologist and His Shortcomings: Distortions in the Attribution Process." In *Advances in Experimental Social Psychology,* edited by Leonard Berkowitz, 10:173–220. New York: Academic Press.

Ross, Lee, T. M. Amabile, and J. L. Steinmetz. 1977. "Social Roles Social Control, and Biases in Social-Perception Processes." *Journal of Personality and Social Psychology* 35:485–94.

Ross, Lee, and Richard E. Nisbett. 1991. *The Person and the Situation: Perspectives of Social Psychology.* New York: McGraw-Hill.

Ross, Stephen L., and John Yinger. 2002. "The Full Story about Gaps in Homeownership." *Hartford Courant*, November 4.

Rothstein, Richard. 2004. *Class and Schools: Using Social, Economic, and Educational Reform to Close the Black-White Achievement Gap.* Washington, DC: Economic Policy Institute and Teachers College Press.

———. 2008. "Whose Problem Is Poverty?" *Educational Leadership* 65 (7): 8–13.

Rothstein, Richard, Rebecca Jacobsen, and Tamara Wilder. 2008. *Grading Education: Getting Accountability Right.* Washington, DC: Economic Policy Institute and Teachers College Press.

Rousseau, C. I., G. Hassan, T. Measham, N. Moreau, M. Lashley, T. Castro, et al. 2009. "From the Family Universe to the Outside World: Family Relations,

School Attitude, and Perception of Racism in Caribbean and Filipino Adolescents." *Health and Place* 15 (3): 751–60.

Rowley, William D. 1970. *M. L. Wilson and the Campaign for the Domestic Allotment*. Lincoln: University of Nebraska Press.

Rubinowitz, Leonard S., and Imani Perry. 2002. "Crimes without Punishment: White Neighbors' Resistance to Black Entry." *Journal of Criminal Law and Criminology* 92 (2): 335–428.

Ruiz-de-Valasco, J., M. Fix, and B. C. Clewell. 2001. *Overlooked and Underserved: Immigrant Students in U.S. Secondary Schools*. Washington, DC: Urban Institute.

Ryan, James. 2004. "The Perverse Incentives of the No Child Left Behind Act." *New York University Law Review* 79:932–39.

Ryan, James E., and Michael Heise. 2002. "The Political Economy of School Choice." *Yale Law Journal* 111:2043, 2062.

Rydell, R. J., R. M. Shiffrin, K. L. Boucher, K. Van Loo, and M. T. Rydell. 2010. "Stereotype Threat Prevents Perceptual Learning." *Proceedings of the National Academy of Sciences* 107:14042–47.

Salzman, Avi. 2006. "NAACP Is Bush Ally in School Suit against State." *New York Times*, February 1.

Sanders, Mavis G. 1997. "Overcoming Obstacles: Academic Achievement as a Response to Racism and Discrimination." *Journal of Negro Education* 66:83–93.

Satter, Beryl. 2009. "Race and Real Estate." *Poverty and Race* 18 (4): 1–2, 8–11.

Sattin Bajaj, Carolyn, and Marcelo Suárez-Orozco. 2010. *English Language Learner Students and Charter Schools in New York State: Challenges and Opportunities*. Albany: New York State Department of Education.

Satz, D. 2007. "Equality, Adequacy, and Education for Citizenship." *Ethics* 117 (4): 623–48.

Sawchuk, Stephen. 2009. "Duncan Presses NEA on Merit Pay, Tenure." *Education Week*, July 2.

———. 2010a. "Emerging Trends Reflected in State Phase I Race to the Top Applications." Emerging Trends Report from Learning Point Associates, June.

———. 2010b. "States Strive to Overhaul Teacher Tenure." *Education Week*, April 5. http://www.edweek.org/ew/articles/2010/04/07/28tenure_ep.h29.html.

Scalabrini Migration Center. 2003. *Hearts Apart: Migration in the Eyes of Filipino Children*. Quezon City, Philippines: Scalabrini Migration Center.

Schapiro, Tamar. 1999. "What Is a Child?" *Ethics* 109 (4): 715–38.

Schein, Bernie. 2008. *If Holden Caulfield Were in My Classroom: Inspiring Love, Creativity and Intelligence in Middle School Kids*. Boulder, CO: Sentient.

Schlesinger, Arthur M., Jr. 1998. *The Disuniting of America: Reflections on a Multicultural Society*. New York: W. W. Norton.

Schmitter, Philippe, and Terry Lynn Karl. 1991. "What Democracy Is . . . and Is Not." *Journal of Democracy* 2 (3): 75–88.

Schnapper, Eric. 1985. "Affirmative Action and the Legislative History of the Fourteenth Amendment." *Virginia Law Review* 71 (5): 753–98.

Schunk, D. H. 1991. "Self-Efficacy and Academic Motivation." *Educational Psychologist* 26:207–31.

Schwartz, Amy Ellen, Ross Rubenstein, and Leanna Stiefel. 2009. "Why Do Some Schools Get More and Others Less? An Examination of School-Level Funding in New York City." Working Paper 09–10. Institute for Education and Social Policy.

Schwarz, N. 2000. "Social Judgment and Attitudes: Warmer, More Social, and Less Conscious." *European Journal of Social Psychology* 30:149–76.

Schwarz, N., H. Bless, F. Strack, G. Klumpp, H. Rittenauer-Schatka, and A. Simons. 1991. "Ease of Retrieval as Information: Another Look at the Availability Heuristic." *Journal of Personality and Social Psychology* 61:195–202.

Scribner, J. D., M. D. Young, and A. Pedroza. 1999. "Building Collaborative Relationships with Parents." In *Lessons from High-Performing Hispanic Schools*, edited by P. Reyes, J. D. Scribner, and and A. P. Scribner. New York: Teachers College Press.

Sedlacek, W. E. 2004. *Beyond the Big Test: Noncognitive Assessment in Higher Education*. San Francisco: Jossey-Bass.

Self, Robert. 2005. *American Babylon: Race and the Struggle for Postwar Oakland*. Princeton, NJ: Princeton University Press.

Sellers, Robert M., Tabbye M. Chavous, and Deanna Y. Cooke. 1998. "Racial Ideology and Racial Centrality as Predictors of African American College Students' Academic Performance." *Journal of Black Psychology* 24:8–27.

Shachar, Ayelet. 2009. *The Birthright Lottery*. Cambridge, MA: Harvard University Press.

Sheldon, S. B. 2002. "Parents' Social Networks and Beliefs as Predictors of Family Involvement." *Elementary School Journal* 102 (4): 301–16.

Sherif, M. 1935. "A Study of Some Social Factors in Perception." *Archives of Psychology* 27:187.

Sherman, D. K., and G. L. Cohen. 2006. "The Psychology of Self-Defense: Self-Affirmation Theory." In *Advances in Experimental Social Psychology*, edited by M. P. Zanna, 38:183–242. San Diego, CA: Academic Press.

Shi, David E. 1985. *The Simple Life: Plain Living and High Thinking in American Culture*. New York: Oxford University Press.

Shirley, Dennis. 1997. *Community Organizing for Urban School Reform*. Austin: University of Texas Press.

Shklar, Judith. 1998. *American Citizenship: The Quest for Inclusion*. Cambridge, MA: Harvard University Press.

Shrader-Frechette, Kristin. 2007. *Taking Action, Saving Lives: Our Duties to Protect Environmental and Public Health*. Oxford: Oxford University Press.

Simon, Bryant. 2004. *Boardwalk of Dreams: Atlantic City and the Fate of Urban America*. New York: Oxford University Press.

Sirin, Selcuk, Patrice Ryce, and Medea Mir. 2009. "How Teachers' Values Affect Their Evaluation of Children of Immigrants: Findings from Islamic and Public Schools." *Early Childhood Education Quarterly* 24 (4): 463–73.

Smaby, Beverly Prior. 1988. *The Transformation of Moravian Bethlehem: From Communal Mission to Family Economy.* Philadelphia: University of Pennsylvania Press.

Smith, David. 1981. *Unemployment and Racial Minorities.* London: POLICY Studies Institute.

Smith, Robert Courtney. 2006. *Mexican in New York: Transnational Lives of New Immigrants.* Berkeley: University of California Press.

Smith, Rogers M. 2003. *Stories of Peoplehood: The Politics and Morals of Political Membership.* Cambridge: Cambridge University Press.

Smith, Ryan A. 1997. "Race, Income, and Authority at Work: A Cross-Temporal Analysis of Black and White Men (1972–1994)." *Social Problems* 44:19–37.

———. 2001. "Particularism in Control over Monetary Resources at Work: An Analysis of Racial Ethnic Differences in the Authority Outcomes of Black, White, and Latino Men." *Work and Occupations* 28:447–68.

———. 2005. "Do the Determinants of Promotion Differ for White Men versus Women and Minorities? An Exploration of Intersectionalism through Sponsored and Contest Mobility Processes." *American Behavioral Scientist* 48: 1157–81.

Snow, C. 1993. "Bilingualism and Second Language Acquisition." In *Psycholinguistics,* edited by J. B. Gleason and N. B. Ratner. Fort Worth, TX: Harcourt Brace.

Solomon, Stephen D. 2009. *Ellery's Protest: How One Young Man Defied Tradition and Sparked the Battle over School Prayer.* Ann Arbor: University of Michigan Press.

Soss, Joe, Jacob S. Hacker, and Suzanne Mettler, eds. 2007. *Remaking America: Democracy and Public Policy in an Age of Inequality.* New York: Russell Sage Foundation.

Spencer, S., C. M. Steele, and D. Quinn. 1999. "Stereotype Threat and Women's Math Performance." *Journal of Experimental Social Psychology* 35:4–28.

Spiro, Peter. 2007. *Beyond Citizenship.* Oxford: Oxford University Press.

Stanton, Cathy. 2006. *The Lowell Experiment: Public History in a Postindustrial City.* Amherst: University of Massachusetts Press.

Steele, Claude M. 2010. *Whistling Vivaldi and Other Clues to How Stereotypes Affect Us.* New York: W. W. Norton.

Steele, Claude M., and J. Aronson. 1995. "Stereotype Threat and the Intellectual Test Performance of African Americans." *Journal of Personality and Social Psychology* 69:797–811.

Steele, Claude M., S. J. Spencer, and J. Aronson. 2002. "Contending with Group Image: The Psychology of Stereotype and Social Identity Threat." In *Advances in Experimental Social Psychology,* edited by M. P. Zanna, 34. San Diego, CA: Academic Press.

Steinberg, Laurence, Sanford Dornbusch, and Bradford Brown. 1992. "Ethnic Differences in Adolescent Achievement: An Ecological Perspective." *American Psychologist* 47:723–29.

Steinhauer, Jennifer. 2010. "Arizona Law Reveals Split within G.O.P." *New York Times*, May 22.

Sternberg, R. J., et al. 2006. "The Rainbow Project: Enhancing the SAT through Assessments of Analytical, Practical, and Creative Skills." *Intelligence* 34: 321–50.

Stolzenberg, Nomi M. 1993. " 'He Drew a Circle That Shut Me Out': Assimilation, Indoctrination, and the Paradox of a Liberal Education." *Harvard Law Review* 581:106.

Strohmeyer, John. 1986. *Crisis in Bethlehem: Big Steel's Struggle to Survive.* Pittsburgh: University of Pittsburgh Press.

Suárez-Orozco, Carola, H. J. Bang, and H. Y. Kim. 2011. " 'I Felt Like My Heart Was Staying Behind': Psychological Implications of Immigrant Family Separations and Reunifications." *Journal of Adolescent Research* 25 (5): 222–57.

Suárez-Orozco, Carola, F. Gaytán, H. J. Bang, J. Pakes, E. O'Connor, and J. Rhodes. 2010. "Academic Trajectories of Newcomer Immigrant Youth." *Developmental Psychology* 46 (2): 602–18.

Suárez-Orozco, Carola, and Marcelo M. Suárez-Orozco. 1995. *Transformations: Immigration, Family Life, and Achievement Motivation among Latino Adolescents.* Stanford, CA: Stanford University Press.

———. 2001. *Children of Immigration.* Cambridge, MA: Harvard University Press.

Suárez-Orozco, Carola, Marcelo M. Suárez-Orozco, and Irina Todorova. 2008. *Learning a New Land: Immigrant Students in American Society.* Cambridge, MA: Harvard University Press.

Suárez-Orozco, Carola, I. Todorova, and L. Louie. 2002. " 'Making Up for Lost Time': The Experience of Separation and Reunification among Immigrant Families." *Family Process* 41 (4): 625–43.

Suárez-Orozco, Carola, Hiro Yoshikawa, Robert Teranishi, and Marcelo Suárez-Orozco. 2011. "Growing Up in the Shadows: The Developmental Implications of Unauthorized Status." *Harvard Education Review*, special issue on immigrant students in education, 81 (3) 438–72.

Suárez-Orozco, Marcelo M., ed. 2007. *Learning in the Global Era: International Perspectives on Globalization and Education.* Berkeley: University of California Press/Ross Institute.

Suárez-Orozco, Marcelo M., and Carolyn Sattin-Bajaj, eds. 2010. *Educating the Whole Child for the Whole World: The Ross School Model and Education for the Global Era.* New York: New York University Press.

Sugrue, Thomas J. 1995. "Crabgrass-Roots Politics: Race, Rights, and the Reaction against Liberalism in the Urban North, 1940–1964." *Journal of American History* 82 (2): 551–78.

———. 2005. *The Origins of the Urban Crisis: Race and Inequality in Postwar Detroit.* Princeton, NJ: Princeton University Press.

Sunstein, Cass. 1992. "On Marshall's Conception of Equality." *Stanford Law Review* 44 (1992): 1267.

———. 2004. "Did *Brown* Matter?" *New Yorker*, May 3.

Suro, Roberto. 2003. *Remittance Senders and Receivers: Tracking the Transnational Channels.* Washington, DC: Multilateral Investment Fund and the Pew Hispanic Center.

Swift, Adam. 2003. *How Not to Be a Hypocrite: School Choice for the Morally Perplexed Parent.* New York: Routledge.

———. 2008. "The Value of Philosophy in Non-ideal Circumstances." *Social Theory and Practice* 34 (3): 363–88.

Sy, S. R., and J. E. Schulenberg. 2005. "Parent Beliefs and Children's Achievement Trajectories during the Transition to School in Asian American and European American Families." *Psychology in the Schools* 34 (3): 505–15.

Taeusch, Carl F. 1926. *Professional and Business Ethics.* New York: Henry Holt.

———. 1938. *Career Training for Agriculture.* Washington, DC: Agricultural Adjustment Administration.

Taylor, Lori, and William Fowler Jr. 2006. *A Comparable Wage Approach to Geographic Cost Adjustment.* Research and Development Report. Washington, DC: US Department of Education.

Taylor, V. J., and G. M. Walton. 2011. "Stereotype Threat Undermines Academic Learning." *Personality and Social Psychology Bulletin* 73:1055–67.

Taylor, William, and Crystal Rosario. 2009. "National Teachers' Unions and the Struggle over School Reform." Citizens' Commission on Civil Rights, July. http://www.cccr.org/doc/NatlTeachersUnionsandtheStruggleOverSchoolReform.pdf.

Temkin, Larry. 1993. *Inequality.* New York: Oxford University Press.

———. 2001. "Inequality: A Complex, Individualistic, and Comparative Notion." *Philosophical Issues* 11:327.

———. 2003. "Egalitarianism Defended." *Ethics* 113 (4): 764–82.

Theilheimer, R. 2001. "Bi-directional Learning through Relationship Building: Teacher Preparation for Working with Families New to the United States." *Childhood Education* 77 (5): 284–89.

Thomas, Anita, and Suzette Speight. 1999. "Racial Identity and Racial Socialization Attitudes of African American Parents." *Journal of Black Psychology* 25:152–70.

Tomaskovic-Devey, Donald, Melvin Thomas, and Kecia Johnson. 2005. "Race and the Accumulation of Human Capital across the Career: A Theoretical Model and Fixed-Effects Application." *American Journal of Sociology* 111:58–89.

Tomlinson, Sally. 1991. "Ethnicity and Educational Attainment in England: An Overview." *Anthropology and Education Quarterly* 22:121–39.

Tonn, Joan C. 2003. *Mary P. Follett: Creating Democracy, Transforming Management*. New Haven, CT: Yale University Press.

"Truman Hails U.N. Flags." 1950. *New York Times*, November 17.

Trumbull, E., C. Rothstein-Fisch, and E. Hernandez. 2003. "Family Involvement in Schooling: According to Whose Values?" *School Community Journal* 13 (2): 45–72.

Turner, Sarah, and John Bound. 2002. "Closing the Gap or Widening the Divide: The Effects of the G.I. Bill and World War II on the Educational Outcomes of Black Americans." Working Paper 9044, National Bureau of Economic Research.

Tversky, A., and D. Kahneman. 1981. "The Framing of Decisions and the Psychology of Choice." *Science* 211:453–58.

Tyson, Karolyn. 2003. "Notes from the Back of the Room: Problems and Paradoxes in the Schooling of Young Black Students." *Sociology of Education* 76:326–43.

Tyyska, V. 2007. "Immigrant Families in Sociology." In *Immigrant Families in Contemporary Society,* edited by Jennifer E. Lansford, Kirby D. Deater-Deckard, and Marc H. Bornstein. New York: Guilford Press.

United Nations Development Programme. 2009. *Overcoming Barriers: Human Mobility and Development*. Human Development Report 2009. New York: United Nations Development Programme.

Urban Institute. 2005. "Young Children of Immigrants in Two-Parent Families Have Triple the Poverty Rate of Children with U.S.-Born Parents." http://www .urban.org/publications/900779.html.

Urrea, Luis Alberto. 1998. *Nobody's Son*. Tucson: University of Arizona Press.

US Census Bureau. 2000. *Profile of the Foreign-Born Population in the United States*. Washington, DC: Government Printing Office.

———. 2009. *Public Education Finances: 2007*.

———. 2010. "American FactFinder, Geographic Comparison. New York— County. GCT-P6. Race and Hispanic or Latino: 2000." http://factfinder.census .gov/home/saff/main.html.

———. 2011. *Public Education Finances: 2009*

US Department of Education. 2007. "Common Core of Data." http://nces.ed.gov /edfin/graph_topic.asp?INDEX=1.

———. 2009. "Digest of Education Statistics 2009." http://nces.ed.gov/programs /digest/2009.

———. 2010. "Duncan, AFT and NEA Call for National Education Reform Conference on Labor-Management Collaboration." Press Release, October 14. http:// www.ed.gov/news/press-releases/duncan-aft-nea-call-national-education- reform-conference-labor-management-collab.

Valdés, G. 1998. "The World Outside and Inside Schools: Language and Immigrant Children." *Educational Researcher* 27 (6): 9.

Valdés, G., and R. A. Figueroa. 1994. *Bilingualism and Testing: A Special Case of Bias*. Norwood, NJ: Ablex.

Wagner, Dennis. 2010. "Mural Gripe Costs Prescott Official Radio Job." *Arizona Republic*, June 9. http://www.azcentral.com/arizonarepublic/news/articles/2010/06/09/20100609prescott-councilman-loses-job-over-mural.html.

Walton, G. M., and M. R. Banaji. 2004. "Being What You Say: The Effect of Linguistic Labels on Attitudes." *Social Cognition* 22:193–213.

Walton, G. M., and G. L. Cohen. 2003. "Stereotype Lift." *Journal of Experimental Social Psychology* 39:456–67.

———. 2007. "A Question of Belonging: Race, Social Fit, and Achievement." *Journal of Personality and Social Psychology* 92:82–96.

———. 2011. "A Brief Social-Belonging Intervention Improves Academic and Health Outcomes of Minority Students." *Science* 331:1447–51.

Walton, G. M., G. L. Cohen, D. Cwir, and S. J. Spencer. 2012. "Mere Belonging: The Power of Social Connections." *Journal of Personality and Social Psychology* 102 (3): 513–32.

Walton, G. M., and S. J. Spencer. 2009. "Latent Ability: Grades and Test Scores Systematically Underestimate the Intellectual Ability of Negatively Stereotyped Students." *Psychological Science* 20:1132–39.

Walton, G. M., S. J. Spencer, and S. Erman. In press. "Affirmative Meritocracy." *Social Issues and Policy Review*.

Walzer, Michael. 1983. *Spheres of Justice: A Defense of Pluralism and Equality.* New York: Basic Books.

Warren, Elizabeth. 2007. "Unsafe at Any Rate." *Democracy* 5. http://www.democracyjournal.org/pdf/5/Warren.pdf.

Warren, Mark R. 2001. *Dry Bones Rattling: Community Building to Revitalize American Democracy.* Princeton, NJ: Princeton University Press.

Waters, J. L. 2002. "Flexible Families? 'Astronaut Households' and the Experience of Lone Mothers in Vancouver, British Columbia." *Social and Cultural Geography* 3:117–34.

Weaver, Robert C. 1948. *The Negro Ghetto.* New York: Russell and Russell.

Weinstein, Rhona S. 2002. *Reaching Higher: The Power of Expectations in Schooling.* Cambridge, MA: Harvard University Press.

Weisberg, Daniel, Susan Sexton, Jennifer Mulhern, and David Keeling. 2009. *The Widget Effect: Our National Failure to Acknowledge and Act on Differences in Teacher Effectiveness.* New York: New Teacher Project.

Wendel, F. C., and K. E. Anderson. 1994. "Grading and Marking Systems: What Are the Practices, Standards?" *NASSP Bulletin*, 79–84.

West, Martin, and Paul Peterson, eds. 2006. *School Money Trials: The Legal Pursuit of Educational Adequacy.* Washington, DC: Brookings Institution Press.

White, Graham, and John Maze. 1995. *Henry A. Wallace: His Search for a New World Order.* Chapel Hill: University of North Carolina Press.

White, Patricia. 1996. *Civic Virtues and Public Schooling: Educating Citizens for a Democratic Society.* New York: Teachers College Press.

Wiggins, Grant P. and Jay McTighe. 2007. *Schooling by Design: Mission, Action and Achievement.* Alexandria, VA: ACSD.

Wilder, Tamara Elaine. 2008. *Is Democratic Participation at Risk—Do Exit Policies Depress Parental Voice?* PhD diss., Columbia University.

Wilkenfeld, Britt. 2009. "Does Context Matter? How the Family, Peer, School, and Neighborhood Contexts Relate to Adolescents' Civic Engagement." CIRCLE Working Paper 64. *CIRCLE*, civicyouth.org.

Williams, Joe, and Pedro Noguera. 2010. "Poor Schools or Poor Kids?" *Education Next* 10 (1): 44–51.

Williams, Melissa. 2003. "Citizenship as Identity, Citizenship as Shared Fate, and the Functions of Multicultural Education." In *Citizenship and Education in Liberal-Democratic Societies: Teaching for Cosmopolitan Values and Collective Identities*, edited by Walter Feinberg and Kevin McDonough, 208–47. Oxford: Oxford University Press.

———. 2006. *Citizenship under Fire: Democratic Education in Times of War.* Princeton, NJ: Princeton University Press.

———. 2009. "Citizenship as Agency within Communities of Shared Fate." In *Unsettled Legitimacy: Political Community, Power, and Authority in the Global Era*, edited by Steven Bernstein and William D. Coleman, 33–52. Vancouver: University of British Columbia Press.

Williams, Raymond. 1984. *The Long Revolution.* Harmondsworth, UK: Penguin.

Williams, Richard, Reynold Nesiba, and Eileen Diaz McConnell. 2005. "The Changing Face of Inequality in Home Mortgage Lending." *Social Problems* 52:181–208.

Williamson, June. 2005. "Retrofitting 'Levittown.'" *Places Journal* 17 (2). http://escholarship.org/uc/item/0r57v5j3.

Wilson, George, Ian Sakura-Lemessy, and Jonathan P. West. 1999. "Reaching the Top: Racial Differences in Mobility Paths to Upper-Tier Occupations." *Work and Occupations* 26:165–86.

Wilson, M. L. 1938. "New Horizons in Agricultural Economics." *Journal of Farm Economics* 20 (1): 1–7.

Wilson, T. D., M. Damiani, and N. Shelton. 2002. "Improving the Academic Performance of College Students with Brief Attributional Interventions." In *Improving Academic Achievement: Impact of Psychological Factors on Education*, edited by J. Aronson. Oxford: Academic Press.

Wilson, William Julius. 1987. *The Truly Disadvantaged: The Inner City, the Underclass, and Public Policy.* Chicago: University of Chicago Press.

Wittgenstein, Ludwig. 1991. *Philosophical Investigations*, translated by G. E. M. Anscombe. Oxford: Wiley-Blackwell.

Wolfe, Barbara, and Robert Haveman. 2001. "Accounting for the Social and Nonmarket Benefits of Education: The Contribution of Human and Social Capital to Sustained Economic Growth and Well-Being." Human Resources Development Canada and Organisation for Economic Co-operation and Development, September.

Wolff, Jonathan, and Avner De-Shalit. 2007. *Disadvantage*. Oxford: Oxford University Press.

Wong, B. P. 2006. "Immigration, Globalization and the Chinese American Family." In *Immigrant Families in Contemporary Society*, edited by Jennifer E. Lansford, Kirby D. Deater-Deckard, and Marc H. Bornstein. New York: Guilford Press.

Wong, Carol A., Jacquelynne S. Eccles, and Arnold Sameroff. 2003. "The Influence of Ethnic Discrimination and Ethnic Identification on African American Adolescents' School and Socioemotional Adjustment." *Journal of Personality* 71:1197–1232.

Woodward, C. Vann. 1955. *The Strange Career of Jim Crow*. New York: Oxford University Press.

Wyly, Elvin, and Daniel Hammel. 2004. "Gentrification, Segregation, and Discrimination in the American Urban System." *Environment and Planning* 36: 1215–41.

Yalof, David A., and Kenneth Dautrich. 2008. "Future of the First Amendment: What America's High School Students Think about Their Freedoms." John S. and James L. Knight Foundation, High School Initiative. http://firstamendment.jideas.org/downloads/future_final.pdf.

Yates, W. Ross. 1992. *Lehigh University: A History of Education in Engineering, Business, and the Human Condition*. Bethlehem, PA: Lehigh University Press.

Yeager, D. S., and G. M. Walton. 2011. "Social-Psychological Interventions in Education: They're Not Magic." *Review of Educational Research* 81:267–301.

Young, Iris Marion. 1990. *Justice and the Politics of Difference*. Princeton, NJ: Princeton University Press.

———. 2007. "Structural Injustice and the Politics of Difference." In *Multiculturalism and Political Theory*, edited by Anthony Simon Laden and David Owen, 60–88. Cambridge: Cambridge University Press.

Yuracko, Kimberly. 2008. "Illiberal Education: Constitutional Constraints on Homeschooling." *California Law Review* 96:123.

Zanesville. 2007. *Kennedy v. City of Zanesville*, U.S. District Court for the Southern District of Ohio, Eastern Division, Case No. 2:03-cv-1047, Opinion, September 7 (2007). http://www.relmanlaw.com/docs/zanesville-order.pdf.

Zhou, M. 2009. "Conflict, Coping, and Reconciliation: Intergenerational Relations in Chinese Immigrant families." In *Across Generations: Immigrant Families in America*, edited by Nancy Foner. New York: New York University Press.

Contributors

DANIELLE ALLEN is UPS Foundation Professor in the School of Social Science at the Institute for Advanced Studies. She is the author of *Why Plato Wrote* (Wiley-Blackwell, 2010), *Talking to Strangers* (University of Chicago Press, 2004), and *The World of Prometheus* (Princeton University Press, 2000).

SIGAL BEN-PORATH is associate professor in the Graduate School of Education at the University of Pennsylvania. She is the author of *Tough Choices: Structured Paternalism and the Landscape of Choice* (Princeton University Press, 2010) and *Citizenship under Fire: Democratic Education in Times of Conflict* (Princeton University Press, 2006).

HARRY BRIGHOUSE is professor of philosophy and affiliate professor of educational policy studies at the University of Wisconsin, Madison. He is the author of *On Education* (Routledge, 2006) and *School Choice and Social Justice* (Oxford University Press, 2000) and an editor of *The Political Philosophy of Cosmopolitanism* (Cambridge University Press, 2005).

ANGEL L. HARRIS is associate professor of sociology and African American studies at Princeton University. He is the author of *The Broken Compass: Is Social Policy on Parental Involvement Misguided?* (Harvard University Press, forthcoming) and *Kids Don't Want to Fail: Oppositional Culture and the Black-White Achievement Gap* (Harvard University Press, 2011).

HELEN LADD is Edgar T. Thompson Professor of Public Policy Studies and professor of economics at Duke University. She is an editor of *Handbook of Research in Education Finance and Policy* (Routledge, 2008), coauthor of *Elusive Equity: Education Reform in Post-Apartheid South*

Africa (Brookings Institution Press, 2004), and author of *Market-Based Reforms in Education* (Economic Policy Institute, 2002).

ANTHONY SIMON LADEN is professor of philosophy at the University of Illinois at Chicago. He is the author of *Reasoning: a Social Picture* (Oxford University Press, 2012) and *Reasonably Radical: Deliberative Liberalism and the Politics of Identity* (Cornell University Press, 2001) and coeditor, with David Owen, of *Multiculturalism and Political Theory* (Cambridge University Press, 2007).

SUSANNA LOEB is Barnett Family Professor of Education at Stanford University, director of the Institute for Research on Education Policy and Practice, and codirector of Policy Analysis for California Education and is the author of numerous papers on the economics of education.

PATRICK MCGUINN is associate professor of political science and education at Drew University. He is the author of *No Child Left Behind and the Transformation of Federal Education Policy, 1965–2005* (University Press of Kansas, 2006) and coeditor of the forthcoming *Rethinking Education Governance for the 21st Century: Overcoming the Structural Barriers to School Reform.*

SETH MOGLEN is associate professor of English at Lehigh University. He is the author of *Mourning Modernity: Literary Modernism and the Injuries of American Capitalism* (Stanford University Press, 2007), and the editor of an edition of T. Thomas Fortune's *Black and White: Land, Labor and Politics in the South* ([1884] Simon and Schuster, 2007).

ROB REICH is associate professor of political science at Stanford University. He is the faculty director of the Program on Ethics in Society, the author of *Bridging Liberalism and Multiculturalism in American Education* (University of Chicago Press, 2002), and a former sixth-grade teacher at Rusk Elementary School in Houston, Texas.

RICHARD ROTHSTEIN is research associate at the Economic Policy Institute and senior fellow at the Chief Justice Earl Warren Institute on Law and Social Policy at the University of California (Berkeley) Law School. He is coauthor of *Grading Education: Getting Accountability Right* (Economic Policy Institute and Teachers College Press, 2008) and author of *Class and Schools: Using Social, Economic and Educational Reform to Close the Black-White Achievement Gap* (Economic Policy Institute and Teachers College Press, 2004).

ANNA MARIE SMITH is professor of government at Cornell University. She is the author of *Welfare and Sexual Regulation* (Cambridge, 2007), *Laclau and Mouffe: The Radical Democratic Imaginary* (Routledge, 1998), and *New Right Discourse on Race and Sexuality: Britain, 1968–1990* (Cambridge University Press, 1994).

CAROLA SUÁREZ-OROZCO is professor of psychological studies at the Graduate School of Education and Information Studies at UCLA. She is coauthor of *Learning a New Land: Immigrant Students in American Society* (Harvard University Press, 2008) and *Children of Immigration* (Harvard University Press, 2001).

MARCELO M. SUÁREZ-OROZCO is dean of the Graduate School of Education and Information Studies at UCLA. He is the editor of *Writing Immigration: Scholars and Journalists in Dialogue* (University of California Press, 2011) and coauthor of *Educating the Whole Child for the Whole World* (New York University Press, 2010) and *Learning a New Land: Immigrant Students in American Society* (Harvard University Press, 2008).

ADAM SWIFT is professor of political theory in the Department of Politics and International Studies at the University of Warwick. He is the author of *How Not to Be a Hypocrite: School Choice for the Morally Perplexed Parent* (Routledge, 2003) and *Political Philosophy: A Beginners' Guide for Students and Politicians*, 2nd ed. (Polity, 2006) and coauthor of *Liberals and Communitarians, 2nd ed.* (Blackwell, 1996) and *Against the Odds? Social Class and Social Justice in Industrial Societies* (Oxford University Press, 1997).

GREGORY M. WALTON is assistant professor in the Department of Psychology at Stanford University. He is the author of numerous papers on the topics of self and identity, stereotypes, motivation and achievement, psychological intervention, and social cognition.

Index